T0234938

Communications
in Computer and Information Science 1049

Commenced Publication in 2007
Founding and Former Series Editors:
Phoebe Chen, Alfredo Cuzzocrea, Xiaoyong Du, Orhun Kara, Ting Liu,
Krishna M. Sivalingam, Dominik Ślęzak, Takashi Washio, and Xiaokang Yang

Editorial Board Members

More information about this series at http://www.springer.com/series/7899

Jerzy Mikulski (Ed.)

Development of Transport by Telematics

19th International Conference
on Transport System Telematics, TST 2019
Jaworze, Poland, February 27 – March 2, 2019
Selected Papers

 Springer

Editor
Jerzy Mikulski
Polish Association of Transport Telematics
Katowice, Poland

ISSN 1865-0929 ISSN 1865-0937 (electronic)
Communications in Computer and Information Science
ISBN 978-3-030-27546-4 ISBN 978-3-030-27547-1 (eBook)
https://doi.org/10.1007/978-3-030-27547-1

This Springer imprint is published by the registered company Springer Nature Switzerland AG
The registered company address is: Gewerbestrasse 11, 6330 Cham, Switzerland

Preface

The 19th International Conference on Transport Systems Telematics (TST 2019) was held in Jaworze, Poland, during February 27 to March 2, 2019.

As usual, the patronage of the conference was given by Mr. Jakub Chełstowski, the Marshal of the Śląsk Province, and Mr. Andrzej Adamczyk, the Polish Minister of Infrastructure. The patronage was also given by the chairman of the Transport Committee of the Polish Academy of Sciences, Prof. Wojciech Wawrzyński.

This year's conference, TST 2019, attracted a large number of participants. The annual meetings gather a group of outstanding scientists from Poland and abroad, and the submitted papers constitute a significant contribution to the issues underlying the conference. I would like to emphasize the participation in the conference of Mr. Sebastian Belz, the General Secretary of the European Platform of Transport Sciences, whose presentation was an introduction to a broader discussion of intelligent solutions in transport.

I am very confident that the best papers presented in these proceedings will be important and interesting material for discussions on the development of Polish and European transport telematics.

March 2019 Jerzy Mikulski

Organization

Organizers

Polish Association of Transport Telematics

Co-operating Universities

Gdynia Maritime University, Poland
Maritime University of Szczecin, Poland
University of Bielsko-Biała, Poland
Warsaw University of Technology, Poland
Wrocław University of Science and Technology, Poland
University of Economics in Katowice, Poland
University of Technology and Humanities in Radom, Poland
University of Lodz, Poland
WSB Schools of Banking in Wrocław, Poland
Katowice School of Technology, Poland
UNESCO Chair for Science, Technology and Engineering Education at the AGH, Poland

Scientific Program Committee

J. Mikulski (Chair)	Polish Association of Transport Telematics, Poland
E. van Berkum	University of Twente, The Netherlands
M. Bregulla	Ingolstadt University of Applied Sciences, Germany
A. Bujak	WSB Universities in Wroclaw, Poland
M. Bukljaš-Skocibušic	University of Zagreb, Croatia
F. Busch	Technische Universität München, Germany
M. Chrzan	University of Technology and Humanities in Radom, Poland
R. van Duin	Delft University of Technology, The Netherlands
M. Franeková†	University of Zilina, Republic of Slovakia
G. Gentile	Universita di Roma La Sapienza, Italy
M. Givoni	Tel-Aviv University, Israel
J. Gnap	University of Zilina, Republic of Slovakia
P. Groumpos	University of Patras, Greece
H. Hadj-Mabrouk	Institut Français des Sciences et Technologies des Transports, France
S. Iwan	Maritime University of Szczecin, Poland
A. Janota	University of Zilina, Republic of Slovakia
U. Jumar	Institut für Automation und Kommunikation, Germany

A. Kalašová	University of Zilina, Republic of Slovakia
R. Kozłowski	University of Lodz, Poland
J. Krimmling	Technische Uniwersität Dresden, Germany
O. Krettek	RWTH Aachen, Emeritus Professor, Germany
A. Lewiński	University of Technology and Humanities in Radom, Poland
M. Luft	University of Technology and Humanities in Radom, Poland
Z. Łukasik	University of Technology and Humanities in Radom, Poland
A. Maczyński	University of Bielsko-Biała, Poland
G. Nowacki	Military University of Technology in Warsaw, Poland
T. Perzyński	University of Technology and Humanities in Radom, Poland
Z. Pietrzykowski	Maritime University of Szczecin, Poland
C. Pronello	Politecnico di Torino, Italy
K. Rástočný	University of Zilina, Republic of Slovakia
M. Siergiejczyk	Warsaw University of Technology, Poland
A. da Silva	Carvalho University of Porto, Portugal
J. Skorupski	Warsaw University of Technology, Poland
J. Spalek	University of Zilina, Republic of Slovakia
J. Szpytko	AGH University of Science and Technology, Poland
M. Ślezak	Motor Transport Institute, Poland
R. Thompson	University of Melbourne, Australia
R. Toledo-Moreo	Universidad Politécnica de Cartagena, Spain
R. Wawruch	Gdynia Maritime University, Poland
W. Wawrzyński	Warsaw University of Technology, Poland
A. Weintrit	Gdynia Maritime University, Poland

Contents

x   Contents

Telematics in Marine Transport

Telematics in Air Transport

General About Telematics

Telematics in Rail Transport

Telematic Applications for the Metropolitan Railway System (MR) in the Górnośląsko-Zagłębiowska Metropolis

Ryszard Janecki[1(✉)], Grzegorz Karoń[2], and Jerzy Mikulski[3]

[1] University of Economics in Katowice, 1 Maja 50, Katowice, Poland
ryszard.janecki@ue.katowice.pl
[2] Silesian University of Technology, Akademicka 2A, Gliwice, Poland
[3] Katowice School of Technology, Rolna 43, Katowice, Poland

Abstract. The subject of consideration in the presented article is the concept of a metropolitan railway system (MR) in the area of the Górnośląsko-Zagłębiowska Metropolis (GZM Metropolis). The content of the publication is divided into two distinct parts. The first presents the assumptions and proposed solutions of the MR system as one of the elements of integrated metropolitan transport. In the second, in the context of the designed solutions in the scope of structure, function and organization of the MR system, the issues of telematic applications for metropolitan passenger transport were discussed. Possible solutions and proposals regarding access of passengers (mainly metropolitan residents) to the metropolitan rail system using individual and network telematics applications were indicated.

Keywords: Telematic application · Metropolitan railway system · Integrated metropolitan transport

1 Introduction

In passenger transport in the Górnośląsko-Zagłębiowska Metropolis (GZM) area, actions are necessary to ensure:

- improvement of the natural environment in the metropolis,
- elimination or reduction of communication congestion,
- increase in the competitiveness of public transport.

The projects that generate the aforementioned benefits include a construction project in the GZM area of the metropolitan rail system (MR). The proposed solutions in the scope of structure, function and organization of the MR system require the implementation of telematics applications for metropolitan passenger transport.

J. Mikulski (Ed.): TST 2019, CCIS 1049, pp. 3–16, 2019.
https://doi.org/10.1007/978-3-030-27547-1_1

2 Basic Assumptions of Metropolitan Rail Conceptions in the Górnośląsko-Zagłębiowska Metropolis Area

The following attributes are proposed in the concept of the MR system:

- it will operate in the Górnośląsko-Zagłębiowska Metropolis with the possibility of expanding the service area outside the metropolis,
- the limits of the system are determined by extreme stations of metropolitan trains, located on rail transport lines served by these trains,
- in the MR system, passenger transport will be carried out on selected lines using the metropolitan rail network, located in the area designated by the system boundaries,
- in order to transport people (residents of GZM, guests and visitors), the system will launch appropriate means of transport, the type of which will be determined by the technology of transports and infrastructure adapted to it,
- in transport by metropolitan railway resources will be used in the form of:
  - rail transport lines, technically or organisationally separated, after which metropolitan trains will move,
  - transport stock suitable for the technologies being implemented and reported transport needs formed in metropolitan trains,
  - infrastructure, equipment and means of transport enabling MR connections on selected sections of the so-called last mile (in deliveries - transfers to check-in points on the MR network) without using rail transport means,
  - adapted to the needs of the technical back-up system,
- the MR system will operate in a continuous, safe and efficient manner, offering the quantity and quality level of transport services accepted by users (mainly GZM residents),
- metropolitan railway will be a system open to development, capable of creating and implementing development processes, depending on the needs, all of its subsystems.

Taking into account the aspirations of MR system stakeholders and currently identified and projected passenger flows, four variants of W0–W3 Metropolitan Railway system were constructed. Figures 1, 2, 3 and 4 present the MR transport network for each of the system variants, and in Tables 1 and 2 their general characteristics (the variant of the W0 omitted, in which no infrastructure investments are anticipated) was omitted.

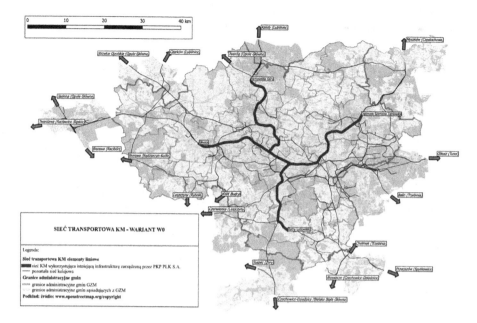

Fig. 1. Variant W0 – MR transport network [1]

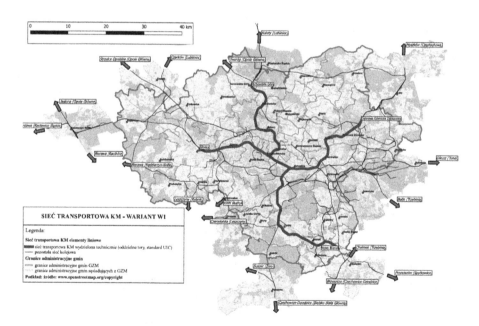

Fig. 2. Variant W1 – MR transport network [1]

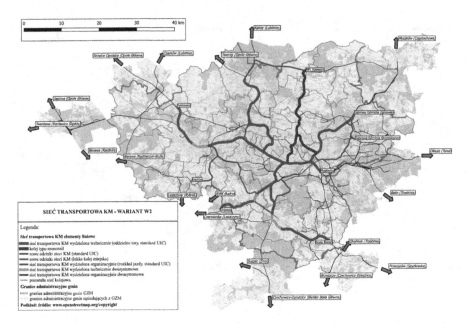

Fig. 3. Variant W2 – MR transport network [1]

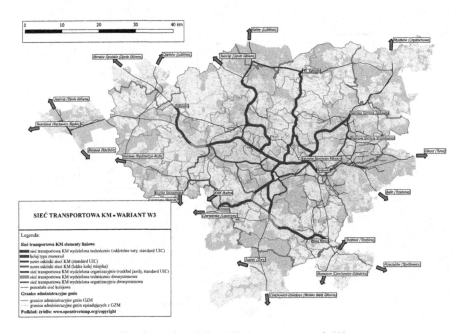

Fig. 4. Variant W3 – MR transport network [1]

Table 1. Characteristics of the variants of solutions W1–W3 proposed in the concept of metropolitan railways in the area of GZM (technical aspect) [1]

MR Variant	Transport technology used in a given MR variant	Selected parameters of the transport network MR			The scope of the most important works on the MR transport network					The size of the required number of means of transport in [number of trains]
		overall length in [km]	the total number of check-in points	the number of metropolitan nodes	construction of new UIC railway tracks in [1]	construction of a light rail line in [1]	construction of monorail type railways in [km]	revitalization / revitalization and construction or reconstruction / modernization of the PKP PLK SA line in [1]	revitalization / construction of passenger check-in counters in [number of objects]	
1	2	3	4	5	6	7	8	9	10	11
W1	a monotechnology variant - a railway that complies with the UIC standards	117,5	58	2	219,7	-	-	15,2	26	33
W2	multitechnological variant - railway in accordance with UIC standards, light city railway, monorail	261,4	100	16	279,0	32,0	35,1	135,0	53	70
W3		312,0	115	22	279,4	61,1	35,1	140,7	69	82

Table 2. Characteristics of the variants of solutions W1–W3 proposed in the concept of metropolitan railways in the area of GZM (organizational aspects) [1]

MR Variant	Selected aspects					
	organization of metropolitan trains				organization of transport	
	target type of traffic	interval between trains in [min]		target daily number of metropolitan trains launched in [train pairs]	organizer of railway metropolitan transport	operator (s) of metropolitan rail transport
		in the day (except transport peaks)	at transport peaks			
1	2	3	4	5	6	7
W1		min. 20 max. 60	min. 10 max. 20	metropolitan mains – 79 metropolitan supplementary lines – 43	Metropolitan Transport Board (ZTM)	an external operator selected by ZTM
W2	equally spaced metropolitan train traffic on technically or organizationally separated tracks	min. 20 max. 60	min. 10 max. 20	metropolitan mains – 79		
W3		min. 20 max. 60	min. 10 max. 20	metropolitan basic lines – 54 metropolitan supplementary lines – 43		

3 Present Applications of ITS Technologies in Metropolitan Transport in GZM Area

ITS technologies in public collective transport allow for the implementation of many goals. Among the most important of them, and thus among the ITS system modules, the following are mainly mentioned [2–6]:

- management of the public transport fleet,
- ensuring the priority of the journey,
- collection of fees (e-ticket, e-card),
- passenger information,
- measurement of passenger flows.

From the above list of functionalities, it appears that they concern two areas of operation of urban public transport. The first one has an operational dimension. It includes the implementation of transport processes resulting from the market transport offer of the organizer of public collective transport. The second is the broadly under-stood system organization, including the passenger-system relation.

The existing state in the scope of using ITS technology in the Górnośląsko-Zagłębiowska Metropolis area can be described as follows:

- there is no metropolitan traffic management system,
- The Metropolitan Transport Authority (ZTM) does not have a public metropolitan transport management system,
- the applied solutions for transport processes in public urban transport have a local character include only metropolitan bus and tram transport,
- the use of ITS technology to service metropolitan public transport passengers covers all types of transport organized by the Metropolitan Transport Authority and the entire metropolitan area,
- many of the applied technologies were implemented by the public transport orga-nizers operating until 31 December 2018 in the area of GZM, i.e. KZK GOP in Katowice, MZK in Tychy and MZKP in Tarnowskie Góry,
- the Koleje Śląskie company that operates regional rail transport has an exclusive passenger service system using regional trains; this system is not integrated with the ZTM system.

Table 3 presents the general characteristics of solutions currently used in the GZM area using ITS technologies and in Fig. 5 their structure.

The current state of ITS applications in the GZM collective transport system is characterized by [16]:

- lack of some components of the ITS core structure in the metropolis, including the metropolitan transport management system,
- a critical evaluation of the solutions of the Silesian Public Service Card system.

An additional circumstance is also the process of creating a metropolitan rail. Both mentioned groups of factors indicate the urgent need to undertake work in the field of ITS in the area of GZM and at the same time define their directions.

Table 3. Description of solutions based on ITS technologies operating in the GZM area [4, 7–15]

Area of application	Operating range	Description of the offered services
1	2	3
1. Ensuring the priority of travel for public collective transport	Local solution	- Priority at intersections for delayed line A4 buses in Gliwice obtained thanks to the synchronization of traffic lights with the timetable and the current registered bus line position; within the extended ITS system it is planned to include a further priority of 150 public transport vehicles - Priority at intersections for trams on the route Katowice-Chorzów-Bytom (line 6) and on the section Katowice Rynek-Katowice Zawodzie Zajezdnia

2. Electronic payment for tickets	Metropolitan area solution	- Purchase of tickets using the Silesian Card of Public Services (ŚKUP):
		  • Purchase of single tickets:
		    - Using the Customer Portal, which is a website at www.kartaskup.pl, which enables the user of the card to remotely access its functions
		    - using the funds accumulated on the account of ŚKUP card (electronic purse) at customer service points, passenger service points, ticket sales points and stationary card recharge machines
		    - in a reader on board the means of metropolitan transport
		  • Purchase of season tickets - all of the aforementioned ways except for the purchase on the reader on the vehicle
		- purchase of tickets using mobile applications:
		  • "mPay Mobile Payments", after the purchase the ticket is assigned to the mobile phone from which the purchase was made
		  • Using the IVR voice mode - making a call to the indicated number and selecting appropriate options according to the voice messages given by the system
		  • Using SMS text mode - sending an SMS message to the indicated number with the content corresponding to the type of ticket purchased
		  • SkyCash - payment by a payment card connected to the system or cash that was previously credited to the account
		- Purchase of tickets in the Open Payment System - tickets are purchased on board vehicles using a contactless voucher card (Visa, Mastercard), which in the system has been given a dual function: a means of payment and at the same time a payment payment identifier; it is a pilot project

(continued)

Table 3. (*continued*)

Area of application	Operating range	Description of the offered services

3. Passenger information	Metropolitan area solution	- In this ITS subsystem:
		  • There is a Dynamic Passenger Information System
		  • Websites are available that provide service functions dedicated to passengers of metropolitan public transport
		  • There is an internal passenger information system
		- Dynamic Passenger Information System:
		  • Provides information to passengers using passenger information boards at bus stops and the Passenger Portal
		  • Real and planned departures of transport vehicles on the basis of data obtained from the system are placed on passenger information boards
		  • Passenger Portal can work in desktop and mobile versions; allows you to obtain current information on the progress of courses on ZTM communication lines (expected departure times from a given stop and the position of the vehicle on the line)
		- ZTM website - OFFICIAL WEBSITE https://rj. metropoliaztm.pl:
		  • Enables the acquisition of the "Find connection" function, thus planning travel by means of ZTM transport, taking into account the actual traffic conditions
		  • Provides timetable information, presents messages, a list of stops and a map of the ZTM network
		  • Provides a link to the Portal of Passenger of the Dynamic Passenger Information System and the jakdojade.pl portal
		- ZTM website at https://www.metropoliaztm.pl/pl/ offers passengers:
		  • Searching for connections
		  • Subpages: Timetable, Tickets, ŚKUP, Airport lines
		- The internal passenger information module consists of directional tables, a table with line numbers, internal information boards and a voice information system; currently, the standards for collective transport solutions in the GZM area are not defined

(a) basic elements

(b) subsystem PROVIDING PRIORITY

(c) subsystem ELECTRONIC PAYMENT

(d) subsystem PASSENGER INFORMATION

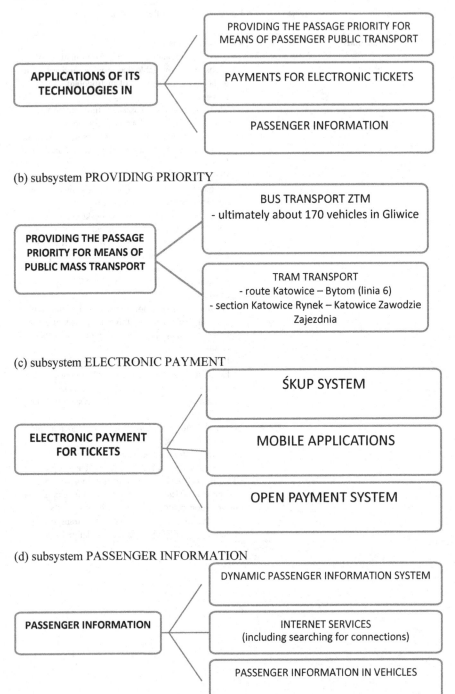

Fig. 5. Applications of ITS technology in collective transport in the Górnośląsko-Zagłębiowska Metropolis area [own study]

4 Telematics for the Metropolitan Railway System in the Górnośląsko-Zagłębiowska Metroplis Area - Proposals of Solutions

The support of the metropolitan rail system being developed by ITS technologies must be harmonized with the activities related to the construction of the target metropolitan transport management system for the needs of ZTM in the area of GZM. At the same time, issues related to the control of metropolitan train traffic are not considered, the issues being the responsibility of the managers (managers) of the MR transport network (inter alia, PKP PLK SA).

An important determinant of the proposed solutions is the chosen approach to the problem. It is possible to distinguish two ways of action in this area, dictated, among others, by the scale and complexity of ITS modules, costs and a relatively long period of implementation of telematics projects:

– an approach that uses existing solutions to the maximum and assumes integration with new system elements,
– building from scratch a new ITS system for collective transport in the metropolis.

First of all, the reduction of funds and the lack of acceptance for duplicating what already exists, speak for choosing the first approach. Accordingly, the ITS project for the metropolitan railways should be constructed in accordance with the following rules:

– the subsystem should be developed to provide the PROVIDING THE PASSAGE PRIORITY of TRANSPORT to the means of metropolitan transport in places where the public transport network serves metropolitan nodes and integrated metropolitan stations/passenger stops, located on the metropolitan rail transport lines; these activities should ensure punctuality of ZTM buses, trams and trolley-buses serving such types of MR check-in desks. The implementation of this task should be carried out in close cooperation with ZTM with the authorities of the metropolitan municipalities concerned,
– in the subsystem ELECTRONIC PAYMENT FOR TICKETS, the purchase of tickets for the metropolitan railways should be considered; the subsystem should be open to use modern forms of payment, constantly developing,
– necessary changes in the ŚKUP system should be made to eliminate existing defects; it is advisable to concentrate first of all on ensuring effective and acceptable forms of implementation of existing functionalities by users and extending them to journeys and journeys by metropolitan railways. Then, the system should be expanded with new functionalities; e.g. optimizing the selection of a fare for travel or travel (ŚKUP II system),
– all components of the PASSENGER INFORMATION module must be extended, including:
  – both external and internal information (among others, the system of visual and auditory information of travellers on platforms is necessary for railway metropolitan transport),
  – functioning access systems to information for passengers,

– information systems (internet services), including, among others, the possibility of planning a trip in the area of GZM by bus, tram, trolleybus and the ZTM metropolitan train taking into account the actual conditions of transport of public transport vehicles.

Figure 6 presents the basic elements of the ITS structure of the Metropolitan Transport Board after the implementation of the metropolitan rail project and the implementation of the ŚKUP II system.

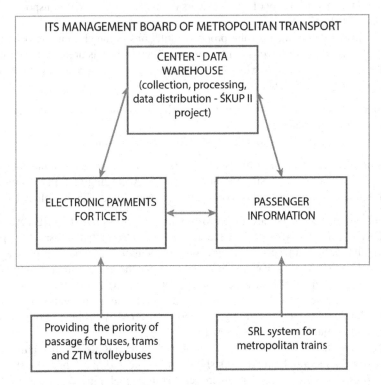

Fig. 6. Basic elements of the ITS structure of the Metropolitan Transport Board after the implementation of the metropolitan railway project and implementation of the ŚKUP II project [own study]

5 Conclusion

1. Undertaking work related to the creation of a metropolitan rail should be the premise for developing a public metropolitan transport management system for ZTM.
2. Particular elements of this system should include all transport technologies (buses, trams, trolleybuses, metropolitan trains and metropolitan bicycles) used in metropolitan transport.

3. An important attribute of the system will be its integration with the ITS system of Koleje Śląskie.
4. The system should use previously functioning ITS elements. At the same time, it is necessary to eliminate outdated ones, modify them and modernize them. If it is rational and effective, new projects should be prepared.
5. Taking into account the current state of ITS applications and the approach to this problem by self-government authorities, it seems justified to design and implement using a modified and improved ŚKUP II system (account-centricity attributes in terms of on-line identification and online work) of the IT platform integrating:

   - all ITS elements of the Metropolitan Transport Board,
   - ITS systems of individual cities Górnośląsko-Zagłębiowska Metropolis at the level of data transmission collected in the ŚKUP II system generated by the system and installed cameras, signalling controllers, passenger information systems, vehicle locations, etc.

References

1. Janecki, R., et al.: Koncepcja kolei metropolitalnej dla Górnośląsko-Zagłębiowskiej Metropolii z wykorzystaniem metod inżynierii systemów, praca naukowo-badawcza NB-29/RT5/2018 Katedra Systemów Transportowych i Inżynierii Ruchu, Wydział Transportu Politechniki Śląskiej, Katowice grudzień (2018)
2. Cichoński, J., et al.: Koncepcja Inteligentnego Systemu Transportowego dla miasta Bielsko-Biała, Gliwice (2014)
3. Koncepcja i architektura Inteligentnego Systemu Zarządzania ruchem na obszarze działania Komunikacyjnego Związku Komunalnego Górnośląskiego Okręgu Przemysłowego, Śląska Sieć Metropolitalna sp. z o.o., wersja 1.4 e, Katowice (2015)
4. Wilczek, M. (ed.): Inteligentny System. Zarządzania Transportem Publicznym. Wydział Transportu Politechniki Śląskiej, Katowice (2007)
5. Mikulski, J.: Innowacje z zastosowaniem telematyki w sektorze TSL. In: Michałowska, M. (ed.): Aktywność podmiotów sektora TSL w tworzeniu i realizacji strategii społecznej odpowiedzialności biznesu. Wydawnictwo Uniwersytetu Ekonomicznego w Katowicach, Katowice (2016)
6. Janecki, R.: Zastosowanie nowoczesnych systemów telematycznych w sektorze TSL na tle zasad CSR. In: Michałowska, M. (ed.) Aktywność podmiotów sektora TSL w tworzeniu i realizacji strategii społecznej odpowiedzialności biznesu. Wydawnictwo Uniwersytetu Ekonomicznego w Katowicach, Katowice (2016)
7. Inteligentny System Transportowy. ZDM Gliwice. www.zdm.gliwice.pl/strona.php?s=31
8. Informacje na temat zrealizowanych i planowanych inwestycji. Tramwaje Śląskie SA. https://tram-silesia.pl/www/index.php/inwestycje. Accessed 12 Jan 2019
9. Usługi komunikacyjne. https://portal.kartaskup.pl/web/10180/59. Accessed 12 Jan 2019
10. Bilety elektroniczne w Metropolii GZM (ZTM). https://www.mpay.pl/usługi/bilety-komunikacji-miejskiej/milety-metropolii-gzm-ztm. Accessed 12 Jan 2019
11. Górny Śląsk, Startuje pilotaż Open Payment System w GZM. https://www.transport-publiczny.pl/wiadomości/gorny-slask-startuje-pilotaż-open-payment-system-w-gzm-60642.html. Accessed 12 Jan 2019

12. SkyCash w KZK GOP. https://www.skaycash.com/aktualności/skycash-w-kzk-gop. Accessed 12 Jan 2019
13. ZTM – OFICJALNA STRONA. https://rj-metropoliaztm.pl. Accessed 12 Jan 2019
14. ZTM. https://www.metropliaztm.pl. Accessed 12 Jan 2019
15. System Dynamicznej Informacji Pasażerskiej – Portal Pasażera. zdip.metropliaztm.pl/web/ml. Accessed 12 Jan 2019
16. GZM/nowa karta ŚKUP. https://www.facebook.com/GZMMetropolia/posts. Accessed 12 Jan 2019

Simulation of the Effect of Selected National Values on the Braking Curves of an ETCS Vehicle

Emilia Koper$^{(\boxtimes)}$, Andrzej Kochan, and Łukasz Gruba

Warsaw University of Technology, Koszykowa 75, Warsaw, Poland
{eko,ako}@wt.pw.edu.pl

Abstract. The ERTMS/ETCS system is intended to provide an interoperable approach to train control and signalling in the EU. Adapting its functionality to the requirements of the different infrastructure managers is to be ensured by national values. The selected variables have an impact on railway safety as their values, together with other parameters form the basis for determining the braking curves of a vehicle running under the supervision of ERTMS/ETCS (ETCS vehicle). Braking curves determine the length of braking distance. The paper presents the results of research on the influence of selected variables on the shape of braking curves. The nature of the tested variables and their application for two models of Gamma and Lambda trains were discussed. The simulation was carried out with the use of the "Braking curves simulation tool" and the assessment of the results on the basis of original criteria.

Keywords: National Values · Braking curves · ERTMS/ETCS

1 Introduction

The integration of the European Union countries requires many activities aimed at achieving technical compatibility and interoperability in the entire territory of the Community. The ERTMS/ETCS system has been designed as a uniform, interoperable approach to controlling train traffic in the European Union. Interoperability means the ability of a rail system to allow the safe and uninterrupted movement of trains which accomplish the required levels of performance [1].

The assurance and verification of the interoperability of the rail system referred to in [1] is based on technical specification for interoperability [10]. General requirements for control-command and signalling subsystems i.e. "control-command and signalling – On-board" and "control-command and signalling – Trackside" are included in [10], and specific requirements - in the so-called subsets and other documents mentioned in the relevant set of specifications.

However, it should be noted that [10] and the documents related to this document specify the European requirements for the implementation of ERTMS/ETCS in areas managed by different infrastructure managers in the European Union.

© Springer Nature Switzerland AG 2019
J. Mikulski (Ed.): TST 2019, CCIS 1049, pp. 17–31, 2019.
https://doi.org/10.1007/978-3-030-27547-1_2

Individual managers shall define among others the operating rules applicable to the infrastructure they manage. The ERTMS/ECTS functionality shall be adapted to the requirements of the different infrastructure managers by National Values.

2   National Values in the ETCS System

The ERTMS/ETCS National Values adapt the functionality of the ERTMS/ETCS system to the requirements of the area or country and are defined and sent as a packet number 3 in the relevant System Requirements Specification (SRS). SRS [11–14] describes National Values and specifies the permissible range of their values, as well as the default value to be used by on-board equipment in the event of unavailability of the values. Table 1 illustrates selected National Values set out in the System Requirements Specification [12, 13] defined for baseline 3 (B3 MR1 - Baseline 3 Maintenance Release 1 and B3 R2 - Baseline 3 Release 2).

Member States are responsible for formulating a set of values of National Values for a given national area, understood as the area of application of a given set of national values. The area of application of a set of National Values is determined by the variable NID_C in packet number 3. The values of the ERTMS/ETCS NID_C parameter, which defines the national areas, are limited. When defining the set of values for National Values, if this set has the same values as other national areas under the responsibility of the same infrastructure manager, it is worth considering extending the area instead of creating a new national area. National areas with the same set need not be geographically adjacent.

2.1   Classification of National Values

Some of the ERTMS/ETCS National Values are directly related to the operational rules of the national area - the so-called 'operating' variable (e.g. V_NVSHUNT - a variable describing the maximum allowable shunting speed under ERTMS/ETCS supervision) and some, especially those introduced by ETCS baseline 3 (B3MR1, B3R2) are linked to the train braking process and the determination of braking curves (e.g. A_NVMAXREDADHx a variable describing maximum deceleration under reduced adhesion conditions).

Tab. 1. Selected National Values and their default values [own study]

Name	Description	Default value	Application (ETCS level)	Application (ETCS mode)
Operating National Values				
V_NVSHUNT	Shunting mode speed limit	30	0, NTC, 1, 2, 3	SH
D_NVROLL	Roll away distance limit	2 m	1, 2, 3	FS, OS, PT, RV, SB, SH, SR, UN

(continued)

Tab. 1. (*continued*)

Name	Description	Default value	Application (ETCS level)	Application (ETCS mode)
T_NVOVTRP	Maximum time for overriding the train trip (Override EoA)	60 s	0, NTC, 1, 2, 3	SH, SN, SR, UN
...	...	...	...	...
National Values affect braking process				
Q_NVSBTSMPERM	Permission to use service brake in target speed monitoring	1	0, 1, 2, 3	FS, LS, OS, SR, UN
...	...	...	...	...
National Values affecting train braking curves				
A_NVMAXREDADH1	Maximum deceleration under reduced adhesion conditions (1) applicable for trains: - with brake position "Passenger train in P", and - with special/additional brakes independent from wheel/rail adhesion	1,0 m/s^2	0, 1, 2, 3	FS, LS, OS, SR, UN
M_NVAVADH	Weighting factor for available wheel/rail adhesion	0	0, 1, 2, 3	FS, LS, OS SR, UN
M_NVEBCL	Confidence level for emergency brake safe deceleration on dry rails	9-99.9999999%	0, 1, 2, 3	FS, LS, UN, SR, OS
A_NVP12	Lower deceleration limit to determine the set of Kv to be used	The SRS does not specify a default value	0, 1, 2, 3	FS, LS, OS, SR, UN
...	...	...	...	...
Other National Values				
Q_NVDRIVER_ADHES	Qualifier for the modification of trackside adhesion factor by driver	0	0, NTC, 1, 2, 3	UN, SN, SR, OS, FS, LS, SH
...	...	...	...	...

The selected National Values have a direct impact on railway safety as their values, together with other parameters, form the basis for determining the braking curves of a vehicle running under the supervision of ERTMS/ETCS (ETCS vehicle). Braking curves determine the braking distance of individual ETCS vehicles. For the purposes of this article, an ETCS vehicle means a train or shunting stock comprising a traction vehicle with ETCS on-board equipment.

2.2 Selected National Values Description

Simulations were carried out for the following National Values: M_NVAVADH, A_NVMMAXREDADH2, M_NVEBCL for Gamma train model. The most important information describing the individual National Values to be simulated is given below.

The M_NVEBCL variable defines Confidence level for emergency brake safe deceleration on dry rails. The value of the variable M_NVEBCL is determined for good adhesion conditions (dry rails), and in the case of reduced adhesion (wet rails), the emergency braking deceleration value is reduced in order to relocate the starting point of the braking process and the possibility of braking before the obstacle/target location [9].

The M_NVEBCL variable is used to set the minimum required probability that the train's braking system could deliver the stated rate of deceleration when commanded. In order to achieve the required confidence level, the appropriate Kdry_rst factor is used to correct the nominal value of the emergency braking deceleration.

The M_NVEBCL variable allows 10 confidence levels, ranging from 50% to 99.9999999%, to be defined. Each confidence level shall have an appropriate speed-dependent value of Kdry_rst parameter, stored on-board. Based on the value of the M_NVEBCL National Value and the estimated train speed, the on-board units select the appropriate Kdry_rst factor, which is used to calculate the emergency braking deceleration. The Kdry_rst factor quantifies the dispersion of the emergency braking performance on dry rails and is determined e.g. by the Monte Carlo method [3, 9].

The M_NVAVADH National Value is a weighting factor for available wheel-rail adhesion. The M_NVAVADH factor defines the weighting to apply to Kwet_rst correction factor. The Kwet_rst parameter quantifies the dispersion of the emergency braking performance on wet rails. In order to determine the safe emergency braking rate, the correction factor Kdry_rst [3, 9] must first be reduced.

The A_NVMAXREDADH National Value defines the maximum emergency brake deceleration rate used for the braking calculation when the low adhesion function is active. The A_NVMAXREDADH 2 National Value applies in the case of reduced adhesion for trains:

- with "brake position" – "Passenger in P",
- without special/additional brakes.

In the case of baseline 3, there are some discrepancies between the SRS in the version 3.4.0 [13] and 3.6.0 [12] with regard to National Values: A_NVMAXRE-DADH2 (and A_NVMAXREDADH1 and A_NVMAXREDADH3):

– according to SRS version 3.4.0 [13] maximum value of the variable A_NVMAXREDADH2, (and A_NVMAXREDADH1 and A_NVMAXRE-DADH3) may be 3,15 m/s^2, but according to SRS version 3.6.0 [12] 3,00 m/s^2,
– SRS version 3.6.0 [12] introduces special values for the variable, and if the special value of variable A_NVMAXREDADH1/2/3 is selected, the maximum deceleration for determining the braking curves does not apply.

For baseline 3, for which a maximum deceleration value is defined and for which the low adhesion function is active, the values of the variable A_NVMAXREDADH2 (and 1, 3) affect only those parts of the EBD curve for which the A_NVMAXRE-DADH2 variable provides a lower deceleration value than the nominal deceleration value defined for the vehicle. As a result, the braking distance of the vehicle, understood as the distance from the starting point of braking as determined by EVC (European Vital Computer) to the target location, may be extended by taking into account the lower deceleration value for part of the EBD (Emergency Brake Deceleration) curve.

3 ETCS Braking Curves

Baseline 2 (B2), corresponding to the first set of specifications defined in [10], formulates the basic principles for generating braking curves and the information displayed to the driver on DMI (Driver Machine Interface), but there is no consistent method for determining these curves. In the absence of consistent requirements, the algorithms used by on-board suppliers/railway undertakings lead to the determination of different braking distances for a given vehicle type [15].

ETCS Baseline 3 introduces a harmonised algorithm and method to compute ETCS braking curves and the associated information displayed to the drivers. In [12, 13] individual ETCS braking curves were specified.

When an ETCS vehicle approaches a supervised target, it enters Target Speed Monitoring (TSM) and it calculates relative locations where ETCS has to perform specific actions as part of its ATP (Automatic Train Protection) functionality. These actions include displaying information to the driver, and issuing commands to the train's traction and braking systems if the driver does not react correctly.

For the purpose of determining braking curves, the locations which initiate individual types of braking are calculated, constituting the starting point of braking for a given curve. Characteristic locations and interpretation of individual curves are shown in the Fig. 1.

EBD - Emergency Brake Deceleration means the latest location from which, if the emergency brake is fully applied and if the braking rate as defined in the train data is achieved, the train will be able to a stop at before the Supervised Location (SvL).

EBI - Emergency Brake Intervention means the latest location from which the emergency brake has to be commanded for the train to follow the EBD curve. This curve takes into account the brake build-up time.

SBD - Service Brake Deceleration means the latest location from which, if the service brake is fully applied and if the braking rate as defined in the train data is

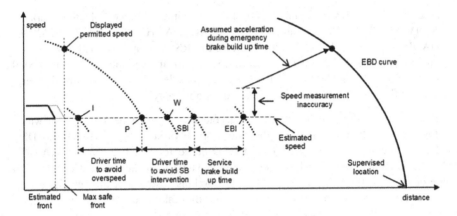

Fig. 1. ETCS braking curves [3]

achieved, the train will be able to a stop at the End of Authority (EoA). SBD is calculated whether or not the service brake command is available for use.

SBI1 - Service Brake Intervention 1 is calculated for an EoA and is the latest location at which the service brake has to be commanded for the train to follow the SBD curve to stop at the EoA. The curve takes into account the brake build-up time for the service brake. This curve shall be taken into account when the on-board computer has the potential to affect the braking system in the event of service braking.

SBI2 - Service Brake Intervention 2 is calculated for an EBD based target and is the latest location at which the service brake is commanded to avoid the train reaching the EBI location, which requires implementation of emergency braking.

W - Warning - the location from which an intervention by the ERTMS/ETCS onboard is two seconds away at current speed. This is indicated to the driver via the DMI. This is the curve beyond which an audible warning is given when the speed limit has been exceeded.

P - Permitted means the location from which an intervention by the ERTMS/ETCS onboard is four seconds away at current speed. This is indicated to the driver via the DMI. The train running speed curve, in excess of which the train driver has sufficient time to apply service braking, not to exceed the position in which the ETCS on-board system will take control of the braking system.

I - Indication means the location from which the ERTMS/ETCS onboard would generate an additional visual curve on the DMI to inform that the start of the P curve is approaching. It shall provide the driver with a sufficient reserve of time to enable him, when applying service braking, not to exceed the permitted speed.

The determination of braking curves can be done according to two models - Gamma and Lambda train models. The article describes the model of the Gamma train and the model of the Lambda train and presents the National Values applicable to the type, but experiments have been carried out for the Gamma model of the train.

In case when:

– the train composition is characterised by known (predefined) fixed parameters (fixed configuration and number of units) or by a finite number of sets of defined parameters,
– all nominal values of braking forces and braking system characteristics are known,
– the values of the correction factors are also known and all these values can be entered in the on-board computer,

then such a train model will be defined as a Gamma train model [3, 4].

If only the percentage of the braking mass is known, which is the quotient of the sum of the braking mass of the train (calculated according to [5]) by the total mass of the train, then this train model will be called a Lambda train.

In practice, in the case of Gamma trains, the following data are entered into the on-board computer: train length, percentage of rotating masses, track and balise location data, National Values and braking system characteristics. In the case of Lambda trains, in addition to the above mentioned parameters, the brake percentage and the values of correction factors are also defined.

The paper focuses on the influence of selected National Values on the SBD and EBD curve. In order to determine individual braking curves in addition to train parameters, including the braking system, route data are also important.

The EBD is a parabolic shaped curve that starts from the target location and is computed with the deceleration resulting from: the guaranteed deceleration due to the emergency brake system itself (A_brake_safe) and the deceleration due to the uphill/downhill slopes (A_gradient) (Fig. 2).

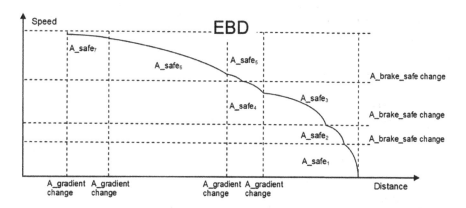

Fig. 2. Determination of the EBD curve [3]

As a general rule, it can be assumed that, for areas with normal adhesion conditions, the value for the safe deceleration of braking shall be determined from the following equation:

$$A\_safe(v, d) = A\_brake\_safe(v) + A\_gradient(d) \tag{1}$$

The A_brake_safe value for the Gamma train model is determined from the equation:

$$A\_brake\_safe(v) = A\_brake\_emergency * Kdry\_rst(M\_NVEBCL)* \\ \{Kwet\_rst + M\_NVAVADH * (1 - Kwet\_rst)\} \tag{2}$$

In the case of areas with reduced adhesion conditions, where the value of the variable A_MAXREDADHx is limited to a speed-dependent maximum value:

$$A\_safe(v, d) = MIN(A\_brake\_safe(v), A\_MAXREDADHx) + A\_gradient(d) \tag{3}$$

Where, for an unknown value of the M_rotating parameter, the A_gradient is determined from the equation: for uphills – formula 4, for downhills – formula 5.

$$A\_gradient(d) = g * grad/(1000 + 10 * M\_rotating\_max) \tag{4}$$

$$A\_gradient(d) = g * grad/(1000 + 10 * M\_rotating\_min) \tag{5}$$

When the value of the M_rotating parameter is specified:

$$A\_gradient(d) = g * grad/(1000 + 10 * M\_rotating\_nom) \tag{6}$$

Figure 3 shows selected data necessary for the determination of braking curves for the Gamma model of train and the general division of responsibilities between infrastructure manager and railway undertaking/onboard equipment supplier. For the Gamma train model, the infrastructure manager or the national authority is responsible

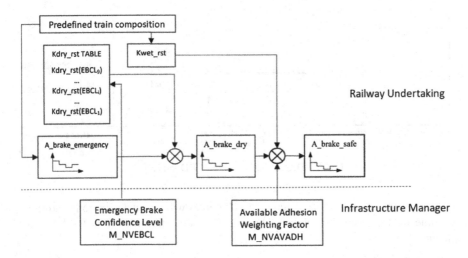

Fig. 3. Determination of braking curves for GAMMA trains - Actors' responsibilities [own study based on 3]

for determining the values of the National Values. For a Gamma type train these are the variables: M_NVEBCL and M_NVAVADH. Railway undertakings are responsible for establishing the relevant brake deceleration rates and values for a given ETCS vehicle.

4 Simulation Tool and Its Parameterization

For the purpose of this article, the influence of values of selected National Values was simulated in a tool developed and made available by European Union Agency for Railways (former ERA) – "Braking curves simulation tool".

Two groups of parameters have been developed for this purpose:

- National Values affecting train braking curves, which are a subtotals of all the National Values defined for baseline 3, with this article focusing on selected variables,
- other parameters relevant to the simulation.

The following assumptions have been made:

- train type – Gamma,
- brake position - Passenger train in P, affecting the delay in the implementation of braking, without additional/special brake (Special/additional brake independent from wheel/track adhesion),
- train length 200 m,
- initial speed – 160 kmph.

From among all the National Values, the first step was to select the variables applicable to the Gamma train. In the next step, this set was limited to variables that potentially affect the shape of the braking curves of a Gamma vehicle. They include: A_NVMAXREDADH1, A_NVMAXREDADH2, A_NVMAXREDADH3, M_NVA-VADH, M_NVEBCL.

For the purpose of conducting the simulation, input data describing the following were introduced [2]:

(a) ETCS vehicle:

- train type model,
- brake position,
- speed inaccuracy, position inaccuracy,
- the existing appropriate interfaces,

(b) track:

- gradient profile,
- initial speed,
- type of target type (LOA or EoA), target speed, distance to target,
- reduced adhesion area,

(c) National Values:

- shared by the Lambda and Gamma trains,
- variables specific to the Gamma train,

(d) braking parameters for the Gamma train model:

- – the deceleration (defined for each speed range) in the case of emergency, service and full service braking, used to determine the corresponding curves,
- – correction factors for Gamma train (Kwet_rst),
- – confidence level for emergency brake safe deceleration on dry rails (EBCL),
- – times from the moment of issuing a braking command (emergency and service commands respectively) until the full efficiency of the brakes is reached: T_be, T_bs.

Figure 4 shows a fragment of the ETCS vehicle braking curve generating algorithm.

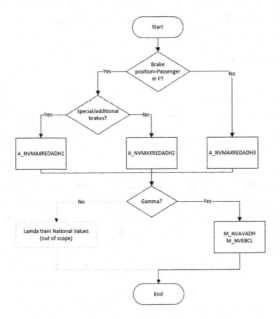

Fig. 4. Algorithm for taking into account National Values for Gamma train model [own study]

This algorithm takes into account the braking curves for the Gamma train model. The article skips part of the algorithm for the Lambda train (which is marked with a dashed line). Input data determines the selection of values of individual parameters taken into account in the determination of braking curves.

Figures 5 and 6 show an example of an input window for a simulation such as Kwet_rst, the deceleration in the case of full service braking applied and the time between the service braking command and the reaching full braking performance (T_bs parameter).

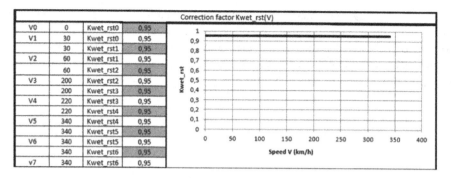

Fig. 5. Input window for KWET_RTS factor [own study]

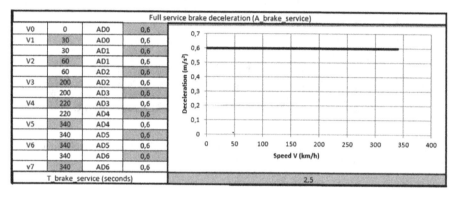

Fig. 6. Input window of the deceleration value parameter for full service braking [own study]

5 Selected Simulation Results

As a result of a single simulation, the SBD and EBD curves determining the braking distance of a given ETCS vehicle resulting from the braking curves were determined [8].

For the purpose of the article, the author's criterion was adopted that a positive evaluation of the simulation results means that the value of a given National Value at a specific combination of input parameters allows for safe stopping of an ETCS vehicle with the implemented emergency and service braking respectively. This means that for a given combination values of National Values, the stopping of the vehicle (V = 0 kmph) from the initial speed (V = 160 kmph), resulting from the length calculated for the SBD and EBD curve, will take place on a distance not greater than the braking distance of a train running at 160 kmph, resulting from national regulations in force in Poland [6, 7] in the absence of the use of Class A systems, i.e. 1300 m. The criterion formulated in this way results from the fact that the key from the safety point of view is stopping the ETCS vehicle before the end of the End of Authority (EoA).

Analyzing the effect of the values of individual National Values on the braking curves SBD and EBD, it can be stated that the M_NVEBCL variable does not affect the braking curve SBD, but influences the EBD curve. It can be observed that the braking distance resulting from the EBD curve is shortened with an increasing value of M_NVEBCL. The dependence of the braking distance on the value of the M_NVEBCL variable is shown in Fig. 7. The braking distance decreases as the value of M_NVEBCL variable increases, which is in line with intuition.

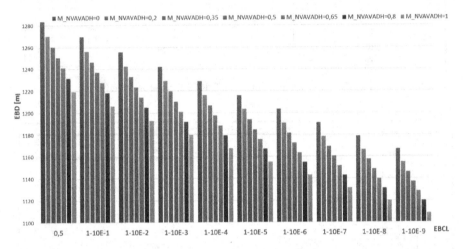

Fig. 7. Braking distance dependence on the value of the M_NVEBCL variable in case of emergency braking [own study]

Similarly, the value of the M_NVAVADH variable does not affect the SBD curve. An increase in the value of the variable results in a reduction of the braking distance in case of emergency braking (EBD curve), as shown in Fig. 8.

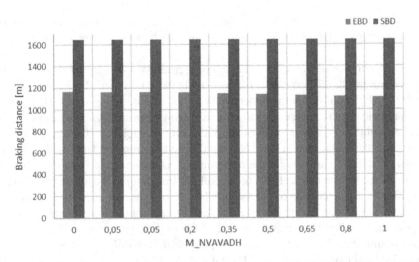

Fig. 8. The relation between braking distance as a function of M_NVAVADH variable for emergency braking (EBD) and service braking (SBD) [own study]

The braking distance resulting from the SBD curve is greater than the length of braking distance resulting from national regulations [6, 7]. This means that for the conditions reflected in the simulation, the ETCS safe stop criterion related to service braking is not met. Moreover, it is noticeable that for such data the braking distance in the case of service braking is 141% (for M_NVAVADH = 0) and 149% (for M_NVAVADH = 1) of the braking distance obtained in the case of emergency braking.

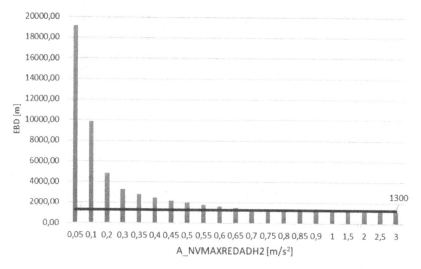

Fig. 9. Dependence of braking distance from a value of A_NVMAXREDADH2 variable [own study]

When analysing the effect of A_NVMAXREDADH2 variable on curves, it can be seen that the parameter does not affect the length of braking distance in the case of service braking (SBD curve), as shown in Fig. 10. The value of the variable affects those EBD curves for which the value of A_NVMAXREDADH2 variable is less than the value of the "emergency brake deceleration" parameter.

For the purpose of the simulation, a deceleration value of 0.9 m/s^2 was assumed. For A_NVMAXREDADH2 in the range (0; 0,85 > the tendency to reduce the emergency braking distance as the value of the variable increases (in the range mentioned above) can be observed. For these data, the braking distance with the manager's regulations [6, 7] was obtained for the value of parameter A_NVMAXREDADH2 greater than or equal to 0,8 m/s^2 (Figs. 9 and 10).

Increasing the value of A_NVMAXREDADH2 variable above the value of the parameter "emergency brake deceleration" (0,9 m/s^2) does not affect the braking distance in the case of emergency braking (EBD), as can be seen in Figs. 9 and 10.

It should be noted that the results of the simulation are some kinds of guidance to determine those combinations values of National Values which, under the conditions described by the simulation, ensure that the ETCS vehicle is stopped before EoA/SvL.

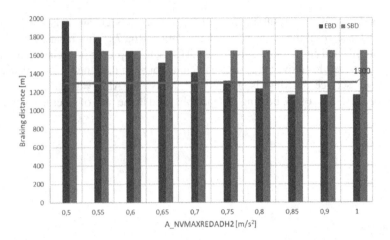

Fig. 10. The dependence of braking distance on selected values of A_NVMAXREDADH2 variable for emergency (EBD) and service braking (SBD) [own study]

In practice, the selection of specific Values of National Values should be preceded by dynamic tests carried out in different areas with different characteristics (e.g. wheel-rail adhesion), using different types of rolling stock with different characteristics and technical condition.

6   Conclusion

The issue of determining the braking curves of an ETCS vehicle and the influence of values of National Values on curves is complex and especially important in the context of the implementation of ERTMS/ETCS system compliant with the 3rd ETCS baseline. The braking curves of an ETCS vehicle (in particular SBD and EBD) are of major importance for the safety of a vehicle operating under ETCS supervision.

Polish infrastructure managers and railway undertakings have little experience in determining the values of these variables. Knowledge of the nature of braking distance characteristics is important from the point of view of awareness of the ranges of values ensuring that the required braking distance resulting from the regulations is maintained.

Parameters important from the point of view of determining curves are diversified. Obtaining reliable input data for simulation requires the involvement of infrastructure managers, railway undertakings and on-board equipment and rolling stock suppliers. In determining the values of National Values, it is essential that infrastructure managers, railway undertakings, rolling stock and on-board manufacturers work together to ensure that the values of the National Values associated with the braking process and the corresponding braking parameters of the rolling stock allow safe operating and the timetable to be realised.

Determination of curves is done differently for Gamma and Lambda train models. The choice of train model depends on the type of known train parameters.

Analysis of the results of simulation of the influence of value selected National Values on braking curves shows that some National Values affect only the EBD curve.

The simulated values of the variables indicate the possibility of defining ranges for which it is possible to achieve a braking distance consistent with the values of classical control systems.

It should be underline that the same values of National Values give different results in terms of braking curves for vehicles with different characteristics.

The tests carried out gave positive results with the assumed criterion for specific parameter values (e.g. Kwet_rst). There is a necessity to continue research in order to find correlations of variables, in order to define spaces for determining safe braking behaviour of a train.

References

1. Dyrektywa Parlamentu Europejskiego i Rady 2008/57/WE z dnia 17 czerwca 2008 r. w sprawie interoperacyjności systemu kolei we Wspólnocie
2. ERA: Braking curves simulation tool handbook, ERA-GUI-05, wersja 4.2 (2018)
3. ERA: Introduction to ETCS braking curves, ERA ERTMS 040026, V.1.4
4. Ilczuk, P., Zabłocki, W.: Wybrane zagadnienia wyznaczania krzywych hamowania pociągów. Prace Naukowe Politechniki Warszawskiej. Transport 95, 167–177 (2013)
5. Międzynarodowy Związek Kolei UIC: Karta UIC 544-1, Hamulec - Hamowność, wyd. 4 (2004)
6. PKP Polskie Linie Kolejowe S.A., Instrukcja o prowadzeniu ruchu pociągów Ir-1 (R1), wrzesień (2017)
7. PKP Polskie Linie Kolejowe S.A.: Wytyczne techniczne budowy urządzeń sterowania ruchem kolejowym Ie-4 (WTB-E10), sierpień (2018)
8. PN-EN 13452-1:2003 Kolejnictwo—Hamowanie – Systemy hamowania w transporcie publicznym—Część 1: Wymagania eksploatacyjne
9. R. I. Standard and R. S. and S. B. RIS-0708-CCS, ERTMS/ETCS National Values, September 2017
10. Rozporządzenie Komisji (UE) 2016/919 z dnia 27 maja 2016 r. w sprawie technicznej specyfikacji interoperacyjności w zakresie podsystemów "Sterowanie" systemu kolei w Unii Europejskiej
11. Unisig: Subset -026 System Requirements Specification – wydanie 2.3.0
12. Unisig: Subset -026 System Requirements Specification – wydanie 3.6.0
13. Unisig: Subset -026 System Requirements Specification – wydanie 3.4.0
14. Unisig: Subset-108 Interoperability-related consolidation on TSI annex A documents 1.2.0
15. Vincze, B., Tarnai, G.: Development and analysis of train brake curve calculation methods with complex simulation. Adv. Electr. Electron. Eng. 5, 174–177 (2006)

The Impact of New Telematics Solutions on the Safety of Railway Traffic on the Example of Modern Simulators Railway Traffic Control Devices

Mieczysław Kornaszewski[✉] and Roman Pniewski[✉]

University of Technology and Humanities in Radom,
Malczewskiego 29, Radom, Poland
{m.kornaszewski, r.pniewski}@uthrad.pl

Abstract. Railway carriers notice an increased need to improve the level of railway traffic safety and efficiency. This is achieved through the education of train drivers and increased opportunities to familiarize railway employees with the control systems of railway vehicles and railway traffic. The dynamic development of the computing power of computers and the increasing possibilities of generating realistic images allowed manufacturers to design and manufacture simulators in accordance with the latest technological trends, including based on a virtual three-dimensional environment. Safe and efficient conducting railway traffic requires the use of increasingly new telematics solutions railway traffic control devices and systems. The article presents a series of simulators of railway traffic control devices used in the didactic classes were presented.

Keywords: Transport · Safety · Telematics · Railway traffic control devices · Simulators

1 Introduction

Technological changes in many areas require people to constantly adapt to new civilizational and social conditions. The most cautious learn to meet the challenges that the future will bring. The consequence is the growing need to change, update and improve the originally acquired qualifications. The accession of Poland to the European Union allows for the launch of significant financial resources intended to support the development of human capital. These funds will allow for a greater involvement in the creation and development of training activities, including in the field of railway transport and issues related to *railway traffic control*.

Scientific and technical progress in many areas of life forces technical universities to constantly improve the level of education. Universities competing in the education market must take into account the expectations of future entrepreneurs. They should emphasize both the teaching of practical applications (laboratory) and prepare students in the field of independent thinking as well as innovation and entrepreneurship [6, 19].

© Springer Nature Switzerland AG 2019
J. Mikulski (Ed.): TST 2019, CCIS 1049, pp. 32–43, 2019.
https://doi.org/10.1007/978-3-030-27547-1_3

Faculty of Transport and Electrical Engineering, Kazimierz Pulaski University of Technology and Humanities in Radom has a modern and developed laboratory base. Collected here models of railway traffic control devices and systems, which are currently produced and operated on modernized railway lines in Poland. Faculty of Transport and Electrical Engineering has been cooperating with many railway companies for many years, for example: Bombardier Transportation (ZUS) Poland from Katowice, KOMBUD from Radom (Poland) and Scheidt & Bachmann Poland from Luboń. In recent years, it has enriched its research infrastructure with modern and unique on the European scale laboratories. They are extensively used to develop and test railway traffic control systems and devices [7].

Implementation of modern methods and IT tools in railway transport requires additional equipment of its infrastructure with many technical elements related to the acquisition, processing and distribution of data. They are composed of complementary modules [4, 25]:

- sensors providing source data on the traffic and condition of railway routes (cameras, satellite receivers, etc.);
- transport information transmission devices (stationary and mobile communication, long-distance and short-range systems, specialized communication systems, e.g. GSM-R);
- transport information processing devices (computer systems);
- devices for the distribution and presentation of data for control, management and communication with users (digital radio frequency GSM-R, man machine interface MMI, etc.).

Thanks to such innovations, the creation of simulators of railway traffic control devices is simple and provides an appropriate level of education for future railway transport employees.

2 Local Control Centers as a Special Place for Integration of Railway Traffic Control Systems and Devices

The railway traffic control systems are becoming more and more complex and perform more and more functions. They allow for integration many systems and devices for various purposes. It enables managing from one place cooperation, among others of control devices at the railway traffic station with track occupancy control systems, line block systems, automatic crossing signaling systems, teletransmission, wired and wireless communication, broadcasting systems, closed circuit television, platform lighting, etc. The Local Control Center is such a place [11, 18].

The Local Control Center manages the function of remote control of railway traffic on separate sections of the railway line. It allows conducting railway traffic from one control station in the area of several railway traffic operation position. Local Control Centers are developed under the following assumptions: area size, number of railway traffic operation position, type and technical and technological level of basic railway traffic control devices, communication and power systems, track devices and other. Remote control devices in the Local Control Centers are therefore intended to control and supervise, from a distance, railway traffic control devices located at the railway traffic operation positions and railway routes of the monitored area [3, 13, 21] (Fig. 1).

Fig. 1. View of the dispatcher's station in the Local Control Center equipped with various functional control and railway traffic diagnostics systems: (a) in Drzewica [30]; (b) at the railway station Wrocław Nadodrze [29]

The principle of remote control consists in transmitting controlling commands and reports between remote railway control traffic rooms and objects. The commands entered by the railway operator are verified for syntax and the existence of a real controlled object. When selecting railway route variants, you can also select an appropriate railway line. The commands are coded and sent to the remote control objects, where they are decoded by the interface and further transmitted to the control suitable devices at the railway traffic station. Verification of devices operation is carried out on the basis of control reports, which are sent from remote control facilities together with their status changes. For proper information processing in the remote control room is a dependency computer used [13, 15].

3 The Classic Simulators of Railway Transport Devices

The process of training and professional development of employees in the transport sector is of great importance in the organization of safe transport. It enables creating competences, expanding previously acquired skills and behaviours. It also determines the improvement of the quality and efficiency of the company management as well as the technological capabilities of the organization.

The dynamic technical development of computers and the increasing possibilities of creating realistic images affect a new approach to the design of simulators of railway transport devices.

The classic form of a railway simulator was created as a result of many years of evolution of individual components. Generally, the simulator consists of two basic parts, i.e. physical and graphic. The physical part usually reflects physical devices (e.g. railway traffic control), for example, a typical cabin of a real rail vehicle. The graphic part is the image on the monitor displayed to the trainee person. Its task is to provide the highest possible realism of simulation and create the impression of realism. Among new solutions, an interesting concept is a simulator desktop type. It is a compromise between a full simulator and simulation on a computer screen. This type of simulator including simplified control devices and a screen designed to display a simulation image can be mounted on the ordinary desk [2, 5, 17, 24].

The device simulators can be used to support training in all types of transport, i.e. both in classical railway transport, as well as in metro systems or trams [1, 4].

In 2012, there was a major railway disaster in Szczekociny in Poland. After this incident, the Ministry of Transport, Construction and Maritime Economy, existing in the years 2011–2013, has started the implementation of a program to improve safety on Polish railways. The effect of this program was to build new or improve existing computer simulators, among others by PKP PLK, Koleje Mazowieckie and Przewozy Regionalne (Fig. 2).

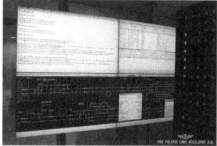

Fig. 2. Simulator of railway traffic control devices of PKP PLK [28]

Currently, all professional simulators intended for train drivers in Poland (Fig. 3) must meet the requirements set out in the Regulation of the Minister of Infrastructure and Development of October 23, 2014. (Dz. U. z 2014 r., Poz. 1566) concerning training and examination centres' for train drivers and candidates for train drivers [28].

Fig. 3. Simulator of traffic control devices and TREsim railway infrastructure modelling [26] and view of the interior of the locomotive simulator of Koleje Mazowieckie [27]

4 Laboratory Base of Railway Traffic Control Devices at the University of Technology and Humanities in Radom

The Faculty of Transport and Electrical Engineering uses three laboratories equipped with modern solutions railway systems and devices for railway traffic control (Fig. 4):

- Laboratory of Railway Traffic Control Elements and Devices (equipped by KOMBUD company and Bombardier Transportation ZWUS Poland),
- Laboratory of Railway Traffic Control Systems (equipped by Bombardier Transportation ZWUS Poland),
- Laboratory of Railway Automation Systems (equipped by Scheidt & Bachmann Poland).

4.1 Selected Simulations Carried Out in Laboratories of Railway Traffic Control at the University of Technology and Humanities in Radom

- designed by Bombardier Transportation ZWUS Poland: automatic crossing signaling SPA-5 type (a); track occupancy counter control system SOL-21 type (b);
- designed by Scheidt & Bachmann Poland: automatic crossing signaling BUES 2000 type (c); traffic operator position in the control system at the railway traffic station ZSB 2000 type (d);
- designed by KOMBUD: track occupancy counter control system SKZR type (e); automatic crossing signaling RASP-4Ft type (f).

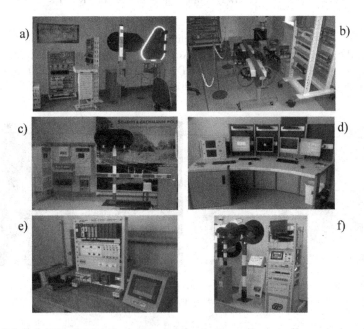

Fig. 4. Selected laboratory stations intended for testing railway traffic control systems and devices from various manufacturers used in Polish railways [own study]:

In the face of the increasing complexity of railway traffic control systems, more and more important are device simulators (using their visual presentation) and simulations installed on them. Most often they contain a complete set of possible equipment variants and situations that may actually exist. Real data from railway traffic control devices significantly improve the accuracy of the simulation and reflect real railway traffic situations and train behaviour.

Laboratory model of the control system at the railway traffic station type Ebilock 950 with STC object controllers (manufactured by Bombardier Transportation ZWUS Poland) and traffic operator position type EbiScreen 2 (Fig. 5) were designed for the example railway station LABORATORY. Its executive elements have been included in the computer application simulating all railway traffic control devices, with the exception of one signalling light and one railway drive, that are real physical objects.

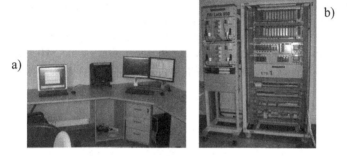

Fig. 5. Laboratory stand of railway traffic operator with the EbiScreen 2 system (a) and installation of the control system at the railway traffic station EbiLock 950 type together with the stand of STC object controllers (b) [own study]

The simulator of the TD 950 railway station (Fig. 6) is a program that runs on a dependency computer and simulates a whole system. The TD 950 station simulation system is based on the Ebilock 950 system's dependency computer. The simulator programme is loaded into one of the dependency computers and emulates the events on the railway station object [23].

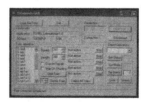

Fig. 6. View of the TD 950 simulator screen for train running and shunting [6, 7]

The TD 950 simulator allows you to:

– simulate railway station objects and enables changing the state of these objects,
– simulate train movement (route, length, speed, etc.).

The TD 950 station simulator system consists not only of software but also of hardware. For its needs were developed special TD-PLC controllers, which replace programmable loop controllers [12, 14].

The TD 950 simulator used has the ability to control the system via the CLT console, which works in "online" mode. It has several important application commands, such as: loading the system, activating the system, shutting down the system, changing the state of the object [6].

The computer SHL-12 line block system is designed for automatic regulation of train consequences on the railway line. The model of SHL-12 line block system is placed between the virtual LABORATORY railway station and the N station.

Connection to the LABORATORY station is physically realized for the needs of didactics, while the N station is operated using the computer simulator of a line block (Fig. 7). Under laboratory conditions, the function of the actual steering panel is taken over by a computer programme simulating the operation of the SHL−12 line block system (Fig. 8a), which uses analogous graphic symbols like the original EAB−61401 desktop [16].

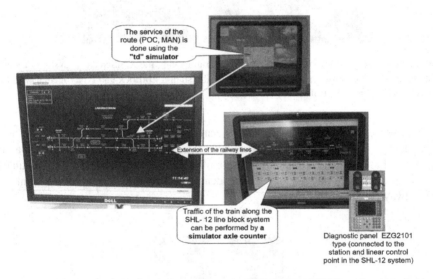

Fig. 7. Logical combination of train routes between the LABORATORY station (the desktop with the EbiScreen system) and the N station by the SHL-12 automatic line block system (simulator of the SHL-12 line block system) [own study]

In the case of SHL-12 line block devices, it is possible to retrieve diagnostic data remotely which provide information needed to monitor the work of the system and efficiently remove any defects [9, 20].

a)    b)

Fig. 8. View of the SHL-12 line block system simulator (a) and contactors steering the work of railway traffic control devices on the N station in logical connection with in this railway line block system (b) [own study]

After preparing and setting the direction of the line block system SHL-12 type, it is possible to carry out train running tests through the railway route in both directions using the simulator of railway axle counters, shown in Fig. 8a. Railway station N is preceded by an entry signalling lights C, where information on possible speeds (colours of displayed signals) are used for the needs of the Railway Traffic Control Systems' Laboratory using contactors (Fig. 6b). Since it is a computer-type line block system, data must be provided in a redundant manner using two channels [6].

a)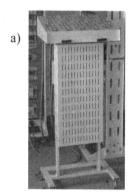

 b)

Fig. 9. View of stand of the control panel for simulation of the level crossing signalling devices SPA-5 type (a) and only control panel (b) [6]

On the model of automatic crossing signalling SPA-5 type (Fig. 4a), after setting the signalling lights in the automatic mode and using the simulation desk of this signalling, it is possible to verify all functional possibilities of the system with its activation and switching off by a passing simulated train. The simulator of SPA-5 automatic crossing signalling is equipped with a number of different colour LEDs and stable two-state switches (Fig. 9). Among the devices intended to safety the level crossing, one set consists of physical devices placed in the laboratory (N1, S1, Top1).

Using the SPA-5 level crossing signalling simulator, it is possible to carry out train driving tests in both directions, with dependence on control devices at the railway traffic station or without addiction. When simulating the train running through a railway level crossing, one must remember about the proper sequence of occupying the zones of individual railway sensors and about the proper order of closing and opening the railway barrier drives located on the right and the left side of the road [8, 10].

The next laboratory exercise involves the functional testing of control system at the railway traffic station of the ZSB 2000 type manufactured by Scheidt & Bachmann Poland. The main plane of connections in the ZSB 2000 system is the route logic. The route is a collection of elements (Fig. 10). Each element fulfils its special task in route. All logical dependencies between elements are implemented using routes. Thus, the main task of the route is to select elements for their proper use according to the user's requirements [22].

Fig. 10. Monitors with a detailed railway station image and messages (alarms) of the ZSB 2000 control system [own study]

Fig. 11. Simulation computer for setting routes for the ZSB 2000 system [own study]

The simulation model of the ZSB 2000 system includes the following components:

– control cabinet for a diagnostic/control computer and a management plane,
– control panel,
– ZSB 2000 simulation computer (logic panel of the ZSB 2000 system) with the possibility of the modular setting of the route (Fig. 11),
– signalling light with LED light points.

The track occupancy control counter system SKZR-2 type (manufactured by KOMBUD from Radom) replaces track circuits while providing more information about the railway traffic situation. To operate laboratory stand of the SKZR system (Fig. 4f), the operator panel is used (Fig. 12). The industrial computer monitor presents the configuration of SKZR devices, which is used to functional test the system and check the system's response to selected faults [8].

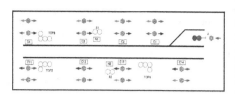 

Fig. 12. Simulation (control) panel of the level crossing signalling devices RASP-4Ft type [own study]

The wheel sensors (Ci – markings on the desktop – Fig. 12) define limits of the section in the controlled area of impact of the rolling stock. The wheel sensor is a device detecting the movement of the train's wheel above the sensor's head. The operation of these sensors has been simulated through switches on the control panel. They enable simulation of the train running with the coded number of axes. The train movement simulation is implemented out by moving the switch in the direction of the train movement. The order of the track sections occupied is important.

5   Conclusion

The paper presents the characteristics of selected simulators of modern railway devices, including the traffic control devices. All test stands in the railway traffic control laboratories at the Faculty of Transport and Electrical Engineering at the Kazimierz Pulaski University of Technology and Humanities in Radom correspond to real systems and devices operated on Polish railways. Based on the presented railway traffic control laboratories, there are didactic classes with students in the field of railway transport education and many scientific research studies. Models of railway traffic control systems have been designed and constructed in such a way that in the future they may constitute a didactic and training base for railway traffic dispatchers.

Simulators of railway traffic control devices can be used in a wide range of scenarios, ranging from trainings on railway traffic dispatchers to validation of new solutions. Trainings on these simulators allow raising the qualifications of the traffic dispatchers and employees responsible for railway traffic safety (manual and psychophysical capability). They enable scenarios to be carried out on many difficult situations related to devices operation and with train traffic controlling. Employees' training without consequences and verification of behaviour in difficult situations allows for better preparation for work. Also thanks to such simulators it is possible to check whether the planned modernizations or investments will bring the expected results [5, 26].

The latest solutions of simulators already use the so-called virtual reality and a virtual three-dimensional environment. Virtual reality solutions allow reducing the space for the simulator, while providing the greatest possible immersion.

References

1. Astengo, G., et al.: A new approach to model signalling systems on railway networks. In: Computers in Railways VI. Advances in Transport, vol. 2, pp. 1077–1084. Computational Mechanics Publications LTD, Southampton (1998)
2. Bartnik, W.: Najnowsze trendy w rozwoju symulatorów kolejowych, Transport Kolejowy 2017. Przeszłość – Teraźniejszość – Przyszłość, Urząd Transportu Kolejowego, Warszawa (2017)
3. Chrzan, M., Nowakowski, W., Sobiczewski, W.: Współczesne systemy prowadzenia ruchu pociągów na przykładzie Linii E-20. Technika Transportu Szynowego Nr 9/2012
4. Ciszewski, T., Nowakowski, W.: Interoperability of IT systems in the international railways. In: Proceedings of 16th International Scientific Conference Globalization and Its Socio-Economic Consequences, Part I, pp. 312–320. University of Zilina, Rajecke Teplice, Slovak Republic, October 2016. ISBN 978-80-8154-191-9
5. Ciszewski, T., Nowakowski, W., Wojciechowski, J.: Symulator pulpitu maszynisty, Logistyka, vol. 4, pp. 2819–2824 (2015)
6. Dyduch, J., Kornaszewski, M., Pniewski, R.: Proces kształcenia specjalistów z zakresu Sterowania Ruchem Kolejowym na przykładzie Politechniki Radomskiej. Problemy Kolejnictwa, zeszyt 155, Warszawa (2012)
7. Dyduch, J., Kornaszewski, M., Pniewski, R.: Rozwój infrastruktury badawczej UTH Radom o nowe urządzenia automatyki kolejowej. AUTOBUSY Technika, Eksploatacja, Systemy Transportowe Nr 6 (196), Radom (2016)
8. Dyduch, J., Kornaszewski, M.: Komputerowe systemy sterowania ruchem kolejowym. Wydawnictwo Uniwersytetu Technologiczno-Humanistycznego, Radom (2014)
9. Galaverna, M., Savio, S., Sciutto, G.: A railway operation simulator for line traffic capacity evaluation. In: Computers in Railways III, vol. 1, pp. 15–24. Computational Mechanics Publications LTD, Southampton (1992)
10. Kim, I., et al.: Integration of driving simulator and traffic simulation to analyse behaviour at railway crossings. In: Proceedings of The Institution of Mechanical Engineers, part F-Journal of Rail and Rapid Transit, vol. 227, no. 5, pp. 427–438. SAGE Publications LTD, London (2013). https://doi.org/10.1177/0954409713489117. ISSN: 0954-4097
11. Kornaszewski, M., Chrzan, M.: Charakterystyka systemów kierowania i sterowania ruchem stosowanych w kolejnictwie polskim. Technika Transportu Szynowego 9/2012
12. Kornaszewski, M., Chrzan, M., Olczykowski, Z.: Implementation of new solutions of intelligent transport systems in railway transport in Poland. In: Mikulski, J. (ed.) TST 2017. CCIS, vol. 715, pp. 282–292. Springer, Cham (2017). https://doi.org/10.1007/978-3-319-66251-0_23
13. Kornaszewski, M.: Lokalne centra sterowania w procesie prowadzenia ruchu pociągów. AUTOBUSY Technika, Eksploatacja, Systemy Transportowe Nr 3(159), Radom (2013)
14. Kornaszewski, M.: Microprocessor technology and programmable logic controllers in new generation railway traffic control and management systems. Arch. Transp. Syst. Telematics 11(2), 18–23 (2018). ISSN 1899-8208
15. Kornaszewski, M.: Zdalne sterowanie ruchem w transporcie kolejowym w Polsce. Technika Transportu Szynowego Nr 9/2012
16. Kornaszewski, M., Pniewski, R.: Impact of new informatics solutions using in railway transport on its safety. In: Proceedings of the 22nd International Scientific on Conference Transport Means 2018, vol. 2008-October, Part II, pp. 996–1001, Trasalis - Trakai Resort and SPAGedimino str. 26Trakai; Lithuania, 3–5 October 2018 (2018). ISSN 1822-296 X (print), ISSN 2351- 7034 (online)

17. Krivka, J., et al.: Hardware for rail traffic simulator. In: Proceedings of Conference: 21st Telecommunications Forum (TELFOR), Belgrade, Serbia, 26–28 November 2013, pp. 590–593. IEEE, New York (2013)
18. Mera, J.M., et al.: Simulation of the railways control and protection ERTMS/ETCS; level-0, level-1 and level-2. In: Computers in Railways VIII. Advances in Transport, vol. 13, pp. 1119–1128. WIT Press, Southampton (2002)
19. Mikulski, J., Bogacki, D., Sobanski, M.: Computer models of simulation of the railway traffic control system operation as a didactic aid. In: Advances in Intelligent Systems. Frontiers in Artificial Intelligence and Applications, vol. 41, pp. 262–266. IOS Press, Van Diemenstraat (1997)
20. Nowakowski, W., Ciszewski, T., Łukasik, Z.: The concept of railway traffic control systems remote diagnostic. In: Mikulski, J. (ed.) TST 2017. CCIS, vol. 715, pp. 471–481. Springer, Cham (2017). https://doi.org/10.1007/978-3-319-66251-0_38
21. Pniewski, R., Kornaszewski, M., Chrzan, M.: Safety of electronic ATC systems in the aspect of technical and operational. In: Proceedings of 16th International Scientific Conference Globalization and Its Socio-Economic Consequences. Part IV, pp. 1729–1735. University of Zilina, Rajecke Teplice, October 2016. ISBN 978-80-8154-191-9
22. Scheidt & Bachmann GmbH: Elektronische Stellwerk ZSB (2000). http://www.scheidt-bachmann.de/de/systeme-fuer-signaltechnik/stellwerkstechnik/. Accessed 2 Dec 2017
23. Sondi, P., et al.: Toward a common platform for simulation-based evaluation of both functional and telecommunication sub-systems of the ERTMS. In: Proceedings of ASME 2012 Joint Rail Conference, Philadelphia, 17–19 April 2012, pp. 351–359. AMER SOC Mechanical Engineers, New York (2012). https://doi.org/10.1115/jrc2012-74049
24. Vlasek, J., et al.: Software for rail traffic symulator. In: Proceedings of Conference, 21st Telecommunications Forum (TELFOR), Belgrade, Serbia, 26–28 November 2013, pp. 594–596. IEEE, New York (2013)
25. Wydro, K.B.: Usługi i systemy telematyczne w transporcie. Telekomunikacja i Techniki informacyjne Nr 3-4, Wydawnictwo Instytutu Łączności w Państwowym Instytucie Badawczym, Warszawa (2008)
26. http://symulatory.net.pl/art,106,symulator-urzadzen-sterowania-ruchem-i-modelowania-infrastruktury-kolejowej-tresim. Accessed 5 Jan 2019
27. http://symulatory.net.pl/art,5,symulator-koleje-mazowieckie-km-sp-z-oo. Accessed 19 Dec 2018
28. http://symulatory.net.pl/art,8,symulator-urzadzen-sterowania-ruchem-kolejowym-pkp-plk-sa. Accessed 19 Dec 2018
29. http://wroclaw.wyborcza.pl/wroclaw/51,35754,19482171.html. Accessed 9 Nov 2018
30. https://www.rynek-kolejowy.pl/wiadomosci/srk-i-automatyka-polem-dla-polskich-innowacji-77057.html. Accessed 9 Nov 2018

The Software Framework for Simulating Railway Automation Systems Failures

Waldemar Nowakowski[✉], Tomasz Ciszewski[✉],
and Zbigniew Łukasik[✉]

University of Technology and Humanities in Radom,
Malczewskiego 29, Radom, Poland
{w.nowakowski, t.ciszewski, z.lukasik}@uthrad.pl

Abstract. Railway automation systems, like other technical systems, despite the constant development are vulnerable to failures. However, due to the fact that they belong to the group of safety-critical systems, also called safety-related systems, they are required to be highly reliable. For this purpose the appropriate maintenance measures and operational tests are carried out. The results of these tests provide some valuable knowledge that allows to improve railway automation systems and modify their operation processes. The implementation of this task requires the development of IT tools that support diagnostics enabling the assessment of the technical condition of a given system, the evolution of this state and the resulting consequences. The software framework developed, by the paper's authors to simulate failures in railway automation systems is helpful in testing diagnostics tools.

Keywords: Railway automation systems · Failures simulation · Safety

1 Introduction

The basic function of railway automation systems is allowing a safe and fluent traffic control [2, 9, 14, 15, 17]. Along with the technical progress, these systems are constantly being improved. As a result, they are made in various technologies, from mechanical, electromechanical and relay to computer solutions. Therefore, maintaining them in the state of technical efficiency is an enormous challenge. The issue of railway automation devices and systems exploitation can be presented on the example of Polish railway market. PKP Polskie Linie Kolejowe S.A., which is the infrastructure manager of railway, has managed (at the end of 2016):

- 18.513 km of railway lines (15.861 km of lines are equipped with signalling block system),
- 46.530 railway switches,
- 5.166 railroad level crossings (2.436 cat. A, 1.171 cat. B, 1.397 cat. C, 121 cat. F, 41 cat. E),
- 307 km of lines are equipped with ETCS L1,
- 84 km of lines are equipped with ETCS L2.

© Springer Nature Switzerland AG 2019
J. Mikulski (Ed.): TST 2019, CCIS 1049, pp. 44–56, 2019.
https://doi.org/10.1007/978-3-030-27547-1_4

The structure of selected railway automation systems exploited in Poland, taking into account the type of technology, is presented in Fig. 1.

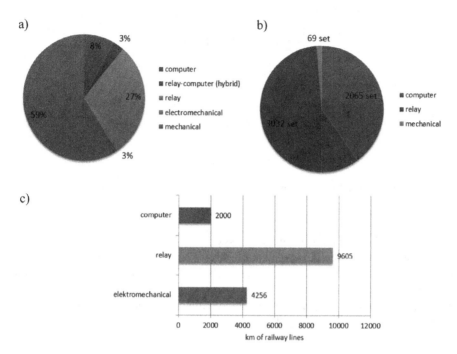

Fig. 1. Structure of railway automation systems (at the end of 2016) (a) interlocking system, (b) railroad level crossings, (c) signalling block system [own study based on 13]

During the exploitation of railway automation systems there are dependent processes of changes in technical condition and changes in exploitation conditions. Railway traffic control devices may be in different operating states. It results from the process of their wearing, which is related to the devices lifetime, the intensity of use and the quality of maintenance [9, 11, 13]. Managing the operating process requires the renewal of individual subsystems at optimum time. The problem of choosing renewal methods is significant in this situation, especially for large integrated systems.

The current level of failures for selected types of railway automation devices used in Poland is presented in Table 1.

Table 1. The failure rate of railway automation devices (at the end of 2016) [own study based on 13]

Type of device	Number of failures
Interlocking system devices	10.365
Block system devices	5.905
Level crossings devices	7.830
Total number of failures	**24.100**

The technical condition of railway automation devices for most solutions is not satisfactory, as shown in Fig. 2.

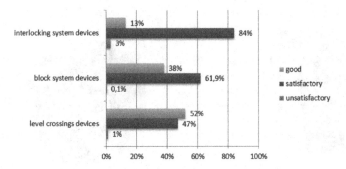

Fig. 2. Technical condition of railway automation devices (at the end of 2016) [own study based on 13]

Operational tests of railway automation systems are a source of valuable knowledge that has an impact on the improvement of railway traffic control devices construction and on the course of their operation process [3, 6, 7]. This results in the need to develop software tools supporting the maintenance process [4, 10, 12, 16, 18]. The failures simulator dedicated to railway automation systems, proposed by the authors of the article, may be helpful in testing this tools.

2 Failures Simulator

The basic task performed by the failures simulator is generating random variables according to the assumed probability distribution resulting from the analysis of real data carried out earlier. In addition, the failures simulator's cooperation with railway automation systems using the proposed data exchange protocol was foreseen. The dedicated server collects data on the failures of the railway traffic control devices and allows it to be uploaded to the MS SQL database. The failures simulator software consists of two cooperating components, i.e.: "Failures simulator - server" and "Failures simulator - client". The server component provides a function of data upload from one or many clients, which initiates requests for such services. Communication between clients and the server is carried out using the TCP/IP protocol. In order to ensure communication safety, the information exchanged between the client and the server is encrypted using the AES (Advanced Encryption Standard) block cipher. Additionally, each of system components enables manual editing of data. The scope and form of the transmitted data is consistent with the structure of the database. The structure of the failures simulator system is shown in Fig. 3.

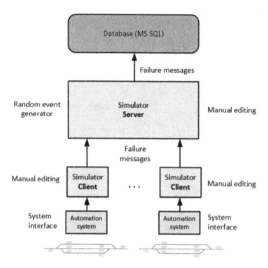

Fig. 3. Block diagram of the failures simulator system [own study]

2.1   Failures Simulator - Server

The "Failures simulator - server" software, in short called server, is the main element of the simulation system. Initial configuration is the first step that must be performed after starting the server. This activity includes configuration of access to the MS SQL database and contains definition of following parameters:

– provider,
– user,
– password,
– the IP address of the database server,
– database server port,
– database names.

Other parameters that need to be defined are the TCP/IP server listening port, information about sending "echoes" to clients after receiving messages (acknowledgement of data reception), as well as encryption parameters, including: encryption password, key length and mode. The data encryption parameters for the client and server should be set to be identical. System parameters set during the initialization are saved in configuration files. An example screen with the active "Parameters" tab is shown in Fig. 4.

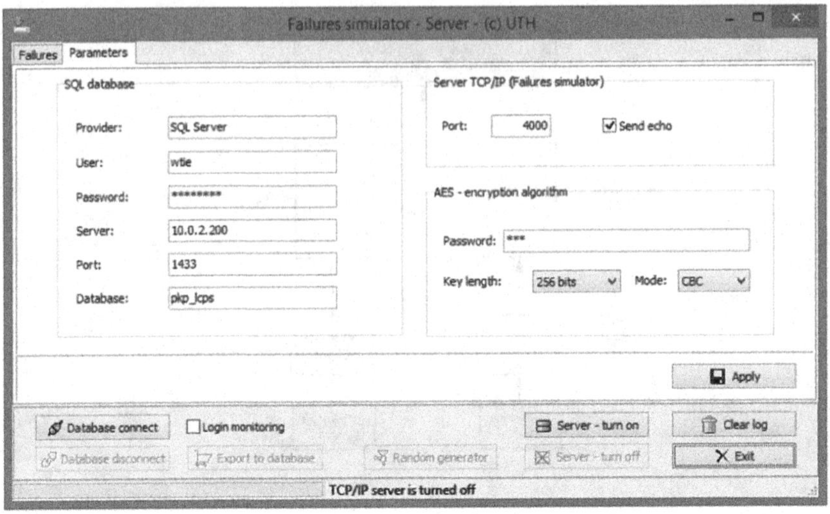

Fig. 4. Configuration of the failures simulator server [own study]

In order to generate random variables (failures of railway automation systems), the server should be turned-on. As a result of this operation a table containing the following fields is displayed in the main application window:

- subsystem,
- device,
- device_type,
- element_type,
- date_of_failure,
- date_of_repair,
- duration,
- activity.

The user is notified about the current state of the simulator with a message in the event log: "TCP/IP server has been turned on" and the "Server - turn off" button is activated. After activating the server, you can start generating failure by selecting the "Random generator" button. The generator window will then be displayed.

The user should set the following parameters (Fig. 5):

- type of distribution (exponential, normal, logarithm-normal),
- number of events (in the range from 1 to 100 000),
- start date,
- period (in years from 1 to 100).

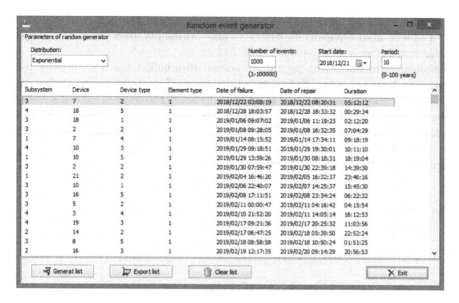

Fig. 5. Failure generator window - exponential distribution [own study]

All fields (subsystem, device, device_type, element_type, date_of_failure, date_of_repair), except for the duration of the failure are calculated on the basis of numbers from a random generator. The number generation function is based on a method called Linear Congruential Generator (LCG). It consists in calculating consecutive pseudo-random numbers: $x_1, x_2, ..., x_n$ with a value range of $0 ... m - 1$ based on the following formula:

$$x_i = (ax_{i-1} + 1) \bmod m$$

where: x_1 is the initial value that the generator initiates - the so-called seed.

In the analyzed case, the random function assumes the following parameter values: $a = 2^{32}$, $m = 134775813$.

Generating the duration of failure depends on the selected type of distribution. As already mentioned, one of the possible distributions is exponential distribution, which is commonly used for modelling time intervals between successive random events [1, 5, 8, 19]. This distribution describes the time between events in the Poisson process, i.e. events that happen continuously, independently of each other, with a constant average frequency. Another of the accepted distributions is the normal (Gaussian) distribution. This distribution is the theoretical probability distribution commonly used in statistical inference as an approximation to sampling distributions [20]. It is assumed to be a good model for the distribution of a random variable in a situation where:

- there is a strong tendency for the variable to take values close to the central value,
- positive and negative deviations from the central value of the distribution are equally probable,
- the quantity of deviations decreases sharply as their size increases.

The last of the possible distribution is logarithmic-normal distribution. In general, if x is a sample from a population with a normal distribution, then $y = e^x$ is a sample in logarithmic-normal distribution.

Normal distribution and logarithmic-normal distribution are described by two parameters: "average value" and "standard deviation". Therefore, in case of choosing such a distribution, it is necessary to additionally set the average value and standard deviation in the range from 1–24 h and from 1–60 min respectively (Fig. 6). Practical implementation of the generation of failure duration, according to the accepted schedule, was possible as a result of using the "*AMRandom*" package (by Alan Miller's), distributed as "open source" software [21].

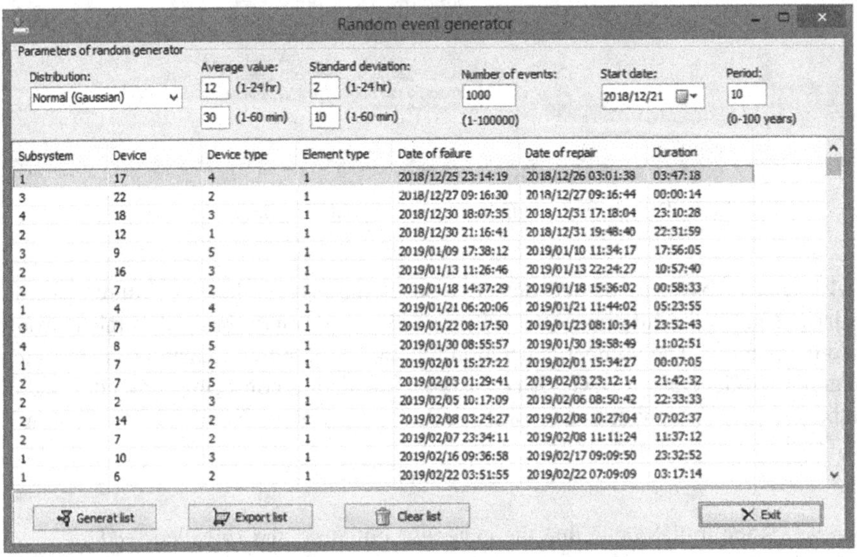
Random event generator
Parameters of random generator
Distribution:
Normal (Gaussian)
Average value:
12 (1-24 hr)
30 (1-60 min)
Standard deviation:
2 (1-24 hr)
10 (1-60 min)
Number of events:
1000
(1-100000)
Start date:
2018/12/21
Period:
10
(0-100 years)
Subsystem Device Device type Element type Date of failure Date of repair Duration
1 17 4 1 2018/12/25 23:14:19 2018/12/26 03:01:38 03:47:18
3 22 2 1 2018/12/27 09:16:30 2018/12/27 09:16:44 00:00:14
4 18 3 1 2018/12/30 18:07:35 2018/12/31 17:18:04 23:10:28
2 12 1 1 2018/12/30 21:16:41 2018/12/31 19:48:40 22:31:59
3 9 5 1 2019/01/09 17:38:12 2019/01/10 11:34:17 17:56:05
2 16 3 1 2019/01/13 11:26:46 2019/01/13 22:24:27 10:57:40
2 7 2 1 2019/01/18 14:37:29 2019/01/18 15:36:02 00:58:33
1 4 4 1 2019/01/21 06:20:06 2019/01/21 11:44:02 05:23:55
3 7 5 1 2019/01/22 08:17:50 2019/01/23 08:10:34 23:52:43
4 8 5 1 2019/01/30 08:55:57 2019/01/30 19:58:49 11:02:51
1 7 2 1 2019/02/01 15:27:22 2019/02/01 15:34:27 00:07:05
2 7 5 1 2019/02/03 01:29:41 2019/02/03 23:12:14 21:42:32
2 2 3 1 2019/02/05 10:17:09 2019/02/06 08:50:42 22:33:33
2 14 2 1 2019/02/08 03:24:27 2019/02/08 10:27:04 07:02:37
2 7 2 1 2019/02/07 23:34:11 2019/02/08 11:11:24 11:37:12
1 10 3 1 2019/02/16 09:36:58 2019/02/17 09:09:50 23:32:52
1 6 2 1 2019/02/22 03:51:55 2019/02/22 07:09:09 03:17:14
Generat list
Export list
Clear list
Exit

Fig. 6. Failure generator window - normal distribution (Gaussian) [own study]

After selecting the "Generate list" button, a list of failures will be generated, and their duration is a function described according to the assumed distribution (Figs. 5 and 6).

The generated data can be sent to the main failure list (Fig. 7) by selecting the "Export list" button (Figs. 5 and 6).

Another functionality of the software is the ability to upload information about randomly generated failures into a prepared database (MS SQL). After activating the server, (using the TCP/IP protocol for communication), clients can connect and send messages about the failure of railway traffic control devices. Railway automation systems can also play the clients role and upload information into the database. This information updates the list of failures in the main application window, where the list's records are sorted by the "date_of_failure" field.

Fig. 7. List of generated random values in the software main window [own study]

The user can keep track of the current number of records that are on the failure list. In addition, the server software provides a group of buttons that allows to change the active position in the list, manually add, delete and modify the indicated records. If the server receives incorrect data from the client resulting, for example, from faulty failure and repair dates, such records are displayed in red (Fig. 8). Before exporting data to the database, such records must be deleted or modified.

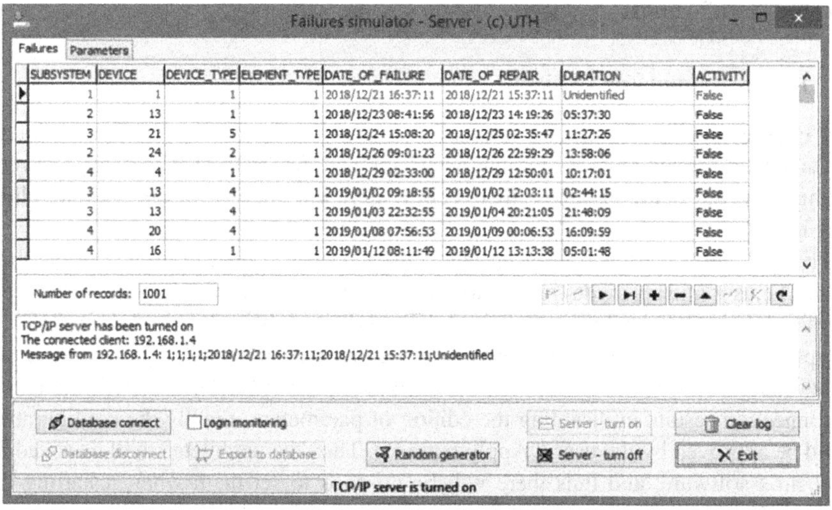

Fig. 8. Incorrect failure information obtained from the client [own study]

In order to transfer the records held in the failure table, a connection to the MS SQL database is required. The connection can be made without prompting the login, based on the data set during the initial configuration or with login prompting, during which the user can edit the logging parameters (Fig. 9).

Fig. 9. Logging into the MS SQL database [own study]

If the connection to the database is successful, the user will receive the message: "The connection to the database is active" and the "Export to database" button will be activated. After exporting the data to the database, the failure list is cleared and the user receives the message: "Export process has been completed". If the user does not plan to perform another data export, he should disconnect from the MS SQL database, about which he will be informed by an appropriate message. Disconnection with the database takes place after selecting the "Database disconnect" button. After disconnection, the server can be turned off by pressing "Server - turn off" button and then select the "Exit" button.

2.2 Failures Simulator - Client

The "Failures simulator - client" software, hereinafter named the client, ensures data exchange between the railway automation system and the "Failures simulator - server". For this purpose, it was assumed that each system will work with the separate client (see Fig. 3).

The first step, that need be taken after the client has started up, is initial configuration. The user must provide the IP address and port of the failure simulator server, the interface port of the railway automation system, as well as parameters related to encryption, including: encryption password, key length and mode. These parameters can be changed only in the state of lack of communication with the server. Establishing the connection results in disabling the edition of parameters. Finally the configuration should be approved by the user ("Apply button"). Then the parameters will be saved by the client's software, and thus there will be no need to set them when restarting the software. The parameters are stored in an encrypted file, which further increases the security of the developed simulation environment. An example client configuration screen is shown in Fig. 10.

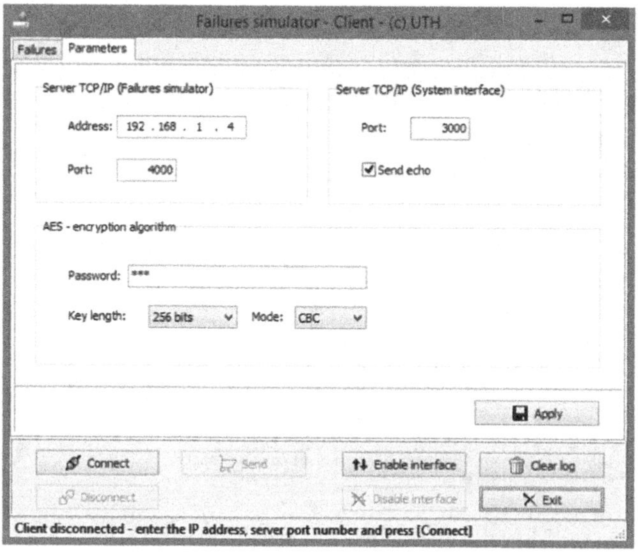

Fig. 10. View of the "Parameters" tab of the client software [own study]

After the configuration is complete, it is possible to establish a connection with the failure simulator server by pressing the "Connect" button. When connection to the server is established, the "Failures" tab is activated and the message "Client connected to the server: ..." is displayed in the "Log" window. In addition, the "Connect" button becomes disabled, while the "Disconnect" and "Send" buttons are activated. The next step is activating the interface of the railway automation system, which is carried out by pressing "Enable interface" button. As a result, the client is ready to cooperate with the railway automation system interface. All failure messages received from the railway automation system are checked by the client's software and automatically redirected to the server (Fig. 11).

Manual events data edition is carried out as a result of handling fields located on the "Manual editing of events" tab. The user can choose appropriate element from the drop-down list:

- subsystem,
- device,
- type of device,
- type of element.

Then the date of the failure and the date of repair must be indicated. These fields can be changed as a result of editing or as a result of selection. The last field "Duration" is calculated automatically as a result of comparing the date of failure and the date of repair. Incorrect indication of the dates leads to the display "Date of repair is earlier than the date of failure" message. Any change of the simulation data leads to updating the message sent to the server, the form of which can be observed in the "Plain message" field. The result of the example simulation is shown in Fig. 12.

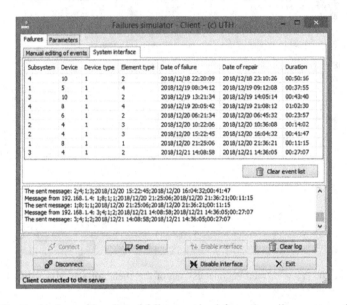

Fig. 11. Client's window with a list of failure received from the railway automation system [own study]

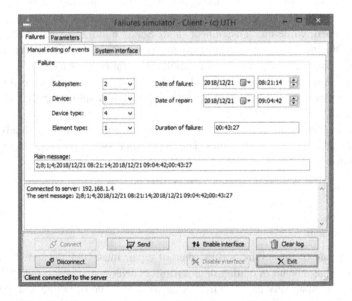

Fig. 12. View of the "Manual editing of events" tab [own study]

After editing, the user can send the message to the server by selecting the "Send" button. This option is available only if the client connection to the server is established. If the server is set to send "echoes", the user receive the following message back: "The sent message: ..." displayed in the "Log" window.

At any time user can clear the "Log". To terminate the program, you must first disconnect from the server and then select the "Exit" button.

3   Conclusion

A characteristic feature of railway automation systems is their presence in various operational states. Many years of experience in the operation of these systems indicate the dependence of their correct functioning on the reliability of the systems and components from which they are built. Therefore, operation tests of railway traffic control devices are the most effective source of information necessary to determine the reliability indicators for railway automation systems. The variety of railway traffic control devices and adopted technical solutions, as well as their failure rate, mean that the operation of railway automation systems must be supported by technical diagnostics. By technical diagnostics we have in mind a set of methods and means used to assess the technical condition of the device, the causes of this condition, its evolution and possible consequences. Information obtained from diagnostics about changes in the technical condition of railway traffic control devices enables their effective renewal to the usable state. Therefore, in the field of railway automation the activities related to the implementation of new diagnostic methods are undertaken. A failure simulator presented in the paper can be helpful in testing diagnostic tools.

In this paper the proprietary computer software used to simulate failures associated with the operation of railway automation systems is described. These events are stored in the MS SQL database prepared for this purpose. The software can be used, among other things, for testing diagnostic tools. It is assumed that the presented IT tools will be used in operation tests of railway traffic control devices, which may allow for the implementation of modern methods of their maintaining and servicing.

References

1. Bojarczak, P., Nowakowski, W., Łukasik, Z.: Application of R package to prediction of the time to failure of elements of automatic railway level crossing system. In: Proceedings of 22nd International Scientific Conference "Transport Means 2018", Part II, pp. 879–882 (2018)
2. Ciszewski, T., Nowakowski, W.: Life-cycle cost analysis for rail control systems. In: Proceedings of the 17th International Scientific Conference Globalization and Its Socio-Economic Consequences, Part I, Rajecke Teplice, Slovakia, pp. 284–291 (2017)
3. Ciszewski, T., Nowakowski, W.: Interoperability of IT systems in the international railways. In: Proceedings of the 16th International Scientific Conference Globalization and Its Socio-Economic Consequences, Part I, Rajecke Teplice, Slovakia, pp. 312–320 (2016)
4. Hei, X., et al.: Design and implementation of a distributed railway signalling simulator. WIT Trans. Built Environ. **114**, 81–88 (2010)

5. Kapur, K.C., Pecht, M.: Reliability Engineering. Wiley, Hoboken (2014)
6. Kornaszewski, M., Bojarczak, P., Pniewski, R.: Introduction of world innovative technologies to railway transport in Poland. In: Proceedings of the 16th International Scientific Conference Globalization and Its Socio-Economic Consequences, Part III, Rajecke Teplice, Slovakia, pp. 1036–1043 (2016)
7. Kornaszewski, M., Chrzan, M., Olczykowski, Z.: Implementation of new solutions of intelligent transport systems in railway transport in Poland. In: Mikulski, J. (ed.) TST 2017. CCIS, vol. 715, pp. 282–292. Springer, Cham (2017). https://doi.org/10.1007/978-3-319-66251-0_23
8. Kuo, W., Zuo, M.J.: Optimal Reliability Modeling: Principles and Applications. Wiley, New York (2003)
9. Lewinski, A., Perzyński, T.: The reliability and safety of railway control systems based on new information technologies. Commun. Comput. Inf. Sci. **104**, 427–433 (2010)
10. Łukasik, Z., Nowakowski, W.: Sieciowe narzędzia diagnostyczne systemów sterowania ruchem kolejowym. Technika Transportu Szynowego (TTS) 12/2015, pp. 2715–2718 (2015)
11. Łukasik, Z., Nowakowski, W., Ciszewski, T.: Bezpieczeństwo danych w diagnostyce systemów sterowania ruchem kolejowym. Autobusy Tech. Eksploat. Syst. Transp. **17**(6), 264–267 (2016)
12. Łukasik, Z., et al.: A fault diagnostic methodology for railway automatics systems. Procedia Comput. Sci. **149**, 159–166 (2019). ICTE in Transportation and Logistics 2018 (ICTE 2018)
13. Nowakowski, W.: Diagnostyka systemów automatyki kolejowej jako metoda poprawy bezpieczeństwa. Wydawnictwo Uniwersytetu Technologiczno-Humanistycznego w Radomiu, Seria Monografie, Nr 218, Radom (2018)
14. Nowakowski, W., Bojarczak, P., Łukasik, Z.: Verification and validation of railway control systems using an expert system. In: Kováčiková, T., Buzna, Ľ., Pourhashem, G., Lugano, G., Cornet, Y., Lugano, N. (eds.) INTSYS 2017. LNICST, vol. 222, pp. 43–50. Springer, Cham (2018). https://doi.org/10.1007/978-3-319-93710-6_5
15. Nowakowski, W., Bojarczak, P., Łukasik, Z.: Performance analysis of data security algorithms used in the railway traffic control systems. In: Proceedings of the International Conference on Information and Digital Technologies 2017, vol. 1, pp. 281–287. IEEE Xplore (2017). Slovak Computer Sciences and Informatics Journal
16. Nowakowski, W., Ciszewski, T., Łukasik, Z.: The concept of railway traffic control systems remote diagnostic. In: Mikulski, J. (ed.) TST 2017. CCIS, vol. 715, pp. 471–481. Springer, Cham (2017). https://doi.org/10.1007/978-3-319-66251-0_38
17. Nowakowski, W., Ciszewski, T., Młyńczak, J., Łukasik, Z.: Failure evaluation of the level crossing protection system based on fault tree analysis. In: Macioszek, E., Sierpiński, G. (eds.) TSTP 2017. LNNS, vol. 21, pp. 107–115. Springer, Cham (2018). https://doi.org/10.1007/978-3-319-64084-6_10
18. Ozturk, V., Rende, F.S., Ince, O., et al.: A general railway data model for simulations and simulators. Simul. Trans. Soc. Model. Simul. Int. **90**(7), 833–849 (2014)
19. Rausand, M., Høyland, A.: System Reliability Theory: Models, Statistical Methods, and Applications. Wiley, Hoboken (2004)
20. Rogowski, A.: Compliance of the results of hypothesis testing with exponential distribution for selected statistical tests. Arch. Transp. **24**(4), 531–551 (2012)
21. AMRandom. https://www.esbconsult.com/download.htm. Accessed 3 Jan 2018

Railway Safety and Security Versus Growing Cybercrime Challenges

Marek Pawlik[✉]

Warsaw Railway Research Institute, Chlopickiego 50, Warsaw, Poland
mpawlik@ikolej.pl

Abstract. Paper presents how safety and security of the railway system have changed over the years taking into account both internal and external factors. It takes into account internal changes in railway technology itself including more and more shifting to electronic, programmable and database systems and shifting from closed to open data communication systems. It also takes into account external changes pointing environmental circumstances, vandalism and terrorism challenges as well as cybercrime changes. Paper is focusing on cybercrime and cybersecurity. It identifies functions of the railway systems which are supported by IT based solutions. Paper subdivides identified IT based solutions by their influence on the safety and security as well as by their susceptibility to external influences including unauthorised attempts to influence the way they work. It shows how much susceptibility depends on internal and external data communication. Paper analyses different types of hazardous events influencing communication starting from relationships between possible undesirable events and threats, which are defined by RAMS railway standards. Conclusions are pointing sensitive IT solutions areas together with descriptions of the related challenges.

Keywords: Railway · Cybersecurity · Communication · Control command · Signalling

1 Introduction

Railways' safety was treated as doubtless requirement from the very beginning. It was obvious, that moving hundreds and thousands of tons would not be acceptable if safety would not be proven. At the same time it was obvious, that technical solutions may eventually malfunction especially as they were foreseen for long time operation in difficult circumstances (high stress, fatigue loading, dust, etc.) and also that the railway staff is not infallible. As a result from the very beginning it was necessary to define safety rules for technical constructions as well as safety related rules for operational purpose and verification of staff competences.

The key safety rule which was used from the beginning was a fail-safe concept. All technical solutions, which are safety critical, are constructed in a way, that ensures safe operation in case of degraded situations, disregarding technical part which is malfunctioning and the way it is damaged. The fail-safe concept was defined for mechanical solutions. This is why horizontal position of the arm of a mechanical

© Springer Nature Switzerland AG 2019
J. Mikulski (Ed.): TST 2019, CCIS 1049, pp. 57–68, 2019.
https://doi.org/10.1007/978-3-030-27547-1_5

semaphore had to mean STOP, while vertical position was not acceptable as reflecting permissible signal. It was so, as broken semaphore wire could result with dangerous situation – showing permissible signal, when route is not set or occupied by rolling stock. Accepting half-up semaphore position as proceed ensures STOP meaning for broken wire thanks to gravity (horizontal position – STOP, 45° angle – proceed).

Fail-safe principle was adopted for mechanical solutions, but it was working perfectly also for electromechanical and electrical solutions. For instance it was, and still is, checked whether short-circuits or lack of electrical connection do not cause dangerous situation. However for electronic solutions fail-safe concept had to be supplemented with additional rules, as it was reasonable to apply it only to general failures like lack of power supply for individual modules. It became not reasonable to apply fail-safe principle for wide range of errors which may occur within individual modules. That's why new safety concept was defined in early 1990s, and is known as Safety Integrity Level SIL-4.

Presently, after nearly thirty years railways are facing new challenge – ensuring cybersecurity. The question is whether SIL-4 is good enough for today risks associated with utilisation of off-shelf electronic components and using publicly known transmission technics, open transmission systems and considering cloud data storage together with cloud computing. Cybersecurity is a question for today.

2 Cybersecurity – How Far It Is a New Challenge

Railway traffic safety was important from the very beginning. The present cyber-crime risks could be compared to risks already present in old technical solutions. For instance the single-line token principle, which was frequently used in the past, which was based on singularity of the device assigned to specific section, could be encroached by preparation of the fake-token. However preparation of such token was really difficult. It was much easier to impose driver to pass signal at danger by forcing then by misleading the driver.

Presently, passing signal at danger (passing STOP without authorisation) is more and more difficult. Many lines are equipped with protection functionalities e.g. by applying automatic train control (ATC) systems like ETCS (European Train Control System imposed by EU law for all railway lines when signalling is upgraded especially when it takes place with use of EU funds). Such ATC systems including ETCS are using electronic, programmable elements and technologies which are considerably known to non-railway experts. That creates risk which is not comparable to fake-token. Railways have to be prepared for different kinds of cyber-crime including attempts to generate fake electronic signals allowing trains to run in dangerous situations.

3 What for Railways Are Using IT Technologies

In order to discuss railway cybersecurity it is important to identify what for railways are using IT technologies. Of course they are presently used for different purposes.

Looking on the railway lines and stations:

- IT support is utilized for design e.g. for planning tracks geometry, calculations of amounts of materials e.g. amount of ballast, verification of appropriateness of place for storage of the materials, technology planning e.g. design of technological roads, design of power stations, subdivision of tracks into sections appropriate for foreseen speed, etc.
- IT support is utilized for construction both for new railway lines and for upgrading existing lines and stations, e.g. for measurements of the tracks, structure gauges, overhead lines, for semi-automatic and automatic construction equipment e.g. for levelling, lifting, lining and tamping machines, for after construction verifications, etc.
- IT support is utilized for operation e.g. for setting proceed signals at the trackside signals, for preparation and transmission of the electronic movement authorities, for authentication of the received authorities, for checking train runs against envelopes, for displaying passenger information, for voice announcements, for emergency braking systems, for continuous collecting of the data reflecting the state of equipment, for diagnostic, etc.
- IT support is utilized for supporting degraded operation e.g. for supporting decision processes, for collecting data about incidents, accidents and near misses for identification of reasons and for elimination of such reasons in the future, for supporting accident commissions by credible data showing all information relevant for accident analyses.

Looking on the railway rolling stock:

- IT support is utilized for design e.g. for individual components and for overall vehicle design, e.g. for calculations and verifications of power equipment, engines, braking systems, doors control, movable steps, ticketing, passenger information systems, passenger emergency calls for establishing communication with driver, passenger emergency brakes, air conditioning and heating, lights, etc.
- IT support is utilized for construction both for new railway vehicles and for renewal of existing ones, e.g. for verification of cabling and wiring, for checking functionalities and their interconnections, etc.
- IT support is utilized for operation e.g. for traction steering, running, braking, and on-board equipment continuous verification for diagnostic purpose and on-board equipment steering e.g. air conditioning, voice announcements, doors opening and closing, etc.
- IT support is utilized for supporting degraded operation e.g. for emergency stop and communication with line-side staff, as well as for collecting credible data showing all information relevant for accident analyses.

Out of that wide range article focuses only on cybersecurity of the solutions supporting operation. However it is more and more reasonable and required to take cybersecurity into account for all different types of systems utilizing IT based and electronic, programmable components.

3.1   Operating Railway Lines with IT Supported Functionalities

Operation starts with timetabling and have to be supported by diagnostic functionalities. However it seems reasonable to focus on three key groups of functions which are supported nowadays by electronic programmable components and IT based algorithms – on signalling, communication and emergency systems and devices. They are marked in a symbolic way on Fig. 1, which is showing urban rail in one of the Italian cities.

Signalling is composed by interlocking, co-working track occupancy checking system, point machines, trackside signals, block centre preparing electronic movement authorities and trackside equipment sending authorities.

Communication ensures operational voice connections between trackside staff and drivers as well as voice announcements. It is composed by many devices interconnected by fibre optic and copper cables as well as by radio.

Additional devices dedicated for emergency are influencing signalling and communication ones as well as braking, lighting, emergency announcements, etc.

Fig. 1. Signalling, communication and emergency components funicolare between Petraio and Fuga [own elaboration]

A set of devices for signalling, communication and emergency support together with their purposes and interconnections which are defined in design phase, constructed during building or re-building and verified during commissioning have to be checked regularly to ensure appropriate functioning which could be corrupted by different kinds of failures, misuses as well as by inappropriate maintenance or unauthorised interventions e.g. cyber-crime.

3.2   Operating Railway Rolling Stock with IT Supported Functionalities

Operation starts with timetabling and have to be supported by diagnostic functionalities. However it seems reasonable to focus on three key groups of functions which are supported nowadays by electronic programmable components and IT based algorithms – on steering, driving & braking and passengers' support components. They are marked in a symbolic way on Fig. 2, which is showing Koleje Mazowieckie train at the Siedlce station in Poland.

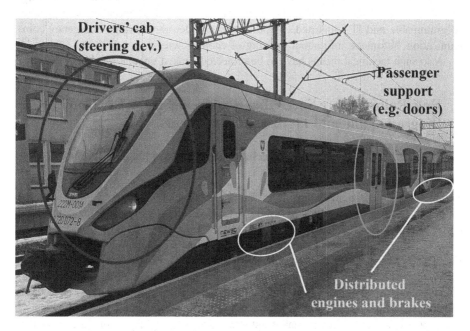

Fig. 2. Steering, driving & braking and passengers' support components Koleje Mazowieckie train at Siedlce station [own elaboration]

Steering devices are operated by driver from driving cab. It covers pantographs, engines, brakes, horn, vigilance as well as signalling, communication and emergency, namely voice and data communication, emergency stop by radio, receiving and using movement authorisations, verification of running parameters, etc.

Key role is played by engines and braking systems, which are also not free from electronic, programmable and IT based solutions. In case of diesel and electrical multiple units both engines and brakes are distributed. In case of classic train composed by locomotives and wagons or coaches engines are located in locomotives, but brakes are distributed.

Passenger trains are also equipped with passengers' support devices like on-board broadcasting and passenger information systems, ticketing, air-conditioning and heating, lights, passenger emergency brakes, etc.

All devices and their interconnections are precisely defined for each type of vehicle, and verified during commissioning for each individual vehicle. Design, construction as well as commissioning are supported by IT based systems. However they have to be checked regularly to ensure appropriate functioning which could be corrupted by different kinds of failures, misuses as well as by inappropriate maintenance or unauthorised interventions e.g. cyber-crime.

3.3   IT Support for Transport Security

Ensuring traffic safety is not enough. Railways have to ensure also transport security. That is based on dedicated staff and procedures, which are also supported by electronic, programmable and IT supported components e.g. video-monitoring, emergency communication, automatic info about opening of cabinets, etc.

Also such technical means have to be protected against unauthorised interventions.

4   How Railways Are Specifying Requirements for Electronic, Programmable and IT Based Components

4.1   Requirements for IT Based Technical Systems Supporting Traffic Safety

Traffic management, namely signalling and control command components are covered by one of the RAMS standard - EN 50129 [8] dedicated for railway signalling reliability, availability, maintainability and safety. Works on software components are required to respect dedicated requirements described in another RAMS standard – EN 50128 [7]. All utilized communication means have to follow requirements applicable to communication systems for rail transport signalling described in another RAMS standard – EN 50159 [9]. Overall signalling and control command have to be covered by safety proving document, called safety case, which is proving safety integrity level SIL-4. Proving takes into account the way how software has been prepared, the way how communication has been established and all components together with their relationships taking into account operation, maintenance and overall system conditions. The overall dependencies are shown at Fig. 3 and is described in the main railway RAMS standard – EN 50126 [5, 6].

Proven SIL-4 is a must, however additionally railways are defining availability requirements. It is not enough that probability of a failure affecting safety is very low. It is also required, that in case of failure system can be put in operation after repair in adequately short time. Availability, which mainly depends on repair times in reality also depends on operating, maintenance and overall system conditions, which are not only related to systematic and random failures but also to human factors, operational and maintenance procedures and logistic circumstances, as well as to external disturbances, preventive and corrective maintenance.

Random failures affecting safety cannot occur more then 10^{-8} times per hour for SIL-4 systems. Proving is usually based on technical structure and mean times between failures MTBF.

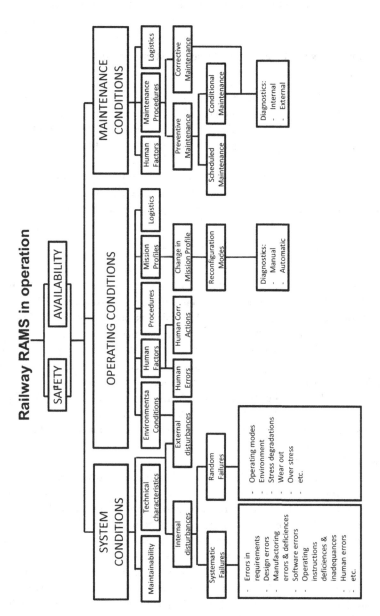

Fig. 3. Safety and availability relationship to operational, maintenance and overall system conditions as depictured in EN 50126 [5]

Systematic failures are more difficult to be taken into account. Verification in that respect is based on quality management and a set of technics which are subdivided into strongly recommended and recommended for different SIL levels. Railway traffic safety was important from the very beginning in nineteen century safe principle and the safety integrity levels.

4.2   Requirements for IT Based Technical Systems Supporting Transport Security

Methodology which is shortly described above in Sect. 4.1 up to now applies only to signalling and control command equipment. It is not legally required for all other types of technical solutions which are dedicated for supporting railway transport security. It is not applicable e.g. for passenger information systems, fire protection systems, electrical protection systems, etc.

All such systems are seen as potential source of troubles starting from traffic disturbances, but requirements are defined case by case, and there is no standard even in relation to the way how such requirements have to be defined and communicated.

4.3   Enlarging Applicability of RAMS Standards

RAMS standards [5÷9] are seen on the European level as a key for cross-acceptance of technical solutions for railways for all solutions which are utilizing electronic, programmable and IT based components. That's why their applicability is just being enlarged. Basic RAMS standard EN 50126, which is pointed by Polish legal documents as the one issued in 1999, has been recently replaced on a European level by a set of two standards EN 50126-1:2017 [5] and EN 50126-2:2017 [6]. It is already agreed, that their applicability will be enlarged. It was officially accepted in January 2019 by Member States, and will be in force since June this year.

Enlargement of the applicability of the RAMS standards covers individual pointed solutions in design and construction of the infrastructure, power supply and rolling stock. Those solutions are pointed in an annex linking standards with Technical Specifications for Interoperability (TSI) issued as annexes to binding European Commission Regulations.

Moreover TSI specifications, due to rapid changes in electronic and programmable components technologies as well as IT technologies, are stating, that all changes in the RAMS standards will be binding without a need to reflect them in the TSI specifications.

As an addition TSI specifications are also changing requirements for the bodies, which are verifying safety cases. Since June such verifications can only be performed by entities which are accredited as Assessment Bodies for risk acceptance under railway safety directive [1]. That is reflected also in a change of the directive, which took place in 2016 within so called fourth railway package. A new directive regarding railway safety [2] will be introduced in Polish law in the mid of June 2020. This directive will heighten requirements for the risk acceptance and further enlarge RAMS standards applicability.

The question is whether it is good enough for ensuring cybersecurity for IT based solutions utilized by railways. It seems it is certainly not. It is enough to point some examples. First, railway freight operators pay for infrastructure, which was requested, even if it was not used. That was necessary to end blocking infrastructure by some operators few years ago. Presently as a result freight operators request paths for trains only when they are sure, that the trains will be ready. As a result Polish Railway Lines are using internet based system for timetabling (SKRJ) offering freight operators an interface for ad-hoc setting of the paths. Presently about seventy operators are using that system, but legally speaking it has to be opened for all freight operators in the European Union latest in 2020 in the light of the fourth railway package.

Polish Railway Lines are using multilevel database containing all data necessary for asset management (SILK). System contains data necessary for dispatching, for maintenance and renewals: ortofotomaps, buildings, public roads and roads owned by railways, land attitude, tracks, switches, bridges, viaducts, signals, are put over maps, which were made available by the main country geodesist. All kinds of documents like feasibility studies, reports reflecting state of the constructions, maintenance recommendations, reasons for local speed restrictions, etc. are also put into SILK as a main database ensuring relations between documents and geographical coordinates of the infrastructure elements. This system is accessible only for infrastructure manager employees, but it is accessible over public network.

Such systems cannot be treated as cyber-crime resistant without appropriate prove.

5 Cybersecurity – What Is Being Done on the European Level

Complex IT based systems are supporting different sectors of national economy. Cybercrime challenge has already been seen many times, even in railway environment – e.g. German railway timetabling and passenger information systems were corrupted causing hundreds hours of delay. As a result dedicated directive concerning measures for a high common level of security of network and information systems has been accepted [3] as a measure supplementing directive dedicated for electronic communications networks and services [4]. Special safety measures are defined on one side for the companies producing and ensuring distribution of the electricity, oil production and managing oil transmission pipelines, and gas supply. On the other side similar requirements regarding cybersecurity are defined for banking and credit institutions, for entities ensuring financial market infrastructure, for health care sector including hospitals and clinics, as well as for drinking water supply and distribution and digital infrastructure together with authentication services raising cyber-crime immunity. The most common attracts are those ones which are blocking systems by rapidly growing amount of requests.

Directive [3] is covering also transport systems: air transport carriers, airport managing bodies and entities operating ancillary installations contained within airports and traffic management control operators providing air traffic control services, as well as inland, sea and coastal passenger and freight water transport companies, ports' managing bodies and entities operating works and equipment contained within ports, as well as road authorities responsible for traffic management control. It covers also railway transport. It that respect it is pointing at rail transport infrastructure managers and railway undertakings, as the ones which are due to introduce safety measures against cyber-crime and which are due to be involved in national and European exchange of cybersecurity relevant alerts and best practices.

6   Cybersecurity – What Is Being Done by Individual Companies

All entities belonging to pointed types are obliged to undertake works ensuring better preparation for cybersecurity related risks. Polish Railway Lines as well as railway transport operators had to identify all IT based systems which could be affected (example are shown above in Subsect. 4.3), and analyse their immunity taking into account the way they were purchased.

There are two general ways to purchase software based systems – selection based purchasing and specification based purchasing. Many systems were bought by selection based processes in the past. Nowadays practically all such systems are purchased by specification based processes. The key questions regarding cyber-security are first – how to define required, necessary security?, second – how to check whether declared security is true?, third – how to ensure, that required security is useful and sufficient? This questions are common disregarding whether software based system is for oil company, air traffic or health care sector. Therefor railway companies have to learn the lesson already learnt by others. The overall process already established for specification based IT purchase processes is shown at Fig. 4.

Fig. 4.   Specification based IT purchase process utilizing verification of the security target by use of protection profile [10]

Customer is due to define in a formal language, described in a 15408 standard [10], cybersecurity related requirements in a form of protection profile. Such PP profile is given to developer, which is preparing a separate document describing in the same formal language achieved, ensured security targets. Verification of the software based systems is performed by authorised evaluating entities, which are cross-accepted under cybersecurity directive [3]. Such entity has already been established in Poland on a national level, but did not performed any work for railway sector up to now.

7 Conclusion

There is no doubt, that RAMS standards have to be applied not only for signalling and control command but also for wide range of technical electronic, programmable and IT based solutions utilized by railway companies. This is however not enough for ensuring cybersecurity. Additional measures have to be undertaken especially for IT based systems which were constructed without defining protection profiles and without verifications of the security targets against protection profiles. It is necessary to verify cybersecurity of systems in use, especially for SKRJ and SILK, but also for a number of others, and to change the way they are developed in the future.

The RAMS standards have to be learnt and adopted by companies undertaking construction works for railway lines and stations as well as by rolling stock producers. Probably Polish versions of the EN 50126-1 and EN 50126-2 [5, 6] will be available at the end of 2019. This however is waiting for confirmation from the Polish Committee for Standardization PKN.

Polish entity authorised for evaluation of the security targets against protection profiles has to be accredited and has to start cooperation with Polish Railway Lines as an infrastructure manager and with key railway operators like PKP Cargo, Intercity, Przewozy Regionalne as well as with key railway IT service providers, especially with Informatyka Kolejowa.

References

1. Directive 2004/49/EC of the European Parliament and of the Council of 29 April 2004 on safety on the Community's railways and amending Council Directive 95/18/EC on the licensing of railway undertakings and Directive 2001/14/EC on the allocation of railway infrastructure capacity and the levying of charges for the use of railway infrastructure and safety certification (Railway Safety Directive) (Official Journal of the European Union, L 164/44, 30.4.2004)
2. Directive (EU) 2016/798 of the European Parliament and of the Council of 11 May 2016 on railway safety (Official Journal of the European Union, L 138/102, 26.5.2016)
3. Directive (EU) 2016/1148 of the European Parliament and of the Council of 6 July 2016 concerning measures for a high common level of security of network and information systems across the Union (Official Journal of the European Union, L 194/1, 19.7.2016)

4. Directive 2002/21/EC of the European Parliament and of the Council of 7 March 2002 on a common regulatory framework for electronic communications networks and services (Framework Directive) (OJ L 108, 24.4.2002, p. 33), amended by: Regulation (EC) No 717/2007 of the European Parliament and of the Council of 27 June 2007 (OJ L 171/32, 29.6.2007), Regulation (EC) No 544/2009 of the European Parliament and of the Council of 18 June 2009 (OJ L 167/12, 29.6.2009) and Directive 2009/140/EC of the European Parliament and of the Council of 25 November 2009 (OJ L 337/37, 18.12.2009)
5. European Standard EN 50126-1:2017, Railway applications – The specification and demonstration of reliability, availability, maintainability and safety (RAMS) – Part 1: Generic RAMS Process
6. European Standard EN 50126-2:2017, Railway Applications - The specification and demonstration of reliability, availability, maintainability and safety (RAMS) – Part 2: Systems Approach to Safety
7. European Standard EN 50128:2011, Railway applications – Communication, signalling and processing systems – Software for railway control and protection systems
8. European Standard EN 50129:2003/AC:2010, Railway applications - Communication, signalling and processing systems - Safety related electronic systems for signalling
9. European Standard EN 50159:2010, Railway applications - Communication, signalling and processing systems - Safety-related communication in transmission systems
10. ISO/IEC 15408-1:2009 Information technology – Security techniques – Evaluation criteria for IT security – Part 1: Introduction and general model

Safety and Availability – Basic Attributes of Safety-Related Electronic Systems for Railway Signalling

Karol Rástočný and Emília Bubeníková$^{(\boxtimes)}$

University of Žilina, Univerzitná 8215/1, 010 26 Žilina, Slovak Republic
{karol.rastocny, emilia.bubenikova}@fel.uniza.sk

Abstract. At the moment, we are exposed to very rapid technological changes. Railway industry must adequately respond to these changes. New technologies will require new approaches, with the result that gradually there is a change of views on processes related not only to the development of these systems but also to their operation and maintenance. Validation that the requirements for the dependability and safety of the safety-related electronic system for railway signalling have been satisfied (i.e. parameters RAMS) is a necessary condition for its implementation to operation. This article provides a conceptual view of the changes in risk analysis, definition requirements for availability and safety, and in particular, the safety evaluation safety-related electronic systems for railway signalling.

Keywords: Signalling system · Risk · Safety · Availability

1 Introduction

Transport of passengers and goods by railway is associated with some risk as an undesirable event that may result in personal injury, significant material damage, environmental damage and other adverse consequences. Various safety measures can be used to eliminate (reduce) the occurrence of these undesirable events. Requirements for these measures and their implementation and evaluation of their quality have always been and are also dependent on the existing technology, knowledge and opinions.

According to [1] is a railway signalling system (RSS) considered a safety-related system, which operates in a continuous mode of operation.

Dependability and safety are two distinct quality attributes of the RSS and must be distinguished between them. Although these are different RSS attributes, they affect each other and are related to each other. The dependability properties of the restored object being (hence RSS also) are comprehensively evaluated through the availability.

There are cases where there is "overlap" of dependability and safety requirements (e.g. safety reasons) are under the continuous mode of process control desired the greatest possible availability of the RSS. If the RSS is capable of operation, responsibility is assumed by a person, and its error rate is usually substantially greater than the

© Springer Nature Switzerland AG 2019
J. Mikulski (Ed.): TST 2019, CCIS 1049, pp. 69–82, 2019.
https://doi.org/10.1007/978-3-030-27547-1_6

failure rate of the RSS. There are also some cases where it is desirable to terminate the service provision, which is contrary to the dependability requirement - to continuously provide the required service. Meeting these conflicting requirements for safety and availability leads to a compromise that affects the choice of the RSS architecture.

The safety and dependability features of the RSS are characterized by the RAMS (Reliability, Availability, Maintainability, Safety) parameters. The relationship between these parameters is illustrated in Fig. 1.

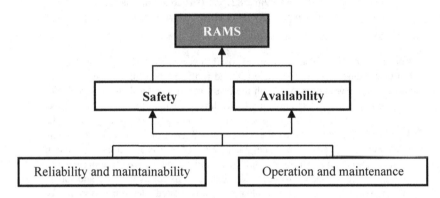

Fig. 1. The relationship between the RAMS parameters [2]

2   Safety and Availability of Railway Signalling Systems

2.1   Current View On the Safety of Railway Signalling Systems

Historically, railway signalling technique largely developed as a separate field of technology. A characteristic feature of classic RSSs was the use of special structural elements whose features were proven by long-term practice and the required safety was achieved by appropriate methods and procedures for applying these elements. The safety evaluation of such RSSs was based only on a qualitative analysis of the consequences of failure modes of the RSS and the verification of the correct the RSS functionality using tests and proofs.

The essence of qualitative analysis of the impact of failure modes on the RSS safety is that the relationship between credible failure modes of the individual RSS components and features of this system (looking for the answer to "What happens if ..."). RSS is considered safe if there is no believable type of credible failure modes (or a combination of credible failure modes), which would result in a dangerous activity RSS. This objective can be successfully used analysis of failure modes and their consequences (FMEA - Failure Modes and Effects Analysis). A qualitative evaluation of the consequences of failure modes of hardware for the RSS safety is based on the assumption that a set of credible failure modes is known for individual components of this system. If none of the credible failure modes does result in a hazardous state of RSS, then the RSS is considered be safe must valid, that

$$E_{HR} = 0, \tag{1}$$

where E_{HR} is a set of credible failure modes.

Such an approach to creating and qualitative evaluation of RSS to lead to the claim that if the RSS does not have any credible failure modes, it has absolute safe and therefore risk analysis is not required and not even done. This is a simplified view of safety because, in addition to credible failure modes (types of failure that are real and probable), there are also incredible failure modes whose occurrence is considered to be unreal, but the probability of their occurrence is not zero (Fig. 2). It should take into account the fact that due to non-compliance with technological procedures (or for other reasons) can significantly increase the probability of credible failure modes.

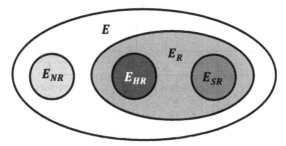

E – a set of failure modes
E_{NR} – a set of incredible failure modes (unreal failure modes)
E_R – a set of credible failure modes (real failure modes)
E_{HR} – a set of credible hazardous failure modes
E_{SR} – a set of credible safe failure modes

Fig. 2. The principle of qualitative analysis of failure modes of an RSS [own study]

In the second half of the last century, electronic components are gradually being deployed also in the field of railway signalling technique and there was effort to avoid the use of special components in the development of an electronic railway signalling system (E-RSS) and to apply the components and subsystems available in the commercial market called commercial off the shelf (COTS) products. Increasing the integration of electronic elements and the use of processor technology has led to the development of the programmable E-RSSs. Because E-RSSs use components with a certain degree of integration, creating a list of credible failure modes for these components is not real.

Developing and evaluating the safety of E-RSS requires the application of new methods and procedures that must (among other things) give answers to questions:

– how to define safety requirements;
– how to evaluate safety.

In connection with an E-RSS, there is a new term - safety integrity. Safety integrity is the ability of a safety-related system to achieve its required safety functions under all the stated conditions within a stated operational environment and within a stated duration [1]. Safety integrity is expressed through Safety Integrity Level (SIL) and consists of two components - the random failure integrity (the quantifiable part of the safety integrity which relates to hazardous random faults) and the systematic failure integrity (the non-quantifiable part of the safety integrity and relates to hazardous systematic faults). Various factors influence the safety integrity, as shown in Fig. 3.

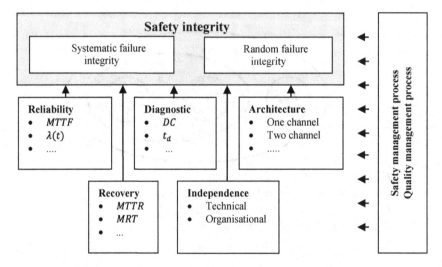

Fig. 3. Factors affecting the safety integrity of an E-RSS [3]

These factors include safety management and quality management that covers all stages of the E-RSS life cycle [2]. Other factors (reliability, diagnostics, recovery, architecture and technical independence) are among the technical and operational parameters of the RSS. Many of these RSS technical and operational features can be referred to as RSS dependability features.

The safety functions of the E-RSS are generally implemented by the fail-safe composite technique, which is characterized by the use of multi-channel architecture. Does not evaluate the safety of the E-RSS as a whole, but is evaluating the level of the SIL of the individual safety function (SF), which implements the E-RSS. When evaluating the safety must be submitted evidence that each the SF of the E-RSS meets the safety requirements for integrity against systematic failure and against random failure (Fig. 4).

Achieving the desired SIL of the SF against systemic failures can be demonstrated in particular by testing and, to a very limited extent, using calculations. The achievement of the required level of the SIL of the SF against random failure must be demonstrated by means of quantitative methods (calculating the probability of a hazardous failure or a hazardous failure rate of the SF) [1]. Testing can only be used to a limited extent, e.g. to evaluate the impact on the safety of those hardware components for which are defined as credible failure modes. To demonstration to prove they have been met other safety requirements need to use testing and/or calculations, depending on the nature of these requirements.

The need to use quantitative methods (probabilistic approach) to evaluate the random failure integrity results from the SIL-table in [1]. This SIL-table defines the tolerable hazard rate (THR) for the SF and its required SIL. For example, if the SIL4 of the SF is required, so the tolerable value of time to the hazardous failure rate of the safety function $TTFF_H > 10^8\,\mathrm{h}^{-1}$, it means over 11 416 years. It is obvious that the verification of RSS in operation cannot say that RSS is safe if during the safety qualification test there has been no hazardous failure [4].

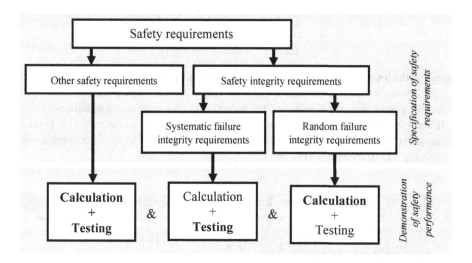

Fig. 4. Evaluation of the safety requirements of SFs of an E-RSS [own study]

In relation to THR (SIL-table in [1]), a logical link between safety and risk is created (safety is defined as freedom from unacceptable risk [1]), because, based on the results of the risk analysis (3rd phase of the life cycle of the E-RSS) define the safety requirements for the individually SF and, ultimately, the safety requirements for the E-RSS [5]. Here it is the evident transition from absolute to the relative view at the safety of a system. The E-RSS safety evaluation cannot be realised only using qualitative methods, but quantitative methods based on probability should also be used (looking for the answer "What is the probability that …"). This historical transition in the development of RSSs and the evaluation of their safety is illustrated in Fig. 5.

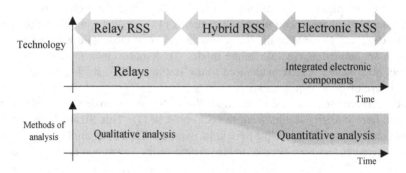

Fig. 5. The transition from classic (relay) RSSs to E-RSSs [own study]

It is clear that absolute safety is unattainable and that the railway transport process contains some inherent risk. In general, the risk can be expressed in a relationship

$$R = \sum_{i=1}^{n} r_i = \sum_{i=1}^{n} (h_i \times C_i), \tag{2}$$

where R is the total risk associated with the railway transport process, n is the number of identified hazards (undesirable events), r_i is the risk associated with the i-the hazard and can be calculated as a combination of the hazard rate (h_i) and its consequences (C_i).

If the risk associated with the controlled process (calculated or estimated) is greater than an acceptable risk, the risk must be reduced to the minimal level of acceptable risk by applying safety measures (Fig. 6).

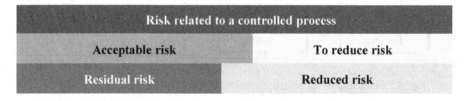

Fig. 6. The principle of a risk reduction [6]

This principle of view at risk (in relation to safety) is of general application and can, therefore, be applied to E-RSS. It should be appreciated that RSS is just one of the factors affecting the safety of the railway transport process (Fig. 7).

This principle of viewing on risk (in relation to safety) is of general application and can, therefore, be applied to the E-RSS [6]. A gradual objectification of the risk analysis process due to the unification of procedures and rules for risk analysis within

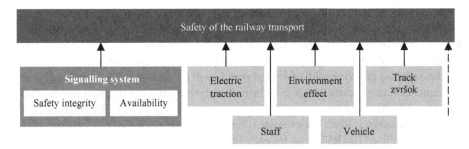

Fig. 7. Factors affecting the safety of the railway transport [own study]

the EU should be considered as a positive change. It has been shown that there are differences in the safety concepts of the individual EU Member States and, therefore, efforts have been made to establish common safety targets and common safety methods, to ensure the maintenance of a high level of safety and create the conditions for its increasing - the pursuit of a coherent approach to problems related to railway safety [7–10]. The risk which is incurred for passengers in the use of railway transport should be the same and independent of the one in the which EU country is passenger located (or not greater than the generally accepted risk).

In Fig. 8 illustrates the principle of reducing risk by means of safety measures. In general, safety measures together provide the required level of safety for the railway transport process by providing accident prevention (reducing the hazard rate; h_{iR} is the reduced hazard rate) and/or mitigating the consequences of a possible accident (C_{iR} are reduced the consequences of an accident caused by i-the hazard).

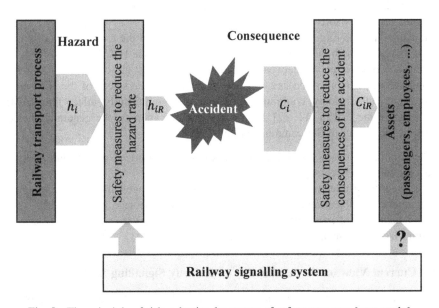

Fig. 8. The principle of risk reduction by means of safety measures [own study]

Since RSS is involved in ensuring the safety of the railway transport process (the process of transporting people and goods), it can be seen as one of the safety measures designed to minimize the hazard rate. However, it cannot be considered as a safety measure to reduce the consequences of an accident because in the event of an accident, it is to be expected that the health of several people will be impaired and consequently the consequences are basically the same as the risk analysis carried out in phase 3 of the RSS life cycle. This has the consequence that in evaluating the safety of the RSS does not talk about on risk analysis (does not evaluate is what is the risk associated rail transportation process, when used and RSS), but for each SF of the RSS assesses the hazard rate (*HR*) and is confronted with the tolerable hazard rate (*THR*). Is must valid, that

$$HR_{SF} \leq THR_{SF}, \tag{3}$$

where HR_{SF} is the hazard rate of the SF (hazardous failure rate of the RSS); THR_{SF} is the acceptable hazard rate of the SF and related to the random failure integrity. The safety functions and associated *THRs* are defined based on risk analysis (3rd phase of the RSS life cycle).

An integral part of programmable E-RSS is the software. While the influence of hardware random failures on the Confidentiality of transmitted safety of the RSS may be relatively well evaluated using qualitative and quantitative methods, the influence of software errors on the E-RSS safety integrity (whether due to bad specification requirements or programmer errors) cannot be quantitatively assessed but only qualitative - especially by testing. Since performing a full test of more complex software is problematic and difficult to implement, it cannot be claimed after tests ending that the software is error-free, but it can only be said that the error was not detected during the tests, so after the test or is not possible to claim that the software is error-free, but it is only possible to say that during the tests the error was not detected. Obviously, the larger the demands on the safety integrity of the E-RSS, the more stringent requirements for testing its software.

It cannot also be forgotten the fact that the realization of the required SFs of the E-RSS is associated with the transmission of information inside E-RSS and also with the transmission of information between the considered E-RSS and cooperating systems. For this reason, it is also necessary to take into account the safety of the used communication, called safety communication that can significantly affect the RAMS parameters of the E-RSS [11, 12]. Safety of communication can be generally characterized as the ability of the communication to guarantee:

- the confidentiality of transmitted messages (only authorized objects/entities have access to data or messages);
- the integrity of transmitted messages (transmitted messages may only be modified by authorized objects/entities and the origin of each message is verifiable);
- the availability of transmitted messages (transmitted messages are accessible to an authorized object/entity within a certain time).

2.2   Current View on the Availability of Railway Signalling Systems

In principle, we should be not interested in the RSS safety but in the safety of the process control (railway) transport process. RSS is only a technical tool (technical measure) that allows us to achieve the required level of safety of the transport process.

Since RSS [1] is considered to be a system operating in a continuous mode of operation, which means that the safety of the transport process (the controlled process) has an impact not only on the integrity of the RSS safety but also on its availability [13]. This fact is illustrated in Fig. 9.

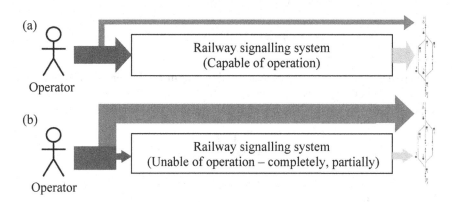

Fig. 9. Operator's impact on railway safety [4]

·   If the RSS is capable of operation (Fig. 9a), almost all operator commands are controlled by the RSS and, if the command is not in conflict with railway safety, it is done. If the execution of the command was dangerous to railway transport, the RSS would reject such a command. Often, a very small part of the operator's commands (usually emergency commands) is executed directly without controlling RSS and only the operator is responsible for their correctness. Figure 9b illustrates a situation where RSS is unable of operation - completely or partially. Since the probability of operator error is generally substantially greater than the probability of a hazardous failure of the RSS, it is desirable that the time of the malfunctioning RSS state be as short as possible. It is obvious that the availability of the RSS affecting the safety of the controlled railway process.

Availability is defined as the ability of an object to be in a state capable of operation the required function under the given conditions and at a given time or within a given time interval, provided that the required external means (maintenance means) are available [14]. To expression of the availability in practice most often used the coefficient of asymptotic availability. Under certain conditions (constant failure rate and constant recovery rate) is valid, that

$$A = \lim_{t \to \infty} A(t) = \frac{MUT}{MUT + MDT}, \tag{4}$$

where $A(t)$ is instantaneous availability, MUT is mean up time and MDT is mean down time.

Because of the objective evaluation of reliability properties of the different RSS, in practice, there is a distinction between the inherent availability of the RSS and operational availability of the RSS.

Inherent availability of the RSS is a value determined by the ideal support environment of maintenance and operation of the RSS (basically given by the RSS features). The inherent availability is defined as follows

$$A_I = \frac{MTBF}{MTBF + MRT}. \tag{5}$$

Operational availability of the RSS is a value determined by realistic operating and support environment operational conditions (it is impacted not only by the RSS properties but also by users). The operational availability is defined as follows

$$A_O = \frac{MTBF}{MTBF + MTTR}, \tag{6}$$

where $MTBF$ is mean operating time between failures, MRT is mean repair time and $MTTR$ is mean time to recovery.

Meaning of parameters in (5) and (6) and the impact of technical and operational properties of the RSS to these parameters is shown in Fig. 10.

In many cases, producers RSSs indicate the value of availability without specifying that this value is the value of inherent availability. Such a custom value could be misleading to the customer because it is valid

$$A_I \geq A_O. \tag{7}$$

It is also important to note, as are defined boundaries of the RSS and to which parts of the system the indicated value of the availability is related. The difference is that the value of availability refers only to the internal part of the E-RSS (the parts which are located in a building) or to the entire E-RSS, including the external elements (signals, points, …). The availability of the E-RSS external elements is significantly more dependent on preventive maintenance than the internal part of the E-RSS. Electronic elements de facto do not require preventive maintenance.

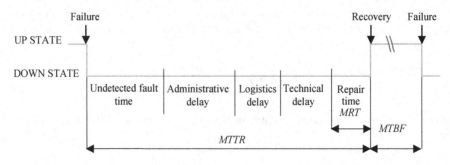

Fig. 10. Availability concept and related terms [14]

3   The Evaluation of the Random Failure Integrity and Availability of SF of the E-RSS

A suitable quantitative method should be used to calculate the observed integrity parameters against random failure and availability of SFs. The most commonly used methods include Fault Tree Analysis (FTA) and Reliability Block Diagram (RBD) [15, 16]. The great advantage of these methods is that they are supported by many software tools that provide not only the means to solve but also the appropriate presentation of the results achieved. The disadvantage of these methods is that they do not allow for a comprehensive evaluation of the current impact of several factors (the impact of the diagnostic coverage, the impact of the recovery, the impact of the change of the architecture of the SF, ...) on the monitored SF parameter.

The most commonly used state-oriented methods include the Markov chains with continuous time (CTMC) method either alone or in combination with Markov chains with discrete time (DTMC) [17].

In Fig. 11 is a CTMC that describes SF transition from operational state (without failure/OK) to the disabled state (**H** or **S**). It is a general model for the analysis of random failure integrity of the SF, which may include the following states:

An operating state

– without failure (one state);
– with failure (one or more states).

A disabled state

– a safety state (one absorption state);
– a hazard state (one absorption state).

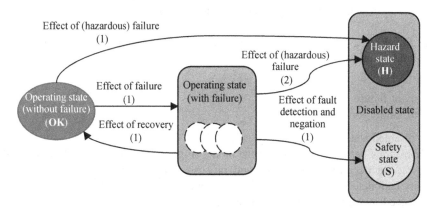

Fig. 11. A general model for analysis of random failure integrity of SF [own study]

In general, the E-RSS is considered a non-recovery system when calculating *HR* of the SF (due to the hazard state). But the real need to consider the recovery E-RSS from the state **S** or state **H**. However, this recovery will not be reflected in the model nor in the *HR* calculation as it occurs at a time when the E-RSS is inoperable and isolated from the controlled process.

Recovery from the state **H** is a specific recovery case. In general, it is necessary to determine the cause of the occurrence of the state **H**, which usually leads to changes in the E-RSS and, given the extent of the changes, all the procedures and measures within the life cycle phases have to be applied as appropriate, as if it were a new system [1]. In such a case, the recovery has its specific features, for example, also depends on the fact that these changes are subject to an independent authority evaluation. After this recovery, the E-RSS is considered as good as new - it starts from the state **OK**.

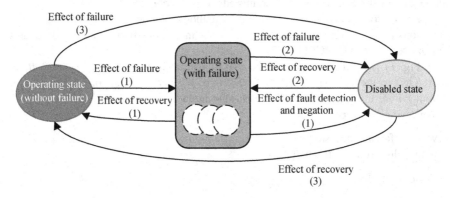

Fig. 12. A general model for analysis of the availability of SF [own study]

Similarly, it is possible to proceed with an analysis of the availability of SF or of RSS. The ideal would be if there was one model to evaluate the safety and availability of SF.

In Fig. 12 is a general state model for analysis of the availability that can include the following states:

An operating state

– without failure (one state);
– with failure (one or more states).

A disabled state.

Transitions between the states of the model (Figs. 11 and 12) should be evaluated based on the occurrence of events and processes (failure rate, intensity recovery, intensity fault detection and negation, …), which relate to those parts of the E-RSS that are involved in the implementation of the SF.

Depending on the specific case of analysis, the use of an individual method or a suitable combination of methods should be considered. For complex systems, modelling is susceptible to analyst error. In order to minimize the probability of an analyst error, a suitable procedure, such as system decomposition [3], should be selected when creating the model.

4   Conclusion

Railway signalling technique has to deal with the new challenges that the current time brings - increasingly demanding customers for services and increasingly more competition from other types of transport. Efforts to meet customer needs and operational efficiency cannot be at the expense of safety. The safety of railway transport must be guaranteed at least at such a level that the risk associated with railway transport is socially acceptable.

It can be assumed, and current trends suggest that the development of RSS will increasingly promote a systematic approach based on unified hardware and software components with clearly defined functional and safety features. The RSS safety evaluation will primarily focus on evaluating the reliability of the application software and evaluating the safety of the interfaces.

If the E-RSS is to be characterized by a high level of safety integrity and high availability, it must include mechanisms that are capable of detecting a failure and consequently negating its potentially undesirable impact on the safety and availability of railway transport.

Acknowledgement. This paper has been supported by the Educational Grant Agency of the Slovak Republic (KEGA) Number 016ŽU-4/2018: Modernization of teaching methods of management of industrial processes based on the concept of Industry 4.0.

References

1. EN 50129: Railway application. Communication, signalling and processing systems. Safety-related electronic systems for signalling (2003)
2. EN 50126-1: Railway application. The Specification and Demonstration of Reliability, Availability, Maintainability and Safety (RAMS). Part 1: Generic RAMS Process (2017)
3. Balák, J., Rástočný, K.: Mathematical model for safety evaluation of distributed interlocking system. In: Mikulski, J. (ed.) TST 2018. CCIS, vol. 897, pp. 234–248. Springer, Cham (2018). https://doi.org/10.1007/978-3-319-97955-7_16
4. Rástočný, K., Pekár, L., Ždánsky, J.: Safety of signalling systems - opinions and reality. In: Mikulski, J. (ed.) TST 2013. CCIS, vol. 395, pp. 155–162. Springer, Heidelberg (2013). https://doi.org/10.1007/978-3-642-41647-7_20
5. Rástočný, K., Ždánsky, J., Nagy, P.: Some specific activities at the railway signalling system development. In: Mikulski, J. (ed.) TST 2012. CCIS, vol. 329, pp. 349–355. Springer, Heidelberg (2012). https://doi.org/10.1007/978-3-642-34050-5_39
6. Rástočný, K., et al.: Problémy súvisiace s analýzou rizika zabezpečovacieho systému – 2. časť (Problems related to risk analysis – Part 2). Nová železniční technika. č. 3/2005, ÚVAR Brno, pp. 11–14. ISSN 1210-3492
7. Directive 2004/49/EC of the European Parliament and of the Council of 29 April 2004 on safety on the Community's railways and amending Council Directive 95/18/EC on the licensing of railway undertakings and Directive 2001/14/EC on the allocation of railway infrastructure capacity and the levying of charges for the use of railway infrastructure and safety certification (Railway Safety Directive)

8. Commission DIRECTIVE 2009/149/EC of 27 November 2009 amending Directive 2004/49/EC of the European Parliament and of the Council as regards Common safety indicators and common methods to calculate accident costs

9. Commission Implementing Regulation (EU) No 402/2013 of 30 April 2013 on the common safety method for risk evaluation and assessment and repealing Regulation (EC) No 352/2009

10. Commission Directive 2014/88/EU of 9 July 2014 amending Directive 2004/49/EC of the European Parliament and of the Council as regards common safety indicators and common methods of calculating accident cost

11. Rástočný, K., et al.: Quantitative assessment of safety integrity level of message transmission between safety-related equipment. Comput. Inform. **33**(2), 343–368 (2014). ISSN 1335-9150

12. Rástočný, K., et al.: Modelling of hazards effect on safety integrity of open transmission systems. Comput. Inform. **37**(2), 457–475 (2018)

13. Nagy, P., Rástočný, K., Ždánsky, J.: Influence of operator on safety of the signalling system during emergency operation. In: Mikulski, J. (ed.) TST 2014. CCIS, vol. 471, pp. 205–214. Springer, Heidelberg (2014). https://doi.org/10.1007/978-3-662-45317-9_22

14. EIC-50(191): International Electrotechnical Vocabulary. Chapter 191: Dependability and quality of service (1990)

15. Ding, L., et al.: A novel method for SIL verification based on system degradation using reliability block diagram. Reliab. Eng. Syst. Saf. **132**, 36–45 (2014)

16. Filthri, P., et al.: Safety analysis at weaving department of PT. X Bogor using Failure Mode and Effect Analysis (FMEA) and Fault Tree Analysis (FTA). In: International Conference on Industrial Engineering and Applications (ICIEA), Singapore, pp. 382–385. IEEE (2018)

17. Klapka, Š.: Markovovské modelování v zabezpečovací technice (Markov modelling in railway signalling technique). Dissertation. Charles University, Prague (2002)

Safe Communication for Railway Transport Using the Example of Axle Counter

Przemysław Wołoszyk$^{(\boxtimes)}$ and Mariusz Buława$^{(\boxtimes)}$

voestalpine SIGNALING Sopot, Jana z Kolna 26C, Sopot, Poland
{Przemyslaw.Woloszyk,Mariusz.Bulawa}@voestalpine.com

Abstract. The article shows practical measures of protection techniques in design of a communication system. It refers to EN 50159:2010 European standard, which includes guidelines for definition of categories and risks in telecommunication network and defences used to protect the system against hazards. The design process requires not only choice of proper defences, but also an analysis and proof that the design assumptions are correct. The choice of proper defences is tightly related to the used communication protocol. The article presents also an approach to "safety code" as a defence against failure and false data of telegrams. The proper "safety code" has a key impact on calculation of HR (Hazardous failure Rate). The article presents practical measures used in design of the UniAC2 axle counter system.

Keywords: System · Communication · Safety protocol · HR · Axle counting

1 Introduction

Safety related systems are using transmission systems more and more frequently. This applies also to railway systems. It is a natural decision to replace parallel interfaces with serial interfaces – such approach brings many advantages, but on the other hand, numerous disadvantages as well. In modern electronics systems, several transmission systems can be defined as a part of connection between subsystems and also as connection between internal modules and functional blocks. Some of these systems belong to non safety related transmission systems. Therefore, how to achieve safety related communication between safety related equipment connected to the non safety related transmission system?

Safety requirements are generally implemented in safety related hardware and safety related software. Because of that, on the level of "safety related application" and "safety related transmission function" adequate techniques shall be used to keep safety level according to requirements. Reference architecture for this approach is proposed by the EN 50159:2010 European standard. It combines:

- Safety related applications which exchange safety related information – logic connection.
- Safety related transmission functions which implement measures and techniques to meet the allocated safety integrity requirements.
- Non safety related transmission system which exchange safety related messages (Fig. 1).

J. Mikulski (Ed.): TST 2019, CCIS 1049, pp. 83–92, 2019.
https://doi.org/10.1007/978-3-030-27547-1_7

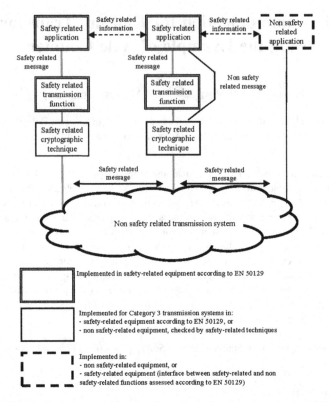

Fig. 1. Reference architecture for safety-related communication [1]

Taking into account hazards which can influence safety aspects of the system, guidelines and a set of basic requirements were defined in EN 50159:2010 standard. The standard collects possible threats, known defences, and defines categories of networks. It contains many detailed rules, but on the other hand, many aspects are only mentioned without strict implementation rules.

The aforementioned standard linked to communication aspects cannot be analysed separately, without the remaining basic standards: EN 50126, EN 50129, EN 50128. Without deep knowledge and understanding what is at the core and main message of all of the mentioned standards, it is not possible to design and analyse a safety protocol and eventually test, verify, and validate results. The most crucial aspect is showed at the end of the standard, in chapter "Guidelines for use of the standard" (Annex D) which includes fundamental rules to guide the process of safety design.

What is more, a good understanding of standards is still not enough. Without knowledge of the system in total, deep understanding of hardware and software architecture as well as details related to design, it is not possible to fulfil requirements of EN 50159 and meet the core requirements related to safety aspects.

The article refers to practical solutions used in safety related systems. Parts of it are based on experiences gained during design process of the UniAC2 axle counting system.

2 Transmission Threats

Threats linked to safety related equipment are considered according to EN 50129. Threats linked to communication and especially non safety transmission system are considered according to EN 50159 and shall be analysed for each project separately, even if chosen defences are the same.

There are many of different hazardous events worth analysis, but the standard groups them all into several basic message errors (threats/defences matrix defined in EN 50159:2010, Table 1):

- telegram repetition,
- telegram deletion,
- telegram insertion by an unauthorized sender,
- telegram re-sequence,
- telegram content corruption,
- telegram receiving delay,
- impersonation of another system (masquerade).

Some of the threats listed above, like lack of integrity (corruption), delay or deletion lead to a temporary break in message flow. In consequence, it can be assumed, that irregularities that can occur during transmission are:

- transmission break,
- telegram error.

Threat analysis shall cover all communication subsystems, e.g. internal communication between safety channels or on board communication to expanders, ADC converters [2]. Different kinds of physical level of communication stack are characterised by different parameter values, e.g. probability that a single bit error in wired transmission systems is lower than in wireless transmission system. For different communication subsystems, other error model can be defined.

The subject of a the analysis conducted for UniAC2 axle counting system was not only the designed protocol, but also hardware configuration and system information flow [3]. In next chapter, practical recommendations can be found.

3 Defences and Adopted Techniques

To ensure transmission in UniAC2 axle counting system on SIL-4 level, data transmission must meet requirements and recommendations described in EN 50159:2010 (for systems in closed and open configuration). According to the standard, that kind of transmission shall be executed in such a way that detection of information errors is possible, and transmission breaks in accordance to the UniAC2 system procedure cause the system to proceed to the safe state. As such, the right behaviour in case of transmission loss and errors should be incorporated.

At an early stage of the project, model of message representation should be chosen. Main aspect which influence it are unauthorised access and malicious attack. One of the most frequently used model of message representation is showed below.

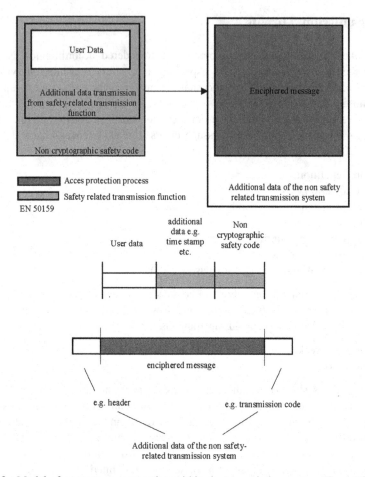

Fig. 2. Model of message representation within the transmission system (Type B0) [1]

To ensure the requested SIL, the following services shall be implemented in safety related transmission function:

- message authenticity,
- message integrity,
- message timeliness,
- message sequence.

The services above can be implemented with the following defences (alone or in combination):

- sequence number,
- time stamp,
- time-out,
- source and destination identifiers,
- feedback message,

- identification procedure,
- safety code,
- cryptographic techniques.

Defences implemented in non safety related transmission system can be taken into account in the analysis, but cannot replace the ones used in safety related transmission function. For example, Ethernet frames use identifiers of sender and receiver which cannot be used as safety identifiers. Additional identifiers have to be added in "additional data" (see Fig. 2). Ethernet frames use code (FCS, CRC-32) which cannot be used as safety code but can be taken into account in safety analyse. [6] Additional code (different polynomial) has to be added as "safety code" (see Fig. 2).

The chosen techniques are presented below.

3.1 Sequence Number

Proper sequence number protects messages against repetition, deletion, insertion, and re-sequence. The safety case shall demonstrate the correctness of sequence number as (see EN 50159):

- proper length,
- proper initialisation and sequence number roll-over procedure,
- proper recovery after interruption of the sequence.

Sequence number has a proper length which ensure that the same value will be repeated after time longer than error detection time (timeout). Taking into account maximum timeout and numbers of frames per second on a specific communication link between two nodes, a proper length of sequence number have to be chosen. For example, for maximum timeout equal 10 s and frames sending every 10 ms:

- 10 000 ms/10 ms = 1000
- 1000 * 1.2 (safety margin) = 1200 frames within 10 s
- Result: data field in the message must be bigger than 1200 (e.g. 2B)

Procedures responsible for initialization, roll-over and recovery can differ depending on implementation. For example, sequence number can be zeroed during initialization procedure, and basing on that, one node has information about restart of the opposite node in the network. Sequence number can be generated as:

- subsequent integers, e.g. 0, 1, 2, 3, …,
- number sequence generated by e.g. linear-feedback shift register with specific polynomial.

Sequence number can be used not only to detect improper sequence of data but also to monitor quality of network. Receiver can easily detect how many frames were lost. Thanks to the feedback message (ACK, NAK), the sender also can monitors quality of the network.

Procedure of recovery after interruption of the sequence also differs, depending on architecture and protocol. Consider an example when the source of information (sender) has data about subsequent activation of a single IN1 input.

In the first implementation, the source of information sends a message each time when input is activated. Based on messages, the receiver counts the number of activations. In this case, lack of one frame (sequence number misalignment) causes improper counting by Receiver; therefore the lack of one message causes an error. What is more, bandwidth of the network shall be analysed and calculated for maximum possible number of activations of IN1.

In the next implementation, the source of information counts the number of activations and share internal counter periodically or on request. The receiver receives the message with the following numbers:

- sequence number 1; counter_in1 = 0
- sequence number 2; counter_in1 = 1
- sequence number 3; counter_in1 = 2
- sequence number 4; counter_in1 = 2
- sequence number 7; counter_in1 = 5

The implementation above is independent from the frequency of IN1 activation, and also it is independent from a short time network break (lack of frames). In point "d", we can see that between subsequent frames (sequence numbers 3 and 4) *counter_in1* has the same value. In point "e", we can see that between subsequent frames (sequence numbers 4 and 7) *counter_in1* increases, and we lost 2 frames (sequence numbers 5 and 6). If a timeout for the next messages meets requirements, it can be accepted without starting *recovery after interruption of the sequence* procedure.

In UniAC2 system, additional frames (the same sequence number) are discarded by the protocol. Older frames (previous sequence number) are discarded by the protocol as well. Lack of a correct telegram for a time longer than the maximal time defined in configuration causes connection closing and subsequent re-opening. Incrementing of the sequence number is done by the receiver of information (in a request frame). As an answer to the request, the source of information sends a frame with the same sequence number as in the request frame. If one telegram is deleted, the second telegram can be accepted by the receiver because all telegrams have the same full information (status). The lack of a correct telegram for a time longer than the maximal time causes communication error.

3.2 Timestamp

A proper timestamp protects the messages against repetition, re-sequence and delay.

The safety case shall demonstrate the correctness of timestamp as (see EN 50159):

- the value of the time increment,
- the accuracy of the time increment,
- the size of the timer,
- the absolute value of the timer (e.g. UTC (universal coordinated time) or any other global clock),
- the synchronism of the timers in the various entities,
- the time delay between originating the information and adding a time stamp to it,
- the time delay between checking the time stamp and using the information.

In many electronic systems (embedded systems), there is no space to complicate architecture and complexity of the solution. Because of that, defenses used by the safety layer of the protocol strictly relate to architecture and implementation of the system. Sometimes it can be hard to fulfill requirements defined in points "d, e, f, g". For example, time synchronization "e" and global clock "d" aspects in all modules of the system together with a small time delay in sending and receiving procedures "f, g" influence architecture of the software and can be difficult to implement if not foreseen at the initial stage. It is not trivial to synchronize many nodes of the system during initialization. During this time, many events are registered in the monitoring system and the correct time is important for further analysis.

Solutions implemented in systems can differ because in some cases old messages can be useless or dangerous; in other cases, old messages can be still valid for a defined time and only then turn useless.

Instead of timestamp defences, many safety related systems use time-out and sequence number. Both of them cover threats as for timestamp: repetition, re-sequence and delay.

Timestamp can be used also to monitor quality of the network. For example, node A sends a timestamp in the request message and node B answers with a message containing this timeout and the requested data. Node B can calculate the time of information flow: from the request to the answer, which is one of the network quality parameters.

3.3 Time-Out

One of the few defence techniques against delay threat is time-out. A proper time-out protects messages against delay.

The safety case shall demonstrate the correctness of timeout as (see EN 50159):

- the acceptable delay,
- the accuracy of the time-out.

This technique is very popular in safety related protocols. In cyclic communication, it is a natural way to check if delay between two messages does not exceed a configured maximum time. If the configured maximum time is exceeded, an error occurs and usually reconnect procedure is run.

In case of one-directional transmission of messages, the receiver monitors the defined maximum time T_{max}. In systems with many logic connections between function blocks, this technique can be highly consuming in terms of resources, especially when accuracy of the timeout is high. For example, when the assumed accuracy of the timeout is 10 ms and there are 256 logic connections between different nodes and different function blocks on a specific module, it means that algorithm shall check status of 256 connections every 10 ms (Fig. 3).

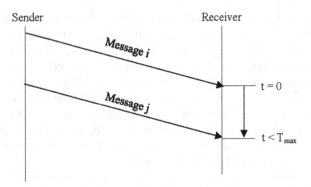

Fig. 3. Cyclic transmission of messages [1]

In case of bi-directional transmission of messages, the sender monitors the defined maximum time T_{max}. One of the implementation starts timer when the sender sends message "i." It can be resource-consuming when there are 256 logic connections and separate timers in the module. Other implementation can be an uptime timer which starts after power up the system. The sender stores the current uptime each time when message "i" is sent. Periodically (depending on the assumed accuracy of the time-out), the sender calculates the difference between current uptime and the stored one for a specific logic connection (Fig. 4).

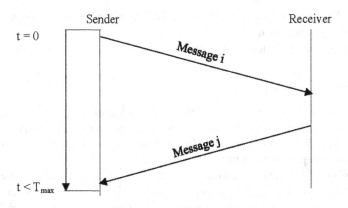

Fig. 4. Bi-directional transmission of messages [1]

3.4 Safety Code

A proper safety code protects messages against corruption.

The safety case shall demonstrate the correctness of safety code as (see EN 50159):

– the capability for detection of expected systematic types of message corruption caused e.g. by hardware, which usually have character of burst errors,
– the probability of detection of random types of message corruption e.g. by EMI.

Safety code can be used to detect corruption and/or correct the messages. Depending on the type of physical medium (wired, wireless) and network length (near, distant), the requested efficiency of safety code can differ. The safety code shall be different than the one used by not safety related transmission systems (in case of UniAC2 system, it is FCS, CRC-32 in Ethernet frames). The whole frame can be secured by the safety code of the safety frame and additional code used by e.g. Ethernet frame. In open transmission systems, it is important to analyse what polynomials are used by commercial transmission systems and choose a different one.

Many different techniques can be used to implement a safety code. One of the most popular is CRC (Cyclic Redundancy Check). The chosen "good" CRC (binary cyclic codes with particular polynomials) is characterised by excellent combating of random errors and burst errors [7–9]. Length of the safety code shall be sufficient for proper level of undetected error probability.

Each polynomial has defined Hamming distance. The Hamming distance (HD) is the minimum number of bits in the code word that must be independently corrupted in order to cause an undetected error. The same length of the safety code e.g. 32 bits can be characterised by a different Hamming distance and maximum number of bits in the message. For example, CRC used by IEEE 802.3 Ethernet standard provides Hamming distance HD = 4 for maximum length of an Ethernet message (1500 bytes). It means that up to 3 bit errors are detected in a corrupted message. The used polynomial can be represents as $x32+x26+x23+x22+x16+x12+x11+x10+x8+x7+x5+x4+x2+x+1$ or 0x82608EDB. In the meantime, we know polynomials which guarantee HD = 6. For example, polynomial 0xBA0DC66B, $x32+x30+x29+x28+x26+x20+x19+x17+x16+x15+x11+x10+x7+x6+x4+x2+x+1$ achieves HD = 6 for up to 16 360 bits, which is more than the length of an Ethernet message [4, 5].

Only for random bit failures due to e.g. EMI, argumentation "the higher the Hamming distance, the lower is the probability of undetected bit failures" is valid. The hazard rates relate to the transmission hardware failures, and faults occurring in the transmission code checker are independent from the Hamming distance, because the failure modes behind these hazards are not related to random (single) bit failures.

The proper "safety code" has a key impact on calculation of HR (Hazardous failure Rate). Tolerable Hazard Rate (THR) per hour and per SIL4 function is $10^{-9} \leq$ THR $\leq 10^{-8}$. The transmission system is a part of the function. The safety target for the transmission system is estimated to be 1% of the safety target of the function, so it equals $10^{-11} \leq$ THR $\leq 10^{-10}$. Using hazardous failure rates obtained for all transmission subsystems results shall be enough to fulfil target hazard rate for SIL4 transmission system and system in total.

4   Conclusion

Practical aspects of design and analysis of communication protocol show that this area requires wide knowledge on the analysed system, as well as the required standards. Yet this knowledge provides visible benefits: on the one hand assuring safety, and on the other hand, it allows to use as simple solution as possible. One of the most complex aspects of the analysis is the choice of the proper safety code and cryptographic techniques. It has to be considered that for open networks with probability of hacker attack, guidelines and recommendations outside of EN 50159 have to be implemented as well. Especially this last area of network and data security is currently undergoing fast changes and getting more complex as we speak.

New solutions are still being introduced to join a wide range of safety related applications and their communication solutions. Highly available industrial networks with high bandwidth are beginning to replace the previously used field bus technologies. In recent decades and years, numerous technologies were developed and introduced for communication networks, providing safe and reliable transmission for the most demanding systems. The struggle with balance against simplicity of solutions resolved with existing techniques and guidelines of EN 50159, which allows to welcome the new challenges with just right assumptions and design ideas.

Combination of non safety-related "black channel" solution with safety related transmission systems [3] bring new opportunities to increase maintainability and configurability of systems without any loss to safety. Systems are then more ready to step into the feature and provide new, better functions. An example of such modern solution is UniAC2, which is a new generation of axle counter systems, designed having in mind the demands of our fast-paced world. It provides safety as well as availability and maintainability in the form of flexible, modular structure for the state-of-art signalling and interlocking systems.

References

1. EN 50159:2010. Railway applications. Communication, signalling and processing systems. Safety-related communication in transmission systems
2. Wołoszyk, P., Buława, M.: Communication in safety systems for railway transport using the example of axle counter. In: Mikulski, J. (ed.) TST 2018. CCIS, vol. 897, pp. 292–302. Springer, Cham (2018). https://doi.org/10.1007/978-3-319-97955-7_20
3. UniAC2 axle counting system documentation
4. Koopman, P.: 32-bit cyclic redundancy codes for Internet applications. In: The International Conference on Dependable Systems and Networks (DSN) (2002)
5. Ray, J., Koopman, P.: Efficient high Hamming distance CRCs for embedded networks. In: Preprint, Dependable Systems and Networks (DSN), Philadelphia, PA, 25–28 June 2006
6. Xu, M., Yang, X.H., Hua, F.C.: The effect of transmission code and safety code on SIL in safety-critical system. In: Second Asia-Pacific Conference on Computational Intelligence and Industrial Applications (2009)
7. Han, J., Siegel, P.H., Lee, P.: On the probability of undetected error for overextended Reed-Solomon codes. IEEE Trans. Inf. Theory **52**(8), 3662–3669 (2006)
8. Wolf, J.K., Michelson, A.M., Levesque, A.H.: On the probability of undetected error for linear block codes. IEEE Trans. Commun. **Com-30**(2), 317–325 (1982)
9. Dodunekova, R., Dodunekov, S.M.: Sufficient conditions for good and proper error-detecting codes. IEEE Trans. Inf. Theory **43**(6), 2023–2026 (1997)

Telematics in Road Transport

Creating a Virtual Environment for Practical Driving Tests

Kristián Čulík[(✉)], Alica Kalašová, and Veronika Harantová

University of Žilina, Univerzitná 8215/1, 010 26 Žilina, Slovak Republic
{kristian.culik, alica.kalasova,
veronika.harantova}@fpedas.uniza.sk

Abstract. From the point of view of road safety, it is necessary to focus the attention to the driver. Despite the increasingly popular topic of autonomous vehicles, the driver is still a central element of the transport system. Human in the transport system causes mistakes and failures that may result in traffic accidents. Testing drivers in real road traffic is in many ways difficult. It is time-consuming and also expensive, because it is necessary to have fully functional vehicle and lot of fuel. Last but not least, experimental drivers may get into dangerous situations in road traffic and there is also risk that they cause a traffic accident. Therefore this article deals with using of driving simulators for driver testing. Due to the limited use of current equipment in University Science Park, it also describes the simple modification of the training driving simulator to a light driving simulator. Simple rebuilding was done to exchange software to enable editing of the virtual environment. The paper describes the modelling of the virtual environment as well as the process of its testing and the initial results of research in the new environment. At the end of the paper are presented the initial results of the graphical recording of the driver's activities together with accurate recording of the actual heart rate during the experimental driving in laboratory conditions.

Keywords: Driving simulator · Simulation · Traffic safety · Driver · Transport system

1 Introduction

Road safety is still a very actual topic. The number of registered vehicles has not yet reached the maximum. The car becomes a part of human's life. The development of the number of registered vehicles in the Slovak Republic is shown in the Fig. 1. With the development of technology and also electronics in vehicles, the driving of vehicle is safer and safer. New electronics safety systems, whether active or passive, are commonly used and some of them are obligatory used. However, it still solves only the technical security issue. More than nine of ten traffic accidents are caused by human error. For this reason, it is especially necessary to focus on the human factor, because the man is faulty and his failure can cause a road accident. Human factor in the driver - vehicle - communication - environment is an important element related to traffic psychology.

© Springer Nature Switzerland AG 2019
J. Mikulski (Ed.): TST 2019, CCIS 1049, pp. 95–108, 2019.
https://doi.org/10.1007/978-3-030-27547-1_8

From the point of view of traffic psychology, the behaviour of the driver during driving can be expressed by the following equation, respectively function [1]:

$$R = f(S - O)$$

where:

R – driver behaviour (response to stimuli)
S – perceived and acting stimuli on the driver
O – personality characteristics of the driver

Behaviour of the driver is running on two levels. At an unconscious level, that is, automated activities of the driver. The second is the conscious level, where the driver connects consciousness with the automated activities according to changes of driving conditions and decides about the most appropriate correct choice of response [1, 2].

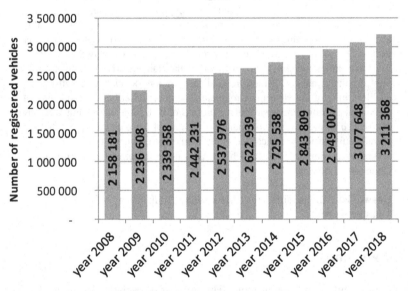

Fig. 1. Numbers of registered vehicles in Slovakia [15]

The transport can be safe, only if all four components of the transport system (the driver, the vehicle, the communication and the environment) are in balance. All of them contribute to achieving the overall system's goal of ensuring the transport and its security. Safe transport have been done without accidents or feeling of danger [16]. The individual partial impacts on traffic safety are shown in the cause and effect diagram in the Fig. 2. The driver factor is connected with his physical and also physical abilities. Vehicle contributes to road safety with its technical parameters, system and condition.

Communication or road ensures the road safety with its conditions, parameters and equipment. Surrounding environment can also affect the safety with visibility and also weather conditions.

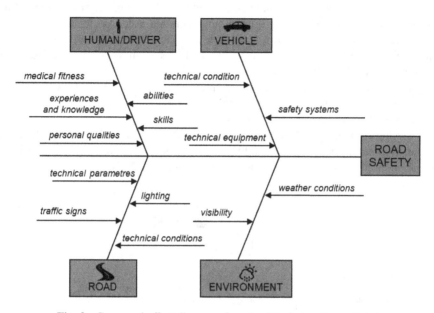

Fig. 2. Cause-and-effect diagram of road safety factors [own study]

In road transport, it is essential to know the factors that can affect the driver's attention. The main reason is the design of environment conditions, driver's work and rest regime, driver training and it also helps to find the causes of traffic accidents. Driver's mistakes need to be identified and driver behaviour examined because, according to the literature, more than 90% of accidents were caused due to human factors [16]. For this reason, exploring the human psyche and the behaviour of the driver while driving is a helpful for society. An effective tool for investigating the driver-vehicle interaction or the driver - transport system interaction, are driving simulators.

2 Virtual Reality and Simulations

Virtual Reality is a term that applies to the artificial environments similar to real world, which has been constructed by computer. Virtual reality has become a common part of many industries and, last but not least, part of driving simulators. The first driving simulators were developed from training flight simulators, which had appeared during World War II. These first simulators have gone from simple mechanical projection techniques to simulated motion picture display systems (MPDS) that show the surrounding environment by projecting a record from a real section of the road. These kinds of simple visual system were used because to the end of 20th century, there was absence of high-performance computers. Over time, technology for creating and displaying virtual reality has become more affordable and better.

Safety and economic benefits from using driving simulators have resulted in their appearance in many areas - the automotive industry, traffic management as well as academic ground. Simple training driving simulators are used also for the training of new drivers in safe conditions. Nowadays there are many commercial driving simulator with high quality graphic and sometimes with motion system, which are used for free-time activities [5, 10, 11].

The biggest benefit of using simulation in experiments is safety and low operating costs. With a driving simulator, it is possible to examine the driver's reactions as well as their behaviour without using a real car.

A driving simulator can be defined as a device that simulates the driving of a road vehicle by imitating the real road traffic environment. The components required for simulation and their communication are shown in the Fig. 3.

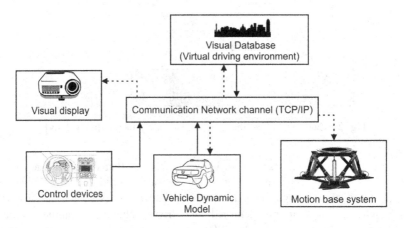

Fig. 3. Components of driving simulator [5]

The components shown in the Fig. 3 can affect the complex validity of simulation. Components are these hardware and software parts:

(a) Control devices – it is an input hardware device. The simplest input device is classic computer keyboard. The driving simulator should have at least the basic controls - the steering wheel, the gear lever, the accelerator pedal and the brake pedal. Other vehicle controls or accessories are required depending on the particular research task.

(b) Visual display – this part is ensured by devices like:

  I. Monitor or large LCD screen or a set of such screens.

  II. Projection screen and projector or multi-projector system. Instead of the classic front projection, sometime it is also used rear projection and with the mirror system, it is possible to reduce the projection distance.

(c) Visual database – this database contains all the models that are in the virtual simulator environment. They are shown by visual display.

(d) Vehicle dynamic model – it is used to create vehicle movement.

(e) Motion base system – often a motion platform with varying degrees of freedom ensures the simulator's movement interaction.

(f) Communication network channel – is a necessary component because the data transfer between components of the simulator is extremely important and any delay time has a negative impact on the simulation validity.

3 Current Equipment and Its Possibility for Use

At present, it is possible to use only one simulator in University Science Park (part of University of Žilina). This device labelled as SNA-211 REN is a training driving simulator. It is shown in the Fig. 4 and it was acquired for road transport research. This simulator is imitation of the Renault Magnum cabin. From the construction design point, it is a stationary simulator without a motion system or vibration platform. Its steering wheel has not force feedback. Seat adjustment and feedback of pedals and parking brake is ensured by a pneumatic system [14].

Fig. 4. Driving simulator SNA – 211 REN [own study]

3.1 Hardware of the Simulator

The training driving simulator is built from the original parts of the truck interior, including the driver's seat. The device consists of the following components [7, 8, 12, 13]:

- driver's cabin,
- display screens,
- instructor's table with computer,

- compressor as a source of compressed air,
- electric and data cables, USB hub and air hoses.

Simulator's controls and indicators are technically good; their interaction with the software is included. The driver's seat with seatbelt is adjustable, as well as the steering wheel and the rear-view mirrors with the control levers identical to the real vehicle. Rear view mirrors are rendered by software on the side LCDs in the driver's field of view. Suspension and adjustment of the driver's seat, pedal force feedback, and parking brake are controlled by the air. The air pressure is provided by an external electric compressor located outside the cabin. The gear lever of the simulator has 5 positions and two switches - one for fast/slow gears and the other one for high/low gears. The training driving simulator also includes: functional dashboard, turn signals all headlamp modes, parking brake, three-position retarder, horn and engine brake. Functional hardware equipment ends with two rotary regulators of sound volume and volume of instructor's voice instructions.

The virtual environment is displayed on three similar GoGen TVF50425 LCD screens with a 1920 × 1080 pixel resolution and a 50″ (127 cm) diagonal, with the two side screens facing the 45° angle to the driver. The settings of the simulator software can be changed via an instructor computer with a separate smaller monitor.

3.2   Software of the Simulator

The training driving simulator SNA – 211 REN includes only two vehicle types. It is not possible to choose any vehicle for any scene. These two vehicles are:

- truck Renault Magnum s with semitrailer or tanker,
- and solo vehicle Renault Midlum.

The simulator software is very simple, so it is difficult to use it for research activities. It allows only the following setup options:

- scene type selection (36 options: training field, motorway, village, etc.),
- visibility setting (3 options: day, fog, night),
- adhesion setting (3 options: 90% asphalt, 50% gravel, 10% ice),
- vehicle load (3 options: 0%, 50%, and 100%).

The evaluation part of the software, which should ensure outputs, is aimed only at the proper driving of the vehicle. It can show only the driver's mistakes during driving a vehicle. All information about the current status of the simulator controls is displayed on-line on the instructor's computer display.

3.3   Problems and Possibilities for Use

The SNA-211 REN is a training device that is not designed for driver-vehicle interaction research. It does not record the position and behaviour of the vehicle and there is not possibility to modify virtual environment. It was necessary to find other way to use the simulator. For few experiments the external recording was used and then the recorded data were processed and evaluated. It is obvious that this process is extremely laborious and may not always provide the required accuracy of output data.

The simulator device has never been used at Department of Road and Urban Transport. First experimental rides were performed by few young drivers. After the experiment, drivers fulfilled the simple questionnaire about their skills and opinions, which can help to enhance the validity of simulation. Results from questionnaire are shown in the Fig. 5 [9].

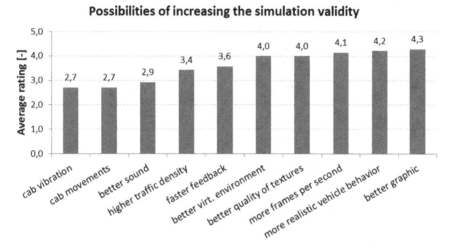

Fig. 5. Possibilities of increasing the simulation validity [own study]

3.4   Alternative Use of the Simulator's Cabin

It is obvious that the original simulation software is not appropriate for research activities. It was necessary to find software, which could be used and which could replace the original software. Therefore the commercial simulation software from the Czech company SCS Software was used for further experiments. Unfortunately, it is possible to use only a central screen of three usable. The simulation software is not customized for more screens with different angles.

Physically, the central LCD LED screen is connected with computer via an HDMI cable, which is reduced to DVI input on the computer. This connection ensures both audio and video transmission. For sound the built-in speakers are used. The keyboard and mouse were also plugged into the new computer to enable simulation software and support programs in a simple way.

The simulator is controlled by the Momo Racing Wheel joystick, which is connected to the computer through the USB interface. It's a steering wheel assembly with a gear lever and pedals. The steering wheel component replaced the original steering wheel on the shaft, and the pedal component was placed instead of the original pedal (brake and accelerator) on the floor of the simulator.

The individual components of the simulator are physically connected according to scheme in the Fig. 6.

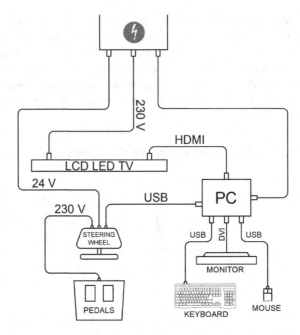

Fig. 6. Scheme of simulator connections [own study]

3.5   Graphic Interface

The narrower field of view, which is caused by using only one screen, is balanced by a high-quality graphic processing of the entire simulation. Graphic is incomparably better and database of individual objects is huge. Also textures and weather simulation has better quality.

In the Fig. 7, there is a graphical comparison of three virtual environments. First on the left is the virtual environment of the current driving simulator SNA – 211 REN from Czech company JKZ Olomouc, in the middle there is virtual reality used by Škoda Octavia simulator at the ČVUT Faculty of Transport in Prague, and on the right is a preview of simulator graphics from SCS Software.

Fig. 7. Graphic comparison of different simulation software [own study based on 16]

4   Creating of Virtual Environment

Map editors in simulators created by SCS Software are basically the same. However, this is a feature that is hidden in the game. To run the map editor, it is necessary to activate the console by editing the settings from uset g_developer "0" and uset g_-console "0" to uset g_developer "1" a uset g_console "1" in the config.cfg file located in the My documents folder. This step allows to press key " ~ " in program, which opens the console. After typing the command "edit", the Map Editor is opened.

For a simple example of virtual environment creating, the SCANIA Driving Simulator and its first exercise map was used. This predefined virtual environment can be edited using the command "edit free_ride_01" after running the console.

After the map editor is started, it is possible to start editing the virtual environment, but it is important to note that the final model of environment is not automatically integrated to the simulator's database. It is necessary to perform multi-step process, during which the model is compressed to special file.

The construction of the transport infrastructure as well as the surrounding objects (for example: natural surfaces, vegetation, buildings etc.) is relatively sophisticated and simple, because the whole virtual environment can be composed of predefined blocks and, moreover, the connection of the communications is intelligent and in some cases the program itself creates the most suitable arc. Virtual environments can be very diverse, even though their creation is time consuming. The final design of environment must be very precise, because we do not want to let drivers ride in virtual world with imperfections, such as deaf places where an infinite space is visible.

Another way of creating a virtual environment is used by the Department of Vehicle Technology of Czech Technical University in Prague. For faster creation of virtual environment there is used a system of virtual blocks with road infrastructure (Fig. 8). Adjacent blocks are compatible – connectable together, so there is simple way to quickly and efficiently create a road without stereotypical surrounding environment. This makes it possible to avoid the unrealistic environment of communication (grass or a simple hill around the path) that occurs in the SNA-211 REN.

Fig. 8. Three square blocks with road connected together [6]

4.1 Infrastructure Creating in Map Editor

In the next part is described an example of creating an infrastructure in the Map editor. This type of environment was used for testing how the type of road affects the driver speed. The different types of road with different horizontal traffic marking were used.

If we do not want to create a whole new map, it is good to open a closed map (for example "free_ride_01" and then begin to create the communication. In this case, there will be 500 m long straight sections connected by the arcs, each straight section being formed by another type of road surface according to Table 1.

Table 1. Names and specifications for selected types of road surface [own study]

Part	Block name Texture name	Road width	Surface and lines	Pattern
1	Road no lanes small y_ground_path1	15 m	gravel	
2	Road no lanes small asphalt2_plates		concrete panels	
3	Road no lanes small asphalt		asphalt, without lines	
4	Road no centre lane asphalt		asphalt, roadside	
5	Road one lane broken asphalt		asphalt, roadside, middle line	

The plan of infrastructure should be prepared before modelling. In the database, there are many patterns, objects and wide range of their properties. If the first type of road for the first segment of road is chosen, it is possible to draw the communication directly in the three-dimensional map editor without interruption. However, in order to make the surroundings of communication realistic, it is advisable to add vegetation or other objects. The creation of the environment is time consuming, but it increases the validity of the simulation.

4.2 Saving and Exporting of Virtual Environment

In this case, it should be noted that the created map can be simply saved through the "Save Map" function, but it is only a save on a disc, not to the simulator's database. For this reason, it is necessary to create a special file that will be inserted into the simulator as a mode. This will automatically overwrite the original map background at each start. The first step is to save the file "free_drive_01.mdb" to the created "map" folder anywhere in computer. Subsequently, the entire folder is archived into a file with the ".zip" file without compression. Then the file extension "zip" must be changed to ".scs", which is internal type of files created by SCS Software Company. This file is uploaded to the "Mods" folder, whose files start overwriting the original files (whether map or vehicle) after starting the program.

5   Practical Measurements

One of the greatest benefits of using a driving simulator is the fact that it is possible to test the behaviour of the driver which is common on the road traffic but is against the law. For example: drunk driving, using a mobile phone while driving, and similar activities not related to driving but also requiring the attention of the driver. Such activity may be the operation of a radio, navigation device or control of the vehicle's air conditioning.

5.1   Measurement of Driver's Behaviour

After connecting the simulator components, a new measurement was performed and new way of record was used. In the past there was performed eye tracking research with old simulator software. Department of Road and Urban Transport does not have an eye tracking device, so it was necessary to look for new methods for analysis of driver's behaviour. For this reason, an external video recording from a digital video camera was used. The video camera was placed on the console (Fig. 8) above the driver's head in the driving simulator.

Figure 9 shows the evaluation of record in software Pinnacle Studio 19. The labels of individual motions of driver are accurate and they mark the start and end of activity of right hand. Subsequently, the time points were exported and converted to the Microsoft Excel.

Fig. 9. Manual evaluation from records [own study]

The individual points are marked on the time axis x of the graph in the Fig. 10. The picture shows activity of right hand: the value "1" means that the hand is on a steering wheel and value "2" says that there is a contact with the gear lever, the time that elapsed between the release of the steering wheel and new fixation.

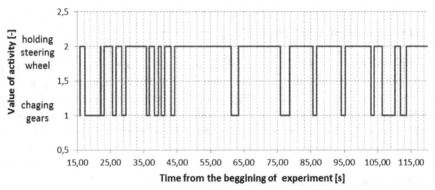

Fig. 10. Record of the driver's activities during free ride [own study]

After the free ride, the driver continued to drive and began the first task. He must to find the address on GPS navigation device and start the voice navigation. This experiment is evaluated in the Excel three-point graph, which is shown in the Fig. 9. The value "3" is added to graph and it means that his hand was touching the device.

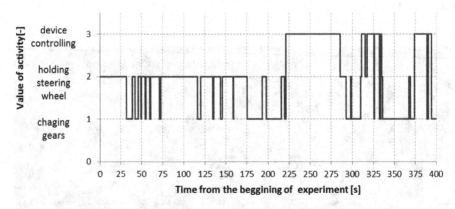

Fig. 11. Record of the driver's activities during task [own study]

During the experimental ride, there was also recorded the driver's heart rate as a stress indicator. The graphs in Figs. 11 and 12 are synchronized. Heart rate was recorded by new device Polar H10, which can measure the human's pulse. Recorded values are transmitted to smartphone via Bluetooth interface and then they are sent on the internet server. Then it is possible to download them with any computer from internet, they could be exported to a .csf file and easily imported into a Microsoft Excel table editor.

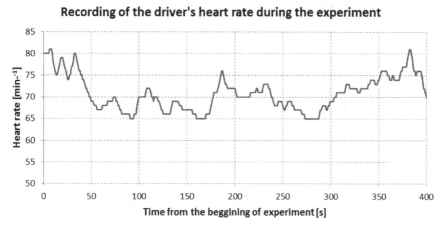

Fig. 12. Record of the driver's heart rate [own study]

6   Conclusion

Previous examples of experiments used the virtual environment created in map editor and new configuration of simulator. It brought some disadvantages connected with new software, which also allows making new virtual environment.

The creating of virtual environment is long-time activity, which can significantly affect the quality of simulation. Off course, the virtual environment is only a means for experiments. For better results, the following rules should be met:

- virtual infrastructure planning before practical modelling,
- decision about surfaces, traffic signs and other equipment,
- created environment should be similar to real part of world,
- a wide database of virtual objects is necessary, it is not possible to create all individual parts of virtual environments (trees, lamps, cars...)
- environment should be tested by independent driver or person, who can identify the mistakes made by creator,
- if the static part of simulation is ready, the dynamic parts can be added (for example sudden obstacle...).

Acknowledgment. This paper was developed under the support of project: MSVVS SR VEGA 1/0436/18 KALAŠOVÁ ALICA – Externalities in road transport, an origin, causes and economic impacts of transport measures.

References

1. Čičáková, K.: Expert system traffic v dopravno-psychologickej praxi na Slovensku: magisterská diplomová práca. Univerzita Palackého, Olomouc, 104 s. (2011)
2. Kubíková, S., Kalašová, A., Černický, Ľ.: Microscopic simulation of optimal use of communication network. In: Mikulski, J. (ed.) TST 2014. CCIS, vol. 471, pp. 414–423. Springer, Heidelberg (2014). https://doi.org/10.1007/978-3-662-45317-9_44
3. Kalašová, A., Krchová, Z.: Telematics applications and their influence on the human factor. Transp. Prob. **8**(2), 89–94 (2013)
4. Čulik, K., Kalašová, A., Kubíková, S.: Simulation as an instrument for research of driver-vehicle interaction. In: Stopka, O. (ed.) 18th International Scientific Conference-Logi 2017, MATEC Web of Conferences, E D P Sciences, Cedex A (2017)
5. Fouladinejad, N., et al.: Modeling virtual driving environment for a driving simulator. In: 2011 IEEE International Conference on Control System, Computing and Engineering, Penang, pp. 27–32 (2011)
6. Orlický, A.: Automatická tvorba silniční infrastruktury ve 3D pro vozidlové simulátory: diplomová práca. ČVUT Praha, Praha, p. 106 (2016)
7. Petro, F., Konečný, V.: Calculation of emissions from transport services and their use for the internalisation of external costs in road. Procedia Eng. [elektronický zdroj] **192**, 677–682 (2017). ISSN 1877-7058
8. Berežný, R., Konečný, V.: The impact of the quality of transport services on passenger demand in the suburban bus transport. Procedia Eng. [elektronický zdroj] **192**, 40–45 (2017). ISSN 1877-7058
9. Gnap, J., Konečný, V., Poliak, M.: Elasticita dopytu v hromadnej osobnej doprave (Demand elasticity of public transport). Ekonomický časopis (J. Econ.) **7**, 668–684 (2006). ISSN 0013-3035. - Roč. 54
10. Poliak, M.: Impact of road network charging system on pricing for general cargo transportation. Promet Traffic Transp. **24**(1), 25–33. https://doi.org/10.7307/ptt.v24i1.263
11. Poliak, M.: The relationship with reasonable profit and risk in public passenger transport in the Slovakia. Ekonomicky Casopis **61**(2), 206–220 (2013)
12. Poliak, M., Semanová, Š., Poliaková, A.: Risk allocation in transport public service contracts. Ekonomski Pregled **66**(4), 384–403 (2015)
13. Gnap, J., Konečný, V.: The impact of a demographic trend on the demand for scheduled bus transport in the Slovak Republic. Commun. Sci. Lett. Univ. Žilina **10**(2), 55–59 (2008). ISSN 1335-4205
14. https://www.minv.sk/?celkovy-pocet-evidovanych-vozidiel-v-sr. Accessed 15 Nov 2019
15. Interné materiály z výskumnej činnosti, ktoré poskytol Ing. Adam Orlický (Ústav dopravních prostředků Fakuty dopravní ČVUT v Prahe)
16. Kalašová, A., Faith, P., Paľo, J.: Dopravné inžinierstvo. Prvé vydanie. EDIS - vydavateľstvo ŽU, Žilina, 194 s. (2006). ISBN 80-8070-634-4

Propagation Loss and Interference Analysis for 5G Systems in the Context of C-ITS System Implementation

Małgorzata Gajewska[(⊠)]

Gdansk University of Technology, Narutowicza 11/12, Gdańsk, Poland
m.gajewska@eti.pg.edu.pl

Abstract. The article presents the concept of implementing subsequent phases of services for the C-ITS system (the Cooperative Intelligent Transport Systems), based on the European Parliament resolution of March 2018. Next, the 5G systems, in the context of their possible cooperation with C-ITS systems, were discussed. Numerical propagation analysis was performed for V2V and V2I type communication based on two different propagation models. Also, rules for the placement of sensors enabling the efficient implementation of data transmission between vehicles and infrastructure were proposed. Next, on the basis of the performed range and interference analysis, the distance between vehicles was estimated at which they could establish communication. It is of vital practical importance as the correct arrangement of the sensors will have a significant impact on the safety of road traffic participants.

Keywords: C-ITS · 5G · V2V · V2I · V2X · NOMA · Propagation model

1 Introduction

Nowadays, the rapid development of the transport systems we are observing. Concepts of new, alternative solutions appear, such as, for example, autonomous vehicles or the use of drones for transporting merchandise and even people. Therefore, safety in transport systems takes on a completely new meaning. That is why we need to look for new, global solutions to improve already bad accident statistics.

On the one hand, a chance gives us the prospect of implementing 5G systems in the near future, in which data transmission will take place, to a large extent, without human participation, and even beyond its awareness. On the other hand, the Cooperative Intelligent Transport System C-ITS seems to be a chance to be implemented in the European Union. It is a system that was created as a response to the Amsterdam declaration, which was signed by the European transport ministers on 12 April 2016 [1].

The combination of these two solutions (5G and C-ITS) opens up new perspectives. The chances of implementing both solutions in practice are very large. First of all, cellular network operators will certainly not let go of the 5G system implementation, because it is a very real prospect of earnings. And the second implementation of the C-ITS system has become a fact because in March 2018 the European Parliament's resolution on the implementation of the Cooperative Intelligent Transport System was

© Springer Nature Switzerland AG 2019
J. Mikulski (Ed.): TST 2019, CCIS 1049, pp. 109–122, 2019.
https://doi.org/10.1007/978-3-030-27547-1_9

officially adopted [1]. The publication of this resolution is the result of many years of commission work that prepared European Parliament recommendations for such a system, based on the results of a variety of research and development work and a big step forward [2, 3]. The proposed C-ITS solutions envisage the possibility of using 5G systems in the future in order to improve travel comfort and safety [4].

2 Concept of C-ITS

The C-ITS system is in principle to improve the safety of all road users. Therefore, standards must be developed that will enable the transmission of signals in such a way as to ensure immediate short-range communication, between vehicles (i.e., basically implementing Vehicle to Vehicle - V2V communication), vehicles and infrastructure (i.e., implementing Vehicle to Infrastructure - V2I) and public transport.

It should be emphasized that the European Parliament wants to quickly implement at least the basic services provided for C-ITS [1] – discussion about this topic will appear in the next paragraph. There is a need to rapidly reduce the number of road deaths and increase the safety of autonomous vehicles appearing on the roads and their full integration into the entire transport system [5]. Work on C-ITS has been ongoing since November 2014 [2], when the European Commission launched the C-ITS platform [2] to identify problems. The work of experts has shown that the basic problem that needs to be addressed already at the planning stage C-ITS is to develop an appropriate communication standard. It was found that the proposed solution should enable the implementation of a very broad and at the same time flexible scope of services, taking into account that the exchange of information will be made up of cars and trucks, autonomous vehicles, public transport vehicles, but also elements of road infrastructure and pedestrian road terminals. Also, it was agreed that data transmission would have to be carried out by many different entities in Europe, in places covered by the range of different cellular systems [3]. Therefore, the use of so-called C-ITS [2, 3] has been proposed as a consensus.

Hybrid communication that will enable the use of various communication technologies that complement each other. Also, according to the documentation [3], the developed solutions should include the non-collision implementation of 5G systems and satellite communications. It was assumed that all messages in C-ITS would be sent transparently, i.e., one that does not require the recognition of communication technology. Currently, it seems that the best chance to meet the set criteria will be hybrid communication based on the combination of the ETSI ITS-G5 (IEEE 802.11p) standard [6] with the standards of local cellular networks. In the future, it will be possible to implement 5G systems efficiently [4]. Thanks to such integration, data will be sent with slight delays [4], while maintaining the ability to operate vehicles located close to each other [3]. Data transmission (in very large quantities) is expected to use the 5.9 GHz frequency band [2, 3] as a band reserved for security systems by the decision of the European Commission (2008/671/EC).

3 Services in C-ITS

As a result of the work of experts gathered around the platform, priorities were adopted in the order of implementation of C-ITS services, which are discussed below [3].

The most important recommendations include the recommendation to maintain the continuity of services, i.e., to ensure that all users in the European Union can use all services offered by C-ITS. It applies both to services that will be implemented on the infrastructure side as well as on the side of the vehicle, i.e., in the variants of the V2V and V2I systems. Already at the stage of the first standardization works, it was pointed out that the implementation of a new, intelligent transport system requires consideration of all problems at the level of horizontal layers, for different industry layers, different types of transport, and not vertical categories such as telecommunications, transport or IT systems. In addition to creating new services, it is necessary to analyze current data, static data and, for example, digital maps [7].

According to the communique of the Committee to the European Parliament, the Council of the European Economic and Social Committee and the Committee of the Regions, the first group of services (being the earliest implemented) of C-ITS are services related to broadly understood notification of the dangerous location of vehicles, compared to other vehicles moving in front of us. It can be, i.e., warning about vehicles in front of us, in particular, information about vehicles moving slowly or standing on the road. Also, drivers are to be informed about ongoing road works and warned about bad weather conditions, which is important, for example, if we remember about last year's collision of a huge number of cars that bumped into each other suddenly entering the fog. Also, the drivers will be informed of oncoming privileged vehicles, especially those left behind the corner, as well as the emergency braking lights. These services are to be implemented as early as in 2019 [3].

In order to implement this first group of services, as shown in [3], it is necessary to perform some changes in a vehicle. Firstly, to install various sensors that will be able to receive the required warning signals from sensors placed in the vehicle engine or tires, and also, devices that give signals about, e.g., the need to provide a green wave and many more.

The second group of services is known as Phase 1.5, i.e., those for which it was assumed that they might not be implemented on a large scale in 2019, due to the lack of full specification or standard. These include, in particular, services related to our comfort of moving around the city, e.g., providing traffic information and intelligent routing, parking support (parking management on and off the street), but also vehicle fleet navigation, intelligent, controlled signaling light. Besides, this group of services will include publicly available information on alternative fuel charging stations, which are currently relatively small [3].

In the further part of the article, a propagation and interference analysis for the C-ITS system based on the 5G system will be carried out.

4   Propagation Model for V2I Communication

In the case when we are considering V2I type communication, in which there is an exchange of information between sensors located in the vehicle and those located on road infrastructure, we can use the WINNER II model to estimate the propagation loss [8]. It is a model that can be used for frequencies in the range from 2 to 6 GHz, so it covers the range of 5G work band.

In this model, we have defined various dependencies to estimate propagation losses in various propagation environments. These dependencies take into account both the case of communication with direct visibility of antennas (transmitting and receiving) (LOS), as well as the case when we do not have such a direct line of sight (NLOS) [8].

The basic dependence modeling propagation loss is as follows

$$L_{prop} = A \log_{10}(d) + B + C \log_{10}\left(\frac{f}{5}\right) + X \tag{1}$$

where: d[m] – distance between the transmitter and the receiver; f[GHz] – signal frequency; A, B, C – constants whose values are defined for different propagation environments; X – parameter, which is defined for specific propagation environments, e.g. it may be related to the width of streets in an urban environment [8].

Various scenarios for the Winner model have been defined in [8]. A few examples (important for our analysis) are shown in the Table 1. As we can see, the Winner II model is suitable for estimating propagation loss for all environments relevant to Intelligent Transport Systems. It takes into account both the difficult urban environment, as well as the suburban environment. In an urban environment, there is a lot of buildings. In the suburban, there are much fewer buildings, and the speed of vehicles is higher. It is important from the point of view of phenomena that occur in the radio communication channel.

Table 1. Different propagation scenarios for ITS in the WINNER II model [8]

Name of the environment	Definition	Micro or macrocells	LOS/NLOS	Acceptable vehicle speed
B₁ Hot Spot	Typical urban environment	Microcell	LOS/NLOS	0–70 km/h
B₂	Bad urban environment	Microcell	Only NLOS	0–70 km/h
C₁	Metropol suburban environment	Macrocell	LOS/NLOS	0–120 km/h
C₂	Metropol typical urban environment	Macrocell	LOS/NLOS	0–120 km/h
C₃	Bad urban environment	Macrocell	Only NLOS	0–70 km/h
C₅	Rural environment	Macrocell	LOS/NLOS	0–200 km/h

In order to further analyze the propagation losses for various radio link parameters, a suitable model for environment B1 was selected. In this environment, according to the WINNER II model, it is assumed that mobile terminal antennas are placed at the height of 1.5 m, and antennas correlated with road infrastructure can be suspended at the height of 5 m to 20 m [8].

In the first step, a case in which the transmitting and receiving antennas remain in the line of direct sight (LOS) will be considered. Then the propagation loss can be represented by the formula

$$L_{prop,LOS} = 22,7 \log_{10}(d) + 41 + 20 \log_{10}\left(\frac{f}{5}\right) \tag{2}$$

for the distance d_1 (which is defined as we can see on Fig. 1) is in the range 10 m up to the d'_{BP} $(10[m] < d_1[m] < d'_{BP}[m])$, where d'_{BP} is a breakpoint defined as

$$d'_{BP}[m] = \frac{4h'_{Tx}h'_{Rx}f}{c} \tag{3}$$

where $h'_{Tx}[m]$ – effective height of the base station antenna (transmitter antenna), $(h'_{Tx}[m] = h_{Tx}[m] - 1[m])$, $h'_{Rx}[m]$ – effective height of the mobile station antenna (receiver antenna), $(h'_{Rx}[m] = h_{Rx}[m] - 1[m])$. Also $h_{Tx.}[m]$ is a real height base station antenna and $h_{Rx}[m]$ is a real height mobile station antenna, f[GHz] is a signal frequency and c – propagation velocity in free space [8].

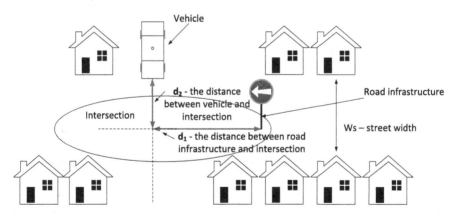

Fig. 1. Geometrical model for communication V2I and transmission LOS and NLOS – model WINNER II [own study based on 8]

If the distance d_1 is in the range d'_{BP} up to 5 km $(d'_{BP}[m] < d_1[m] < 5000[m])$ propagation loss must be calculated [8] with the formula:

$$L_{prop,LOS} = 40 \log_{10}(d_1) + 9,45 - 17,3 \log(h'_{Rx}) - 17,3 \log(h'_{Tx}) + 2,7 \log_{10}\left(\frac{f}{5}\right) \tag{4}$$

In Fig. 2 presented the result of calculations of numerical propagation losses ($L_{prop,LOS}$) for LOS conditions and frequency 6 GHz, h_{Rx} = 1.5 m, h_{Tx} = 10 m. The results were obtained, using the WINNER model, for B_1 environment and different values of distance $d = d_1$. As we can see if the distance d increases, the value of propagation losses also increases.

In the second step, the case is considered in which the transmitting and receiving antennas are not in the direct line of sight (NLOS) [8].

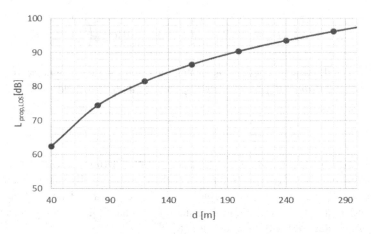

Fig. 2. Propagation loss for V2I communication and LOS condition – WINNER II model [own study]

Then the propagation loss can be calculated using the equation:

$$L_{prop,NLOS}(d_1, d_2) = L_{prop,LOS}(d_1) + 20 - 12,5n_j + 10n_j \log(d_2) + 3 \log_{10}\left(\frac{f}{5}\right) \quad (5)$$

where $L_{prop,LOS}(d_1)$ - radio signal propagation loss in the distance d_1 in condition LOS, d_1[m] – the distance between intersection and infrastructure (look Fig. 1), $n_j = \max(2, 8 - 0,0024d_1, 1, 84)$, d_2[m] – the distance between vehicle and intersection (see Fig. 1), f [GHz] – signal frequency.

This equation is valid for distance d_1 between 10 m and 5 km ($10[m] < d_1[m] < 5[km]$) and $W = 20$ m (see Fig. 1), h_{Rx} = 10 m, h_{Tx} = 1.5 m. However when $0 < d_1[m] < w/2$ the pattern is used scenarios for LOS [8].

In Fig. 3 the result of calculations of numerical propagation losses ($L_{prop,LOS}$) for NLOS conditions for frequency 6 GHz, h_{Tx} = 10 m, h_{Rx} = 1.5 m, W_s = 20 m and different values of d_1 was presented. As we can see with increased distance, d_1 propagation loss was increased. So when designing the C-ITS network, remember that the further the infrastructure element will be set from the intersection, the more difficult it will be to select the other radio link elements and their parameters (i.e., antennas with appropriate profits, transmitted signal power or fiders) to obtain sufficient range.

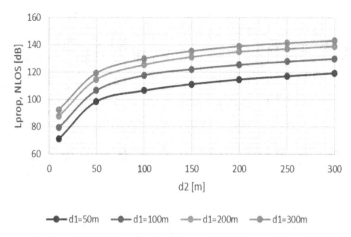

Fig. 3. Propagation loss for V2I communication and NLOS condition – WINNER II model [own study]

5 Propagation Model for V2V Communication

In the case when we are considering V2V type communication, in which there is an exchange of information between sensors located in the vehicles, we can use the University Kangaku model to estimate the propagation loss. It is a model that can be used for frequencies in the range from 400 MHz to 6 GHz [9].

The formula gives propagation loss for the LOS condition:

$$L_{prop,LOS} = [7,2 + 7,1\log(\frac{h_{Tx}h_{RX}}{\lambda})]\log d + 28,3\log(1 + \frac{d}{d_c}) - 1,2\log(f)$$
$$- 19,6\log(W_s) + 65,9 \tag{6}$$

where $h_{Tx}[m]$ – height of the base station antenna (transmitter antenna), $h_{Rx}[m]$ – height of the mobile station antenna (receiver antenna), λ - wavelength, d_C – a critical distance which must be calculated with the formula $d_c[m] = \frac{8h_{Tx}h_{Rx}f}{c}$, W_s – is the street width [9].

The geometry of NLOS transmission (and definition W_1 and W_2) we have shown in the Fig. 4. The formula gives propagation loss for NLOS transmission:

$$L_{prop,NLOS} = [47,6 + 6,6\log((\frac{h_{Tx}h_{Rx}}{\lambda}))]\log(d_{NLOS}) + [89,1 - 33\log(d_1/\lambda)]\log(1 + \frac{d_{NLOS}}{d_b})$$
$$+ 19,9\log f - 11,3\log(W_1W_2) + 2,8 \tag{7}$$

where $d_{NLOS} = d_1 + d_2$ – the distance between the transmitter and the receiver for the situation NLOS [m], and $d_B[m] = \frac{4h_{Tx}h_{Rx}f}{c}$ [9].

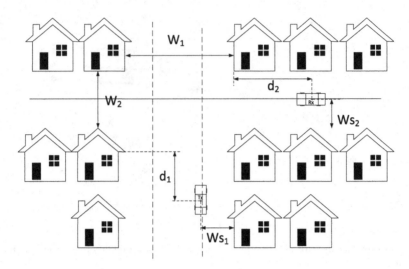

Fig. 4. Geometrical model for communication V2V and transmission NLOS – model University Kangaku [own study based on 9]

In Fig. 5 the result of calculations of numerical propagation losses ($L_{prop,LOS}$) for NLOS for communication V2V is presented.

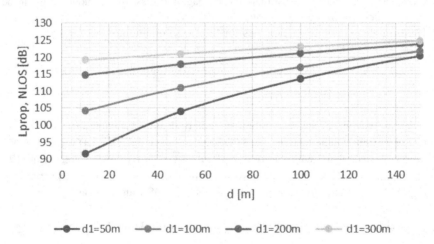

Fig. 5. Propagation loss for V2V communication and NLOS condition – University Kangaku model [own study]

The numerical analysis shows that the increase in the distance between the vehicle and the intersection increases the attenuation of the radio signal. The vehicle is further away from the intersection, and the more obstacles lie on the direct path between them and hence the increase in attenuation. For both models presented, signal attenuation increased with increasing distance from the intersection. It means that for both the LOS and NLOS cases, V2V and V2X signal transmissions, we must try to ensure the smallest distance between the sensors (and/or vehicles). And in case we want vehicles to be able to establish communication from a greater distance, we must provide more signal power.

6 Model to the Interference Analysis in C-ITS

Signal transmission for V2X communication in the C-ITS system, using 5G technology, can in principle be implemented in different modes. The mode of transmission will depend, among others from what kind of services will be implemented. In Table 2 shows how ETSI [10] in the document of November 2018 divided the frequency band to carry out various services.

Table 2. Frequency bands for ITS [10]

Frequency range	Applications
5855 MHz – 5875 MHz	ITS non-safety applications
5875 MHz – 5905 MHz	ITS road safety
5905 MHz – 5925 MHz	Future ITS applications

In principle, we can provide users with data in anycast, unicast, multicast and broadcast modes. The first type of transmission means that one sender sends data to multiple recipients, but in general, the data is received first by one of them - usually the nearest one or the one for whom the connection quality is the highest. With unicast transmission, signals are sent between one sender and one recipient. In multicast mode, the transmission is carried out by one sender to many recipients treated as a certain group, thus in such a way as if the recipient was a group. And in broadcast mode, we send signals to many users from a single point. From the point of view of the C-ITS system, the most important seems to be the unicast type of transmission, in which there will be a signal exchange between, for example, two cars in proximity and broadcast transmission, because we will send, for example, messages about serious incidents to all road users within reach of the network.

Interference analysis for 5G systems in the context of C-ITS system implementation requires consideration of a non-orthogonal method of multiple access to physical resources, called NOMA - Non-Orthogonal Multiple Access. In general, the NOMA method can be divided into the NOMA method with multiplexing in the power domain and the code domain. It raises some doubts whether this classification is fully separable, but so far no better source exists. As with DS CDMA systems, all available physical, time and/or frequency resources are used for each user [11–13].

As reported in [11] for C-ITS, the following scenarios should be considered:

– NOMA for unicast type V2X transmissions,
– NOMA for broadcast V2X broadcasts,
– NOMA for the uplink and V2I transmission
– NOMA for V2V transmission including many operators.

In general, in the NOMA method, signals can be transmitted in the same full frequency channel to two vehicles with different powers. As shown in Fig. 5, in the case of OFDM (i.e., OMA methods), signals are also transmitted in the same channel, but there is a clear separation of subcarriers - i.e., a signal to one user is transmitted on a certain group of subcarriers, and to another on other subcarriers [13, 14].

The model to calculation interference and the method of transmitting signals with the NOMA technique assuming that the base station sends signals to two vehicles marked as A and B is presented in Fig. 6. The signal received at receivers of individual vehicles of user A and B will be a superposition of useful signals intended for a given user and signals constituting internal interference intended for the second user.

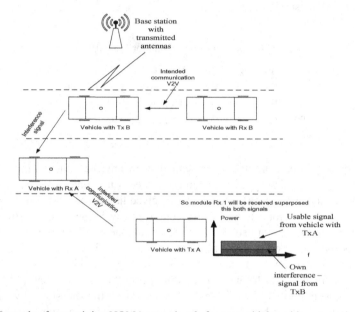

Fig. 6. Example of transmitting NOMA type signals for two vehicles with communication V2X [own study based on 11]

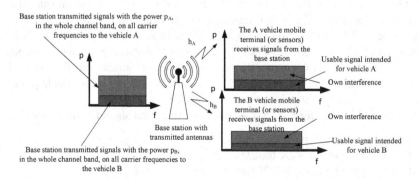

Fig. 7. NOMA in the downlink for V2X transmission [own study based on 13]

Thus, the separation of signals intended for both vehicles must be implemented at the mobile station side, so that each of them can receive the signal sent to it, reduce interference signals and at the same time decode its data properly. It is possible with the use of nonlinear receivers and the use of appropriate SIC (Successive Interference Canceller) algorithms that will allow isolating the signal appropriate for a given user [13].

In order to perform a mathematical analysis of the NOMA method, which will be implemented in C-ITS systems, let us assume that the base station sends a signal s_i the mean value of the square module $E[|s_i^2|]$ is 1, with the total power p_i, for simplicity up to two vehicles A and B (as shown in Fig. 7) [13]. Also, we assume that the transmission of signals takes place in a radio link with a single transmit antenna and a single receiving antenna.

When using the NOMA method, the total signal is a superposition of two signals

$$x = \sqrt{p_A}s_A + \sqrt{p_B}s_B \tag{8}$$

where s_A and s_B these are signals with unit power $\sqrt{p_A}$ and $\sqrt{p_B}$ are the corresponding correction factors resulting from the fact that the power of the signal transmitted in practice is not unitary and different for both signals. Signals received by the receivers of vehicles A and B will have the form, respectively

$$y_A = h_A x + f_A \tag{9}$$

$$y_B = h_B x + f_B \tag{10}$$

Where h_A and h_B they are complex coefficients of radio communication channel influence on transmitted signals that reflect their phase and amplitude changes. In contrast, f_A and f_B are the powers of thermal noise and interference in the receivers of vehicles, A and B, respectively [13, 14].

In the case of a downlink, of course, the process of removing the SIC interference will have to be implemented in the user's receiving mobile station. The process of removing the SIC interference in the mobile station receiver is carried out in order starting from the mobile station, for signals which we achieve the highest ratio of the square root of the channel influence factor to noise power and intercell interference. Based on this principle, each user can decode correctly the signal intended for him and at the same time eliminate interference from other user's signals.

With this in mind and the fact that we are considering a case of two users with the NOMA multiple access methods in which $\frac{|h_A|^2}{N_{o,A}} > \frac{|h_B|^2}{N_{o,B}}$ know that user B will not perform interference elimination because it is in the first place in the decoding order. In other words, the interference is removed in this mobile station, for which the SINR value, is smaller before executing the SIC algorithm, as shown in Fig. 8. Therefore, the user A first decodes the signal s_B and subtracts its components from the received signal y_A before decoding your own signal. However, the literature does not mention the barrier of h_A and h_B knowledge in both mobile stations, which hinders optimal decision-making in the order, and another aspect is the consideration of intercellular interference in the single-frequency network, which may be relevant using different methods of reuse frequencies in cells (frequency reuse) [13, 14].

According to Shannon's theorem, according to which the information throughput of a continuous channel with B [Hz], the frequency band in which additive white Gaussian noise with average power N_0 [W/Hz] occurs, is determined by the formula

$$C = B_s \log_2 \left(1 + \frac{S}{N_o} \right) [b/s] \tag{11}$$

where S[W] is the average power of the received signal, and B_s [Hz] this is the channel band.

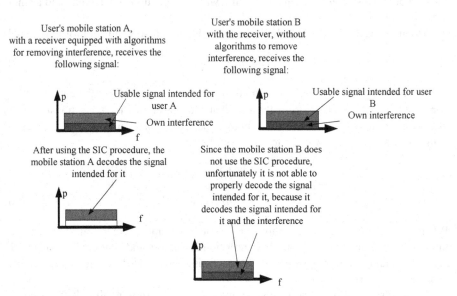

Fig. 8. Decoding signals useful with SIC algorithms and without SIC algorithms with the NOMA method for downlink [own study]

Bearing in mind the above considerations, we can conclude that the information capacity for user A and user B in the bandwidth of B_s is:

$$C_A = B_s \log_2 \left(1 + \frac{p_A |h_A|^2}{N_{o,A}} \right) \tag{12}$$

$$C_B = B_s \log_2 \left(1 + \frac{p_B |h_B|^2}{p_A |h_B|^2 + N_{o,B}} \right) \tag{13}$$

where $\frac{p_A|h_A|^2}{N_{o,A}}$ is the ratio of the signal received to interference and noise in station A, and

$\frac{p_B|h_B|^2}{p_A|h_B|^2 + N_{o,B}}$ is the ratio of signal to noise and interference (including interference from signals for station A) in station B [12–14].

Thanks to the NOMA method, we can obtain better total data throughput in the C-ITS system. Unfortunately, there are no practical recommendations for the implementation of this method yet.

7 Conclusion

The paper presents the concept of implementing the C-ITS system. In the context of the fact that 5G systems will be launched in a moment, it seems that this cooperative system is likely to be gradually put into practice. Car manufacturers are already implementing certain elements of this system for new vehicles – e.g., a parking assistant. It seems that a big problem may be limiting interference because, in the case of systems affecting human life, we cannot allow ourselves to receive signals incorrectly.

References

1. European Parliament resolution of 13 March 2018 on a European strategy for cooperative intelligent transport systems
2. C-ITS Platform Final report Phase II, September 2017
3. EUR-Lex - 52016DC0766 - EN - EUR-Lex, Communication from the committees to the European Parliament, the Council, the European Economic and Social Committee and the Committee of the Regions. A European strategy for cooperative intelligent transport systems- an important step towards the mobility of cooperating, combined and automated vehicles
4. Gajewski, S.: Perspectives of transport systems development in the light of radio communication systems evolution towards 5G. In: Mikulski, J. (ed.) TST 2017. CCIS, vol. 715, pp. 203–215. Springer, Cham (2017). https://doi.org/10.1007/978-3-319-66251-0_17
5. Declaration from Amsterdam on cooperation in the field of combined vehicles and automated vehicles
6. ETSI ITS-G5 (IEEE 802.11p), April 2016
7. Gajewska, M.: Design of M2M communications interfaces in transport systems. In: Mikulski, J. (ed.) TST 2016. CCIS, vol. 640, pp. 149–162. Springer, Cham (2016). https://doi.org/10.1007/978-3-319-49646-7_13
8. Kyösti, P., et al.: WINNER II Channel Models. IST-4-027756 WINNER II, D1.1.2 V1.1, pp. 26–49 (2007)
9. Wang, S.-Y., et al.: Design and implementation of a more realistic radio propagation model for wireless vehicular networks over the NCTUns network simulator, pp. 1–2. National Chiao Tung University, HsinChu, Taiwan
10. ETSI TS 103 613 Intelligent Transport Systems (ITS): Access layer specification for Intelligent Transport Systems using LTE Vehicle to everything communication in the 5,9 GHz frequency band, v 1.1.1, November 2018
11. Boya, D., et al.: V2X meet NOMA: Non – Orthogonal Multiple Access for 5G enabled vehicular networks. IEEE Wirel. Commun. 24(6) (2017)

12. Benjebbour, A., et. al.: Concept and practical considerations of Non-orthogonal Multiple Access (NOMA) for future radio access. In: Proceedings of the IEEE International Symposium on Intelligent Signal Processing and Communications Systems (ISPACS), pp. 770–774 (2013)
13. Higuchi, K.: Non-orthogonal Multiple Access (NOMA) with successive interference cancellation for future radio access. IEICE Trans. Commun. **E98-B**(3), 403–413 (2015)
14. Riazul Islam, S.M., et al.: Power-domain Non-Orthogonal Multiple Access (NOMA) in 5G systems: potentials and challenges. IEEE Commun. Surv. Tutor. **PP**(99), 1–42 (2016)

Traffic Accident Occurrence, Its Prediction and Causes

Veronika Harantová[(✉)], Simona Kubíková, and Luboš Rumanovský

University of Žilina, Univerzitná 8215/1, 010 26 Žilina, Slovak Republic
{veronika.harantova, simona.kubikova}@fpedas.uniza.sk,
Lubos.Rumanovsky@minv.sk

Abstract. A traffic accident represents a stochastic negative event in traffic on road communication network. Sufficiently detailed analysis of traffic accidents and the implementation of some suitable measurements can be helpful to prevent an occurrence of accidents at selected locations where traffic accidents' occurrence is more frequent. It is also important to analyses and understand the environment and events that occurred before and during the accident. The emergence of a traffic accident is always caused by three main factors: a driver, a vehicle and a road communication. The range of causes of traffic accidents is wide, but most accidents are caused by driver inappropriate behavior. Several years, the methods have been developing for traffic accidents prediction. A different view of issue of traffic accidents gave rise to several methods. These methods generally define the probable number of traffic accidents or the number of injured, killed persons at certain section of the road or in a certain area.

Keywords: Traffic accident · Cause of a traffic accident · Probability · Black spots

1 Introduction

Every driving is connected with specific rate of risk. A risk can be defined as some uncertainty or rate of probability that traffic conditions could result into a dangerous situation. A traffic accident occurrence we can understand as a mixture of various consecutive events. Always we should calculate and deal with what can happen. Human failures is predominantly cited as a primary cause of traffic accidents.

Today vehicles are equipped with different safety systems. The main goal of vehicle safety is protection of lives of road users. Traffic safety is a serious traffic, social and economic issue.

2 Traffic Accident in Road Transport

The balance of three factors – driver, vehicle and environment is disrupting when traffic accident occur. According to recorded data most often traffic accident causes in Slovakia including breach of driver's obligations and road users' obligations, unlicensed speed, wrong way of driving, incorrect overtaking and turning. Based on long term

© Springer Nature Switzerland AG 2019
J. Mikulski (Ed.): TST 2019, CCIS 1049, pp. 123–136, 2019.
https://doi.org/10.1007/978-3-030-27547-1_10

analyses it has been found out that driver behavior has an important effect to traffic accident occurrence. The disruption of driver's obligations represents an average 43,1% of the total number of causes in Slovakia in last 5 years (Fig. 1). You can see on the Fig. 1 that the number of traffic accidents per year in Slovakia is approximately the same. However, it is obvious that rising of the number of accidents increases also the human factor effect in accidents. In addition to the behavior and psychological state of driver, the technical state and communications operating conditions (weather conditions) also affect the occurrence of traffic accident.

Fig. 1. Total number of accidents in Slovakia and their main cause [13]

Although the number of fatal traffic accidents is decreasing in Europe, the European Union released a White paper – Roadmap to a Single European Transport area. One of the main goals of this paper is to decrease the number of fatal traffic accident in road transport to 2050 to zero. In line with this objective the EU is working to decrease also the number of accidents at all to halve by 2020 [1, 2, 12, 13].

2.1 Traffic Accident Indicators

The need of comparison of traffic accident rate from different point of view (time and location) gave rise several additional criteria. In general, we called these criteria as criteria of traffic accident rate and they serve to the more detailed evaluation and comparison of traffic accident rate.

Criterion of traffic accident density represents the number of accidents per length unit of communication. It is used most to traffic safety evaluation of main roads when it is possible to compare each section to another and set the riskiest one.

$$H = \frac{N}{t * L} \tag{1}$$

Where:

H – density of accident [TA/(km.year)]
N – a number of traffic accidents in year [TA]
L – a length of a section [km]
t – a time period [year]

Criterion of relative accident rate is the most used criterion to safety evaluation of road communications. Its value represents mainly a probability of traffic accident occurrence on the chosen section of communication which is related to driving performance [4, 5, 7].

$$R = \frac{N * 10^6}{365 * RPDI * t * L} \qquad (2)$$

Where:

R – relative accident rate [TA/(10^6veh.km)]
N – a number of traffic accidents [TA]
RPDI – an average daily intensity per year [TA/24 h]
L – a length of a section [km]
t – a time period [years]

In the project Pilot4Safety were used three mutually independent parameters to identify road sections with high traffic accident rate.

Critical accident rate (CAR) - to the number of accidents per million of vehicle-kilometers traveled per year.

Relatiuve severity index (RSI) - compares accident costs based on standardized statistical valuation of individual types of accidents in individual years (the cost of fatal accidents, severe injuries, light injuries and average material damage without injury) [5, 16].

3   An Analysis and a Probability of Traffic Accident Occurrence

We can make analysis of traffic accident in two ways:

- **Simple analysis** – serves to obtain a basic idea about accident location. We investigate mostly time occurrences of traffic accidents, weather conditions, accident locations, types and causes of accidents.
- **Detailed analysis** – if it is not possible to obtain a certain reason of accidents occurrence, it is necessary to make more detailed investigation. The spatial route guidance is thoroughly examined, the type and quality of road surface, transport load and others [1, 3, 10].

When traffic safety is evaluating by means of statistics, there is one disadvantage that the evaluated accidents have already happened. Therefore, there is a long term process of new methods evolution which would be able to prognoses traffic accidents and evaluate safety on the chosen part of communication before an accident will occur. A different point of view to traffic accident prognosis allows to develop several methods. These methods evaluate safety or predict a number of traffic accidents, number of fatalities and relative or absolute accident rate per the chosen time period [6, 14].

3.1   Prediction Models of a Number of Traffic Accidents

Unified methodology of traffic accident prediction does not exist. Every model is useful only for one specified area. There are several variations of a general relation for accident prediction from simple ones where the risk factor is intensity of vehicles to complex models considering a big amount of crash coefficients.

$$E(k) = \alpha * L^{b1} * RPDI^{b2} \tag{3}$$

Where:

E(k) is an expected number of traffic accidents,
bj represents coefficients which were obtained for model calibration of specific area.

The biggest issue when model formulating is to get correct values of parameters which would be used for specific area. Of course, other models are developing which are based on linear regressive analysis or Poisson distribution [9, 15].

3.2   Bayes Model

This model can be used to estimate a probability of traffic accident occurrence. Classic statistics determines a probability of some event based on known facts from past but when this statistic cannot be used the Bayesian statistics is an alternative. It is a model which takes into account not only available facts but also dependence between them. Bayes' veto is basic sentence in Bayesian statistic. It is used to updating a probability which are the degree of faith after obtaining new data [15].

3.3   Black Spots

When identifying black spots, the basic principle is that traffic accidents (TA) are not evenly distributed on roads but occur more frequently in certain locations (places and sections) than elsewhere. Therefore, from the view of mathematical statistics, the occurrence of traffic accidents on roads could be considered as infrequent unevenly distributed effects. Their occurrence can therefore be considered as a discreetly changing variable. The distribution of such a probability effect on roads can be exactly described by the Poisson distribution [8, 14].

This probability distribution has random variables that describe the number of phenomena with the following properties:

- if a phenomenon in a given interval (time, space) occurs (does not occur), regardless of what happened elsewhere, or another time,

- for each time point, the probability of the phenomenon is the same in a short time interval (the same is true in the space)
- there is no case that two occurrences occur at exactly one time or at a location in the institution.

The average number of occurrences of the studied phenomenon in a given length section is denoted λ [11].

$$P_{(x)} = \frac{\lambda^x}{x!} * e^{-\lambda} \tag{4}$$

Where [14]:

P(x) – is the cumulative probability of the occurrence of x number of critical TA per year on a selected standard length of the road network in a specific territorial unit in empirical population for chosen confidence level,

m – parameter indicating average mean values (average number of TA) on the road network based on a chosen criteria indicator in a specific territorial unit,

x – calculated critical number of TA per year on the unit of length of the road network with certain probability P in a specific territorial administration unit,

e – base of natural logarithm.

4   Evaluation of Traffic Accident Rate on the Selected Section

For analysis of traffic safety, we have used I. class road I/11 which is a part of road E75. This road connects north and south Europe. The road enters Slovakia through the border crossing Svrčinovec and leads to Žilina in 36,8 km of length. It belongs to roads with very high number of accidents per year.

The riskiest section of road I/11 is between border crossing Svrčinovec (SR - ČR) and Čadca city (Fig. 2). According to police records, the chosen section between kilometre of 407,700 and 410,500 (2,8 km) has the highest occurrence on this I. class road.

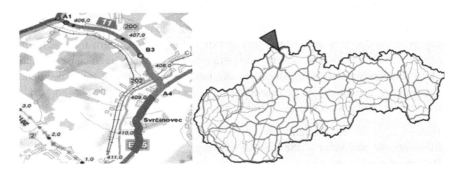

Fig. 2. Selected road section of the communication I/11 [own study]

We analysed factors influencing traffic accidents in last 5 years because of better overview of traffic accident rate on the chosen road section. The number of accidents on the whole communication I/11 represents 290 at all. At the given section, the same time was at 72 accidents which represents approximately 25% of the total. It is a communication which connects Slovakia with two countries (CR and PL) and a transit transportation is available. The composition of the traffic flow is approximately 59% are light vehicles and 41% heavy vehicles. There is a junction on this road section and in this case the road was divided into two parts. First part of 1,2 km length and the second one was 1,6 km of length (Fig. 2). The intersection is situated at 408,900 km (A4). The reason why this road section was divided is a change of averaged daily intensity at the intersection. At the first part of the section there were recorded 53 traffic accidents and at the second one there were 17 traffic accidents. At the mentioned junction there were recorded 2 traffic accidents. There is also a railway crossing and a sharp curve in the section (Fig. 3).

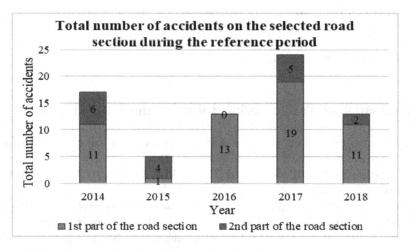

Fig. 3. Total number of accidents on the selected road section [own study]

4.1   The Main Causes and Condition of Traffic Accident

As it is known, the biggest influence to traffic accident occurrence has a human factor. Transport behaviour of a man effects lots of external as well as intern factors. In this case there was a disruption of drivers' obligations mentioned as a main cause of traffic accident. It represents 61% from all causes. Almost every causality of traffic accidents, except weather conditions, were caused by a human failure. At the chosen part of communication there were causes of traffic accidents as follows:

– Disruption of drivers' obligations
– Inappropriate behaviour at the railway crossing
– Breach of road users' duties
– Inappropriate way of driving

- Inappropriate way of driving through an intersection
- Inappropriate overtaking
- Inappropriate turning
- Breach of specific establishments about pedestrians
- Breach of rules of cargo transportation
- Natural force
- Non – observance of distance between two vehicles
- Unsuitable way of driving during winter season.

Their proportion is shown in the Fig. 4. Over 70 traffic accidents have been caused by human factor failures which represents 98,6% and only 1,4% of traffic accidents have been caused by an environment (weather, carriage drive).

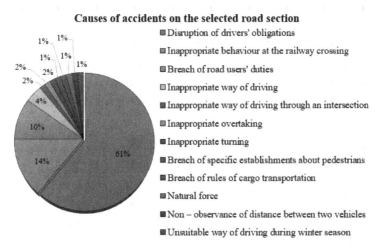

Fig. 4. Main causes of accident on the road section [own study]

Also weather conditions are one of often causes of traffic accidents as well as directional and vertical alignment of route (Fig. 5). Weather conditions which influenced traffic accident rate on the chosen section includes:

- fog,
- rain,
- snowing,
- black ice.

These factors have the biggest impact on increasing traffic accidents occurrence. The highest number of traffic accidents, 89%, was recorded during normal conditions. The rest of TA was influenced mainly by weather which has made operating conditions of transport more difficult. Also directional and vertical alignment of route has an impact on an occurrence of traffic accidents. As you can see in the graphical evaluation, the highest number of traffic accidents – 80%, have caused on the straight section and 17% of TA in curve. On the chosen road section, it is bad outlook behind mentioned curve.

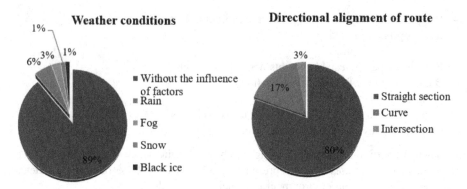

Fig. 5. Influence of weather conditions and directional laying of the roadway on accident [own study]

4.2   Time Occurrence and Culprit of Traffic Accidents

It is also important to find out when during the day a traffic accident happened. Was it day or night as well as in which day the most traffic accidents occurred. The probability of traffic accident is significantly affected by traffic peaks. The following figures show processed values from the records.

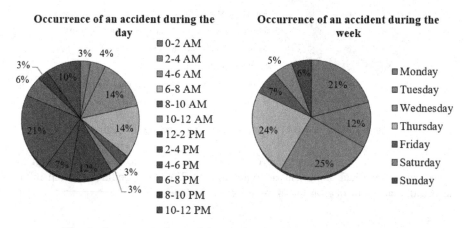

Fig. 6. Occurrence of an accident during the day and week [own study]

As you can see in the Fig. 6, the highest number of TA is recorded during an afternoon from 4 to 6 p.m. It represents 21%. The lowest number of TA was recorded in early morning and from 8 to 12 a.m. The most overloaded day was Wednesday – 25%, then Thursday – 24% and the lowest number was recorded on Saturday – 5%.

Traffic accidents divided according to type of vehicle and culprit you can see in the next figure. It is obvious that drivers of motor vehicles are the most often the cause of traffic accidents – 94%. Then as a culprit are pedestrians and cyclists. In 56% of traffic accidents there were recorded no types of vehicles.

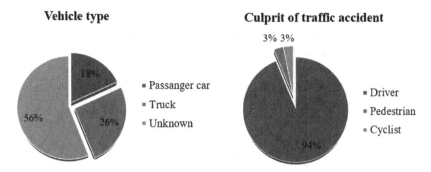

Fig. 7. Vehicke type and person responsible for the TA [own study]

4.3 The Locations of Traffic Accidents on the Chosen Part of a Road Communication

Consequences of traffic accidents on this section are not so serious. In last 5 years there were recorded 4 hard injured people and 4 light injured persons. Material damage achieved 219 470 € at all. The reason of less serious accidents can be a fact that the chosen section is situated in a village and a maximum speed is 50 km/h. Over the last few years, congestions are also part of the daily traffic issues. In the Fig. 7 there are highlighted the places of traffic accidents occurrence for better orientation, because traffic accidents were not spread over the same length each year. The record is created in the system with density of 5 TA per kilometre. The chosen part of road is divided into the same parts with length of 400 m for better processing.

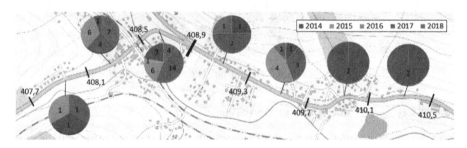

Fig. 8. Total number of accidents on the selected road section during the reference period [own study]

The longest line represents the intersection on the road section. The highest number of traffic accidents was recorded in 2017 (24) and the lowest number was in 2015 (5).

Table 1. Number of TA on a road section with a separation of 400 m [own study]

Road section	2014	2015	2016	2017	2018	Total
407,7-408,1	1	0	1	1	0	3
408,1-408,5	1	0	6	4	7	18
408,5-408,9	7	1	6	14	4	32
Junction (408,9)	2	0	0	0	0	2
408,9-409,3	1	0	0	2	1	4
409,3-409,7	1	4	0	3	1	9
409,7-410,1	2	0	0	0	0	2
410,1,40,5	2	0	0	0	0	2

Figure 8 and Table 1 show that the highest number of traffic accidents was on the section from 408,1 to 408,9 km – 53 TA/1,2 km in 5 years. Riskier section is situated behind the intersection. On this section there is also railway crossing, sharp curve and changing of vertical alignment (Fig. 9).

Fig. 9. Road section with the greatest number of accidents per year [17]

4.4 Safety and Traffic Accident Occurrence

Normal (safe) transportation is when all routes to the destination are made without any accidents and danger. To evaluate traffic safety, we mostly use a criterion of relative accident rate (R). Using this criterion, it is possible to set a probability of traffic accident occurrence related to driving performance. The higher the result of this indicator, the higher the risk of an accident. In the following table there are calculated values of this criterion with the same length of sections per year (Table 2).

Table 2. Average daily intensities per year and relative accident rate [own study]

Years	2014		2015		2016		2017		2018	
Road section	RPDI	R	RPDI	R	RPDI	R	RPDI	R	RPDI	R
407,7-408,1	7119	1.0	7972	0.0	8116	0.8	8257	0.8	8465	0.0
408,1-408,5		1.0		0.0		5.1		3.3		5.7
408,5-408,9		6.7		0.9		5.1		11.6		3.2
Junction	10716	0.5	11465	0.0	11637	0.0	11808	0.0	11894	0.0
408,9-409,3		0.6		0.0		0.0		1.2		0.6
409,3-409,7		0.6		2.4		0.0		1.7		0.6
409,7-410,1		1.3		0.0		0.0		0.0		0.0
410,1,40,5		1.3		0.0		0.0		0.0		0.0

R - relative accident rate [TA/(10^6veh.km)]
RPDI - averaged daily intensities per year [veh/24 h]

Final results are possible to compare to each other because a number of traffic accidents is recorded at the same section every year. The most critical section according to final values is from 408,1 to 408,9 for 2017 and 2018.in this case the number of TA achieve values over 3. If values of criterion R is over 1,6 it points to significant lacks of traffic safety. Regarding the intensity of vehicles are increasing the section becomes riskier in the future. The main cause of accidents is railway crossing. Up to 28 traffic accidents happened right at this railway crossing (year 2017–2018).

Theoretically, we assume that the occurrence of traffic accidents is unevenly distributed in this most overloaded section. Then, the distribution of this probability phenomenon can be accurately expressed in Poisson distribution (formula 4). On this section there were recorded 10 traffic accidents in average per year. Using Poisson distribution, it is possible to estimate a probability (P) of traffic accident occurrence on this section (Table 3).

Table 3. Probability (P) of traffic accident occurrence on this section [own study]

Number of TA	P per year	%	P per half year	%
>0	0.9999	99,99	0.9932	99,32
>1	0.9995	99,95	0.9595	95,95
>2	0.9972	99,72	0.8753	87,53
>3	0.9896	98,96	0.7349	73,49
>4	0.9707	97,07	0.5595	55,95
>5	0.9329	93,29	0.3840	38,40
>6	0.8698	86,98	0.2378	23,78
>7	0.7797	77,97	0.1333	13,33
>8	0.6671	66,71	0.0680	6,80
>9	0.5420	54,20	0.0318	3,18
>10	0.4169	41,69	0.0137	1,37

These estimations are made based on recorded data from last few years. The table shows that probability (P) of traffic accidents occurrence of more than 0 TA per year is almost 100% and for half year it is 99,32%. However, an assumption that more than 10 TA occur, probability decreases to 41,7% per year and 1,37% per half year. As a number of traffic accidents increases, the probability of their occurrence decreases. It is just theoretical calculation. This chosen section could be considered as critical regarding the number of accidents on relative short distance.

5   Decreasing Accident Rate on Selected Road Section

On this black spot a TA causes a congestion in both directions. The congestion is several kilometers long, reaching to Čadca or Czech Republic (CZ). The biggest problem occurs during peak traffic. A long column may cause collapse in Čadca. Decreasing accident rate on this section could be solved by completing highway D3 (Fig. 10).

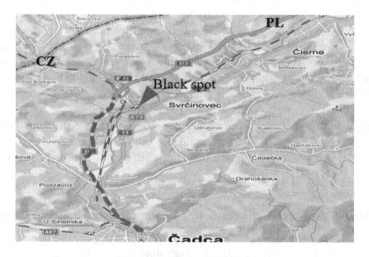

Fig. 10. Highway D3 [17]

Transit transportation will be transferred to highway and our chosen section would by less loaded. A part of vehicles could lead through an intersection Svrčinovec to Czech Republic and other vehicles continue to Poland. Vehicles' intensity on this section would be reduced by approximately 40%. The section of highway between an intersection of Svrčinovec – Poland is already in operation (green colour). Currently the section Svrčinovec – Čadca is in construction. In this case every truck directing to Poland and Czech Republic passing through this accidental section.

6 Conclusion

Traffic accident rate on roads, except serious impacts on safety, represents an important criterion of road conditions level, traffic conditions and quality of road maintenance. Statistics about traffic accidents is basic recourse to finding causes of their occurrence. Based on these data a list of accidental locations is created every year. The goal of this paper was an analysis of traffic accidents on the selected road section. The first step was to determine a causes, time and road conditions of traffic accidents occurrence.

The analysis shows that the main cause of traffic accidents is disruption of drivers' obligations. On the chosen section there are mostly accidents with consequences of material damage. Accidents occur mainly at the railway crossing and in an unclear curve. Next step was to estimate a probability of traffic accident occurrence on this section with using Poisson distribution. We can assume that by improving traffic conditions on the road the number of accidents can be reduced. The possibility of improving the traffic situation is the highway D3. The majority of vehicles (mainly trucks) would be redirected to highway in Čadca. This would reduce the intensity of vehicles passing through the risk area. Then it can be assumed improvement in the traffic situation. However, the biggest impact on traffic accident rate has a human factor. Therefore, every road user can contribute to better safety on our roads by responsible approach to each other.

Acknowledgment. This paper was developed under the support of project: MSVVS SR VEGA 1/0436/18 KALAŠOVÁ ALICA – Externalities in road transport, an origin, causes and economic impacts of transport measures.

References

1. Kalašová, A., Mikušová, M.: Bezpečnosť cestnej dopravy a dopravná psychológia, p. 224. EDIS, Žilina (2017). ISBN 978-80-554-1329-7
2. Poliak, M.: The relationship with reasonable profit and risk in public passenger transport in the Slovakia. Ekon. Cas. **61**(2), 206–220 (2013)
3. Kalasova, A., Krchova, Z.: Telematics applications and their influence on the human factor. Transp. Probl. **8**(2), 89–94 (2013)
4. Culik, K., Kalasova, A., Kubikova, S.: Simulation as an instrument for research of driver-vehicle interaction. In: Stopka, O. (ed.) 18th International Scientific Conference-Logi 2017, MATEC Web of Conferences. E D P Sciences, Cedex A (2017)
5. Poliak, M., Semanova, S., Poliakova, A.: Risk allocation in transport public service contracts. Ekon. Pregl. **66**(4), 384–403 (2015)
6. Berežný, R., Konečný, V.: The impact of the quality of transport services on passenger demand in the suburban bus transport [Vplyv kvality dopravných služieb na dopyt po prímestskej autobusovej doprave]. Procedia Eng. [elektronický zdroj] **192**, 40–45 (2017). ISSN 1877-7058, Accessed 12 Sept 2017
7. Kapusta, J., Kalašová, A.: Motor vehicle safety technologies in relation to the accident rates. In: Mikulski, J. (ed.) TST 2015. CCIS, vol. 531, pp. 172–179. Springer, Cham (2015). https://doi.org/10.1007/978-3-319-24577-5_17

8. Petro, F., Konečný, V.: Calculation of emissions from transport services and their use for the internalisation of external costs in road [Kalkulácia emisií z dopravných služieb a ich použitie na internalizáciu externých nákladov v cestnej doprave]. Procedia Eng. [elektronický zdroj] **192**, 677–682 (2017). ISSN 1877-7058, Accessed 12 Sept 2017

9. Poliak, M.: Impact of road network charging system on pricing for general cargo transportation. Promet Traffic Transp. **24**(1), 25–33. https://doi.org/10.7307/ptt.v24i1.263

10. Gnap, J., Konečný, V.: The impact of a demographic trend on the demand for scheduled bus transport in the Slovak Republic, vol. 10, no. 2, pp. 55–59. Communications - Scientific Letters of the University of Žilina. (2008). ISSN 1335-4205

11. Grinstead, C., Snell, M., Laurie, J.: Úvod do pravdepodobnosti (2 vyd.). Americká Matematická Spoločnosť, Providence (2006). ISBN 978-0-8218-9414-9

12. https://eur-lex.uropa.eu/legal-content/SK/TXT/PDF. Accessed 12 Sept 2017

13. https://www.minv.sk/?kompletna-statistika. Access 12 Sept 2017

14. https://www.ssc.sk. Accessed 12 Sept 2017

15. http://projekt150.ha-vel.cz/node/97. Accessed 12 Sept 2017

16. https://ec.europa.eu/transport/road_safety/sites/roadsafety/files/pdf/projects/pilot4safey.pdf. Accessed 12 Sept 2017

17. https://www.google.sk/maps?hl=sk&tab=wl. Accessed 12 Sept 2017

BIG DATA as Concept for Optimization of the Passage of Privileged Vehicles in City Traffic Network

Kamil Bolek[1]([⊠]) and Kazimierz Liver[2]([⊠])

[1] Polish-Japanese Academy of Information Technology, Al. Legionów 2, Bytom, Poland
s18202@pjwstk.edu.pl
[2] WASKO S.A., Berbeckiego 6, Gliwice, Poland
k.liver@wasko.pl

Abstract. Much has been written about challenges faced by cities of the future. Many of the problems that haven't been solved yet generate further problems. Traffic jams are one of them. They brings many consequences and the biggest one is increasing traffic accident number and problems with fast arrival at the place of emergency services. The goal of this paper is describe and build wireframe for module which will reduce as much as possible the time needed to get the emergency services to the place of the accidents. The main assumption will be blocking intersections located on the route of emergency services. Blocking intersections to facilitate access to the ambulance slows traffic in the city, however, it will help to reduce the number of deaths accident victims. Moreover knowing that cars stop or leave the road to facilitate the passage of privileged vehicles traffic is disturbed anyway so it would be worth taking control over this process.

Keywords: Route optimalisation · RBFS · Traffic management · Privilege vehicle priority

1 Introduction

The problem of traffic jams is getting bigger year by year. They became something common in big cities. As the number of cars increases numbers of collision and road accidents. Traffic jams cause not only air pollution but also generate noise and block roads for the emergency vehicles. The last element is particularly important due to the direct impact of the arrival time of medical assistance and the number of people rescued.

If the victim heart stop, five minutes is enough to significantly reduce its chances of survival. Every driver in Poland have to had first aid course to get driver license. Moreover many people had similar course in high schools or get participations in it for free. Unfortunately, the injured in most cases need professional medical help. Additionally not every person in accident place will take action. Stress and nerves associated with it effectively limits the willingness to help. We can't control people's behaviour, but the intersection yes.

© Springer Nature Switzerland AG 2019
J. Mikulski (Ed.): TST 2019, CCIS 1049, pp. 137–150, 2019.
https://doi.org/10.1007/978-3-030-27547-1_11

Todays traffic management system control the whole city. Every signal for all intersections are recorded and adapted to the current roads conditions. Moreover this system could close lanes and inform drivers about impediments in traffic by VMS. Now when accident happen traffic system operator takes the appropriate steps to minimize its effects. This approach hinders access to emergency vehicles.

To allow privileged vehicles to get to an accident as quickly as possible the intersections in front of ambulance have to been blocked. Only when all lanes will have red light signal then rescuers will be able to pass through them without any problems.

On the one hand idea of blocking intersections it seems to contradict the principle that it is necessary to maximize the flow of traffic, but traffic accident problems affects every inhabitant of the city. Nobody could predict when his life would be threatened.

2   Reporting Information About Accident to the Dispatcher

Traffic accident are everyday life. From the WHO (World Health Organisation) report it follows that every year in cars accidents die 1,35 million people on the world. That's nearly 3 700 people every day. Unfortunately, Poland is in the infamous top of European statistics. In 2017 took fifth place. Every day on average, 11 people die on Polish roads and 100 are injured [1].

The most important for life rescue is time from an accident to provide assistance. If state of the victim is critical that could be only few minutes. Information about accident arrive quite fast. If someone see the serious accident, of take part in it then call to dispatcher and report the whole situation. The further path is much more difficult.

Dispatcher have to get from notifier many information to send specified equipment and get know how many and which type of emergency services are necessary. Dispatcher nowadays get precisely information about notifier localisation, but this person could move away from the moment when he notice the accident.

Nowadays systems working well and also dispatchers are well trained and educated, but helpful would be to inform notifier about the nearest AED localisation. This device are become more popular every year but nobody knows they all localisations in the city. That information could be extremely important if there was a sudden heart stop.

The next functionality is directly related to false notifications which aren't nothing rarely despite fines for unjustified blocking of the emergency number. One of the ways to prevent similar situations are drones, which are relative cheap and give the picture of an accident with the nearest neighborhood as opposed to ordinary cameras located at intersections that have a much smaller view range. After introducing the event into the system by the dispatcher the nearest drone automatically fly to accident place and send streaming video to him. Then dispatcher would verify the situation at the intersection. In the absence of an accident in the indicated location it is worth to call back to notifier-everyone could make mistake in stressful situation. Such a quick verification will allow significant acceleration of the ambulance access to the right place of the accident.

Dispatcher has another extremely important function. After collecting information he transferring the case to the appropriate units together with details necessary to identify which equipment must be taken.

It is possible to reduce time that is needed from the moment when accident took place until the dispatcher received information about it from the inhabitant of the city who saw it.

3 Accident Detection Algorithm

Psychologists have repeatedly proved that the more people see the accident the less chance that one of them will react to it. This applies not only to direct help to the victim, but also to notification of relevant services. As it was mentioned in the first chapter if the victim heart stop, five minutes is enough to significantly reduce its chances of survival. If nobody reacts immediately, emergency services has less time to arrive and rescue the victim.

When accident happen other drivers start behave differently. Accidents are connected with sudden traffic deceleration (it is worth adding that the same effect could be seen on other lanes which the accident shouldn't have any impact). Another thing is completely blocking lane if accident was serious. Listed factors aren't something unusual in the city but based on the prediction model and accident detection algorithm it is possible to detect when the lane is blocked by traffic jams and when it is result of the accident.

Due to the fact that the analysis of traffic which focus on searching accidents requires processing data from many devices simultaneously almost in real time (at most, with an interval of a few seconds, data from all devices in the city should be processed) algorithm must to be fast and easy. Sources of data about actual traffic are:

- induction loop modules (average speed, type of vehicles)
- cameras (queue length, number of vehicle on the lane)
- Automatic Incident Detection (AID) servers (smoke detection, pedestrians on the road)

Induction loop modules send row data about actual loop state (occupied/empty), measure avarage speed and type of passing vehicle. This information are useful in analysis because if the loop state is occupied permanently then it means that on this lane the cars aren't moving. Moreover the type of vehicle which are on the lane determine speed and acceleration of other vehicles on the same lane. This situation is typical. Cars are much more dynamic than trucks or buses so neglect of this parameter could lead to false positives because sudden decreases in speed will result from the loaded, heavy truck, not from accident.

Cameras on intersections has many build-in functions. The main is showing transport system operator actual intersections state. Others are quene length counting, type of vehicle on the lane and their numbers. Nowadays camera systems has good enough result in vehicle detections. However measurement of vehicle type and their speed isn't as precise as induction loop measurement. In case when we will have both of this devices on the intersections (that isn't rare) a complementary value directly from the camera to the automatical accident detection will be only information about number of cars on the lanes and quene length.

AID servers are devices which has implemented neural network which can recognize a few object/situation on the road (Fig. 1).

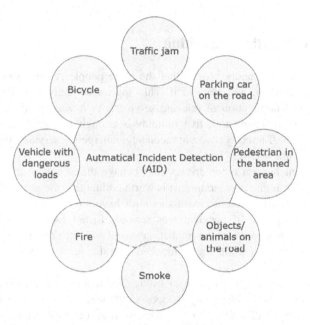

Fig. 1. Incident which could be detected by AID [own study]

Only a few event recognized from AID are useful in accident detection process. They aren't obligatory, but getting them gives a more complex state of the intersections. If induction loop detect on lane sudden speed drop, camera confirms this fact, and will additionally report a constantly increasing queue length but the AID detect object on the road and don't detect car which stop on the lane then is a big probability that it's not accident but only a object which have to been moved to the roadside and taken away by a garbage truck. Without additional information from AID system will wasted the time of the system operator needed to confirm or reject the notification.

Data flow schema (Fig. 2) show details information about source and type of data which are using in accident detection algorithm. All of that data showing actual state on the intersections but the city traffic is a very dynamic environment. Both continuous declines in speed and stopping vehicles on the road are something common and encountered everyday. To detect accident is necessary not only to determine and process actual situation on the road but also check if that situation is predicted by traffic prediction module. If it differs significantly from the predicted one, algorithm will go to a deeper analysis to find a reason of that situation.

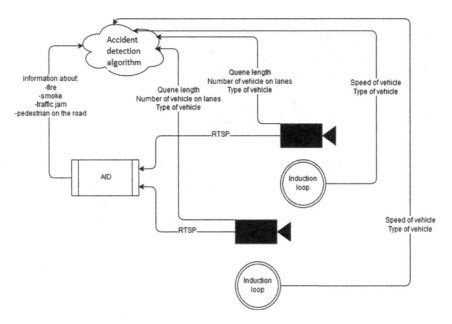

Fig. 2. Accident detection data flow [own study]

To find out if actual situation is anomaly and determine that accident detection algorithm need to build dynamically graph which edge will be calculated using prediction module which will represent typical situation on the crossroads and current data from camera and induction loops. Based on prediction model data and using formula (Formula 3.4) it's easy to count value of edges which will be compared with current values (Table 1). Number of vehicles are determined by type of the vehicle. If vehicle is car or motorbike then the number which is adding to number of all vehicles is one. Otherwise if the vehicle is bus or truck the number is increasing by two (formula 1 show how the number of cars on lane is counting).

$$VN = \sum_{i=1}^{n} T_i \qquad (1)$$

VN – vehicle number
T – type of vehicle, if car or motorbike then T = 1, else if truck or bus then T = 2

Formula (2) show edge values counting in graphs

$$D = \frac{\frac{C_{QL} + C_{VN}*2}{50 - C_{AS}}}{\frac{P_{QL} + P_{VN}*2}{50 - P_{AS}}} \qquad (2)$$

D – difference between modeled traffic and current situation
C_QL – current queue length on lane
C_AS – current average speed on lane (if 0 then set on 0.1)
C_VN – current number of vehicles on lane
P_QL – predicted queue length on lane
P_AS – predicted average speed on lane (if 0 then set on 0.1)
P_VN – predicted number of vehicles on lane

Table 1. Table of values for current and predicted situation [own study]

	Predicted			Current			Difference
	Queue length	Average speed	Number of vehicles	Queue length	Average speed	Number of vehicles	
Lanes 1	26	2	8	30	1	9	0.89
Lanes 2	22	3	7	28	1	11	0.75
Lanes 3	22	5	6	20	5	5	1.13
Lanes 4	22	5	6	20	5	5	1.13
Lanes 5	25	8	7	20	12	3	1.36
Lanes 6	22	12	10	14	17	6	1.40
Lanes 7	15	20	6	18	18	9	0.80
Lanes 8	40	0.1	11	60	1	20	**0.61**
Lanes 9	41	1	13	55	0.1	25	**0.65**
Lanes 10	20	8	7	17	14	7	0.94
Lanes 11	18	6	5	18	5	7	0.89
Lanes 12	15	11	5	15	10	6	0.95
Lanes 13	11	21	3	12	19	4	0.91

Incident detection algorithm depends on accuracy prediction module in the city. The better prediction module the less false alarm about accident. The algorithm in first step get data from the prediction module and from the devices on the intersection. After counting difference between two data source algorithm will focus on lanes which difference is lower or equal 0,7. This value mean that current flow is worse than in predicted model more than 30%. Result of that comparison show in easy way on graph (Fig. 3) on which lane algorithm should focus in next step where will be looking for the potential reason for so big difference.

Knowing about the lanes on which an unexpected slowdown occurred the next step is to check if in the last few minutes AID doesn't recognize anything disturbing. A time of few minutes isn't accidental. Even a temporary, unexpected stopping of one of the vehicles may cause an effect visible for several minutes in the city traffic. After such a stop, algorithm will notice quickly a rapidly growing queue and reduce the average speed of vehicles. If AID server reported recognized fire or smoke on the road then is a big probability that accident happen. Other disturbing signals are animal or pedestrian on the road. Detecting them algorithm should send the current streaming from the camera monitoring the selected lane to the dispatcher for manual verification. Even if very few of the detected events turn out to be a serious accident, every early detection will increase the chances of the victims to get professional help quicker which will increase their chances of survival.

Other idea for arrival time reduction is increasing the number of emergency vehicles, but it is a very expensive solution. Cities need a budget not only for the purchase of a vehicle, but also for its equipment, maintenance and employment of additional employees. It is worth using the existing road infrastructure to reduce travel and return time, thereby increasing the availability of emergency vehicles without the need to increase their number. The algorithm which block the intersections for the ambulance seems to be the ideal solution to achieve it.

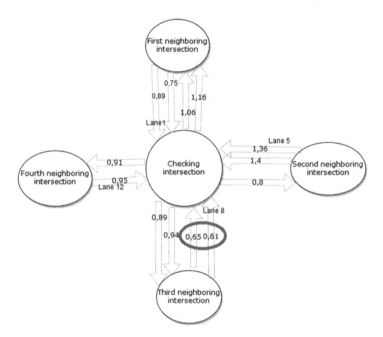

Fig. 3. Graph which is graphical representation of difference between predicted traffic model and actual intersection state [own study]

4   Intersection Blocking Algorithm

Average time of arrival of emergency services in cities is from six to nine minutes. This time is available if only the vehicles are free at the time of notification. Intersection blocking algorithm (IBA) needs for proper working an integrated traffic management system, or an alternative solution allowing to change the signal currently transmitted at the intersection.

Device mounted in preferential vehicles is intended to two-way communication. Information transmitted to the traffic control system will allow identification of the ambulance and designation of an optimal route for it, taking into account changes in the organization of traffic that will be introduced by IBA. Importantly, the basic idea of the system will be to suggest driving route. Many drivers of privileged vehicles thanks to many years of experience can know the topography of the city to find routes that can be faster.

The system needs a few of information from the vehicle to respond appropriately.

The next stage after entering all the necessary information to the system (Table 2), is determining optimal route for the vehicle. When determining the optional route, server are taken a few factors:

– Actual intersections state
– Traffic flow prediction
– Information about other accident which could block the roads

Table 2. Informaton needed for IBA [own study]

Object	Needed information	Description
Dispatcher	Accident localisation	Destination, place where accident takes place
Operator of emergency services	Which units takes action	IBA need information about ID of unit which would be monitored and for which the unit is to optimize the access route
Vehicle	GPS localisation	Exact location. Moreover in case of loss of communication, devices inside privileged vehicles could connect directly with intersections

All of that factors are taken, including the process of stopping vehicles through the IBA algorithm. To make the right decision algorithm performs the following steps:

– Select three alternative shortest routes from the place of departure of the privileged vehicle to the place of the accident.
– Check if there is any road works or other reported accident on the selected route.
– Get current data from all intersections on each route.
– Using the prediction algorithm and current state data, consider the state of the intersection when the privileged vehicle reaches it.
– Select the route that will enable the fastest route to an accident constantly monitor selected route

After make the decision IBA forwards information to privileged vehicle until he reaches his destination. Moreover if selected before path it will stop being optimal the algorithm will inform driver about new route. The traffic management system will, based on the currently received GPS position and the designated route, block the nearest intersections for the time of carriage travel. Intersections will be closed approximately 40 s before the planned ambulance passage to ensure that all cars will be removed from it. What is important, the return of the intersection to normal work will take place immediately after passing the privileged vehicle.

The system, based on the current state of the intersection through which the vehicle has passed and other surrounding intersections, will introduce a modification to program before blocking to maximize the flow of traffic. Full schema shown that IBA can't work at all without many external systems (Fig. 4). All of this information show only in general what IBA is and how it will work, but let's focus on details information about IBA itself.

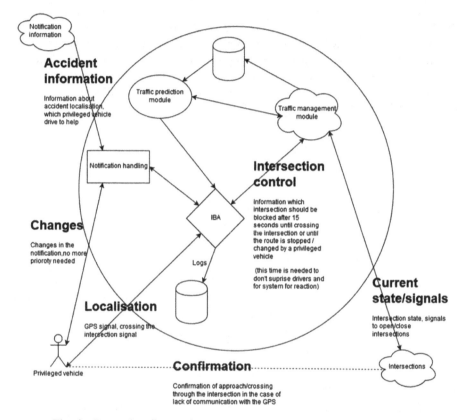

Fig. 4. Connection diagram between external systems and IBA [own study]

5   IBA in Details

IBA start working in the moment when privileged vehicle accepts the notification from operator. Based on vehicle GPS localisation and using Recursive Best First Search (RBFS) algorithm trying to find the fastest route to the accident place. To achieve that the city is converting for dynamically distance and estimates graph. The distance was calculated as:

$$D = (CN/5) + d/L + 50/AS \qquad (3)$$

D – distance
CN – car number on intersection
d – distance between intersections
AS – traffic jam prediction (average speed, if 0 then set to 1)
L – lanes number

This distance is calculated every time when privilege vehicle start drive to/from accident or change the route proposed by system. Proposed from system could be also changed when system will get information about other accident which takes place on the privilege vehicle route. Due to the high probability of blocking the road where the accident took place, this intersection/road should be considered completely impassable and set the distance to the maximum, so that the RBFS algorithm will bypass this place for the vehicles which don't drive there (Fig. 5).

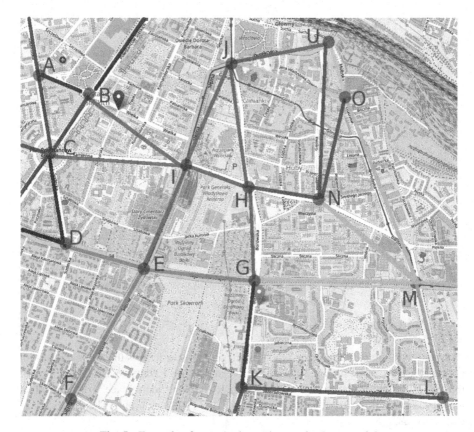

Fig. 5. Example of converted map into nodes [own study]

The easiest way to get the real distance between nodes (Table 3) which are directly connected is to use Google Maps Api which is free for 20 000 distance checking between any two points on the map or Open Street Map Routing Machine [2] which is free for use at all. Both of this solutions will check distance on static map. Any additional factors would be collected from the city in moment when the privilege vehicle start race for the lives of the victims.

RBFS algorithm trying to find the shortest way which is available from two nodes based on edges values [3].

Table 3. Distance in meters between nodes.

	A	B	C	D	E	F	G	H	I	J	K	L	M	N	O	O
A	0															
B	400	0														
C	400	300	0													
D			500	0												
E				500	0											
F					1700	0										
G					800		0									
H							550	0								
I		700	800		700				0							
J							800	750		0						
K							650				0					
L											1300	0				
M							1000	450				700	0			
N								400					850	0		
O										850		1200		800	0	
U								550						1000	650	0

In case of information about accident on the actual route the RBFS algorithm will look for the new best route, bypassing the accident place by setting the biggest distance for the road where accident happen.

Find the best way is one thing, but also important is blocking intersections algorithm which need to know which intersections should be blocked between start and end point. Between the two nodes could be a few intersections in real (Fig. 6). Intersections are identified in city by numbers. Mapping of nodes to real intersections is implemented using a simple two-way list, which is viewed from the front or rear depending on which point the car is moving. Time to start blocking a given intersection will be sent to the traffic control system on a current basis based on the GPS location.

After this short theoretical introduction let's focus on using this module in practice.

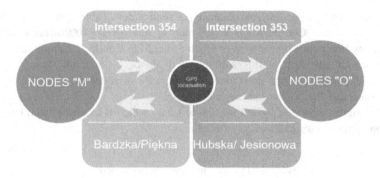

Fig. 6. Two way list of intersections between nodes

6 IBA in Practice

In case of accident happen near "B" intersections (dark grey on Fig. 7) and ambulance starting from near "G" intersections (light grey point) the IBA will on first recalculate connection values (distance) between intersections in the city. That information is necessary to find the shortest way from privilege vehicle position to accident place. Having the values calculated, it should be taken into account that no other accidents have been reported between particular intersections. If so, change their value to a higher one due to the high probability of blocking the road.

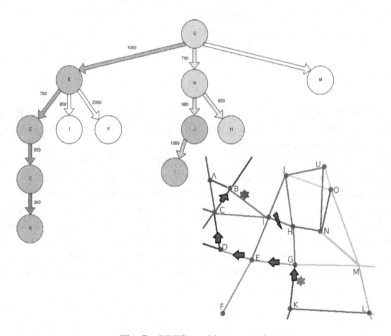

Fig. 7. RBFS working example

Having all necessary data from the city the RBFS algorithm can start looking for the fastest way. The diagram (Fig. 7) shows the next steps performed by the algorithm. The distance between intersections is calculated for a moment when the vehicle statistically reaches the intersection based on traffic prediction module.

After mapping the route to specific intersections, information is sent to the traffic control system which intersection should be closed. The IBA is checking the whole time position of privilege vehicle and send to traffic system id of intersections which should be closed after 15 s. This time is necessary to avoid situation about surprising drivers. Intersections can't change their signals suddenly.

When privileged vehicle crossing the intersection, it starting work normally, and traffic management system trying to achieve as good fluent as possible to avoid paralyze of the whole city.

7 Conclusion

In this paper we have presented one of the possibility how to decrease time necessary to arrival privilege vehicle on the accident place. Using modern traffic management system and IBA this time would be much shorter. Moreover the cost of that solution it is incomparably lower than buying more ambulances and employing more rescuers.

This solution could be used not only by an ambulance but also by a fire truck, which in case of a really serious accident an ambulance must wait. It is not rare situation when victims have to be on first removed from the car wreck before transporting to the hospital. Only firefighters have equipment for cutting metal sheets.

Accident detection algorithm reduce dispacer time reaction and allow for a reaction before any of the residents inform about the incident.

None of the proposed solutions is perfect. Accident detection basen on prediction algorithm and if its effectiveness will be low, the algorithm will be useless due to generating false positives. Furthermore IBA will have a significant impact on reducing the flow of traffic especially in hospital area.

City of the future should focus not only about traffic jams, but many problems which they generate. IBA algorithm represent other way of develop. It don't trying to reduce traffic jams, but maybe when drivers will stop on every intersections they starting to think about public transport as alternative, fastest way of traveling in the city.

We show how in short time build and mapping the town intersections for nodes and edges. Moreover how to use one of the optimisation algorithm in that develop environment. Connection with traffic prediction module and traffic management system provides us with all the necessary data to implement and build module which would be part of future intelligent transport systems.

In further work we will try to full implemented this module and check it working using simulations. This will allow to check the effectiveness of the algorithm and optimization of its weaknesses. It is necessary in the case of later use of this solution in a real city where unnecessary slowdown of traffic isn't permissible.

Irreversible changes in the brain occur after 4–5 min from stopping the heartbeat. After 7 min the victim is dead. We can't control people's behaviour so we can't ensure that someone always helps to the injured, but we can, and we should control intersections and reduce ambulance travel time as much as it is possible.

References

1. Global Status Report On Road Safety 2018, World Health Organization, ISBN 978-92-4-156568-4
2. Huber, S., Rust, Ch.: Calculate travel time and distance with OpenStreetMap data using the open source routing machine (OSRM). Stata J. **16**, 416–423 (2016)
3. Gubichev, A., et al.: Fast and accurate estimation of shortest paths in large graphs. In: Proceedings of the 19th ACM International Conference on Information and Knowledge Management. ACM (2010)

Optimization of Fixed Time Control of Road Intersection by Evolution Strategies

Michal Gregor, Aleš Janota$^{(\boxtimes)}$, and Lukáš Slováček

University of Žilina, Univerzitná, 8215/1, Žilina 010 26, Slovak Republic
{michal.gregor,ales.janota}@fel.uniza.sk,
lukas.slovacek@gmail.com

Abstract. The paper presents how a model of static traffic light control (with predefined fixed duration of phases) can be optimized using evolution strategies. Using an example of a simple intersection configuration the authors show the key steps in design of control script written in the Python programming language. A deterministic model is used to optimize arguments in evolution strategy logics, subsequently used to simulate a stochastic model. Parallel running of two control strategies based on stationary signal-timing plans makes possible to compare results obtained before and after adoption of the artificial intelligence method. The created Python script may be further developed or modified for other model improvements or other optimization methods may be implemented.

Keywords: Model · Simulation · Intersection · Control optimization · Evolution · Strategy · SUMO · Python

1 Introduction

Intersection (junction) control plays a very important role in the urban traffic – to ensure smooth and safe movement of all traffic participants such as vehicles, bicyclists, pedestrians, etc. To accomplish that, a variety of different control systems are used, ranging from simple clockwork mechanisms to sophisticated computerized control and coordination systems having the ability of self-adjusting. Traffic controllers use the concept of phases. The phase is a part of a signal cycle allocated to any single combination of one or more driving directions simultaneously receiving the right-of-way during one or more intervals. Many cities around the world still implement fixed-time control traffic signal systems. These systems operate on a number of fixed or predetermined stationary signal-timing plans, which are put in operation at different times of the day [1]. This approach is attractive for simplicity of design and low cost of initial investment and operation maintenance. The disadvantage is that there is no possibility to respond to changes in traffic demands and the time of the "go" period is wasted if there are no vehicles in the relevant driving directions, which causes useless delays to other traffic participants. It is very hard to get an optimal signal-timing plan based on the real traffic conditions. Therefore there has been a lot of research and studies on the design of proper control methods (e.g. mathematical analyses, analyses based on fuzzy logic, neural networks etc.) and optimization of the obtained models.

© Springer Nature Switzerland AG 2019
J. Mikulski (Ed.): TST 2019, CCIS 1049, pp. 151–164, 2019.
https://doi.org/10.1007/978-3-030-27547-1_12

Many traffic control problems are solved using simulation-based approaches and optimisation via evolutionary algorithms. As an example of available optimized models, discrete event simulation and evolutionary algorithms have been used to optimize a complex urban intersection in [2]; evolutionary algorithms have also been used to optimise a multi-objective simulation-based signal control problem that relies on a 3D mesoscopic traffic simulation approach [3]; a novel agent-based intersection control method has been proposed in [4]. Generally, evolutionary algorithms as a subclass of evolutionary computation [5] use simulated evolution to explore the solutions for complex real world problems. They have become a very popular tool for optimisation but also for searching and solving complex problems [6]. One of separately developed groups of Evolutionary algorithms is a subclass of Evolution strategies (ESs). ES is based on the principle of strong causality: small changes have small effects. It finds a (near-) optimal solution to a problem within a search space and is often used for empirical experiments. Unlike another subclass of Evolutionary algorithms – Genetic algorithms, it is usually faster, can readily find a local maximum, provides a "good enough" solution that is acceptable and the problem parameters are real numbers (which fits well into engineering problems). Our intention is to show how ESs could be used to optimise fixed-time phases in control of a relatively simple light intersection.

Traffic simulation models and software tools have been developed for the purpose of traffic modelling, planning and to analyse different strategies in traffic control during simulations [7]. In our study we use SUMO - Simulation of Urban Mobility [8, 9] – an open source, highly portable, microscopic and mesoscopic road traffic simulation package designed to handle large road networks, that can be found in more studies, e.g. [10–12]. Basic survey of features and abilities of this tool, seen in comparison with other 16 traffic simulation software tools available on the market, can be found in [7].

2 Intersection Model

The purpose of this chapter is to briefly introduce a simple model of road traffic light intersection with known parameters created in SUMO. The reason is to use this model as a reference model for comparison of a conventional control method with newly proposed traffic control solutions. The intersection layout is depicted in Fig. 1 (left), the SUMO-based model containing suffixes with identification numbers for individual traffic lanes is in Fig. 1 (right). The maximum traffic lane speed is set to 13.89 m/s, which corresponds to the real speed limit in urban areas 50 km/h.

Another step comprises settings of the links (interconnections) among individual traffic lanes. The defined settings are summarized in Table 1.

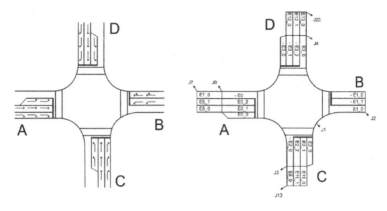

Fig. 1. Intersection layout (left) and SUMO-based intersection scheme (right) [own study]

Table 1. Traffic lane interconnections [own study]

Input branch	Input edge	Driving direction	Output branch	Output edge
A	E0_0	To the right	C	−E2_0
	E0_1	Straight ahead	B	E1_0
	E0_2	To the left	D	E3_0
B	−E1_0	To the right	D	E3_0
	−E1_0	Straight ahead	A	−E0
	−E1_1	To the left	C	−E2_0
C	E2_0	To the right	B	E1_0
	E2_1	Straight ahead	D	E3_0
	E2_2	To the left	A	−E0
D	−E3_0	To the right	A	−E0
	−E3_1	Straight ahead	C	−E2_0
	−E3_2	To the left	B	E1_0

As far as the intersection control is concerned, we suppose a 3-phase control model as indicated by Figs. 2 and 3.

3   Traffic Intersection Control in the SUMO Tool

One of the advantages of the modelling environment SUMO is the availability of its built-in tool Traffic Control Interface (TraCI). Giving access to a running road traffic simulation, it allows to retrieve values of simulated objects and to manipulate their behavior "on-line" [7]. Before running the script, one should make sure that the environment variable SUMO_HOME is set correctly (for details, consult the installation guide to SUMO).

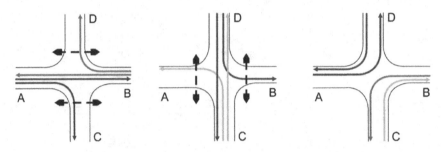

Fig. 2. Definition of signal phases – Phase I (left), II (middle), and III (right) [own study]

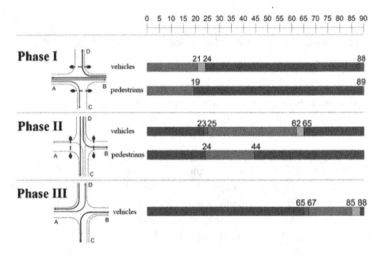

Fig. 3. Definition of signal phases – Phase I (left), II (middle), and III (right) [own study]

3.1   Import of Python Modules

To control an intersection with the use of artificial intelligence we will use TraCI from a Python script. The script must begin with the declaration of paths to several relevant Python modules. An example of such declaration for a Windows environment is given bellow:

Source code 1: Import of Python modules for Windows systems (example)
sys.path.append(os.path.join(os.path.dirname(__file__),'C:\ProgramFiles(x86)\DLR\ Sumo', "tools"))
sys.path.append(os.path.join(os.environ.get("SUMO_HOME", os.path.join(os.path.dirname(__file__), "C:\Program Files (x86)\DLR\Sumo")), "tools"))

3.2   Traffic Generation

Our intersection model includes data on traffic lanes and light signal intersection control. However, it does not say anything about traffic. The traffic data is generated automatically by the script and written into a separate temporary file. This file contains the routes, which define all the pairs of lanes between which vehicles may travel, definitions about the amounts of vehicles arriving from each direction, etc.

In our case, the routes are determined by the geometry of the intersection and they remain fixed for the duration of our experiments. The definitions concerning the vehicles, however, are subject to change. Our procedure is to adhere to a fixed, deterministic scenario when optimizing the phases, so that the utility function optimized by the ES is not stochastic. In the evaluation phase, however, simulations are run with randomized vehicle configurations, which also help to test the ability of the method to generalize.

Source Code 2: Temporary File Creation

```
with tempfile.NamedTemporaryFile('w', delete=False) as routes:
print("""<routes>
<vType id="Car" sigma="0.5" length="5" minGap="2.5" guiShape="passenger"/>
```

The temporary file is created using the "tempfile" library. The root element containing vehicle routes is placed within the tags <routes> and </routes>. The tag "vType" found in the element body specifies parameters of contained vehicles. Then we can create the actual routes:

Source Code 3: Routes Creation

```
<route id="CB" edges="E11 E2 E1" />""", file=routes)
```

In the given example, we create the route for vehicles moving from branch C to branch B. In a similar way, we define routes for all other directions.

Having vehicle parameters and routes defined, we can generate the vehicles themselves:

Source Code 4: Vehicles Generation

```
N = 3600
for i in range(N):
    if random.uniform(0, 1) < pCB:
    print('<vehicle id="CB_%i" type="Car" route="CB" depart="%i" />' % (vehNr,
i), file=routes)
        vehNr += 1
        lastVeh = i
print("</routes>", file=routes)
```

The code is defined for a simulation lasting one hour, i.e. 3600 s with a one-second simulation step. It is possible to generate vehicles at each simulation step, i.e. once per second. Whether to generate a new vehicle with the appropriate direction of movement is decided by sampling from a Bernoulli distribution using a (pseudo-) parametrization by an auxiliary variable representing the vehicle demand per second. In case the algorithm decides that a vehicle is to be generated, it will be registered in the file, along with its identification number, type, route and its time of exit. In addition, some auxiliary variables will be incremented to keep track of the number of vehicles and of when the last vehicle was generated.

Once the vehicles' registration has been completed, it is necessary to close the rooting tag with "routes".

3.3   Creating TraCI Connection

The last step to be done is to define simulation attributes. Since simulation is run by script, we must create the SUMO server using a "TraCI" library at the SUMO command line. The source code given below establishes connection between this server and the client via open TCP port.

```
Source Code 5: TraCI-based Connection
def start(cmd, port=None, numRetries=10, label="default"):
    if port is None:
        port = traci.sumolib.miscutils.getFreeSocketPort()
    sumoProcess = subprocess.Popen(cmd + ["--remote-port", str(port)],
            stdout=DEVNULL, stderr=DEVNULL)
    traci._connections[label] = traci.connect(port, numRetries, "localhost",
sumoProcess)
    traci.switch(label)
    return traci.getVersion()
traci.start = start
```

In addition, in case a firewall is active we should not forget to add the appropriate exception to it, so that it does not block SUMO's open port communication.

4   Simulation

Once all the needed settings have been performed, we are able to create the function that will generate traffic and ensure simulation is run using the source files attributes.

```
Source Code 6: Simulation Start
def run_simulation(params):
    routefile_name = generate_routefile()
    with contextlib.redirect_stdout(None):
        traci.start(["sumo","-c","map.sumocfg","-r",routefile_name,"--tripinfo-
output","tripinfo.xml"])
```

Our intention is to estimate the waiting time of vehicles found in the individual traffic before the intersection. Once a connection with the SUMO server has been established, we can access the simulation parameters online.

Source Code 7: The Waiting Time for Vehicles in Traffic Lane

```
while step < 3600:
traci.simulationStep()
    waitingTimeAC = traci.lane.getWaitingTime("E0_0")
    if (waitingTimeAC < pomE0_0 and pomE0_0 > pom0):totalTimeAC += pomE0_0
    pom0 = pomE0_0
    pomE0_0 = waitingTimeAC
    return (totalTimeAC + totalTimeAB + totalTimeAD + totalTimeBDA +
    totalTimeBC + totalTimeCB + totalTimeCD + totalTimeCA + totalTimeDA +
    totalTimeDC + totalTimeDB)
```

The actual values of waiting times are recorded using auxiliary variables (here denoted as "pom"). The same approach is used for all individual traffic lanes.

Simulation of fixed time intersection control: by fixed time intersection control we understand intersection control based on static signal plans. Since our model is stochastic, we have to perform several simulation runs and obtain the average (across simulation runs) total waiting time values. We will then use these as a baseline against which we will benchmark the evolutionary approach. The average times are indicated in Figs. 4 and 5.

5   Evolution Strategies

The usual goal of an evolution strategy is to optimize some given objective or quality function(s) with respect to a set of decision variables or control parameters (often referred to as object parameters). Evolution strategies operate on populations of individuals. An individual comprises not only the specific object parameter set (or vector) and its objective function value (often referred to as fitness) but usually a set of endogenous strategy parameters. These evolvable parameters are used to control certain statistical properties of the genetic operators, especially those of the mutation operator. Endogenous strategy parameters can evolve during the evolution process and are needed in self-adaptive evolution strategies [13]. In our case, the evolution strategy will not have a direct effect on road intersection control – it will only optimize already existing phases.

After completing all the pre-configurations related to model design, we create a new script. The role of this script is to create control logic for the intersection through parental mutations based on evolution strategies. This script is directly linked to the script whose function we have approached in the previous text. It takes the simulation start function, resulting in a total sum of the vehicle's waiting times. This time has therefore become our target parameter.

In our case the operator of the mutation is represented by the lengths of the phases of the light signals. Phase lengths are randomly generated for each phase, but only individuals with a high level of rating survive when selecting new individuals. The generation of these parameters is displayed below:

Source Code 8: Generating of phase lengths

```
def generate(random, args):
    phase_duration = []
    for i in range (args['num_phases']):
        if i == 1 or i == 2 or i == 8:
            phase_duration.extend([2])
        if i == 3 or i == 4 or i == 11 or i == 12:
            phase_duration.extend([1])
        if i == 7 or i == 10:
            phase_duration.extend([3])
        if i == 0 or i == 5 or i == 6 or i == 9:
            phase_duration.extend([random.randint(args['min_phase_duration'],
args['max_phase_duration'])])
    return (phase_duration)
```

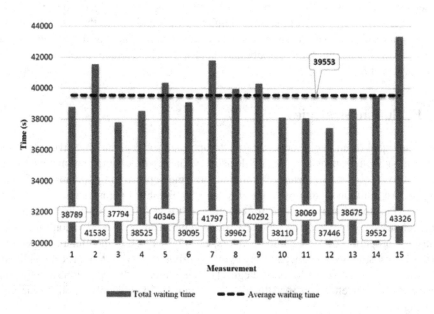

Fig. 4. Simulation of intersection control with fixed time intervals [own study]

We need to realize that the description of phases of light signaling in SUMO does not correspond to that of the real world. In SUMO, the new phase is defined by any change in the state of the light intersection. Therefore, it is necessary to think about phase transitions and setting their lengths statically. The lengths of each phase are initially written in files with the extension ".net.xml". Therefore, they need to be changed every time we start the simulation. We will then write new phase lengths to the temporary file every time we start the simulation, similar to when generating traffic.

Source Code 9: Writing Phases to an Additional File
```
def generate_tlLogic():
    with tempfile.NamedTemporaryFile('w', delete=False) as tlLogic:
        print("""<add>

        """, file=tlLogic)
        for i in range (13):
            if i == 0:
                print('<phase        duration="%d"        state="rrrGGrrrrGGrGrGr"/>'%
(params[0]), file=tlLogic)

        print("""   </tlLogic></add>""", file=tlLogic)
        return(tlLogic.name)
```

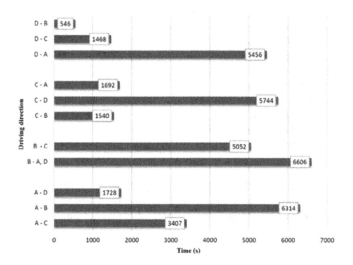

Fig. 5. Values of the average waiting times for individual driving directions at the intersection with fixed time phases [own study]

The output of this function is the name of the file with the newly generated phase lengths. To successfully link this file to our simulation process, it still needs to be associated with the simulation startup parameters using the additional file identifier "a".

Source Code 10: Parameters of a Simulation Run
```
traci.start(["sumo", "-c", "map.sumocfg", "-r", routefile_name, "-a", tlLogic_name])
```

The main logic of the evolution strategy includes several modules. One of them is a terminator. This module provides predefined terminators for evolution calculations. It specifies when to end the development process. The output value of the terminator is a Boolean value, where "True" means that the development should end [14].

Another module is the observer module that provides predefined observers for evolutionary methods. Observer functions have the following arguments: population, num_generations, num_evaluations and args. The "evolve" function creates a population and passes through a series of evolutionary epochs until the terminator is satisfied. The function returns a list of elements representing individuals contained in the final population: generator, evaluator, pop_size, seeds, maximize, bounder, args. The meaning of parameters can be found in [14].

Source Code 11: ES Logics

```
def fitness(params, args):
    return run_simulation(params)
rand = random.Random()
rand.seed(int(time.time()))
es = inspyred.ec.ES(rand)
es.terminator = inspyred.ec.terminators.evaluation_termination
es.observer = inspyred.ec.observers.stats_observer
final_pop = es.evolve(generator=generate,
    evaluator=inspyred.ec.evaluators.parallel_evaluation_mp,
    mp_evaluator=fitness,
    mp_num_cpus=100,
    pop_size=32,
    maximize=False,
    max_evaluations=30000,
    num_phases=13,
    min_phase_duration=5,
    max_phase_duration=45)
```

The graphical representation of the entire control script is depicted in Fig. 6. The intention is to use parallel running of simulations and keep a population of individuals with the best fitness values, i.e. individuals with obtained the minimum waiting times of vehicles.

To optimize the ES arguments in ES logics we have used a deterministic model. The best evaluated parameters have then been used to simulate a stochastic model. We have done simulations with a population of a hundred individuals and observed the shortest waiting times of vehicles. The results are given in a graphical form in Figs. 7 and 8. Figure 7 indicates that there is progress in reducing vehicle waiting times with rising populations. We have also monitored the phases set up using ESs and in particular, we have deduced signal lengths for the best result and averaged the results (Fig. 8).

An average delay of vehicles found at individual traffic lanes is represented by Fig. 9. It shows the average waiting times for particular driving directions for intersection control optimized using evolution strategies. The greatest time losses occurred in traffic from node C to node D, i.e. between the nodes with the most intensive traffic.

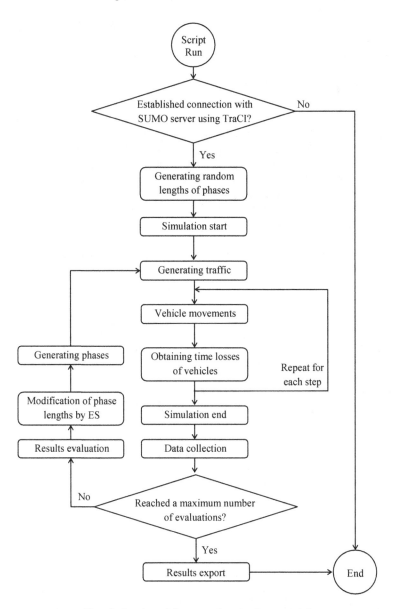

Fig. 6. Logics of the control script [own study]

On a global scale, the phases were designed more effectively with ESs, with less impact on vehicle time losses. Figure 10 shows differences between phase lengths before and after ES optimization.

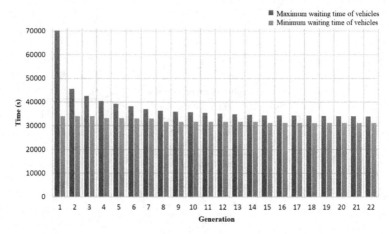

Fig. 7. Simulation of evolution strategies [own study]

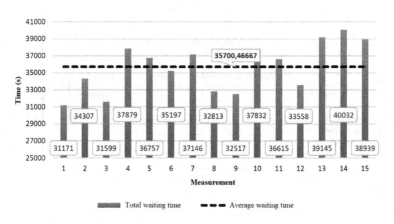

Fig. 8. Stochastic simulations and average values after signal length modifications [own study]

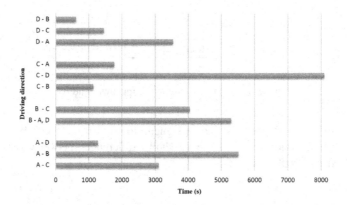

Fig. 9. Average waiting times for driving directions defined at the intersection [own study]

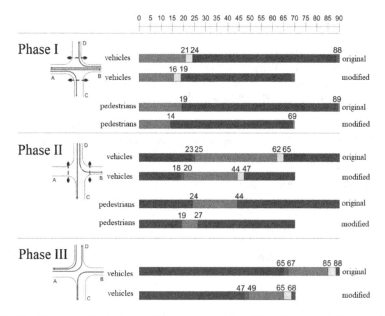

Fig. 10. Phase lengths before and after usage of the AI-based approach [own study]

6 Conclusion

The presented model can serve as a good basis for other custom algorithms of intersection control, whether from the field of artificial intelligence or from others. The model can be further improved, for example, by introducing more randomness or taking a detailed account of pedestrians as well as finding a suitable equilibrium in the traffic network between vehicles and pedestrians waiting for the green light. The generated Python script has the potential to optimize the cross-section phase lengths with known parameters, especially the traffic intensity, which is a key parameter for creating a reliable model. Other results of our work (not included in this paper) indicate that the obtained results for static intersection control are getting closer to but are still not better than results obtained with dynamic intersection control. A future line of work could therefore be concerned with designing dynamic AI-based intersection control methods. These will very likely be able to further reduce the waiting times, but they could also prove much more difficult to verify from the standpoint of safety.

Acknowledgment. This work has been supported by the Educational Grant Agency of the Slovak Republic KEGA, Project No. 014ŽU-4/2018 "Broadening the content in a field of study with respect to the current requirements of the industry as regards artificial intelligence methods and IT".

References

1. Nigarnjanagool, S., Dia, H.: Evaluation of a dynamic signal optimisation control model using traffic simulation. IATSS Res. **29**(1), 22–30 (2005)
2. Mihăiţă, A.S., Camargo, M., Lhoste, P.: Optimization of a complex urban intersection using discrete event simulation and evolutionary algorithms. IFAC Proc. Vol. **47**(3), 8768–8774 (2014)
3. Mihăiţă, A.S., Dupont, L., Camargo, M.: Simul. Model. Pract. Theory **86**, 120–138 (2018)
4. Zhu, Y., Duan, J., Yin, H.: A novel agent-based intersection control method for urban traffic. In: 2016 World Automation Congress (WAC), IEEE, Rio Grande, Puerto Rico, 31 July–4 August, pp. 1–5 (2016)
5. Vikhar, P.A.: Evolutionary algorithms: a critical review and its future prospects. In: 2016 International Conference on Global Trends in Signal Processing, Information Computing and Communications (ICGTSPICC)
6. Yao, X.: Global optimisation by evolutionary algorithms. IEEE Trans. Evol. Comput. **3**(2), 82–102 (1999)
7. Pell, A., Meingast, A., Schauer, O.: Trends in real-time traffic simulation. Transp. Res. Procedia **25**, 1477–1484 (2017)
8. SUMO – Simulation of Urban MObility. http://www.sumo.dlr.de/userdoc/Sumo_at_a_Glance.html. Accessed 12 Dec 2018
9. Gudwin, R.R.: Urban Traffic Simulation with SUMO. A Roadmap for the Beginners. DCA-FEEC-UNICAMP, 44 p. (2016)
10. Metev, S.M., et al.: Urban Traffic Simulation with SUMO. Springer, Berlin (1998)
11. Dias, J.C., et al.: Preparing data for urban traffic simulation using SUMO. In: The SUMO User Conference (SUMO2013), May 2013
12. Behrisch, M., et al.: Sumo-simulation of urban mobility – an overview. In: SIMUL 2011, the Third International Conference on Advances in System Simulation, pp. 55–60 (2011)
13. Beyer, H.G., Schwefel, H.P.: Evolution strategies. A comprehensive introduction. Nat. Comput. **1**, 3–52 (2002)
14. inspyred 1.0 documentation. Library Reference. https://pythonhosted.org/inspyred/reference.html. Accessed 12 Dec 2018

Organizational Changes Related to the Launch of ITS on the Example of Lodz

Remigiusz Kozlowski[1]([✉]) and Per Engelseth[2]([✉])

[1] University of Lodz, Matejki 22/26, Lodz, Poland
rjk5511@gmail.com
[2] Molde University College, P.O.Box 2110, 6402 Molde, Norway
peen@himolde.no

Abstract. Managing city logistics in large cities is a challenge. As a rule, this is done by several organizational units appointed by the territorial self-government as well as units belonging directly to the structures of the city office. The management system is constantly changing under the influence of various factors such as legal requirements, the strategy implemented by the local government or technology. Research in this area has been subject to a scientific inquiry for decades and these results are still interesting both because of their academic as well as business practice contribution. Contingency theory combined with network theory is together applied as an approach to consider the complementary roles of interaction, interdependence and integration in the studied network. The implementation of intelligent transportation systems (ITS) necessitates further changes in the urban logistics management system. The article contains the results of research in this area on the example of Lodz, where the largest ITS system in Poland operates.

Keywords: Networks · Intelligent transport systems · Organizational changes

1 Introduction

The use of information technology has over the past years expanded to include a wide range of business and societal functionalities. In this study, the focus is directed to the practical application of information technology (IT) to control urban traffic. This study provides empirical evidence form the Polish city of Lodz based on a case study of intelligent transportation systems (ITS) development end following use at this location. In this study, we focus not on the technology itself, but on organizing over time as a process the application to secure traffic control. This means that rather than technology, it is ITS as an innovation embedded on a network of actors that is focused upon and how this collective of networked actors together facilitated the implementation and use of ITS and its results. This leads us to the following research question: *"How the organization structure changed through the use of Intelligent Transportation Systems? Also, we consider why these changes took place?"*

© Springer Nature Switzerland AG 2019
J. Mikulski (Ed.): TST 2019, CCIS 1049, pp. 165–176, 2019.
https://doi.org/10.1007/978-3-030-27547-1_13

2 Organizing ITS as a Networked Process

The research question directs us to consider what features inter-organizational cooperation. Perceptions of value creation drive customer-centric production. Since interaction is the foundation of value creation, it is a complex phenomenon. Pettigrew [13] proposes a working definition of the process as: "A sequence of individual and collective events, actions and activities unfolding over time in a context". Processes are in their fundamental nature unfolding through synchronized sequentially interdependent decision-making events in a network interconnected by mutual interactions that unfold over time in specific contexts [7, 13, 15]. Value is created and uncertain, likewise, the quality features of what is produced in its final form, is likewise subject to uncertainty, before and after its implementation. Furthermore, implementation is not the process ends since it is followed by further improvements to the system. Production, in this case of ITS development, implementation and is a process that creates value in its network of different interdependent actors. This value creation involves forming the ITS as well as regarding value perception of its use. This study applies the contingency theory together with the industrial marketing group (IMP) network approach to shed light over the role of interaction in facilitating the development of traffic control systems. Three concepts, following Janusz et al. [9], are revealed in relation to creating and sustaining customer value in the industrial network; (1) interaction, (2) interdependency and (3) integration. Interaction concerns action, interdependency: "the reasoning" for and/or "the result" of interaction in a network structure, and integration helps characterize the quality of activity links and resource ties in the network.

One of the prime topics of contingency theory is about organizations coping with environmental uncertainty [14]. In their experienced network actors, perceive production because of interaction with agents as well as artefacts affecting managing to produce. The importance of interaction reduces a manager's ability to plan production creating a need to continue solving production, including purchasing issues, through interaction. In line with this consideration, from the IMP literature, Cantu et al. [1] state that "solutions (i.e., resource combinations) always emerge as a consequence of interaction among actors. This interaction makes the actual combination dependent on the web of actors involved and, therefore, difficult to predict" [1]. Production is therefore networked and emergent; complex. Following Cantu et al. [1], this complexity is rooted in that (1) solutions (the outcome of production) can be interpreted differently by different actors in the network, (2) actors usually have dual roles, as resource provider and also user, (3) the dual perspectives of actors as resource user and provider are confronted in business relationships through interaction. Håkansson and Johanson [5] state that much due to interaction "networks are, by their very nature, in imbalance". Thompson states that [14], "...human action emerges from the interaction of (1) the individual, who brings aspirations, standards, and knowledge or beliefs about causation; and (2) the situation, which presents opportunities and constraints". Interaction is according to contingency theory embedded in its environment. Although they in time seem linear in form, this unfolding of meaning, sensemaking, usually involves many interacting processes and many interacting people as well as artefacts. "There is, therefore, no stop in interaction, events unfold following a timeline, and this continuity impacts on how actors perceive one-another in the industrial network in an ever-changing manner" [9]. This provides an assumption that in its networked state traffic control systems are in general not to be considered as a finished resource entity. They are subject to a continuous change impacted by networked interaction. This is the same view found as the Kaizen understanding of continuous improvement in Lean manufacturing systems. This implies also a theoretical consideration that contingency theory is in general well fit to analyse Kaizen systems in use.

"Interdependency" is a key concept in contingency theory, and concerns yet another aspect of production; why networked actors interact to produce embedded in their environmental context [14]. Parsons [12] classifies organizations as having three distinct levels of responsibility and control: technical, managerial and institutional. Interdependency is a feature of network structure. This changes more slowly; it is the experienced context of the interaction. In networks, there is an abundance of such linkages, and each business is a node in its own network [6]. This manifold interdependence characterizes the supply networks structure. "The institutional aspect of networks is key to understanding its interdependencies; it is perceived and interdependency is an important perception held by various actors in a more or less collective network organizational structure" [9]. When producing a new ITS, its vital in describing the network structure to consider this reasoning for interaction based on considering the nature of interdependencies in the different business relationships that comprise the studied network. The prevailing development question concerns how can this collective of heterogeneous actors together in an optimal fashion produce the ITS.

"Integration" is weakly conceptually considered in IMP literature. It is a key SCM concept [8], a norm and value of interaction in the "supply chain". The IMP wording points more to "relationship ties". Integration is conceptually wider than "ties". A supply network is composed of more or less heterogeneous actors that do business with each other or compete with each other based on perceptions of degrees of complementarity [4]. In this network, the strength of integration may change affecting the state of interdependency. "This state is fragmented since integration is measured in business relationships, that the importance of these may change as interdependencies fluctuate, or are simply chosen by managers to alter the characteristics" [9]. Organizations involved in the production are heterogeneous entities harnessing the economies of complementarities through integration. Heterogeneity is a core reasoning as to why firms network and gradually integrate. Interdependence is also an expression of network-founded power [2]. Interdependence, reasoning for production accomplishments, rather than a foundation for coercive behaviour. Since a network consists of many business relationships, following IMP network thinking: "The manager becomes someone who must operate within multiple dependencies" [3]. In the network, each firm manages, following Håkansson and Persson [6], a set of supplier and customer relationships. Interaction, interdependence and integration concerns all the relationships, and these features are different when comparing a purchaser's different supplier relationships. This is also a reason why the strengthening of relationships ties is never clear-cut. They may grow, weaken or remain much the same based on a perceived change of the value of the relationships. This value perception is in motion and it is network contingent. "This description provides thus the foundation for considering reasons for how interaction changes based both on changes in the contextual factors interdependency and integration" [9]. In cases of strong integration, dependent on strong interdependency, interaction is then facilitated by strong organizational ties that bind in varying strengths heterogeneous and therefore complementary actors. In the case of ITS development, this means that not all the relationships are to the same degree integrated, and this aspect of stronger weak ties, together with its reasoning founded in considerations of interdependency, spells out how interaction is strongly or weakly facilitated by the relationship itself. This reasoning also may point out relationships that should be strengthened or weakened. The network structure must be designed, and this endeavour is continuous since the nature of these relationships is not stable. The studied network should, therefore, be considered an unstable entity. Changes in interdependency are the main reason for the structural change. Changes in integration may reflect changes in interdependency as well as strategic drive to change the network. Interaction is impacted by features if interdependency and integration. These two factors comprise the context for interaction, in this case, the development, implementation and networked use of ITS.

3 Methodology

The case study method was applied. The information was collected based on analysis of documents, personal open-ended interviews and participant observation. The case study research strategy implies observing in the case the real ITS implementation and uses in its context in the municipality of Lodz in Poland. The case study approach is here qualitative, meaning limitation are associated with generalizability. The strength is providing detailed descriptive information about the Lodz ITS case. However, learning from this case for use in other organizational setting is limited to theoretical transferability. This means that the findings in this case, to the degree they are conceptualised, maybe consider with scrutiny applied to develop ITS in other societal contexts.

4 Findings

The beginning of Lodz ITS took place on April 3, 2007, when the municipal transport company MPK Lodz Sp. z o.o. signed a contract with a consortium of companies Tyco Fire & Integrated Solutions, Alcatel-Lucent and R & G Plus regarding the construction and installation of the Area Traffic Control System (SOSR), which was to ensure priority transport through the city for the Lodz Regional Tram (LTR) and provide so-called passenger information. This project costs about 92.5 million Euro and covered 50 stops and the route length is almost 30 km. The LTR construction took place in the period from July 7, 2007 to August 31, 2009. The project will be further developed - the current course is shown in the figure below (Fig. 1).

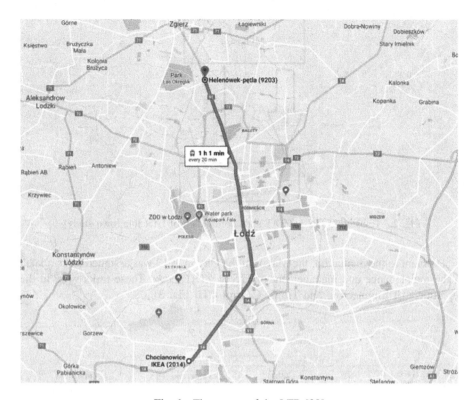

Fig. 1. The course of the LTR [20]

It was, therefore, an investment accompanying LTR and at the beginning covered 70 intersections on the route of this tram, but it was already the largest system of this type in Poland.

It soon turned out that the possibilities of this ITS went beyond the area of public transport that MPK dealt with. It was decided that this technology will be transferred to Zarząd Dróg i Transportu (ZDIT), which deals more widely with road traffic management and is able expand its use (Fig. 2).

In the next steps, ITS tasks were extended to coordinate all public transport. It was possible thanks to placing terminals in all public transport vehicles and special sensors in the elements of linear and point infrastructure. Thanks to this, the ITS system had accurate information about the location of these vehicles. This in turn made it possible to prepare a forecast on the arrival of a given means of transport for subsequent stops. All this information was in the possession of ZDiT, who had to send it to MPK Lodz, which directly managed these vehicles. Another important task was information for passengers, which was also generated by ITS operated by ZDiT and then sent to the boards installed at MPK's stops. Therefore, moving ITS from MPK to ZDiT resulted in the need for close cooperation between these units. As a result, tasks were changed for individual employees both at ZDiT and at MPK.

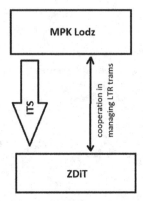

Fig. 2. Transferred ITS to ZDiT and coordination of LTR line [own study]

Pursuant to the regulation, the Mayor of the City in 2013 was assigned tasks related to the maintenance and management of ITS to ZDiT Lodz. These tasks were in the department of Engineering and Traffic Control - TI (Fig. 3).

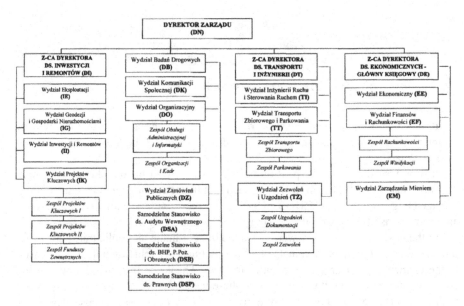

Fig. 3. The organizational structure of ZDiT from 20/09/2013 [17]

TI's tasks include typically related to ITS support - including: (1) organizing and conducting traffic volume measurements and safety analyzes; (2) implementing and maintaining elements of the Municipal Information System; (3) maintenance and maintenance of traffic lights and traffic control systems; (4) maintaining the Intelligent System for the Protection of Restricted Traffic Zones and (5) approval of technical documentation and traffic organization projects in the area of traffic lights and traffic control systems. In 2014, in connection with the modernization of the W-Z route in Lodz, the tasks implemented by TI were updated. These changes were intended to prepare for the inclusion of this route, especially the ITS tunnel. The completion of the modernization of the WZ route and the inclusion of traffic control in ITS in the tunnel resulted in further replacements (Fig. 4).

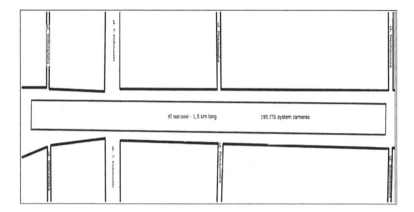

Fig. 4. Diagram of the W-Z route tunnel [own study]

Next, the system was extended further. By the end of November 2015, all target crossings to the ITS system in the number of 240 were fully connected. The employees had appropriate training. All tasks implemented by the system were divided into six groups and individual employees assigned to them. These groups are responsible for subsystems such as management of:

– public transport,
– a tunnel on the WZ route,
– traffic lights,
– cameras at intersections, etc.

It turned out that it was necessary to move the management center of this system into a new location that meets all the conditions, i.e.:

– has enough space to set the required number of monitors and to install the number of workstations required by the system,
– large enough places for meetings of proctors in order to solve emerging problems,
– areas for installing the necessary technical elements,
– adequate physical and IT security.

The change of location took place at the beginning of 2016 and resulted in significant accumulation of working conditions and, consequently, the efficiency of the entire system. As a result of this in 2016, a number of organizational changes took place. ZDiT has been divided into three units: ZDiT, Zarząd Inwestycji Miejskich (ZIM) and Shared Services Center [Centrum Usług Wspólnych]. In the "new" ZDiT,

the structure was expanded (Fig. 5) by separating three teams in the TI Faculty:
(1) Traffic Engineering Team, (2) Traffic Control Team and (3) the Maintenance Team.

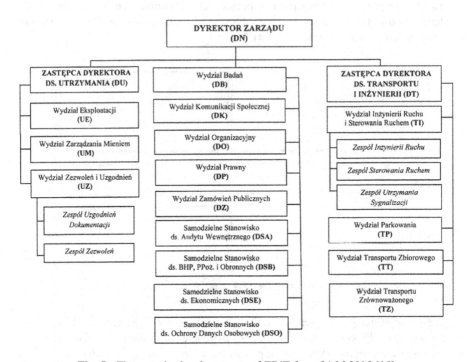

Fig. 5. The organizational structure of ZDiT from 24.06.2016 [16]

The tasks have been expanded and at the same time divided between three separate
teams. The implementation of the Urban Information Systems was assigned to the
Traffic Engineering Team. The Traffic Light Maintenance Complex has been assigned
specialized tasks related to the broadly understood tasks related to traffic lights. The last
of the Teams, which is the Traffic Control Team, has ITS focused tasks and includes,
among others: (1) supervision of subsystems: area traffic control, information for drivers as well as CCTV and ANPR cameras; (2) traffic control in emergency situations
and informing relevant services and drivers; (3) development and implementation of
new traffic light programs, including expansion of the existing Area Traffic Control
System. At present ITS Łódź is functioning in the organizational structure as Fig. 5.
The territorial range of this system is the largest in Poland and includes the intersections marked in Fig. 6 red dots.

Fig. 6. The ITS territorial range in Lodz [21] (Color figure online)

A very important function is the generation of information for drivers by ITS. The information is collected both about the repairs carried out in accordance with the plan, as well as about accidents that stopped traffic. This information is posted on the map and published on the website (Fig. 6). It is very valuable functionality for drivers but from the organizational side it also requires very close cooperation with the Police and with the unit Management of the City Inventors. This required that all the listed organizational units should be included in the tasks of the practioners (Fig. 7).

Fig. 7. Map for drivers generated by ITS [21]

Lodz ITS will definitely have to be further developed, which will involve implementation of both new technologies and new functionalities. The formal structure will also have to be adapted to cooperation with other oraganizations with divergent strategies [19]. The effect of this will also be a necessity to introduce organizational changes. Based on the experience of other Polish and foreign cities, it will be necessary to cooperate with many partners who have knowledge in the areas of specialists in ZDiT and municipal units. Research results made by R. Kozlowski and M. Matejun indicate, that in the practice the cornerstone of technology entrepreneurship development is the contract cooperation of a partner character with the representatives of the world of science [10]. Therefore, the further development of technology and especially the possibilities of practical application offered by ITS in Lodz will be closely related to the necessity of cooperation, among others with universities.

5 Conclusion

The case exemplifies the development of ITS in Lodz as an inter-organizational task. No actor in the described network is an unconnected island in its industrial network. Examples of this are, among others:

(1) the takeover of the ITS system service by ZDiT Lodz - it caused the necessity of extensive and limited cooperation with the previous ITS owner, which was MPK Lodz,
(2) the division of ZDiT in 2016 into three units also caused the need for close cooperation in the implementation of tasks not only related to the ITS system; this cooperation has disappeared from intra-organizational to inter-organizational character.

These developments are interconnected in an industrial network. This network is as already discussed, the context of interaction to develop the studied ITS development in Lodz. This is again supported by improved of integration as mutual organizational and technical investments economize interaction based on more smooth trust-founded interaction. The development of the actual ITS and its following use can be described as an emergent process. The network positions of the involved actors changed over time with the variation in their network roles. These roles were clearly emergent through their networked interaction. The case therefore shows how the actors are interdependent and therefore the state of integration between the shown heterogeneous set of actors facilitates the quality of networked interaction. This study mainly describes the structure change of the network. This network structure is the context of the interaction. The study, therefore, substantiates that the network structure, the context of the studied ITS development, implementation and use is complex based on the sheer number of actors needing to interact. This shows why the network developed. This interaction is necessarily a process. It will, therefore, be emergent in character. This study may, therefore, may be followed by more detailed process description of ITS implementation and use - Such studies provide detailed descriptions of interaction to develop the ITS in Lodz. Similar studies may also be carried out in other network contexts.

To summarize the analysis undertaken in this article (concluding remarks), the issues raised require further research in two areas:

(1) analysis of the impact of new functions on changes in both the organization of processes and changes in the organizational structure of ZDiT Lodz, which directly supports ITS,
(2) provoking changes in structures and processes that have taken place in all cooperating organizations for which ITS is a tool for carrying out tasks (MPK Lodz, Police, Municipal Police, ZiM, etc.).

Acknowledgements. We would like to thank Mr Michał Sarnacki, the Head of the Department of Traffic Engineering and Traffic Control Board of Roads and Transport in Lodz for help in preparing empirical materials used in this article.

References

1. Cantu, C., Corsaro, D., Snehota, I.: Roles of actors in combining resources into complex solutions. J. Bus. Res. **65**(2), 139–150 (2012)
2. Emerson, R.: Power-dependence relations. Am. Sociol. Rev. **27**(1), 31–41 (1962)
3. Ford, D., Mattson, L.G., Snehota, I.: Management in the interactive business world. In: Håkansson, H., Snehota, I. (eds.) No Business Is an Island. Emerald Publishing, Bingley (2017)
4. Gadde, L.-E., Håkansson, H., Persson, G.: Supply Network Strategies. Wiley, Chichester (2010)
5. Håkansson, H., Johanson, J.: The network governance structure: interfirm cooperation beyond markets and hierarchy. In: Grabher, G. (ed.) The Embedded Firm: On the Socioeconomics of Industrial Networks. Routledge, London (1993)
6. Håkansson, H., Persson, G.: Supply Chain Management: the logic of supply chains and networks. Int. J. Logist. Manage. **15**(1), 11–26 (2004)
7. Halinen, A., Medlin, C.J., Törnroos, J.Å.: Time and process in business network research. Ind. Mark. Manage. **41**(2), 215–223 (2012)
8. Halldorsson, A., Kotzab, H., Skjott-Larsen, T.: Inter-organizational theories behind Supply Chain Management – discussion and applications. In: Seuring, S., Müller, M., Goldbach, M., Schneidewind, U. (eds.) Strategy and Organization in Supply Chains. Physica Verlag, Berlin (2003)
9. Janusz, A., et al.: Networked interdependencies and interaction in a biotechnology research project (2018). https://doi.org/10.1108/imp-01-2018-0009
10. Kozlowski, R., Matejun, M.: Forms of cooperation with the business environment in the process of technology entrepreneurship development. Res. Logist. Prod. **2**, 91–101 (2012)
11. Kozlowski, R., Palczewska, A., Jablonski, J.: The scope and capabilities of ITS – the case of Lodz. In: Mikulski, J. (ed.) TST 2016. CCIS, vol. 640, pp. 305–316. Springer, Cham (2016). https://doi.org/10.1007/978-3-319-49646-7_26
12. Parsons, T.: Structure and Processes in Modern Society. Free Press of Glencoe, New York (1960)
13. Pettigrew, A.M.: What is processual analysis? Scand. J. Manag. **13**(4), 337–348 (1997)
14. Thompson, J.D.: Organizations in Action. McGraw Hill, New York (1967)

15. Van De Ven, A.H.: Suggestions for studying strategy processes: a research note. Strateg. Manag. J. **13**(S1), 169–188 (1992)
16. Zarządzenie Prezydenta Miasta Łodzi nr 3842/VII/16 24.06.2016 r.
17. Zarządzenie Prezydenta Miasta Łodzi nr 4982/VI/13 20.09.2013r.
18. Zarządzenie Prezydenta Miasta Łodzi nr 6718/VI/14 17.07.2014 r.
19. Mnich, J., Wisniewski, Z.: Strategy and structure in public organization. In: Kantola, J.I., Nazir, S., Barath, T. (eds.) AHFE 2018. AISC, vol. 783, pp. 351–358. Springer, Cham (2019). https://doi.org/10.1007/978-3-319-94709-9_33
20. Google maps. Accessed 03 May 2019
21. Website of ITS Lodz: www.its.lodz.pl. Accessed 03 May 2019

Using Wireless Sensor Networks for Vehicles and Pedestrian Movement Tracking

Wiktoria Loga$^{(\boxtimes)}$, Artur Ryguła, and Justyna Sordyl

University of Bielsko-Biała, Willowa 2, Bielsko-Biala, Poland
{wloga, arygula, jsordyl}@ath.bielsko.pl

Abstract. The increasing popularity of Smart City concept and constant traffic intensity growth in urban areas has caused the need for searching more effective and economic measuring methods. Wireless sensor networks have become the answer to that demand. The solution enables continuous and low-cost road network monitoring in selected area. Authors of the research evaluated the usefulness of Wi-Fi technology detection system for pedestrian and traffic streams tracking. The presented measurement results were obtained due to devices and systems integrated by ITS testing ground located in University of Bielsko-Biała. The research is a continuation of a previous work regarding wireless multi-sensor networks usage for traffic flow detection. As a part of analysis specific traffic parameters were determined and authors made an attempt to classify the vehicle and pedestrian flow on discussed area.

Keywords: TS · Bluetooth detection · Wi-Fi detection · Traffic flow detection

1 Introduction

Along with the population growth and progressing urbanisation, the need for sustainable development began to be noticed. This concept has been evolving since the 1980s [1] in order to respond to changing needs of the community and following the technological progress. Nowadays, one of the most dynamically developing issues inherent to sustainable development is a Smart City concept [9]. There are many definitions of this concept, but most of them consider the use of digital information and communication networks as crucial to integrate urban systems in order to improve their efficiency and interactivity [6, 12]. As the result, intelligent transport systems (ITS) has been introduced and developed in urban areas. They become a tool for providing information on traffic conditions as well as traffic control, therefore they require modern and effective measurement methods. Due to these conditions, the popularity of mobile solutions is increasing, as they enable to easily relocate the detector. The example of those solutions may be Wireless Sensor Networks (WSN). In these systems, traffic detection data is sent through the wireless sensor network to a central unit. Part of the technologies used in WSN are solutions based on detecting the activity of devices equipped with Wi-Fi or Bluetooth modules [4, 5].

The paper is a continuation of a study on the detection of traffic flows. The authors have taken steps to develop a method for estimating the volume and profile of traffic streams (including pedestrian flow) in selected areas of the transport network. This has

© Springer Nature Switzerland AG 2019
J. Mikulski (Ed.): TST 2019, CCIS 1049, pp. 177–187, 2019.
https://doi.org/10.1007/978-3-030-27547-1_14

been achieved through the implementation of the concept of WSN (Wireless Sensor Network) based on Wi-Fi detection in traffic analysis. The research on determining the traffic distribution on the basic sections within the network field was based on the observation of vehicle and pedestrian streams characteristics. The streams were generated by detecting road traffic participants' active devices equipped with Wi-Fi module.

Clear identification of the same device at several measuring points is possible due to the use of MAC addresses (Medium Access Control) unique for each device. It allows to determine the most frequent routes selected by vehicles and pedestrian streams and also provides information about the average time of residence of a vehicle or a pedestrian within the sensor field. Moreover, the application of the filtering algorithm allows to extend the observation e.g. by the characteristics related to [2]:

- number of objects detections vehicle and pedestrian traffic volume,
- the average time of passage through the defined measuring points,
- the average speed at the defined measuring points,
- the distribution and intensity of traffic,
- the occurrence of traffic obstructions.

Nowadays, it is estimated that a system using Bluetooth detection, implemented on the municipal transport network is able to detect from 10% to 35% of all vehicles [7, 8]. On the other hand, systems using Wi-Fi detection detect 30% to 70% of devices, which corresponds to the percentage of users travelling in a traffic flow with Wi-Fi active devices [3]. Taking the above into account, the characteristics obtained with the detection of devices with Wi-Fi module were compared to the results of tests based on the detection of devices using Bluetooth, carried out on the same testing ground [11]. It allowed to verify the reasonableness and effectiveness of using these technologies in traffic analysis.

2 ITS Testing Ground

2.1 Description of a Testing Ground

An example of a pilot implementation of a Bluetooth activity detection system can be the ITS testing ground, launched in 2016 on the campus of the University of Bielsko-Biala. It was created for both, didactic and research purposes. The training ground consists of the following elements of road infrastructure [7]:

- freely programmable VMS in RGB technology,
- 3D scanner for classification and obtaining in-motion vehicle contours,
- set of inductive loops enabling vehicle classification according to 8 + 1 standard,
- measuring the passing vehicle speed,
- weigh-in-motion (WIM) station based on tensometric technology,
- integrated weather station with advanced road sensor,
- combination of ANPR and CCTV cameras,
- subsystem of Bluetooth sensors used for tracking traffic flows on campus.

In 2019, in order to extend the research capabilities, the testing ground was upgraded with a new functionality - a system of Wi-Fi activity sensors.

The spatial distribution of the infrastructure of the testing ground is presented in Fig. 1.

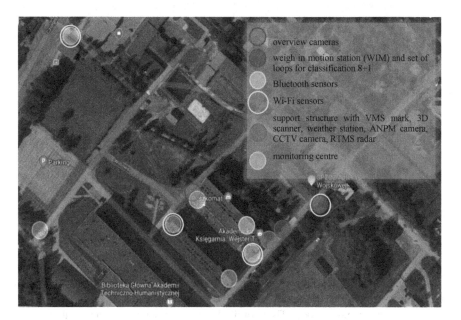

Fig. 1. An infrastructure of the ITS testing ground [own study based on 13]

2.2 Wi-Fi Detection System

The design and deployment of WSN based on Wi-Fi activity monitoring was intended to supplement the ITS testing ground traffic detection systems. The implementation enable the continuation of the studies on Wireless Sensor Networks suitability for detection and traffic flow tracking. Authors previous findings [11] concerning Bluetooth activity detection has focused on detecting mostly hands-free sets and vehicle on-board devices. Authors assumed that the usage of Wi-Fi monitoring could allow to extend the observation to greater amount of pedestrian due to detection of mobile devices, including smartphones.

As shown in Fig. 1, the WSN is formed by 4 sensors located on university campus area. Each of the devices consists of:

- IEEE 802.11 Wireless USB Adapter,
- 4 dBi external antenna,
- Raspberry Pi microcomputer,
- power cord and Ethernet cable,
- sensor enclosure.

All sensors are connected in one network by dedicated software. Figure 2 presents described device.

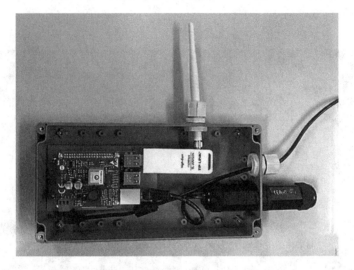

Fig. 2. Wi-Fi activity sensor [own study]

Wi-Fi sensor network operating principle comes down to Wi-Fi wireless radio activity monitoring. Each sensor listens to 802.11 traffic and detects all mobile devices in active Wi-Fi scanning mode. The mobile device is registered in the database along with its identifier (individual MAC address) and precise timestamp of device appearance in detection area.

Every mobile device equipped in network interface controller has a 48-bit MAC address, which is globally unique. The address may be divided into two-layer hardware identifier. In order to guarantee the uniqueness, each MAC address is assigned to a manufacturer. A MAC Address Block Large (MA-L), widely known as an Organizationally Unique Identifier (OUI) is a 24-bit prefix that precisely identifies the organisation. The manufacturer is free to assign any character string to the remaining 24 bites. However, modern mobile devices increasingly use locally assigned MAC with a universal bits in the prefix layer. Locally assigned MACs are randomized for the privacy issues and need not be unique or used in a persistent manner [10].

3 Analysis

3.1 Devices Manufacture Analysis

As an element of the presented study, authors carried out an analysis regarding the type of detected devices. According to the assumptions, the system should detect mobile devices of users who are present and moving within a sensor field (university campus). However, it should be taken into account that due to the specificity of the research area (administrative facilities, numerous measuring apparatus and workstations), some of the measurements may be distorted by units continuously connecting with individual network nodes. Therefore, it was necessary to implement certain boundary conditions and data pre-selection.

In order to check the generic structure of devices detected by the sensor network, authors have attempted to identify individual manufacturers. Analysis of the MAC address prefix allowed to identify part of the devices manufacturer. It should be emphasized that a large part of the detected MAC addresses started with the universal prefix DA:A1:19, owned by Google. Due to addresses randomization it was possible to identify the device as a mobile device, but it was impossible to precisely determine the manufacturer. The analysis of the generic structure included one average traffic measurement day - 18.01.2019. All observations were cleared of distortion by separating only and exclusively unique MAC addresses. Figure 3 shows the 73% share of identified MAC addresses that can be certainly recognised as mobile devices.

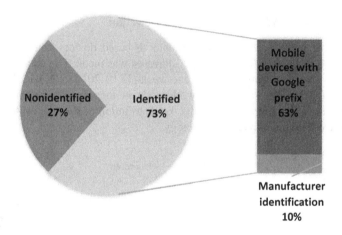

Fig. 3. Share of identified MAC addresses [own study]

The remaining 27% of the observations can represent both mobile devices with randomized, locally assigned MAC address as well as university office devices or remaining measuring apparatus. Out of all detected devices, 63% could be identified as Android or iOS device (judging by randomized Google prefix), while 10% of devices could be precisely identified and assigned to a specific manufacturer.

In the next step, an analysis of the popularity of individual manufacturers among the registered devices was carried out, the result is presented in Fig. 4. The largest share in the detected devices, with the amount of 29%, is held by Samsung. A relatively high number of detections was also noted for Huawei Technologies (14%) and LG Electronics (10%).

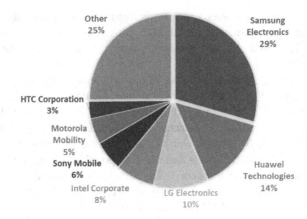

Fig. 4. Share of individual manufacturers among the identified MAC addresses [own study]

3.2 Comparison of Wi-Fi and Bluetooth Detection

To compare the number of Wi-Fi and Bluetooth based devices detection, the comparison of each technology unique MAC addresses was made. The data samples were obtained from 160 measuring node and one-week (17.01.2019 to 24.01.2019) analysis period was chosen. The selected network node is located near the main campus entrance (Willowa St.). Figure 5 presents the distribution of detected MAC addresses for each wireless communication technology.

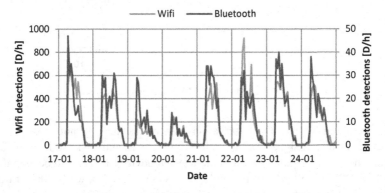

Fig. 5. Distribution of unique MAC addresses for Wi-Fi and Bluetooth on node no. 160 within 17.01 - 24.01.2019 analysis period [own study]

In the presented graph (Fig. 5) the typical daily traffic distribution may be observed. Moring and afternoon pick hours are clearly visible, also the decrease in intensity of detection can be notice during the weekend (19.01 and 20.01). Additionally, to illustrate the interdependence of selected wireless communication technologies, Fig. 6 presents the registered data correlation. The coefficient of determination R^2 amounted to 0,78, which is the evidence of satisfactory distribution matching. What is worth mentioning is the fact, that in the case of Wi-Fi detection nearly 20-times greater amount of data samples have been registered.

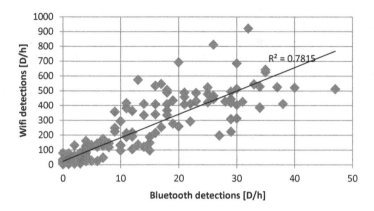

Fig. 6. Correlation of unique MAC addresses for Wi-Fi and Bluetooth on node no. 160 within 17.01 - 24.01.2019 analysis period [own study]

3.3   Vehicle and Pedestrians Detection Using Wi-Fi

As the next part of the study, authors performed pedestrian and vehicle flow analysis regarding morning (7 am – 9 am) and afternoon (2 pm – 4 pm) peak hours during selected day (18.01.2019). The measurement were conducted on a link section between sensor no. 160 (Willowa st.) and sensor no. 183 (building located directly at VMS gantry). Described road section is one-way street (the traffic is moving only towards the university buildings). Tested road section is presented in Fig. 7.

Fig. 7. The test road section between 160-183 nodes [own study]

Figure 8 presents the number of pedestrians and the number of Wi-Fi detections on the road section in the direction from campus to the entrance. Due to aforementioned organisation of traffic flow, no vehicles were noted on discussed direction. The number of Wi-Fi detections was divided into two data sets, where t > 0 and t = 0. First case concerns situation when mobile device logged sequentially to sensor no. 183 and then sensor no. 160, also the time between logging exceeds 0. In the latter case, the device logged onto both sensors simultaneously – this scenario occurs when object during the detection was located in-between sensors and its movement direction is impossible to determine.

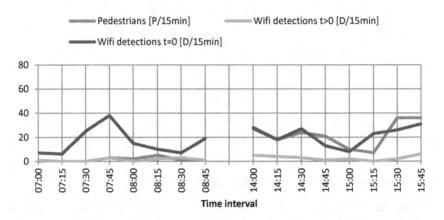

Fig. 8. The number of detection on 183-160 test road section during rush hours on 18.01.2019 [own study]

Analysis of discussed traffic direction has shown a significant relationship for Wi-Fi detection in afternoon peak hours, where t = 0 and the movement direction was undetermined. The above may be a result of relatively short test section and insufficient amount of Wi-Fi detections (single logging observations prevailed).

In Fig. 9 the number of Wi-Fi detections was summarised with pedestrian and vehicle traffic volume on the campus access route (sensor 160 – sensor 183). Also in this case, there was relevant relation between pedestrian traffic volume and amount of Wi-Fi detections, where Δt = 0.

To determine the correlation between overall pedestrian, vehicle and Wi-Fi detections volume, the data was summarised in the Fig. 10. Presented data indicate explicit relation for traffic (both vehicle and pedestrian) flow and objects detected by Wi-Fi sensors.

Additionally, to examine the correlation between registered datasets, the relation between pedestrian flow, traffic flow and the number of Wi-Fi detections is presented separately in Fig. 11.

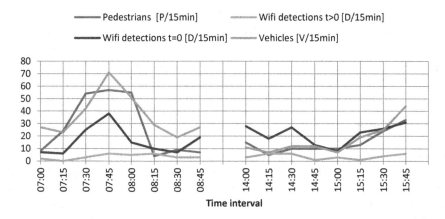

Fig. 9. Comparison of detections samples on 160-183 test road section during rush hours on 18.01.2019 [own study]

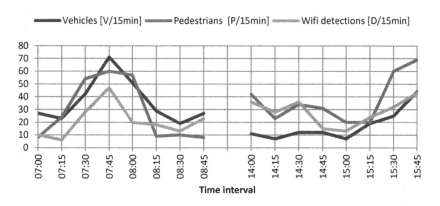

Fig. 10. Comparison of detections samples on 18.01.2019 – cross-section of data [own study]

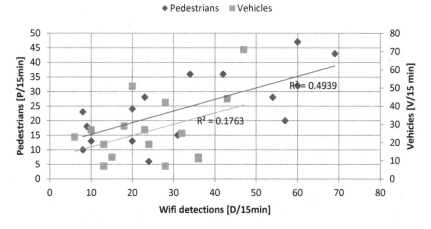

Fig. 11. Comparison of Wi-Fi detections and number of pedestrians on 160-183 test road section during rush hours on 18.01 – cross-section of data [own study]

Presented results showed significantly higher level of correlation between pedestrian flow and Wi-Fi detection than between vehicle flow and Wi-Fi detection. The above may be the result of residence time on the test section, especially the limited applicability of active Wi-Fi devices registration, as vehicles pass the sensor field in relatively short time.

4 Conclusion

All analyses presented in this paper have preliminary nature due to recent implementation of new functionality and lack of continuous and long term measurements. Conducted research reviled few imperfections of Wi-Fi detection technology and indicated the direction of future works. However, even preliminary tests confirm the suitability of Wi-Fi based WSN in traffic measurements.

Comparative analyses of Wi-Fi and Bluetooth wireless communication technologies has shown high degree of correlation. The coefficient of determination R^2 reached 0,78 which is the evidence of satisfactory distribution matching. Moreover, the number of unique Wi-Fi detection samples was nearly 20-times higher than Bluetooth based devices. The daily traffic volume distribution obtained by both wireless communication technologies was consistent with typical daily traffic variability, including morning and afternoon peak hours.

The major share of randomized MAC addresses (63% of total) was observed within the analysis period. It indicates growing popularity of users privacy protection policies. However, the randomization does not eliminate the possibility of device detection on the selected test link. It is worth mentioning that 73% of all detections was proven to be mobile devices which are the subject of the study. Among identified devices about 14% could be precisely assigned to manufacturer.

It was observed that significant part of detected devices was spotted simultaneously by both network nodes. In this scenario it is not possible to explicitly assign users moving direction. While analysing link data between two sensors on both directions, the major relationship between pedestrian flow and detected devices was noted. It legitimise the Wi-Fi WSN suitability for pedestrian detection and tracking. Moreover, the coefficient of determination for pedestrian flow and Wi-Fi detection was significantly higher than for vehicle traffic.

Performed analyses helped to identify the future work line. Next studies will focus on determining boundary conditions and cleansing data samples. Among future tasks it is planned to estimate detection range area of each sensor and identify external factors that may affect:

- device detection/possible lack of detection,
- spotting time,
- residence time within sensor field,
- WSN efficiency performance with diversified data samples intensity.

Authors intend to extend further research on pedestrian traffic flows. The clue of those actions will be enhancing the precision of identifying pedestrian streams from general traffic flow.

References

1. Brundtland, G.H.: Our Common Future, WCED. Oxford University Press, Oxford (1987)
2. Brzozowski, K., Maczyński, A., Ryguła, A.: The air quality monitoring results in the conditions of morning and afternoon rush hours for the Bielsko-Biala city area. Autobusy: technika, eksploatacja, systemy transportowe, r. 17, nr. 11 (2016)
3. Du, Y., et al.: Exploration of optimal Wi-Fi probes layout and estimation model of real-time pedestrian volume detection. Int. J. Distrib. Sens. Netw. (2017). https://doi.org/10.1177/1550147717741857
4. Fernández-Ares, A., Arenas, M.G., Mora, A.M., Castillo, P.A., Merelo, J.J.: Comparing wireless traffic tracking with regular traffic control systems for the detection of congestions in streets. In: Alba, E., Chicano, F., Luque, G. (eds.) Smart-CT 2016. LNCS, vol. 9704, pp. 42–51. Springer, Cham (2016). https://doi.org/10.1007/978-3-319-39595-1_5
5. Fernández-Lozano, J., et al.: A wireless sensor network for urban traffic characterization and trend monitoring. Sensors **15**(10), 26143–26169 (2015)
6. Giffinger, R., et al.: Smart cities: ranking of European medium-sized cities. Centre of Regional Science (SRF), Vienna University of Technology, Vienna, p. 11 (2007)
7. Grabara, A., Płosa, J., Ryguła, A.: The evaluation of the efficiency of determining traffic volume using Bluetooth systems. In: Transport Problems' 2015: VII International Scientific Conference, IV International Symposium of Young Researchers: Proceedings, pp. 149–156 (2015)
8. Konior, A., et al.: A concept of extension of the OnDynamic system with module for monitoring road traffic impact on the urban environment. Arch. Transp. Syst. Telematics **9** (2), 22–25 (2016)
9. Kuder, W.: Smart Cities, Eurogospodarka, nr 9 (2013)
10. Martin, J., et al.: Study of MAC address randomization in mobile devices and when it fails. https://doi.org/10.1515/popets-2017-0054
11. Ryguła, A., Loga, W.: The Bluetooth system utilization to detect vehicle and pedestrian streams. Autobusy: technika, eksploatacja, systemy transportowe, r. 18, nr 12 (2017)
12. Smart Cities Study: International Study on the Situation of ICT, Innovation and Knowledge in Cities, red. I. Azkuna, The Committee of Digital and Knowledge-based Cities of UCLG, Bilbao (2012)
13. https://www.google.com/maps. Accessed 12 Dec 2018

Modelling of the Movement of Designed Vehicles on Parking Space for Designing Parking

Miroslava Mikusova[1]([✉]), Jamshid Abdunazarov[2],
and Joanna Zukowska[3]

[1] University of Žilina, Univerzitná 8215/1, 010 26 Žilina, Slovak Republic
miroslava.mikusova@fpedas.uniza.sk
[2] Jizzakh Polytechnic Institute, Islam Karimov Avenue 4, Jizzakh, Uzbekistan
jamshid1986_86@list.ru
[3] Gdansk University of Technology,
Gabriela Narutowicza 11/12, Gdańsk, Poland
joanna.zukowska@pg.edu.pl

Abstract. Nowadays, in all cities there is an acute problem of lack of parking spaces. The vehicles are becoming more and more not only in megacities, but also in small cities of the country, and there are no more parking places - the pace of solving the problem is several times slower than the speed of transport growth among the citizens. The article is dedicated to determination of the optimum sizes parking place for designing vehicles on parking space which is an element of the roads. On example of the passenger cars and trucks are determined optimum amount parking place. The results of research on the dimensioning of parking spaces, recommendations to use of the results for the design of objects of transportation infrastructure.

Keywords: Passenger car · Truck · Auto train · Trajectory · Parking space · Design vehicle · Software AutoTURN · Turning radius of vehicles

1 Introduction

Trends in the size of cars in traffic flow, an acute shortage of parking space requires a more careful attitude to the design of the size of parking place and parking space [1–4]. Unfortunately, the design of parking does not take into account the composition of the traffic flow that takes shape on a specific road, transport infrastructure object (requirements are obvious here, in the USA where the size of cars is larger than in Europe, the size of parking space is larger), the duration of parking is not taken into account short-term parking near shops, banks, etc., requires more space for maneuvering upon arrival and departure from the parking space than during long-term parking) [5–9]. The most acute problem manifested itself when a ban was imposed on the transit movement of vehicles weighing more than 12 tons in the daytime along the Moscow Ring Road

© Springer Nature Switzerland AG 2019
J. Mikulski (Ed.): TST 2019, CCIS 1049, pp. 188–201, 2019.
https://doi.org/10.1007/978-3-030-27547-1_15

(Resolution of the Mayor of Moscow dated November 15, 2012 No. 650-PP "On Amendments to Legal Acts of the Government of Moscow" [10]). According to the Moscow mayor's office, more than 150 thousand trucks with a maximum weight of more than 3.5 tons are moving through the city streets during the daytime. About 40 thousand trucks arriving daily from the regions.

At the Moscow Ring Road, large trucks make up 30% of the flow, half of which are transit and do not serve the needs of the capital [11]. At this time, there was no experience in designing parking place for cars arriving in Moscow or following in transit.

In the domestic regulatory and procedural documents, the dimensions of parking spaces for road infrastructure facilities are defined in the Methodological Recommendations of the SRC MDRS MIA [12], IRM 218.4.005-20101 и SS P 52289-20042. The dimensions in these documents were borrowed from the Handbook for Automobile Transportation and Traffic Management [13] published in the USSR in 1981, which, in turn, was a translation of the American Road Traffic Management Handbook of 1965 and the recommendations given in the third edition of the Transportation and Traffic Engineering Handbook [14].

Requirements for parking geometry in regulatory documents contain ambiguous, sometimes contradictory information that may adversely affect the level of road safety [15]. Thus, in the "Methodological recommendations on the design and equipment of highways to ensure traffic safety" [16], the turning radius of passenger cars is 8 m, and for truck is 9–12 m. When approximate calculation of the total area of coverage in parking place, including the area of maneuvering and parking, it is recommended to proceed from the average area per one passenger car of 25 m^2, on a truck –40 m^2. At the same time, in the album of typical projects "Cross-sectional profiles of highways passing through settlements" (TP503-0-47.86) 4, the average parking area for a truck should be 92.4 m^2, not 40 m^2, as stated in the methodological recommendations. The dimensions of the parking space given in the Regulations for the placement of multifunctional zones of road service on roads [17] take into account the size of modern cars, but this is not enough to develop a complete planning solution, since the parking maneuvers are not taken into account, and only the dimensions of the parking space are given. The passenger car and truck placement schemes used in the United States and the dimensions of parking spaces shown in Fig. 1 provide more complete information. The planning solution for placing parking spaces for trucks, which provides the simplest conditions for entering and leaving a parking space, recommended in the USA, is shown in Fig. 2. The sizes on the scheme presented on Fig. 3, correspond to a parking angle of 45°, while it is indicated that at angles of 30°, the width of the passages can be reduced to 6.0 m, and the width of each parking space - by 30 cm. For large trucks, the length of the longitudinal parking space must be at least 41 m, width by 5.2 m. The same values are specified in the regulations of the United Arab Emirates for large trucks on parking spaces [18].

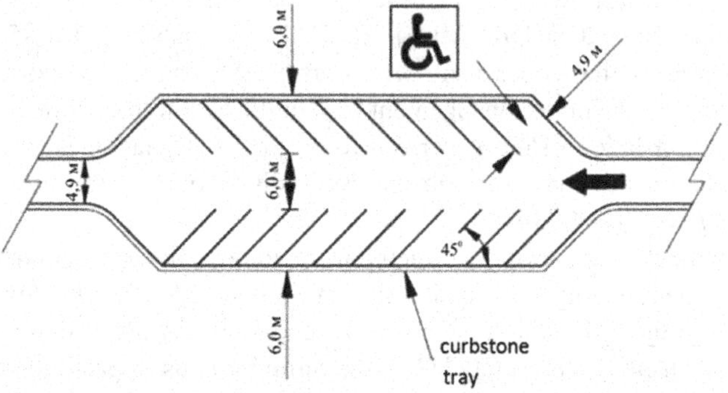

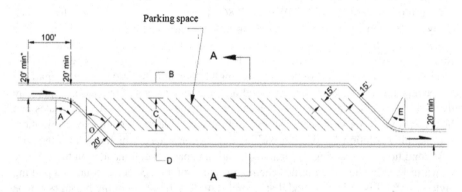

Fig. 1. Schemes of planning of parking spaces for passenger cars with one-sided (a) and two-sided (b) placement [own study]

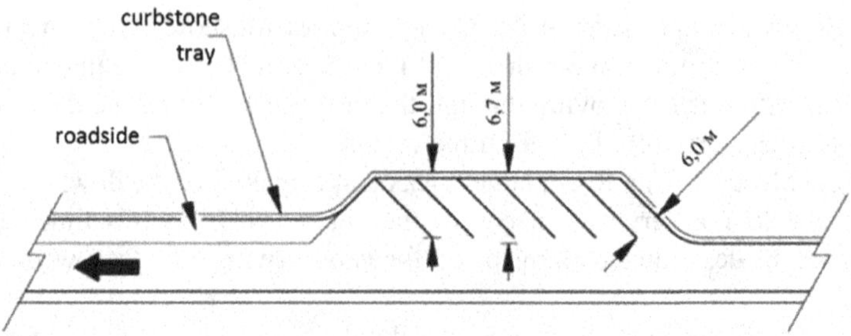

Fig. 2. The fundamental planning of the placement of parking spaces for trucks, recommended in the US: Ø [own study]

– 30–45°; A – 25,9–30,5 м; B – 9,1–13,7 м; C – 15,2–18,8 м; D – 9,1–13,7 м; E – 30,5–35,0 м.

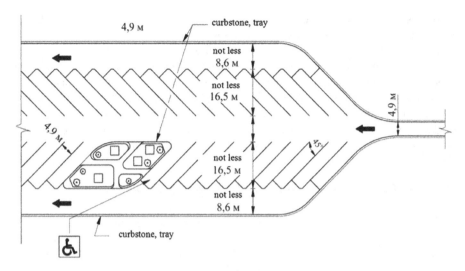

Fig. 3. Scheme of parking spaces for trucks [own study]

At the Department of Survey and design of roads MADI have been conducted research to justify the size of parking spaces for vehicles, taking into account the characteristics for modern traffic on the roads of the Russian Federation [19].

This research work included: monitoring parking maneuvers, studying the real situation when setting up parking spaces and modeling parking maneuvers of passenger cars and trucks using the AutoTURN software, which allows to simulate the movement and maneuvering of vehicles at speeds up to 60 km/h, and also to model three-dimensional movement on a 3D surface, localize modeling for various groups of vehicles; graphically represent the dynamic dimensions indicating the dynamic dimensions of the vehicles (external and internal wheels, characteristic points of the body); create vehicle reversal patterns [20].

Parking space for vehicles includes parking spaces for vehicles and a maneuvering area, designed for the entrance to parking spaces, exit and setting cars [21]. The dimensions of the parking space must ensure unhindered entry, opening the doors of the vehicles, unloading or loading luggage, and then unimpeded exit without hitting other vehicles [22].

The dimensions of the car parking space determine its type and size (length, width, turning radius of the inner rear wheel, overhang, base, gauge). To be able to bypass and open the doors of the car, the parking dimensions should be 0.5 m larger than the corresponding dimensions of the designing vehicles [23].

The "Methodological guidelines for the design and equipment of highways to ensure traffic safety" [24] indicated that parking at large recreation areas, at roadside catering establishments, motels and campgrounds should be placed between the highway and buildings with vehicle separation by types and sizes. Parking areas for trucks and passenger cars should be demarcated and provide for each type of vehicle a separate entrance to the appropriate temporary parking area [25–29].

In this case, passenger cars and buses are recommended to have on the left, and trucks on the right in the direction of travel [30].

It is recommended to place the parking of trucks parallel to the axis of movement, while parking of passenger cars mainly should be arranged according to an oblique angle at an angle of 45–60°. For long stays in the parking place, as well as in cramped conditions, when the parking place have one exit, it is recommended to install vehicles perpendicular to the direction of the axis of movement. Recommendations are given for the designation of the average area of coverage for one vehicle, taking into account the area of the exit and entry zones and the area of the parking space itself.

2   Modelling of the Movement of Designed Vehicles

To determine the width of the maneuvering of parking spaces, the authors took into account the minimum turning radius of the design vehicle and its dynamic clearance. To do this, studies have been conducted that allowed us to determine these characteristics [31, 32]. In the study, the width of the passage was determined as follows. When designing the parking space and the entrance vehicles at parking spaces, the following schemes and provisions were applied in the calculations:

  1 - the road train leaves the parking space in the forward direction;
  2 - auto train drives backwards in a parking space;
  3 - road train drives forward;
  4 - the road train leaves the parking space in reverse.

It was found that for reversing a large maneuvering lane is needed than in other variants. This maneuver is a common parking method for road train drivers. With this in mind, the width of the maneuvering strip was determined.

The design vehicle made a maneuver at the location of a parking space at an angle of 90°, 60° and 45° (see Fig. 4). After each maneuver, the parking length, maneuvering lane, and parking width were determined.

Studies have shown that for one passenger car, taking into account maneuvering, 28.7 m^2 of parking space is needed. For a road train length of 16.5 m, this value is 143.1 m^2 of area.

From Fig. 5 it follows that with more than five parking spaces, the area of parking space for one vehicle does not increase (depending on the angle). When the parking space is located at an angle of 90°, and if there are less than 5 parking spaces in the parking, the parking space is reduced by one car. At the location of parking spaces at angles of 60° and 45°, the indicator is 4 parking spaces. Similar values are obtained for cars and for trucks. Proceeding from this, it can be concluded that, when parking places at an angle of 90°, designing less than five parking spaces is ineffective for any type of car, and if placed at angles of 60° or 45°, up to four parking spaces are considered ineffective.

a.

b.

c.

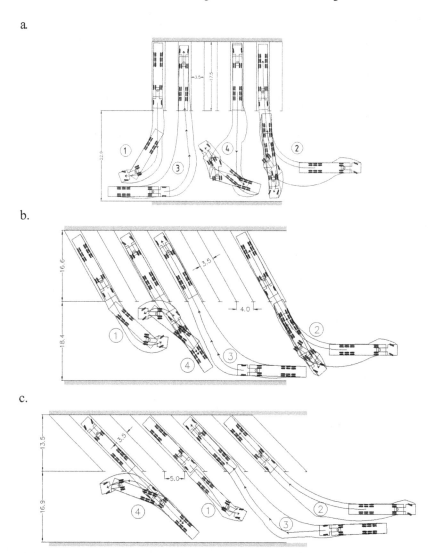

Fig. 4. Maneuvering schemes for a train (16.5 m) in a parking; (a) the location of the parking space at an angle of 90°; (b) the location of the parking space at an angle of 45°; (c) the location of the parking space at an angle of 60°; 1-way forward; 2- backing; 3- forward ride; 4 – reversing [own study]

a.

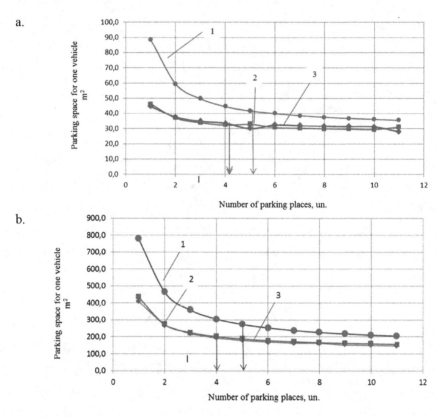

b.

Fig. 5. The dependence of the area of parking space on the number of parking spaces for passenger cars (a) and for a train 16.5 m long (b) when set at the corners: 1 – 90°; 2 – 60°; 3 – 45° [own study]

3 Conclusion

Based on the above data, we can draw the following conclusions:

1. Less than 5 parking places at an angle of 90° is economically inefficient for any type of vehicle;
2. When located at angles of 60° or 45°, up to 4 parking places are considered to be economically inefficient.

Table 1. Recommended size of the design vehicles [own study]

Type of design vehicles	Designation		Wheelbase, m	Dimension, m			
				General		Overhang	
	RD[1)]	TR[2)]		Length	Width	Front	Rear
Passenger car	P	L	2,90	4,90	1,90	0,90	1,10
City bus	CB	M_2	6,20	12,0	2,50	2,75	3,05
Bus	B	M_3	6,90/1,30	15,0	2,50	2,60	4,20
Articulated bus	AB	M_3	5,96/6,05	18,4	2,55	2,68	3,71
Truck	T	N_3	6,80	12,0	2,50	1,50	3,70
Road train	A16	N_2+O_4	3,80/7,02	16,50	2,50	1,43	2,98
Road train	A20	N_3+O_4	6,80/4,30	19,80	2,50	1.50	0.70

Note
RD[1)] – vehicle designation adopted in the article.
TR[2)] – designation of cars in accordance with the Technical Regulations "On the safety of wheeled vehicles" (approved by the decision of the Commission of the Customs Union of 9 December 2011 No. 877)

Table 2. Minimum turning radius of the design vehicle [own study]

Type of design vehicles	Minimum turning radius, m	Minimum outer radius, m	Minimum inner radius, m
Passenger car (P)	6,55	6,85	4,42
City bus (C)	9,20	10,54	5,40
Bus (B)	10,32	11,52	6,40
Articulated bus (A)	13,12	14,21	10,10
Truck (T)	11,07	11,82	6,15
Road train (A16)	9,69	10,19	6,20
Road train (A20)	12,06	12,63	8,50

The following types of design vehicles were recommended as most frequently encountered on the roads for Russia Federation: passenger car (P); city bus (CB); bus (B); articulated bus (AB); truck (T); road train consisting of truck tractor and semi-trailer (A16); road train consisting of a truck and a trailer (A20). The main dimensions of the specified design vehicle are given in Table 1, the minimum turning radius - in Table 2. The resulting sizes of parking spaces and the scheme of their breakdown are

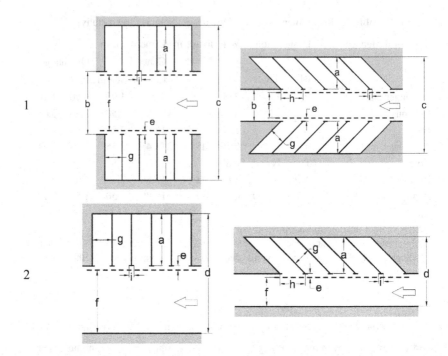

Fig. 6. Possible layouts of parking space 1- two-way parking; 2- one-way parking a - the depth of the parking space; b - the width of the passage between the rows of parking spaces; c - the distance occupied by the strip for parking and travel; d - the distance occupied by the strip for parking and travel; e - security band; f - maneuvering strip; g - the width of the parking space; h - the width of the parking module; i - markup line length 1.1; [own study]

given in Table 3 and Fig. 6. Recommended lengths of parking spaces for longitudinal placement of design vehicles are presented in Table 4. Recommended schemes and dimensions of parking of buses (type of rated car B) with longitudinal, saw tooth and perpendicular device of aprons are shown in Fig. 7. Considering the foreign experience of organizing parking spaces for large-sized vehicles, which provides for entry and exit to a parking without reversing (Fig. 8), as a result of research, it is recommended to take the dimensions of parking spaces in accordance with the values in Table 5.

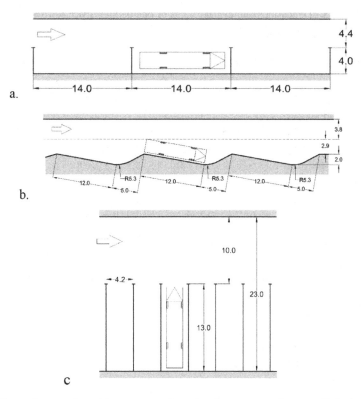

Fig. 7. The scheme of parking spaces for city buses: a- when parallel; b-sawtooth; c-perpendicular placement in relation to the driveway or maneuvering zone [own study]

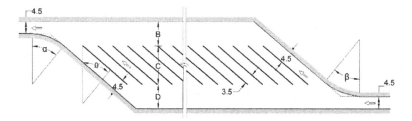

Fig. 8. Elements of breakdown of parking space for trucks α – β – parking angle; Ø – vehicle installation angle; B – D – maneuvering strip; C – parking module length [own study]

Table 3. Dimensions and average areas of one parking space [own study]

Vehicle installation angle, degree	Sizes of elements, m									Average area for 1 vehicle, m^2	
	a	b	c	d	e	f	g	h	i	Without maneuvering	With maneuvering
1	2	3	4	5	6	7	8	9	10	11	12
One-way car parking (**P**)											
90	5,0	7,0	17,0	11,5	0,5	6,0	2,5	2,5	0,5	12,5	28,7
60	5,2	4,2	14,6	8,9	0,5	3,2	2,5	2,9	0,5	15,1	25,8
45	4,8	4,0	13,6	8,3	0,5	3,0	2,5	3,5	0,5	16,8	29,0
Two-way car parking (**P**)											
90	5,0	8,0	18,0	12,5	0,5	7,0	2,5	2,5	0,5	12,5	22,5
60	5,2	5,2	15,6	9,9	0,5	4,2	2,5	2,9	0,5	15,1	22,6
45	4,8	5,0	14,6	9,3	0,5	4,0	2,5	3,5	0,5	16,8	25,5
Truck Parking (**T**)											
90	13,0	16,1	42,1	28,6	0,5	15,1	3,5	3,5	0,5	45,5	100,1
60	11,8	12,4	36,0	23,7	0,5	11,4	3,5	4,0	0,5	47,2	94,8
45	10,5	8,7	29,7	18,7	0,5	7,7	3,5	5,0	0,5	52,5	93,5
City bus parking (**CB**)											
90	13,0	16,1	42,1	28,6	0,5	15,1	3,5	3,5	0,5	45,5	100,1
60	11,8	12,4	36,0	23,7	0,5	11,4	3,5	4,0	0,5	47,2	94,8
45	10,5	8,7	29,7	18,7	0,5	7,7	3,5	5,0	0,5	52,5	93,5
Bus parking (**B**)											
90	16,0	19,0	51,0	34,5	0,5	18,0	3,5	3,5	0,5	56,0	120,7
60	14,3	16,1	44,7	29,9	0,5	15,1	3,5	4,0	0,5	57,2	119,6
45	12,4	11,7	36,5	23,6	0,5	10,7	3,5	5,0	0,5	62,0	118,0
Articulated bus parking (**AB**)											
90	19,5	25,1	64,1	44,1	0,5	24,1	3,5	3,5	0,5	68,3	154,3
60	17,3	20,3	54,9	37,1	0,5	19,3	3,5	4,0	0,5	69,2	148,4
45	14,9	18,5	48,3	32,9	0,5	17,5	3,5	5,0	0,5	74,5	164,5
Road train parking (**A16**)											
90	17,5	23,9	58,9	40,9	0,5	22,9	3,5	3,5	0,5	61,3	143,1
60	16,6	18,9	52,1	35,0	0,5	17,9	3,5	4,0	0,5	66,4	140,0
45	13,5	17,4	44,4	30,4	0,5	16,4	3,5	5,0	0,5	67,5	152,0
Road train parking (**A20**)											
90	21,0	33,0	75,0	53,5	0,5	32,0	3,5	3,5	0,5	73,5	187,2
60	18,6	23,8	61,0	41,9	0,5	22,8	3,5	4,0	0,5	74,4	167,6
45	16,0	21,1	53,1	36,6	0,5	20,1	3,5	5,0	0,5	80,0	183,0

Table 4. The length of parking spaces for longitudinal settlement cars [own study]

Design vehicle	Passenger car (P)	Truck (T)	Buses			Road Train	
			(CB)	(B)	(AB)	(A16)	(A20)
Parking space length, m	6,0	14,0	14,0	17,0	22,5	20,0	24,0

Table 5. Sizes of parking spaces at different corners of the parking of trucks [own study]

Installation angle, degree			Sizes of parking spaces, m (see Fig. 8)		
Ø	α	β	B	C	D
A 16					
30	30	30	7,5	12,0	7,5
35	35	35	8,5	13,0	8,5
40	40	40	8,7	13,5	8,7
45	45	45	9,5	15,5	9,5
A 20					
30	30	30	8,0	13,0	8,0
35	35	35	9,0	15,5	9,0
40	40	40	9,2	16,5	9,2
45	45	45	10,0	17,7	10,0

Acknowledgment. This paper was supported by the Project 586292-EPP-1-2017-1-PL-EPPKA2-DBHE-JP - INTRAS - Intelligent Transport Systems: New ICT – based Master's Curricula for Uzbekistan, co-funded by the ERASMUS+ scheme under grant agreement n. 2017-3516/001-001 and by the project 5/KCMD/2019 Vytvorenie metodiky pre analýzu priechodov pre chodcov z hľadiska ich bezpečnosti ako nástroja pre implementáciu revidovanej Smernice Európskeho parlamentu a Rady 2008/96/ES o riadení bezpečnosti cestnej infraštruktúry.

References

1. Mikusova, M., Gnap, J.: Experiences with the implementation of measures and tools for road safety. CIT 2016: XII congreso de ingenieria del transporte, Valencia, Spain, pp. 1632–1638 (2016)
2. Horalek, J., Sobeslav, V.: Analysis of software routing solution based on mini PC platform for IoT. In: Nguyen, N.T., Pimenidis, E., Khan, Z., Trawiński, B. (eds.) ICCCI 2018. LNCS (LNAI), vol. 11055, pp. 455–466. Springer, Cham (2018). https://doi.org/10.1007/978-3-319-98443-8_42
3. Mikušová, M., Torok, A., Brída, P.: Technological and economical context of renewable and non-renewable energy in electric mobility in Slovakia and Hungary. In: Nguyen, N.T., Pimenidis, E., Khan, Z., Trawiński, B. (eds.) ICCCI 2018. LNCS (LNAI), vol. 11056, pp. 429–436. Springer, Cham (2018). https://doi.org/10.1007/978-3-319-98446-9_40

4. Varik, V., Gregor, M., Grznar, P.: Computer simulation as a tool for the optimization of logistics using automated guided vehicles. In: 12th International Scientific Conference of Young Scientists on Sustainable, Modern and Safe Transport - TRANSCOM 2017, vol. 192, pp. 923–928 (2017)

5. Jamroz, K., et al.: Tools for road infrastructure safety management - Polish experiences. In: 17th Meeting of the EURO-Working-Group on Transportation, Transportation Research Procedia, vol. 3, pp. 730–739 (2014). https://doi.org/10.1016/j.trpro.2014.10.052

6. Jankowska, D., Mikusova, M., Wacowska-Słęzak, J.: Mobility issues in selected regions of Poland and Slovakia – outcomes of international project SOL (Save Our Lives) survey. Period. Polytech. Transp. Eng. **43**(2), 67–72 (2015). https://doi.org/10.3311/pptr.7580

7. Mikusova, M.: Joint efforts needed to prevent traffic accidents, injuries and fatalities. Safety Secur. Eng. V. 503–514 (2013). https://doi.org/10.2495/safe130451

8. Mikušová, M.: Value of networking in transport policy related to the road safety. In: Mikulski, J. (ed.) TST 2011. CCIS, vol. 239, pp. 70–77. Springer, Heidelberg (2011). https://doi.org/10.1007/978-3-642-24660-9_8

9. Rievaj, V., Mokrickova, L., Synak, F.: Benefits of autonomously driven vehicle. Transp. Commun. Sci. J. **4**(2), 15–17 (2016)

10. Information and legal portal Garant. Electron. Dan. (2018). http://www.garant.ru/hotlaw/moscow/430367. Accessed 27 Jan 2018

11. Buranov, I.: Mayor shifted the burden of responsibility to the region. Newspaper "Kommersant", vol. 218(5003) (2012)

12. Monitoring compliance with the norms, rules and standards when designation and construction of roadside facilities (service facilities). Methodical recommendations. SIC STSI of the Ministry of Internal Affairs of Russia, p. 28 (2004)

13. Rankin, V.U.: Automobile transportations and the organization of traffic. Transport, p. 592 (1981). Reference book. Per. from English V.U. Rankin, P. Klafey, S. Halbert, and others

14. Baerwald, J.E.: Transportation and Traffic Engineering Handbook, 3rd edn. p. 717. Institute of Traffic Engineers, Washington, D.C. (1965)

15. Mikusova, M.: Crash avoidance systems and collision safety devices for vehicle. DYN-WIND2017, vol. 107 (2017). Article no. 00024. https://doi.org/10.1051/matecconf/201710700024

16. Design and equipment of highways to ensure traffic safety. Methodical recommendations. Transport (1983)

17. Regulations for the placement of multifunctional road zones of the service on the highways of the State company "Russian highways" (Approved by the order of the State company "Russian highways" 24 June 2013, no. 114). http://www.rhighways.ru/for_investor/road_service/multifunctional_road_service_area/. Accessed 27 Jan 2019

18. Machado, L., Merino Dominguez, E., Mikusova, M.: Proposta de índice de mobilidade sustentável: metodologia e aplicabilidade. Cadernos Metrópole, 14 (July–December) (2012). ISSN 1517-2422. http://www.redalyc.org/articulo.oa?id=402837818011. Accessed 27 Jan 2019

19. Zukowska, J., Mackun, T.: Monitoring of drivers' behaviour in real conditions. In: CMDTUR 2018 - Proceedings of 8th International Scientific Conference, pp. 173–178 (2018)

20. AutoTURN. Advanced vehicle simulations, Transoftsolution. http://store.softline.ru/transoft/transoft-autoturn. Accessed 27 Jan 2018

21. Mikusova, M., Zukowska, J., Torok, A.: Community road safety strategies in the context of sustainable mobility. Commun. Comput. Inf. Sci. **897**, 115–128 (2018)

22. Abdunazarov Nurmuhumatovich, J., Mikusova, M.: Application of GIS in automobile-road sector (Using the ArcGIS example). In: CMDTUR 2018 - Proceedings of 8th International Scientific Conference, pp. 324–327 (2018)
23. Help for guests. Guidelines. Elektron. data, 2013. http://www.gosthelp.ru. Accessed 18 Dec 2018
24. The Methodical recommendations on designing and equipping the highways for road safety, Minavtodor RSFSR, M.: Transport (1983)
25. Callejas-Cuervo, M., Valero-Bustos, H.A., Alarcón-Aldana, A.C., Mikušova, M.: Measurement of service quality of a public transport system, through agent-based simulation software. In: Huk, M., Maleszka, M., Szczerbicki, E. (eds.) ACIIDS 2019. SCI, vol. 830, pp. 335–347. Springer, Cham (2020). https://doi.org/10.1007/978-3-030-14132-5_27
26. Zukowska, J., Mikusova, M., Michalski, L.: Integrated safety systems - the approach toward sustainable transport. In: Archives of Transport System Telematics, vol. 10, no. 2, pp. 44–48 (2017). ISSN 1899-8208
27. Alsobky, A., Hrkút, P., Mikušová, M.: A smart application for university bus routes optimization. In: Kováčiková, T., Buzna, Ľ., Pourhashem, G., Lugano, G., Cornet, Y., Lugano, N. (eds.) INTSYS 2017. LNICST, vol. 222, pp. 12–20. Springer, Cham (2018). https://doi.org/10.1007/978-3-319-93710-6_2
28. Mikusova, M.: Sustainable structure for the quality management scheme to support mobility of people with disabilities. Procedia Soc. Behav. Sci. 160, 400–409 (2014). https://doi.org/10.1016/j.sbspro.2014.12.152
29. Mikusova, M.: Proposal of benchmarking methodology for the area of public passenger transport. Periodica Polytech. Transp. Eng. 47(2), 166–170 (2019). https://doi.org/10.3311/PPtr.10271
30. Abnunazarov, J., Mikusova, M.: Testing trajectory of road trains with program complexes. The Archives of Automotive Engineering – Archiwum Motoryzacji, AMO-00003-2018-02
31. Abdunazarov, J.N.: Justification the parameters of design vehicles for the design geometric elements of highways, Ph.D thesis, Moscow, MADI, pp. 143 (2015)
32. Bobkowska, K., Ignolt, A., Mikusova, M., Tysiac, P.: Implementation of spatial information for monitoring and analysis of the area around the port using laser scanning techniques. In: Polish Maritime Research: The Journal of Gdansk University of technology, vol. 24, no. 1, pp. 10–15 (2017). ISSN 1233-2585

Selected Telematics Solutions in City Transport

Tomasz Perzyński[✉] and Andrzej Lewiński[✉]

University of Technology and Humanities in Radom, Malczewskiego 29,
Radom, Poland
{t.perzynski,a.lewinski}@uthrad.pl

Abstract. The article presents selected solutions of urban telematics systems, which also belong to the city ITS. The concept of a system supporting mobility in the urban area of emergency vehicles was presented. The paper also contains a mathematical analysis of selected solutions carried out using stochastic processes in the form of Markov processes.

Keywords: Management of city transport · ITS solutions · Markov process

1 Introduction

The growing number of motor vehicles causes the need to introduce solutions allowing for better management of the transport process. The big challenge is also a solution the problem of crowded cities. The investments in road infrastructure are insufficient in order to needs. It is necessary to use tools in the form of telematics systems, including ITS systems [7, 14]. Telematics of transport allows for better transport management. The basic tasks carried out by transport telematics systems are, among others:

- increasing road safety,
- optimization of transport costs,
- increasing road capacity,
- reducing the negative effects of road transport on the natural environment.

By using transport telematics it is possible to collect, analyse and process information that can enable better management of the transport process [6]. This applies to both a given section of the road as well as the area supervised by the telematics system. Another element is the use of tools restricting the mobility of motor vehicles in congested agglomerations. One of the elements of transport policy, especially in urban areas, is the implementation of tasks related to the reduction of individual road transport, which is also related to traffic safety. Urban development is possible due to the reversal of the trend associated with the movement of private vehicles in their centers. Solutions dedicated to public transport, including priority transport systems or additional buses lanes, make getting around by urban public transport more convenient and faster [14]. Telematics in public transport systems is also a source of precise passenger information, which contributes to its attractiveness. This allows passengers to plan their trip, especially in cities with different means of transport. The example of

J. Mikulski (Ed.): TST 2019, CCIS 1049, pp. 202–215, 2019.
https://doi.org/10.1007/978-3-030-27547-1_16

such solution is the Dynamic Passenger Information System (SDIP – in PL), which has been operated in the city of Radom (Poland) since 2014. Authors of the paper made a description of the main elements of the system was made. Ultimately, the presented system will be an element of urban ITS.

The paper also presents the concept of a system allowing faster passage through a selected intersection of privileged vehicles (e.g. fire brigade, ambulance). Creation of the so-called - green line - allows EV to shorten the drive time through the intersection and thus faster to reach to the place of the event or to people in need of help. The proposed concept is a solution dedicated to local small intersections with traffic lights and can be an alternative to systems included in the ITS or V2I solutions. One of the tools which give the opportunity to analyze the impact of new solutions on transport-related indicators, including safety or better organization of vehicle traffic is modelling. The systems' modelling allows getting approximate results already at the design level. Thanks to modeling, it is possible to analyze many scenarios of events. As a modeling tool, dedicated software [1] is used, or e.g. universal methods based on queue theory [9] or Petri networks [3]. In the paper, models based on Markov processes were proposed for analysis [2]. The proposed models reflect working a intersection with traffic light in relation to the passage of a privilege vehicle by the intersection. Authors proposed in the paper an analysis including an additional system enabling the privileged vehicle to passage the intersection with traffic light faster using the so-called green line (green light).

2   Telematics in Management of Public City Transport

Modern public transport management systems allow to obtain detailed information about the vehicle, its location on the route or the time of travel from the bus stop to the bus stop. The use of telematics systems in such solutions gives detailed information to the infrastructure manager, to the owner of the transport company and to the driver. On-line information for the bus driver allows him to adjust the speed of vehicle so that the bus travel time could be compatible with assumed passage time from one stop to the next one. An example of an urban telematics system that may comprehensively manages public transport is the Dynamic Passenger Information System launched in 2014 in Radom (Poland).

The Dynamic Passenger Information System is an example of a transport telematics system that uses modules of wireless terrestrial data transmission, a computer information processing system and a satellite GPS system. Each bus has an on-board computer, a GSM transmission module and a GPS location module. Based on the data received from the satellite, the on-board computer of the bus transmits data about the location of the vehicle to the main server. The main server is located in the building of the road infrastructure manager - City Road Authorities and Communication. The server room consists of computers:

– database and application computers,
– TMC server computers (Traffic Monitoring Center) and on-line services.

The basic scheme of Dynamic Passenger Information System is shown in Fig. 1.

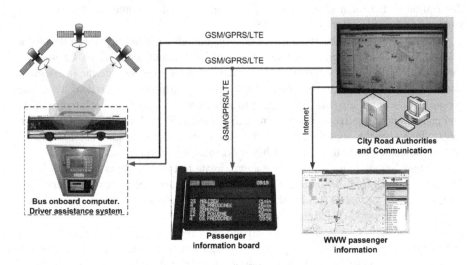

Fig. 1. Basic functionality scheme of the SDIP [own study]

The data sent by the computer installed in the bus allows to determine the position of the bus on the route and determine the position relative to the bus stop. Ultimately, the data sent from the bus can be used by the urban ITS system, thanks to which it will be possible to set the priorities of the bus crossing through the intersection. The main server has connectivity with information boards located at stops. Each information board has a built-in computer and a GSM module. Data sent by the server to the information board at the bus stop allow for display information regarding the actual arrival time of the bus to the bus stop. Figure 2 shows an example screen from the SDIP system [2].

In the case of a transmission or server failure, data displayed on the information board on the stop are downloaded from the inside computer memory. In this case theoretically assumed bus arrival times are displayed. The transmission modules (GSM modules) installed in the information boards works in every GSM network on each range. Data to the system is sent and updated every 30 s. In the event of problems on the road section, the operator can send messages which will be displayed on the bus driver's computer, [2].

The software installed on the server also allows to create various statistics. One of them is the possibility to view the punctuality of bus arrivals at any stop. Table 1 presents an example of a combination for the selected bus stop (1905 Roku/Kościuszki street in Radom), analysis over in period time from 10.00 to 11.00.

The data presented in the Table 1 shows that the average bus delay is 92 s. One of the elements of the system is also passenger access to an interactive map of bus connections. Access of the passengers to the data is possible via a website or through a

a)

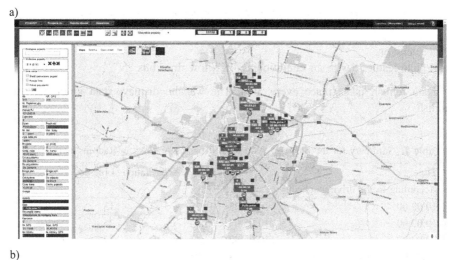

b)

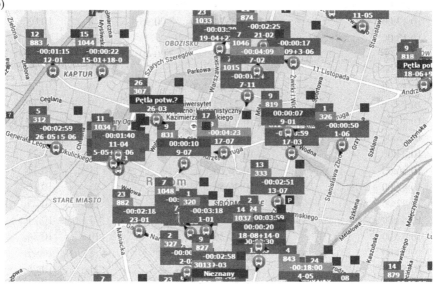

Fig. 2. Printscreens of SDIP [own study]

mobile application. An exemplary preview is shown in Fig. 3. The application has a search mode:

– by route number,
– by bus stop name,
– by street name.

The direct preview allows to read such information as:

- delay,
- acceleration,
- vehicle features: with air conditioning "K", low-floor bus "N".

Data refresh takes place every 30 s. The website displays data in Polish and English.

Table 1. Summary for the bus stop 1905 Roku/Kościuszki street in Radom [own study]

Time		Delay	Acceleration	Line no.	Course
According to the driving schedule	Departure				
10:02:00	10:03:28	01:28	–	13	09:45
10:02:00	10:05:04	03:04	–	25	09:36
10:03:00	10:06:32	03:32	–	7	09:51
10:06:00	10:06:04	00:04	–	10	09:50
10:13:00	10:12:24	–	00:36	8	10:03
10:13:00	10:15:40	02:40	–	7	10:01
10:14:00	10:13:20	–	00:40	14	09:54
10:16:00	10:16:28	00:28	–	11	09:57
10:22:00	10:22:48	00:48	–	13	10:08
10:23:00	10:25:08	02:08	–	7	10:11
10:26:00	10:25:52	–	00:08	14	10:06
10:33:00	10:35:32	02:32	–	7	10:21
10:33:00	10:34:38	01:38	–	8	10:21
10:36:00	10:38:16	02:16	–	11	10:17
10:42:00	10:46:58	04:58	–	25	10:16
10:42:00	10:42:08	00:08	–	13	10:25
10:43:00	10:43:26	00:26	–	7	10:31
10:52:00	10:52:26	00:26	–	10	10:36
10:53:00	10:54:40	01:40	–	8	10:43
10:53:00	10:53:10	00:10	–	21	10:46
10:53:00	10:55:32	02:32	–	7	10:41
10:54:00	10:54:38	00:38	–	14	10:34
10:56:00	10:59:36	03:36	–	11	10:37

Fig. 3. Window of the interactive bus connection map [13]

3   The Concept of Priority System for Emergency Vehicles

In the event of an accident requiring the participation of emergency services (fire brigade, ambulance, police), it is necessary to allow fast arrival of emergency vehicles. Short arrival time is a priority task in such situations. According to the Polish Journal of Laws [8], a privileged vehicle is a vehicle which sends light signals in the form of blue flashing lights and at the same time tone signals with variable pitch, driving with dipped beams or main-beam headlights on. If there is such a vehicle other vehicle drivers are obliged to facilitate his passage. Unfortunately, there are situations where the number of vehicles on a given stretch of road or intersection is so large that it prevents the free movement of a privileged vehicle. Currently, there are already solutions on how to enable faster passage through the intersection of privileged vehicles. Most often, these solutions are a combination of the urban ITS or V2I infrastructure and telematics solutions allowing to determine the position of the privileged vehicle in relation to the intersection, [1, 4]. Such solutions are usually an automatic traffic light switching systems for emergency vehicles in relation to the position on the road and distance to the intersection. However, each intersection should be approached individually. Analyzes carried out, in particular the time of crossing through the intersection during the communication summit or the number of vehicles within an hour, allow to determine whether the installation of the proposed systems and solutions allowing for the passage of emergency vehicles is justified.

As a research object, the authors proposed a crossing with traffic lights of Malczewskiego and Wernera streets in Radom (Poland). The traffic light simplified scheme at the intersection of Wernera, Malczewskiego, Kelles Krauza and view of the intersection are shown in Fig. 4a and b.

a)

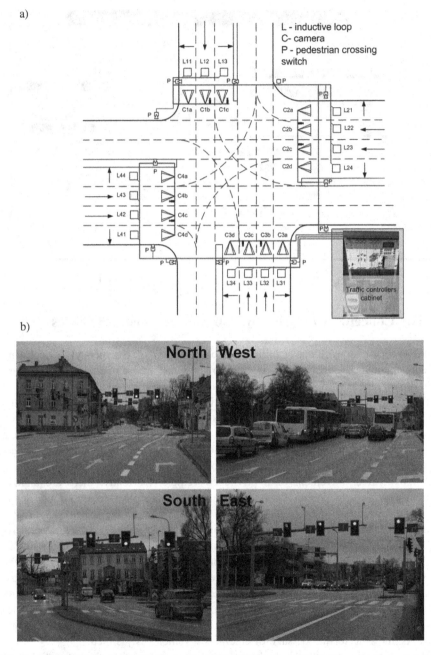

b)

Fig. 4. (a) traffic light plan at the intersection of Malczewskiego/Kelles Krauza streets, (b) view of the intersection [own study]

The intersection has been equipped with acyclic signaling, where the operation of the system is entirely dependent on signals received from motion detectors. Traffic lights work as accommodative characterized by a sequence of phases depending on the intensity of vehicle traffic at a given moment. Inductive vehicle presence detectors and video detection cameras have been located at each entering of the intersection. The control of traffic lights is carried out with MSR Traffic controllers [10].

For emergency vehicles - fire brigade, ambulance - having their bases in the center of Radom, the analyzed intersection is the first main on the route toward north direction of the city. The analyzed intersection, especially during rush hour, is a problem for the free passage of privileged vehicles. The authors of the study [5] have measured the time needed to passage a privileged vehicle through the analyzed intersection. The analysis of times was made during congestion hours, in two directions - north and south, and on different days. The results of the analysis are presented in the Table 2, [5]. The carried out measurements show that the time of passage by a privileged vehicle in the case of green light is shorter to 20% in relation to the passage time at a red light, [5]. If the red signal is displayed at the intersection, the privileged vehicle must slow down, sometimes stop and go only when the driver of the vehicle considers it safe to cross the intersection. Unfortunately, passing through several such intersections may finally extend the arrival time, e.g. to the injured. A way to partially solve this problem is the use of telematics solutions, which in the event of problems with passing through the intersection will allow appropriate switching of traffic lights creating the so-called - green line. Therefore, the authors propose a solution that allows the privileged vehicle to pass together with other road users, using the permission for passage - green light.

Table 2. The results of measurements of passage time through the intersection [5]

Towards north								
	11.03.15r (08:00–09:00)	11.03.15r (15:00–16:00)	09.04.15r (08:00–09:00)	09.04.15r (15:00–16:00)	05.05.15r (08:00–09:00)	05.05.15r (15:00–16:00)	09.06.15r (08:00–09:00)	09.06.15r (15:00-16:00)
Red light	18 s	20 s	17 s	22 s	16 s	19 s	20 s	21 s
Green light	14 s	17 s	12 s	18 s	11 s	16 s	15 s	17 s
Towards south								
Red light	20 s	19 s	18 s	20 s	21 s	18 s	22 s	20 s
Green light	15 s	16 s	13 s	14 s	15 s	12 s	16 s	15 s

The authors assumed that there is not always a need to intervene in the existing cycle of changes in traffic lights at the analyzed intersection. During the green light for the south-north direction, the privileged vehicle overcomes the intersection in time about 10 s. Therefore, the proposed concept boils down to the independent activation of a change in the signaling cycle by the driver of a privileged vehicle, setting the green line, especially when the driver considers such a change necessary. As it results from the tests carried out (Table 2), the maximum time required for a passage of vehicle was 22 s, therefore the authors proposed the duration of the mode - green line - at about time 20 s. Figure 5 shows a simplified algorithm of system operation.

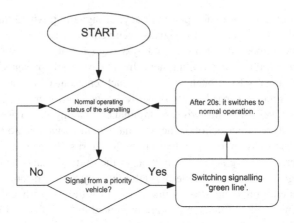

Fig. 5. Simplified operation algorithm [own study]

In the presented concept, the authors assumed that the priority for a privileged vehicle is to leave the city center as soon as possible and go to the place of the incident. To implement the system, the authors proposed modules: ATmega128 (L) microcontroller, wireless module with a range of up to 1 km. The prototype of the device was presented in [11]. At the current stage of work, modifying the prototype may allow implement it as a system for the analyzed intersection.

4 Models of Systems

One of the elements of the analysis of the proposed solutions is the analysis of models reflecting the operation of the system, [2, 3]. From among the various available tools and methods of analysis, the authors proposed a mathematical analysis based on Markov processes. The first of the proposed models reflects the work of traffic lights with automatic notification of the upcoming emergency vehicle. The model for the system with priority passage for the privileged vehicle is shown in Fig. 6.

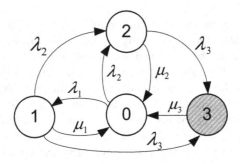

Fig. 6. Model for the system with the priority [own study]

In the model shown in Fig. 6, we can distinguish:

- State 0 – the status of the normal operation of the signaling, the system works, the state of waiting for vehicles,
- State 1 – vehicles appears, standard vehicles service by the system,
- State 2 – appears priority vehicle, the system service the emergency vehicle,
- State 3 – failure of the control system, vehicles are moving in accordance with traffic law.

The model uses the following designations:

- λ - intensity of transition to the state,
- μ - the inverse of the return time from the state.

State 3 in the model is an undesirable state. Despite the failure to the system in state 3, the vehicles move in accordance with the applicable regulations, but depending on the traffic it may generate an extended passage time through the intersection. The failure intensity of the control module was assumed at the level of typical failure to electronic components. For the presented model (Fig. 6), we can write the equations:

$$\begin{cases} \frac{dP_0(t)}{t} = -(\lambda_1 + \lambda_2) \cdot P_0(t) + \mu_1 \cdot P_1(t) + \mu_2 \cdot P_2(t) + \mu_3 \cdot P_3(t) \\ \frac{dP_1(t)}{t} = \lambda_2 \cdot P_0(t) - \mu_1 \cdot P_1(t) - \mu_4 \cdot P_1(t) - \lambda_3 \cdot P_1(t) \\ \frac{dP_2(t)}{t} = \lambda_2 \cdot P_0(t) - \mu_2 \cdot P_2(t) + \mu_4 \cdot P_1(t) - \lambda_3 \cdot P_2(t) \\ \frac{dP_3(t)}{t} = -\mu_3 \cdot P_3(t) + \lambda_3(P_2(t) + P_3(t)) \end{cases} \quad (1)$$

The limit value of the probability of being in state 3 estimated on the symbolic formulas equal:

$$P_3(t)_{t\to\infty} = \frac{\lambda_3(\mu_2\lambda_1 + \mu_1\lambda_2 + (\lambda_1 + \lambda_2)(\lambda_2 + \lambda_3))}{\mu_1(\mu_2\mu_3 + \lambda_2\lambda_3 + \mu_3(\lambda_2 + \lambda_3)) + \mu_2(\lambda_1\lambda_3 + \mu_3(\lambda_1 + \lambda_2 + \lambda_3)) + (\lambda_2 + \lambda_3)((\lambda_1 + \lambda_2)\lambda_3 + \mu_3(\lambda_1 + \lambda_2 + \lambda_3))} \quad (2)$$

Assuming:

- traffic at the intersection of 1,500 vehicles per hour,
- service of all arriving vehicles,
- arrival of a privileged vehicle in the amount of four per hour,
- intensity of system failure at the level 1E-04,
- time of repairing the traffic light system after a failure – 5 per hour,

system availability equal:

$$A = 1 - P_3(t)_{t\to\infty} = 0,995 \quad (3)$$

For the model proposed in Fig. 6, the greatest impact on the accessibility value is the intensity of failure the traffic light system and the time of return to full functionality. The model shown in Fig. 7 is an analysis of the passage of a privileged vehicle through the intersection with traffic lights, where the passage times are taken into account in red and green light (data included in Table 2).

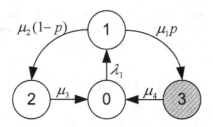

Fig. 7. System model for data from Table 2 [own study]

In the model shown in Fig. 7, we can distinguish:

- State 0 – normal operation of the signaling,
- State 1 – a privileged vehicle appeared,
- State 2 – green light, the vehicle passage faster,
- State 3 – red light, difficulties in passing.

For the presented model (Fig. 7), we can write the equations:

$$
\begin{cases}
\frac{dP_0(t)}{t} = -\lambda_1 \cdot P_0(t) + \mu_4 \cdot P_3(t) + \mu_3 \cdot P_2(t) \\
\frac{dP_1(t)}{t} = \lambda_1 \cdot P_0(t) - \mu_1 \cdot p \cdot P_1(t) - \mu_2 \cdot (1-p)P_1(t) \\
\frac{dP_2(t)}{t} = \mu_2 \cdot (1-p)P_1(t) - \mu_3 \cdot P_2(t) \\
\frac{dP_3(t)}{t} = -\mu_4 \cdot P_3(t) + \mu_1 \cdot p \cdot P_1(t)
\end{cases}
\tag{4}
$$

Solving the Eq. (4) for the model from Fig. 7, the limit value of probability of finding oneself in state 3 was calculated:

$$
P_3(t)_{t\to\infty} = \frac{\mu_1\mu_3\lambda_1}{\mu_1\mu_3(\mu_4+\lambda_1)+\mu_4(\mu_3\lambda_1+\mu_2(\mu_3+\lambda_1))}
\tag{5}
$$

Assuming:

- λ_1_4 privileged vehicles per hour,
- μ_1 – the inverse of the vehicle's passing time on green light, $t_1 = 10$ s.,
- μ_2 – the inverse of the vehicle's passing time at a red light, $t_1 = 20$ s.,
- μ_3, μ_4 – time to return to normal working condition, $t_3 = 1$ min,
- p – the probability of the vehicle appearing at a red light, $p = 0.5$,

the calculated value of availability equal:

$$
A = 1 - P_3(t)_{t\to\infty} = 0,866771
\tag{6}
$$

The model shown in Fig. 7 has been supplemented with an additional state related to the possibility of switching the signaling by the privileged vehicle driver, as shown in Fig. 8.

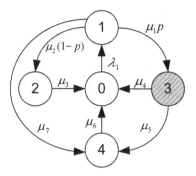

Fig. 8. The model from Fig. 7 supplemented with an additional state [own study]

For the presented model (Fig. 8), we can write the equations:

$$\begin{cases} \frac{dP_0(t)}{t} = -\lambda_1 \cdot P_0(t) + \mu_4 \cdot P_3(t) + \mu_3 \cdot P_2(t) + \mu_6 \cdot P_4(t) \\ \frac{dP_1(t)}{t} = \lambda_1 \cdot P_0(t) - \mu_1 \cdot p \cdot P_1(t) - \mu_2 \cdot (1-p)P_1(t) - \mu_7 \cdot P_1(t) \\ \frac{dP_2(t)}{t} = \mu_2 \cdot (1-p)P_1(t) - \mu_3 \cdot P_2(t) \\ \frac{dP_3(t)}{t} = -\mu_4 \cdot P_3(t) + \mu_1 \cdot p \cdot P_1(t) - \mu_5 \cdot P_3(t) \\ \frac{dP_4(t)}{t} = \mu_5 \cdot P_3(t) + \mu_7 \cdot P_1(t) - \mu_6 \cdot P_4(t) \end{cases} \qquad (7)$$

In this model, state 4 is additionally introduced, which is the switching state of the signaling. The vehicle can appears - state 1 - and passaged on green light or appear during a cycle of red light - state 3. In case of red light the driver can switch the signaling - establishing a green line for 20 s. - state 4. The proposed model corresponds to the intersection shown in Fig. 3. Solving the system of Eq. (7) for the model from Fig. 8, the limit value of the probability of finding oneself in state 3 equal:

$$P_3(t)_{t\to\infty} = \frac{p\mu_1\mu_3\mu_6\lambda_1}{(p(-\mu_2(\mu_4+\mu_5)\mu_6(\mu_3+\lambda_1) + \mu_1\mu_3(\mu_1\mu_6 + \mu_6\lambda_1 + (\mu_6+\lambda_1))) (\mu_4+\mu_5)(\mu_2\mu_6(\mu_3+\lambda_1) + \mu_3(\mu_7\lambda_1 + \mu_6(\mu_7+\lambda_1))))}$$

$$(8)$$

Assuming parameters as for the model from Fig. 7 and:

- μ_5 – the inverse of the transition time to state 4, $t_5 = 2$ s.,
- μ_6 – the inverse of the return time to the "0" state, $t_6 = 10$ s.,
- μ_7 – the inverse switching time to provide additional green light, $t_7 = 2$ s.,

the calculated value of availability equal:

$$A = 1 - P_3(t)_{t\to\infty} = 0,8908 \qquad (9)$$

Figure 9 is a graph showing the dependence of the probability p of vehicle appearance at red light on the function of availability of the model from Figs. 7 and 8

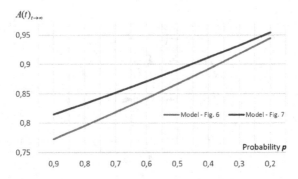

Fig. 9. Dependence A(p) for models from Figs. 7 and 8 [own study]

The graph presented in Fig. 9 shows that the use of an additional system improves the efficiency of passing through the intersection, especially when the probability of the priority vehicle appearing in the red light cycle increases.

5 Conclusion

Contemporary urban road infrastructure should ensure a safe and continuous transport process. Today, congestion is a big problem, which is a problem not only for large urban agglomerations but also for smaller cities. The problem of congested roads concerns both main roads and smaller roads, sometimes small residential roads. Current road infrastructure does not fulfill its functions in many places. The increase in the wealth of the society and the related increase in the number of vehicles means that the state of congestion in cities is increasing. The transport telematics systems are a tool to limit road paralysis. Telematics of transport, as a tool, allows for better control of vehicle traffic, it also gives the possibility of dynamic and adaptive traffic management. The greatest impact on the creation of road congestion has insufficient capacity of road infrastructure. Therefore, another tool that helps reduce this problem is public transport. The work presents an exemplary system that allows full control of the passenger transport process. Such solutions make public transport an attractive and punctual means of urban transport. It should be emphasized that in many cities public transport is free, which is an additional argument for leaving a private vehicle at home. The best example is Luxembourg, which is set to become the first country in the world with free, not only city public transport, but all its public transport [12].

The work also presents the concept of a local system allowing faster passage of a privileged vehicle through the intersection. A mathematical apparatus in the form of Markov processes was proposed for the analysis. The analysis confirmed the rightness of using such solutions.

References

1. Nellore, K., Hancke, G.P.: Traffic management for emergency vehicle priority based on visual sensing. Sensors **16**(11), 1892 (2016)
2. Perzyński, T.: Selected telematic systems in safety and management in land and inland transport. Monographs Series, no. 201. Publishing House Kazimierz Pulaski University of Technology and Humanities in Radom, Radom (2016)
3. Yi-Sheng, H., Jang-Yi, S., Jiliang, L.: A traffic signal control policy for emergency vehicles preemption using timed petri nets. IFAC-Pap. Online **48**(3), 2183–2188 (2015). ISSN 2405-8963
4. Wang, Y., et al.: Design and implementation of an emergency vehicle signal preemption system based on cooperative vehicle-infrastructure technology. Adv. Mech. Eng. **5**, 1–10 (2013). https://doi.org/10.1155/2013/834976
5. Winiarski, M., Chrzan, M.: The strategy paving the way for passing emergency vehicle. Autobusy 6/2016, pp. 465-457 (PL)
6. Siergiejczyk, M., Paś, J., Rosiński, A.: Evaluation of safety of highway CCTV system's maintenance process. In: Mikulski, J. (ed.) TST 2014. CCIS, vol. 471, pp. 69–79. Springer, Heidelberg (2014). https://doi.org/10.1007/978-3-662-45317-9_8
7. Grochowski, A.: Architektura FRAME w projektach ITS Opis metodyki opracowania architektury ITS. Centrum Unijnych Projektów Transportowych pl. Europejski 2, 00-844 Warszawa (2017)
8. Journal of Laws: Dz.U. 1997 Nr 98 poz. 602, Art. 2, pkt. 38
9. Wei, H., et al.: Signal priority control for emergency vehicle operation. In: 2nd International Conference on Models and Technologies for Intelligent Transportation Systems, Leuven, Belgium, 22–24 June 2011
10. Project: RAD EX E SE 9_401 00 – MZDiK Radom
11. Perzyński, T., Lewiński, A.: The influence of new telematics solutions on the improvement the driving safety in road transport. In: Mikulski, J. (ed.) TST 2018. CCIS, vol. 897, pp. 101–114. Springer, Cham (2018). https://doi.org/10.1007/978-3-319-97955-7_7
12. https://www.theguardian.com/world/2018/dec/05/luxembourg-to-become-first-country-to-make-all-public-transport-free. Accessed 1 January 2019
13. http://rkm.mzdik.radom.pl/Default.aspx?lang=PL. Accessed 1 January 2019
14. Mikulski, J.: The possibility of using telematics in urban transportation. In: Mikulski, J. (ed.) TST 2011. CCIS, vol. 239, pp. 54–69. Springer, Heidelberg (2011). https://doi.org/10.1007/978-3-642-24660-9_7

System for Planning and Monitoring Driving Strategy

Maciej Gwiżdż and Wojciech Skarka[✉]

Silesian University of Technology, Konarskiego 18A, Gliwice, Poland
maciej.gwizdz1994@gmail.com, wojciech.skarka@polsl.pl

Abstract. The article presents a computer application for planning and monitoring the driving strategy of an energy-saving vehicles. The system is an element of the Monitoring Center of the energy-efficient vehicle and is used by the team participating in competitions of energy-efficient vehicles. The application has a number of functions that allow to define any track profiles and visualize pre-set control data enabling easy tracking of the driver's driving strategy in relation to the planned one. The description of the whole system and its operation is presented in the context of the entire telematics system of the vehicle. The system is used in real time to supervise the implementation of the previously calculated strategy, but it can be used with a strategy that is calculated in real time while driving. In addition, the application is also used to analyze various aspects of already completed racing and test rides, thanks to the visualization functions of any tracks and recorded telemetry data from races, it allows easy analysis of track data after the race and their comparison with strategies obtained in various rides and data from computer simulations. The results of these analyzes are used to correct planned driving strategies and to adjust vehicle design and settings.

Keywords: Driving strategy · Monitoring · Computer application · Energy efficient vehicle

1 Introduction

The reduction of energy consumption used to power a moving vehicle is done by optimizing the design of the vehicle during the design and adjusting the vehicle settings as well as by choosing the appropriate driving strategy. Especially the last issue brings quite big effects when the vehicle route is known. In Shell Eco-marathon competitions, energy-efficient vehicles drive along a well-known route and our special attention is paid to choosing the right driving strategy and research related to this issue becomes the main research tasks carried out by the teams involved. Simulation models or specially dedicated software for simulation purposes are used for design purposes as well as for vehicle development [1, 4, 8, 13]. The selection of our case strategy takes place through time-consuming simulation calculations [13], [18, 19] before the races for the conditions of the given route and the current weather conditions. They are implemented using the vehicle simulation model and route as well as race conditions. It is true that there are real-time driving optimization methods, but they do not give such

© Springer Nature Switzerland AG 2019
J. Mikulski (Ed.): TST 2019, CCIS 1049, pp. 216–229, 2019.
https://doi.org/10.1007/978-3-030-27547-1_17

good results as the aforementioned offline optimization calculations in this case. The Smart Power team [12] since their first competitions in Shell Eco-marathon [17] (SEM) races optimizes the racing vehicle driving strategy [13, 19] especially for the last vehicle *Hydro*GENIUS (Fig. 1) which is UrbanConcept Category vehicle with Hydrogen Fuel Cell Stack used as promising electric energy source [20]. During the race it is necessary to oversee this driving strategy and verify its implementation. It is accomplished by the center supervising the work of the race driver and driving parameters in relation to the calculated strategy. So far monitoring has been implemented through:

- familiarizing the driver with the strategy and earlier training of the driver's implementation of this strategy,
- supervising driving parameters by the monitoring center, identifying deviations from this strategy and instructing the driver to alter the driving corrections,
- monitoring driving parameters through the use of appropriate software to identify deviations from the strategy in a quantitative manner [2]
- recording driving parameters and analyzing these results by a team of strategists on a regular basis during the race and between subsequent races

Fig. 1. A vehicle of the UrbanConcept category of the Smart Power team taking part in the Shell Eco-marathon competition [own study]

In particular, the latter method brought a lot of benefits [1, 4, 13] and had a decisive impact on the quality of strategy implementation. Using the experience of previous years of starts, it was decided to develop new modular and developmental software that will allow to easily and quickly supervise driving during a race and implement driving strategies. The software should enable easy development and in particular integration with the dynamic driving strategy implementation system, which is planned to be developed in future years. In addition to work related to vehicle optimization and driving strategies, Smart Power team conducts a number of works related to, among others, building support and driver systems and driving automation [6, 7], using generative modeling to automate the design process.

2   Overview of Vehicle Monitoring Systems

Systems for monitoring vehicle motion parameters and driving strategies used for sports purposes, especially those highly specialized, are developed or adjusted only for the objectives and characteristics of the team or vehicle and are not widely available. However, it is widely common to use systems that monitor vehicle operational parameters for commercial purposes, they are primarily used to manage a fleet of vehicles.

The SAT-DOG [3] system is an example of a vehicle monitoring system. It is a system that collects data on company servers, which are secured through client authentication based on a special encryption. The SAT-DOG device enables monitoring the current location of the vehicle based on the GPS system and much technical information using sensors, circuit breakers, measuring probes and alarm systems. The Map Center produced by the Polish company E-Map is used to visualize the location of vehicles.

The system also allows fuel measurement. Additionally, it allows to control the amount of fuel in the tank by measuring the fuel from the float of the measuring system in the vehicle's tank. A very accurate measurement is possible if an additional fuel probe in the tank is installed. Thanks to this, it is possible to analyse the average fuel consumption.

Another example of vehicle monitoring systems is the Globtrak system [9] with monitoring and system functions.

Monitoring functions: Indications available from the vehicle's CAN, Fuel level, Opening/closing the door, Driver identification, Private ride, Using air conditioning.

System functions: Summary of fuel consumption in any time interval, Archiving routes and data from monitored functions, Implementation of the route plan, Reporting to a spreadsheet or text file.

The presentation of data read from vehicles also applies to applications for mobile devices. An example of such an application is DashCommand. It reads the data through the vehicle diagnostic connector. It allows tracking selected vehicle parameters. The system allows the analysis of vehicle diagnostic data in real time, thanks to the connection to the OBD II module (ELM 327) via Wi-Fi or Bluetooth.

The examples of parameters that can be observed include:

Speed, Engine speed, Fuel consumption data, Acceleration, Torque, Display of temperature sensors, Display of pressure sensors, Location, Number of stops, Driving time.

Most of the available systems for monitoring vehicles are based on the GPS (Global Positioning System) system - satellite navigation system for detecting position on the map.

In addition to the GPS system, various types of sensors installed in vehicles and CAN (Controller Area Network) information technology are also used. It is a two-wire bus, where the transmission takes place in real time at speeds up to 1 Mb/s. It enables communication between electronic modules.

3 Supporting Vehicle Driving Strategies

So far, the strategy has been calculated on the basis of complex calculations of optimization simulation carried out with MBDO (Model Based Design and Optimization) techniques [13, 18], using a simulation model built in the Matlab/Simulink software. The simulation model created for this purpose included:

Simulation model of the vehicle itself reflecting the equations of moving vehicle motion, aerodynamic characteristics, characteristics of subsystems affecting driving and energy consumption, i.e. engine, drive system, drive transmission system, track simulation model, its geometrical configuration and type of surface, external conditions, weather and weather conditions.

Simulation calculations led to obtaining a driving strategy which included mainly the speed profile and corresponding moments of driving the drive system as a function of the position on the track. In addition, the strategy was directly verified during test drives on the track and tuned directly before the race.

Implementation of the strategy is a task carried out by the driver and the control center and is based on experience, learning the driver's strategy and its supervision and correction by the persons supervising the ride. It is extremely difficult because the rides are held in racing conditions and the main factors disrupting the strategy implementation process are other racing vehicles moving on the track. In the peak moments there is quite a lot of traffic on the track and the attention of the driver must focus on avoiding collisions and at the same time on implementation of the strategy. In addition, there are problems in updating the current position and there is a delay in responding to the supervision center. Based on the experience of the supervision center and drivers and the application of the previous software and used good practices, assumptions and concepts of the currently implemented application supporting the work of the strategists' center were developed. So far, during the competition, the crew set some checkpoints to optimize the travel time on which the team members were. They communicated using walkie-talkies with a strategist, announcing that the vehicle is at a given control point. The strategist checked the current time on the stopwatch and wrote it down on a piece of paper, and then analyzed it. The developed application was to include a system in which this process would be automated.

3.1 The Impact of Driving Strategies on Fuel Consumption

During the design process, the built simulation model was used to optimize the design features [13]. Under operating conditions, the model was used to determine the settings of the vehicle, e.g. the transmission of the main transmission and the development of the driving strategy [18]. Doubts as to the rationale of determining the driving strategy and its impact on the result of the race were examined during the first simulation calculations where a comparison between the strategy calculation results obtained from the simulation model and the strategy selected based on experience and principles of energy-efficient driving was made [19]. Additionally, the same verification was carried out once more while racing. Because the number of racing trials is significantly limited, in practice, verification has been made only once. The results obtained by simulation calculations were significantly better than those obtained during rides and simulations based on the driver's experience and skills. In extreme cases, the differences between the optimal strategy results from the simulation model were twice as good. Typically, the results of optimization gave a few-dozen percent improvement in results obtained in relation to the strategy invented by the driver [19].

3.2   Assumption and Concept of the Application

The main assumptions for the application resulted from the needs of the driving strategy verification center. The assumptions adopted for creating the application included:

- Application of the software during the race to the current analysis and monitoring and then after the race to analyze the saved data and compare it with simulation data
- Simple interface for working during the race
- Complex comparative analyzes conducted after the race
- Visualization of driving during the race in graphic mode on the track model based on data transmitted online from the vehicle via the telematics system
- Defining checkpoints allowing verification of positions based on real observations
- Bidirectional data transmission
- Access to detailed data in various comparison modes, e.g. current deviation from the planned strategy
- Monitoring technical data and parameters of the operation of the sub-assemblies
- Implementation of corrections and recommendations for the driver directly by the strategy based on the observation of results
- Possibility of extending the application in particular by integrating the module to automatically propose corrective actions for the current driving mode with the possibility of automatic feeding of vehicle control signals

Based on these general assumptions, the following detailed technical requirements were defined and application concepts were proposed.

Data to be available in period of time: Speed, Power (current, voltage), Detailed assumptions:

- Frequency of data downloading - 1 s
- The method of representation of data collection - a graph
- Type of data downloaded - floating point numbers (float/double)
- Type of data project - natural numbers (int)
- Move data on the chart for available reading it in real time
- Possible changes in the size of the chart
- Offering the current state of the chart, as image and csv file

Assumptions about the location of the vehicle on the map:

- The position of the vehicle on the track by coordinates x, y
- Representation method - map
- Map refresh rate - 1 s

In the assumptions of the race, it is required to drive a certain number of laps in a given time. Therefore, it is necessary to select a few checkpoints on the map and define for them the desired average speed with which the car should move. If the actual average speed is too low, we should get a message to make the driver speed up, whereas if the speed is too high, let the driver release it.

An additional facilitation will be the timing difference from the set average value at a given control point. In the transmission, when the driver, exceeding the control point, is late by 5 s, we will receive a message of +5 s, while if it is 5 s late for the given average speed we will receive a message of −5 s.

Current state of vehicle sensors allows to measure the following data:

Velocity, Current, Voltage, Vehicle position.

In the future it is planned to have the following measuring parameters:

Hydrogen consumption measurement, Cell temperature, Fan speed.

The speed measurement is carried out by means of a magnetic encoder mounted on the wheel. The present measurement is carried out thanks to a special measuring system with the use of current measurement sensors connected directly to the electrical system. The voltage measurement was realized on the principle of a simple voltage divider.

At present, in each car the GPS module is assembled by the organizers of the competition. Nevertheless, the plans are to implement our own module enabling tracking of the current position of the vehicle.

Hydrogen consumption measurement will be possible due to the use of a flow sensor. This sensor is now available and requires integration with the current system.

There are plans to add the ability to measure the temperature of the hydrogen cell and control the speed of the fans and to supply air to the cell in order to reduce energy consumption and at the same time prevent the cell from overheating. The temperature will be read by the Arduino UNO using the NTC 110 thermistor, and the fans will be controlled by the PWM signal.

The programming language that was used to create the application was C++.

In order to write a window application monitoring the vehicle's driving, it was necessary to use a library that made it possible. For this task a set of portable Qt libraries was chosen. It is a programming tool dedicated to other languages for C++, which consists of classes for building GUI (Graphical User Interface). It allows for multi-threaded programming and file operations. It also enables network communication - sockets and HTTP, FTP and SSL protocols.

One of the ways to visualize data were graphs. They have been used both to display the received data in the time domain and to create a graphical representation of the race route [5]. For this purpose, it was necessary to use a library to create charts, It was decided to use the QCustomPlot library [14]. QCustomPlot is a widget dedicated to Qt [15, 16], written in C++ for the drawing and visualization of data. It is very well documented, allowing to create nice looking graphs and visualize data in real time.

4   Description of the Application

The main tab (Fig. 2) contains the most important data. It consists of the following elements: Graph monitoring, Track monitoring, Time monitoring, Laps time viewer, Checkpoints monitoring.

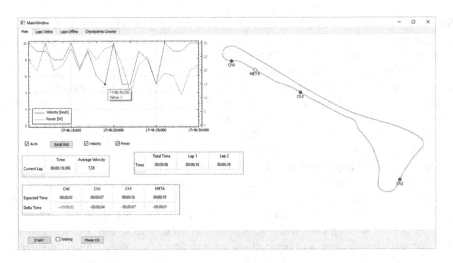

Fig. 2. Main window tab of the application [own study]

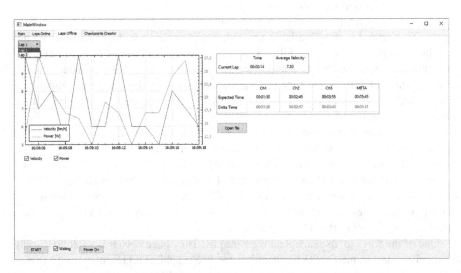

Fig. 3. Laps Offline tab of the application [own study]

The Laps Online and Laps Offline tabs (Fig. 3) are very similar to each other. The difference is that the Laps Online tab allows you to analyze data from the current race, while the Laps Offline tab allows you to analyze data from a race that has already ended. Laps Online includes a 'Save As' button that allows you to save the current data to a file, while Laps Offline has an 'Open File' button that allows you to read the data you want to analyze from a file.

This is a tab (Fig. 4) that allows you to create checkpoints on the trajectory that supervise the optimal vehicle speed.

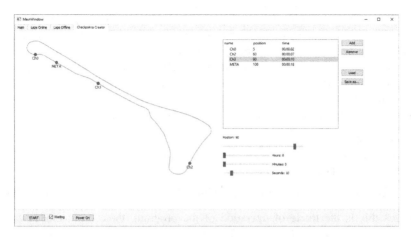

Fig. 4. Checkpoints creator tab of the application [own study]

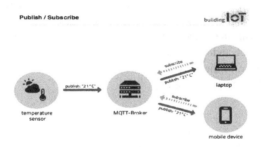

Fig. 5. Idea of operation in publisher/subscriber mode [own study]

For wireless data transfer, the MQTT protocol was selected [11]. MQTT (MQ Telemetry Transport) - is designed for devices that do not require high bandwidth. It ensures high reliability and energy saving, which in our case is a very big advantage. It was created by Andy Stan-Ford-Clark from IBM, and by Arlene Nipper of Arcom (now Eurotech) in 1999. MQTT uses the Facebook and Messenger protocol for data transmission.

MQTT works on the basis of the publisher/subscriber pattern (Fig. 5). It is based on the fact that each client connects to the broker. Clients can subscribe to a given topic and publish data on a given topic. When the client publishes information on the given topic, each of the clients who subscribes to this topic downloads this data.

5 Application Tests and Verification

In order to guarantee the correct operation of the application, a detailed test plan was prepared. It happens quite frequently, for this type of application, that tests are skipped or neglected, which contributes to the poor reception of the application. During the detailed tests described below, not only the obvious errors were corrected but the functionality of the application itself was also improved, adding better detailed solutions and the user-friendliness and transparency of the interface. The tests were carried out in an iterative manner for particular revised and improved software versions. The previously planned and systematic testing procedure enabled efficient and rapid software prototyping.

The test of the application has been divided into three parts:

– Manual test
– Data transmission test
– Test on actual race data

Configs.txt file (Fig. 6), was created for testing which contains the following data:

– state - this is the mode of operation of the program, three basic modes can be distinguished- Offline, Online and OnlineRandom mode, where Offline mode means offline simulation when generating random data, OnlineRandom is a test using random data that is sent over the network using the MQTT library whereas online mode is the intended operation of the application during the race, if the application connects to the broker and waits for the data provided to it
– simulatingDt - means the speed at which data should be generated during simulation in Offline or OnlineRandom mode
– brokerName - name of the broker
– topicName - the name of the topic

Fig. 6. Exemplary configs.txt file for the offline testing of the application [own study]

In order to carry out the tests, the Received Data tab (Fig. 7) has also been added, which displays the received data. This is very important for the Online test to see if we receive data and if received data is correct.

The manual test consisted in checking the correct operation of available program functions. The Offline mode was set in the configs.txt file during this test.

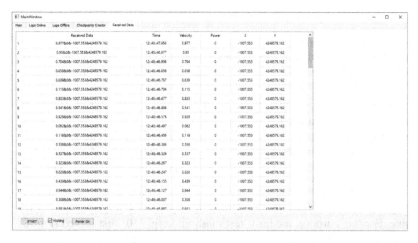

Fig. 7. Additional window tab – Received Data – displaying current received data for verification in test application process [own study]

The main tab test plan:

1. Pressing the START button - the graph should display a motion with a value between 0 and 1 and a constant power value of 0.
2. Pressing the Power On button - a vertical green line marking the beginning of a new lap should appear on the graph, speed and manual power take random values from the specified range.
3. In the Time Monitoring table, the current lap time and average speed can be observed.
4. On the route, a moving white and red point symbolizing the vehicle can be observed
5. We can also observe the Checkpoints Monitoring table and check if the time deviation appears in the table when the point symbolizing our vehicle crosses the green dot marking the control point in the table.
6. Vehicle reached finish line - the vehicle stops moving, a vertical red line should appear on the graph symbolizing the end of the lap, the counter calculating the current lap time is stopped, the total time and time of the last lap is added to the Laps Time Viewer table. The Waiting checkbox is cleared. Data from the last lap will be saved to the backup file.
7. To simulate the next round, select the Waiting check box and then press the Power On button again.

The plan to run the Laps Offline and Laps Online tabs test is as follow:

1. The vehicle shall be simulated for at least two laps.
2. In the Laps Online tab, check if there is a possibility of previewing the laps that have been passed.
3. Then save the file anywhere on the disk.
4. Next, go to the Laps Offline tab, load the previously saved file and check if it has been loaded correctly and whether we can observe the data.

Plan to test Checkpoints Creator tab is as follow:

1. Use the Add and Remove buttons to add a specific number of control points.
2. Then, using the slider responsible for the position of the point on the map, set the positions of all control points in such a way that the control point with the larger index is further away from the one with the lower index.
3. Using the sliders responsible for time, set the waiting times for all control points.
4. Then save our set checkpoints to give the disk.
5. We can also load any saved control points and modify them and save them again.
6. If we want to use other settings with the control points in the Main tab, we need to replace the file checkpoints.txt in the folder. Then turn the application off and on.

Conducting a data transmission test consists in setting in the file configs.txt the operating mode of the application on OnlineRandom and setting appropriate host and any topic. For this purpose, the host 'test.mosquitto.org' [10] first served (Fig. 8). The test was similar to the previous one, with the difference that the generated data was placed in the character string according to the following system: time & velocity & power & x & y, where: time - the current time taken from the computer, velocity, power, x - vehicle position from the GPS module at position x, y - vehicle position from the GPS module at position y.

Then, the data was sent thanks to the use of the MQTT protocol.

Unfortunately, during the test lap, sometimes there was a temporary loss of connection (Fig. 8). At the moment when communication was recovered, everything returned to normal and this did not cause any critical errors for the operation of the entire application.

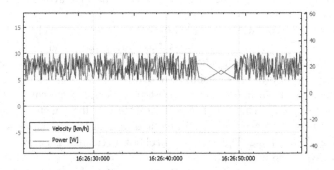

Fig. 8. Test result of the downloaded data using the 'test.mosquitto.org' host. Observed problem resulting from temporary loss of connection [own study]

This problem drew our attention to a certain situation. At the moment when the vehicle is just before the checkpoint and the connection is broken, then after a few seconds, when the car has passed the control point and will be behind its radius, the detection checkpoint will not be passed and we will not receive information about the time deviation for given control point. To avoid such a situation, it is necessary to introduce a security system that will cope with such an event. Another idea was to test another broker. A host named 'broker.hivemq.com' [11] has been subjected to the tests. The test result for this broker was very satisfactory.

As you can see in the figure above (Fig. 9), no disturbances occurred during the test. However, there is such a probability, so the safety button has been added to the application.

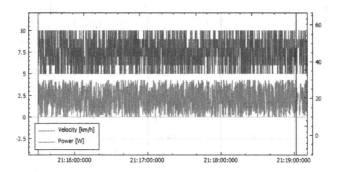

Fig. 9. Test result of the downloaded data using the 'broker.hivemq.com' host [own study]

In the Main tab, the REACH CHECKPOINT button has been added. It allows to manually pass the checkpoint. At the moment when there are disturbances, as a result of which the vehicle will pass through the checkpoint, when it is not noted, then the person supervising the crossing may manually mark the checkpoint.

6   Conclusion

The purpose of the work was to develop a usable version of the *Hydro*GENIUS vehicle monitoring system. This system is to be used as a driving control center during the route during the Shell Eco-marathon competition. It should enhance the construction of the most energy-efficient vehicle.

Its main task was to be real-time visualization of downloaded data and their interpretation by a strategist who communicates with the driver during the race. This would help a driver to be able to focus more on driving. In addition, it will allow the analysis of data that the driver would not be able to observe and analyze while driving.

The main assumptions have been fulfilled. Conducted detailed and systematic tests confirmed that the basic functions of the application work correctly and also enabled the improvement of the application. While testing the application, one of the brokers has a temporary loss of signal, which may cause the lack of calculated time deviation at the control point. For this purpose, a button has been added that allows to pass the checkpoint manually.

Additionally, the problem of different data format received by the GPS module and the points that form the route was encountered. Therefore, it is necessary to harmonize them.

In the future, this system will be capable of extending which should allow vehicle diagnostics in real time. The list of planned works includes wider collection of information on the technical parameters of the vehicle subsystems and the extension of the monitoring system on the vehicle. In addition, it is planned to implement a system that, instead of manually, by changing the points.txt file, will allow you to load the route from the application level automatically. It is also possible to change the current way of presenting the route by using Google Maps, which will allow for the correct operation of the application anywhere without having to know the GPS coordinates of the entire route. It is also intended to add functionality that allows to change the application mode, data download frequency during simulation, broker and topic settings. In the future, the system will be expanded with a real-time strategy system that, based on the vehicle speed profile, will be able to determine the optimal speed of the car between the control points. It is also prearranged to add a tab with a chart, to which you can download any diagnostic data. From the user's point of view, it is also worth thinking about designing the graphic design of the application.

It should be noted that although the application works correctly, in the next seasons of the race it is planned to systematically develop the application including, on the one hand, increase of diagnostic functionality through the ability to display subsequent data and, on the other hand, the introduction of intelligent diagnostic and strategic functions. Particularly these latter tasks, however, require advanced research in this area, which is currently being carried out by the team members and supervisors. From the beginning, such systematic and planned development of the application will facilitate future tasks. The already developed working application is an excellent help for the strategy supervision center and is a base for integration of new intelligent functions.

References

1. Anh-Tuan, N., Reiter, S., Rigo, P.: A review on simulation-based optimization methods applied to building performance analysis. Appl. Energy **113**, 1043–1058 (2014)
2. Cichoński, K., Skarka, W.: Innovative control system for high efficiency electric urban vehicle. In: Mikulski, J. (ed.) TST 2015. CCIS, vol. 531, pp. 121–130. Springer, Cham (2015). https://doi.org/10.1007/978-3-319-24577-5_12
3. Description of the system. Sat-dog. http://www.sat-dog.pl/opis.php. Accessed 1 June 2018
4. Gao, D., Wenzhong, M.C., Emadi, A.: Modeling and simulation of electric and hybrid vehicles. Proc. IEEE **95**(4), 729–745 (2007)
5. Google Maps in LabVIEW. Forum National Instruments. https://forums.ni. Accessed 1 June 2018
6. Jezierska-Krupa, K., Skarka, W.: Design method of ADAS for urban electric vehicle based on virtual prototyping. J. Adv. Transp. Article Number: 5804536 (2018). https://doi.org/10.1155/2018/5804536
7. Jezierska-Krupa, K., Skarka, W.: Using simulation method for designing ADAS systems for electric vehicle. In: 23rd ISPE Inc. International Conference on Transdisciplinary Engineering, Federal University of Technology, Curitiba, Brazil, 03–07 October 2016. Transdisciplinary Engineering: Crossing Boundaries Book Series: Advances in Transdisciplinary Engineering, vol. 4, pp. 595–604 (2016)

8. Markel, T., et al.: ADVISOR: a systems analysis tool for advanced vehicle modeling. J. Power Sources **110**(2), 255–266 (2002). Article Number: PII S0378-7753(02)00189-1 AUG 22
9. Monitored functions. Globtrak. https://www.globtrak.pl/floty-handlowe/. Accessed 1 June 2018
10. Mosquitto. Mosquitto. https://test.mosquitto.org/. Accessed 1 June 2018
11. MQTT 101 – How to Get Started with the lightweight IoT Protocol. HiveMQ. https://www.hivemq.com/blog/how-to-get-started-with-mqtt. Accessed 1 June 2018
12. Smart Power. Smart Power Team. http://185.201.112.44/. Accessed 1 June 2018
13. Skarka, W.: Reducing the energy consumption of electric vehicles transdisciplinary lifecycle analysis of systems book series: advances in transdisciplinary. Engineering **2**, 500–509 (2015)
14. QCustomPlot. Introduction. http://www.qcustomplot.com/. Accessed 1 June 2018
15. Qt-based Clients for Google APIs. Ics. https://www.ics.com/technologies/qt/qt-based-clients-google-apis.com/t5/Example-Programs/Google-Maps-in-LabVIEW/ta-p/3512488. Accessed 1 June 2018
16. Qt Charts. Qt. https://doc.qt.io/qt-5/qtcharts-index.html. Accessed 1 June 2018
17. Shell eco-marathon. Shell. http://www.shell.com/energy-and-innovation/shell-ecomarathon.html. Accessed 1 June 2018
18. Targosz, M., Skarka, W., Przystałka, P.: Model-based optimization of velocity strategy for lightweight electric racing cars. J. Adv. Transp. Article Number: 3614025 (2018). https://doi.org/10.1155/2018/3614025
19. Targosz, M., Szumowski, M., Skarka, W., Przystałka, P.: Velocity planning of an electric vehicle using an evolutionary algorithm. In: Mikulski, J. (ed.) TST 2013. CCIS, vol. 395, pp. 171–177. Springer, Heidelberg (2013). https://doi.org/10.1007/978-3-642-41647-7_22
20. Tyczka, M., Skarka, W.: Optimisation of operational parameters based on simulation numerical model of hydrogen fuel cell stack used for electric car drive. In: Conference: 23rd ISPE Inc. International Conference on Transdisciplinary Engineering, Federal University of Technology, Curitiba, Brazil, 03–07 October 2016. Transdisciplinary Engineering: Crossing Boundaries Book Series: Advances in Transdisciplinary Engineering, vol. 4, pp. 622–631 (2016)

Liquefied Petroleum Gas Transport Service Improvement via Telematics Support

Janusz Szpytko[2(✉)], Lenier Aleman Hurtado[1,2(✉)],
and Yorlandys Salgado Duarte[2(✉)]

[1] Cuban Petroleum Company, Santa Clara, Villa Clara, Cuba
lenier.aleman34@gmail.com
[2] AGH University of Science and Technology,
Ave. Mickiewicza 30, Krakow, Poland
{szpytko,salgado}@agh.edu.pl

Abstract. In developing countries, there are cases where the transport fleets are not subjected to scheduled services/maintenance or there are no maintenance procedures. The observed situation is the result of a shortage of required exploitation resources. The subject of the paper are solutions aimed at improving the service of the liquefied petroleum gas (LPG) transport with the use of telematics applications (information and communications technology, ICT). As result of the analysis of various strategies, a predictive maintenance type model was selected. The method of designing a predictive maintenance model of transport devices was presented, in which tele-information techniques (telematics) were proposed (to obtain information on the technical condition device). The operational parameters were identified, which will be the subject of registration, and then analysis and synthesis for decision-making purposes.

Keywords: LPG transport · Maintenance schudule · Telematic

1 Introduction

Oil industry is undoubtedly one of the most important worldwide. The refining process produces a multitude of products, from liquefied gases such as propane or butane to products to produce plastics or asphalts that obviously pass through fuels such as gasoline, gas oil or kerosene. Essential derivatives in the current life model and in the world economy.

Liquefied petroleum gas (LPG) was first identified as a significant component of petroleum in 1910 by Dr. Walter Snelling, who built a contraption that could separate the gasoline into its liquid and gaseous components. LPG describes flammable hydrocarbon gases including propane, butane and mixtures of these gases. Liquefied through pressurization, comes from natural gas processing and oil refining. Since them LPG is frequently used for fuel in heating, cooking, hot water and vehicles, as well as for refrigerants, aerosol propellants and petrochemical feedstock. From its obtaining to the long supply chain that takes it to the final customer, the effective use of transportation in all its types is required. LPG can be transported in several ways, including by ship, rail, tanker trucks, intermodal tanks, cylinder trucks and pipelines. All of them need the proper maintenance management.

© Springer Nature Switzerland AG 2019
J. Mikulski (Ed.): TST 2019, CCIS 1049, pp. 230–249, 2019.
https://doi.org/10.1007/978-3-030-27547-1_18

In general, the equipment is supposed to be subject to failures, and to a time-dependent process of degradation. Maintenance strategies and planning can be properly updated based on the feedback data extracted from the transport equipment performances [9].

The study of the maintenance management is very important because the impact in the final transport equipment cost. But we must also think about the losses that they produce to companies when the team is not available to carry out its mission. In delivery companies when the equipment is not available, it can also lead to unattended orders.

The target of this research is to improve the LPG transport service with the help of telematics application and the preventive maintenance approach to the scheduling of the necessary transport equipment.

2 Research Problem and Research Methodology

One of the supply main aspects of fuel is its transport and distribution, this has a special meaning to know where, when and how much is transported and delivered to the end customer; however, the measurements made in them guarantee the evaluation and control of the operational status in real time [5]. The maintenance plans play a fundamental role in the prevention of faults that frequently occur in the transport equipment, one of the main problems that we present in the LPG distribution system in Cuba for not carrying out an effective maintenance and does not taking in account the customers demand.

Currently Cuban transport fleet does not perform the maintenance planning using the existing database. Sometime the equipment is not available, when we have the highest demand, because they are on maintenance or are broken. The transports equipment is very frequent failures because they have many years of operation. In most cases these failures or maintenance cause stock outs at the points of sale, because the fleet design is very tight. If the demand goes beyond the availability, we will have a failure in the system that is why we must always try to achieve the maximum possible availability. We propose to apply telematics for the predictive maintenance in the transports equipment to resolve this problem.

The research goal is improvement liquefied petroleum gas transport service. Maintenance planning of transport equipment does not consider the demand for the service. The research aims to improve the planning of maintenance, achieving the greatest possible availability for each demand.

3 Methodology

3.1 Data Mining

Data mining also popularly referred as knowledge discovery from data (KDD) is the automated extraction of patterns representing knowledge implicitly stored in massive information repositories or data streams. Data mining is a sub field of artificial intelligence, drawing work from areas including database technology, machine learning, statistics, pattern recognition, information retrieval, neural networks, knowledge-based systems, artificial intelligence, high-performance computing, and data visualization. This multidisciplinary field emerged during the late 1980s, made great advances during the 1990s, and continues to attract increasing attention over the last decade [11].

However, before attempting a definition of data mining, let us emphasize some aspects of its genesis. Data mining has three generic roots, from which it borrowed the techniques and terminology.

Statistics: Its oldest root, without statistics, data mining would not have existed. The classical statistics have well-defined techniques that we can summarize as Exploratory Data Analysis (EDA), used to identify systematic relationships between different variables, when there is no enough information about their nature. Among EDA classical techniques used in DM, we can mention:

- Computational methods: descriptive statistics (distributions, classical statistical parameters (mean, median, standard deviation, etc.), correlation, multiple frequency tables, multivariate exploratory techniques (cluster analysis, factor analysis, principal components & classification analysis, canonical analysis, discriminant analysis, classification trees, correspondence analysis), advanced linear/non-linear models (linear/non-linear regression, time series/forecasting, etc.).
- Data visualization: aims to represent information in a visual form and can be regarded as one of the most powerful and, at the same time, attractive methods of data exploration. Among the most common visualization techniques, we can find frequency histograms.
- Artificial Intelligence (AI) that, unlike statistics, is built on heuristics. Thus, AI contributes with information processing techniques, based on human reasoning model, towards data mining development. Closely related to AI, Machine Learning (ML) represents an extremely important scientific discipline in the development of data mining, using techniques that allow the computer to learn with 'training'. In this context, we can also consider Natural Computing (NC) as a solid additional root for data mining.
- Database systems (DBS) are considered the third root of data mining, providing information to be 'mined' using the methods mentioned above [4].

In principle, when we use data mining methods to solve concrete problems, we have in mind their typology, which can be synthetically summarized in two broad categories, already referred to as the objectives of data mining:

- Predictive methods which use some existing variables to predict future values (unknown yet) of other variables (e.g., classification, regression, biases/anomalies detection, etc.).
- Descriptive methods that reveal patterns in data, easily interpreted by the user (e.g., clustering, association rules, sequential patterns, etc.).

We briefly present some problems facing the field of data mining and how they can be solved to illustrate in a suggestive manner its application field.

Among the most popular classification models (methods), we could mention, although they are used, obviously, for other purposes too:

- Decision/classification trees.
- Bayesian classifiers/Naive Bayes classifiers.
- Neural networks.
- Statistical analysis.
- Genetic algorithms.
- Rough sets.
- k-nearest neighbor classifier.
- Rule-based methods.
- Memory based reasoning.
- Support vector machines [4].

We intend to use the maintenance historical data of the transport fleet for the design of predictive maintenance model; therefore, we will have to use data mining. This is very useful to find some patterns of behavior that can be used in the model construction.

3.2   Mathematical Modeling

The aim is to use mathematical modeling to obtain an objective function related to the different variables and parameters that influence in the system, considering the external influences and giving us as output the maximum availability of the system.

Mathematical model can be found as the most frequently used model in optimization research area. It is an abstract model that uses mathematical language to describe the system. It is very useful to estimating the nature systems state by using limited information. By using the stochastic principle, the possible condition including system itself and variables that influence the system can be predicted. Optimization process can be conducted along with the predicted information [13].

The first step is to create a model from the real object or real problem by developing an abstract representation of the reality. As explained above, an appropriate model type and modeling restrictions need to be determined in this step. Afterwards, the model is analyzed, calculated, or modified in order to gain the desired insights. In the third step, the findings are interpreted regarding the real object. Finally, the findings of the model analysis are transferred to the real object. At this point, the effects of model simplifications need to be examined [10].

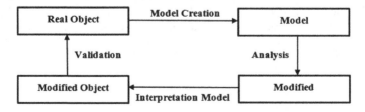

Fig. 1. Modeling process (adapted from [10])

Becker et al. define the following general principles of proper modeling, which may be used to assess the quality of model construction:

- Correctness.
- Relevance.
- Efficiency.
- Clarity.
- Comparability and systematic structure.

The application of the modeling process to a practical problem is a complex task, which is supported by general guiding principles [3]:

- Precise determination of the real object.
- Description of applicable regularities.
- Definition of relevant information.
- Transfer of existing approaches.
- Identification of appropriate modeling parameters.

3.3 Optimization

Traditional optimization techniques and methods have been successfully applied for years to solve problems with a well-defined structure/configuration, sometimes known as hard systems. Nowadays, manufacturing industries are aiming higher operation efficiency, effectively, and economically to survive in the fiercely competitive global economy. Proper maintenance has been drawing more and more attention in contributing industries towards prolonging the system's effective operational lifetime and improves the system reliability/availability to ensure the delivery of high-quality product to customers on time. Overall, maintenance can be described as a combination of all technical and administrative actions including supervision, action intended to retain or restore the system into a state in which system can perform a required function [15].

The optimization techniques can be classified into two distinct types as given below:

- Traditional optimization techniques: These are deterministic algorithms with specific rules for moving from one solution to the other. These algorithms have been in use for quite some time and have been successfully applied to many engineering design problems. Examples include nonlinear programming, geometric programming, quadratic programming, dynamic programming, generalized reduced gradient method, etc.
- Advanced optimization techniques: These techniques are stochastic in nature with probabilistic transition rules. These techniques are comparatively new and gaining popularity due to certain properties which the deterministic algorithm does not have [12].

In this paper, we focus the attention in the advanced optimization techniques because they are more useful for the problem solution proposal. Some of the most used algorithms in the literature are described below:

- Genetic Algorithm (GA): Genetic algorithms guide the search through the solution space by using natural selection and genetic operators, such as crossover, mutation and the selection. GA encodes the decision variables or input parameters of the problem into solution strings of a finite length. While traditional optimization techniques work directly with the decision variables or input parameters, genetic algorithms usually work with the coding. The most popular genetic operators are selection, crossover and mutation [12].

- Differential Evolution (DE): The algorithm was first proposed by Storn and Price [14]. There are only three real control parameters in the algorithm. These are: (1) differentiation (or mutation) constant F, (2) crossover constant Cr and (3) size of population. The rest of the parameters are (a) dimension of problem S that scales the difficulty of the optimization task; (b) maximal number of generations (or iterations) G, which serves as a stopping condition in our case and (c) high and low boundary constraints, x_{max} and x_{min}, respectively, that limit the feasible area. DE also starts with a set of random population which consist the initial solution to the problem. Mutant vector $v_{i,m}$ is generated from three different randomly chosen target vectors. This process can be mathematically written as $v_{i,m} = x_{i,3} + F(x_{i,1} - x_{i,2})$ [17].

- Harmony Elements Algorithm (HEA): According to Chinese philosophy, the five kinds of substances (wood, fire, earth, metal and water) are essential things in the daily life of mankind. Among the five elements, there exist the relations of generation and restriction [8]. The order of generation is: (1) wood generates fire, (2) fire generates earth, (3) earth generates metal, (4) metal generates water and (5) water, in its turn, generates wood. Relationship of restriction for the five elements works in the following order: wood restricts earth, earth water, water fire, fire metal and metal wood. So, they oppose each other and at the same time cooperate with each other, thus a relative balance is maintained between generation and restriction, to ensure normal growth and development of things in nature. Harmony elements algorithm follows the generation and restriction rules between the elements of the string. It starts the procedure with a random population. Like GA, each individual in the population is made up of string which represents the design variables. Dissimilar to GA, the algorithm initializes the solutions as strings of $0s$, $1s$, $2s$, $3s$ and $4s$ to represent 'earth', 'water', 'wood', 'fire' and 'metal', five elements, respectively. Population is modified according to generation and restriction rules to reach its harmonious state [12].

- Biogeography Based Optimization (BBO): Biogeography-based optimization (BBO) is a population-based optimization algorithm inspired by the natural biogeography distribution of different species [16]. In BBO, each individual is considered as a "habitat" with a habitat suitability index (HSI). A good solution is analogous to an island with a high HSI, and a poor solution indicates an island with a low HSI. High HSI solutions tend to share their features with low HSI solutions.

Low HSI solutions accept a lot of new features from high HSI solutions. In BBO, each individual has its own immigration rate λ and emigration rate μ. A good solution has higher μ and lower λ and vice versa. The immigration rate and the emigration rate are functions of the number of species in the habitat. They can be calculated as $\lambda_k = I(1 - k/n)$ and $\mu_k = E(k/n)$ where, I is the maximum possible immigration rate, E is the maximum possible emigration rate; k is the number of species of the kth individual and n is the maximum number of species. In BBO, there are two main operators, the migration and the mutation [12].

- Artificial Bee Colony (ABC): Is an optimization algorithm based on the intelligent foraging behavior of honey bee swarm. The colony of artificial bees consists of three groups of bees: employed bees, onlookers and scouts [2, 7]. An employed bee searches the destination where food is available. They collect the food and return to its origin, where they perform waggle dance depending on the amount of food available at the destination. The onlooker bee watches the dance and follows the employed bee depending on the probability of the available food. This principle of foraging behavior of honey bee is used to solve optimization problems by dividing the population into two parts consisting of employed bees and onlooker bees. An employed bee searches the solution in the search space and the value of objective function associated with the solution is the amount of food associated with that solution. Employed bee updates its position using equation and it updates new position if it is better than the previous position, i.e. it follows greedy selection.

- Artificial Immune Algorithm (AIA): The immune system defends the body against harmful diseases and infections. B cells recognize the antigens which enter the body. B cells circulate through the blood. Each antigen has a shape that is recognized by the receptors present on the B cell surface. B cells synthesize and carry antibodies on their surfaces molecules that act like detectors to identify antigens. B cell with better fitting receptors and binding more tightly the antigen replicate more and survive longer. The immune response represents solutions and antigens represent the problem to solve. More precisely, B cells are considered as artificial agents that roam around and explore an environment. In other words, the optimization problem is described by an environment of antigens. The positive and negative selection mechanism is used to eliminate useless or bad solutions [12].

- Particle Swarm Optimization (PSO): Inspired by animal behavior proposed in 1995 an optimization method called Particle Swarm Optimization (PSO). In this approach, a swarm of particles simultaneously explore a problem's search space with the goal of finding the global optimum configuration [6].

The particle swarm concept was originated as a simulation of a simplified social system. The original intent was to graphically simulate the graceful but unpredictable choreography of a bird group [12].

In PSO the position x_i of each particle i corresponds to a possible solution to the problem, with fitness $f(x_i)$. In each iteration of the search algorithm the particles move as a function of their velocity v_i. It is thus necessary that the structure of the search space allows such movement. For example, searching for the optimum of a continuous function in R^n offers such a possibility [1]. Also, each particle keeps track of its coordinates in the problem space, which are associated with the best solution (fitness) it has achieved so far. This value is called '*pBest*'. Another "*best*" value that is tracked by the global version of the particle swarm optimization is the overall best value and its location obtained so far by any particle in the population. This location is called '*gBest*'. The particle swarm optimization concept consists of, at each step, changing the velocity (i.e. accelerating) of each particle toward its '*pBest*' and '*gBest*' locations (global version of PSO). Acceleration is weighted by a random term with separate random numbers being generated for acceleration toward '*pBest*' and '*gBest*' locations. The updates of the particles are accomplished as per the following equations:

$$V_{i+1} = w \cdot V_i + c_1 \cdot r_1(pBest_i - X_i) + c_2 \cdot r_2(gBest_i - X_i) \tag{1}$$

$$X_{i+1} = X_i + V_{i+1} \tag{2}$$

Equation (1) calculates a new velocity (V_{i+1}) for each particle (potential solution) based on its previous velocity, the best location it has achieved ('*pBest*') so far, and the global best location ('*gBest*'), the population has achieved. Equation (2) updates individual particle's position (X_i) in solution hyperspace [12].

The model to be used will depend on the characteristics of the objective function. But we intend to propose the use of a heuristic model based on group intelligence, better known in the literature as Particle Swarm Optimization (PSO).

3.4   Conclusions of Review

Data mining is useful to find some patterns of behavior that can be used in the construction of the model.

Mathematical modeling allows us: knowing how the system works, what are its critical components, find the system parameters identification and obtain a model proposal that represents the real problem that we are trying to solve.

PSO optimization method is chosen for the problem solution, because it is simple, practical, effective and easy to apply.

4   Result and Discussion

LPG deliveries in Cuba have, like all systems, targets and restrictions that we need consider for the elaboration of the methodological scheme: the system main target is satisfying clients demand; the human, economic and technological resources are inputs to the system, but also the disturbances that can be caused by the environment (all these inputs have influence in the final target); the maintenance process as a support to the LPG delivery operating system maximizes the availability of transports equipment and this fact makes the accomplishment of the mission much easier.

Based on the previous comments, we decided to build a model that improve the system efficiency with a maintenance planning effective strategy, which maximizes the system availability based on customer demand, as illustrated by the framework of the Fig. 2 (Truck maintenance supporting LPG deliveries system).

4.1   LPG Delivery Operation System (Demand-Availability Relation)

The main component of the LPG delivery operating system is deliveries planning. The deliveries planning process is carried out considering three elements, the customers demand, the availability of products (LPG) and the availability of transport equipment. The first two elements we cannot control, but if we improve the availability of transports equipment, we are improving the delivery process. *So, if we have achieving maximum availability of transport equipment; we have a mayor margin in the decision-making process.*

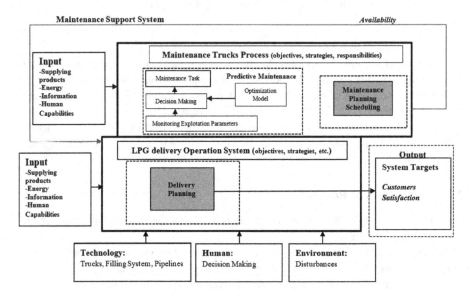

Fig. 2. Truck maintenance supporting LPG deliveries system [own study]

4.2   Load Capacity-Demand Relation

Generally, the transport equipment makes an average of two trips per day, so the trips schedule of the transport's equipment considers the days of coverage, the distance and the clients schedules.

The number of travels depends on the distance traveled on each trip, when the deliveries are concentrated in the sales points within the city, the number of trips may increase. The second trip in the day is made at large distances outside the city. Trucks characteristics (Table 1) are also consider selecting the trip they will take. For example, the load capacity and the fuel consumption index are one of the most used criteria to achieve a more efficient planning.

Other strategies in the delivery planning are to use *the equipment of greater load capacity to cover the large orders of the customers.* Also, the transport equipment with a lower fuel consumption index is also used to make longer trips.

Table 1. Truck fleet characteristic [own study]

Index	Brand-Model	Year	Capacity (t)	Load Cap. Use (%)	Fuel Cons. Index
Truck 7047	Hyundai-H35	1997	4.1	76	4.55
Truck 7048	Hyundai-H45	1998	4.1	76	4.50
Truck 7052	Hyundai-H65	2004	4.2	80	4.60
Truck 7061	Hyundai-H78	2000	5.5	70	4.70
Truck 7156	Hyundai-H65	1999	4.2	80	4.60
Truck 7309	Zil - 130	1977	7	46	3.80
Truck 7358	Kamaz - 43118	1983	8	56	2.85
Truck 7445	Zil - 130	1977	7	42	3.65
Truck 7720	Roman 8.135 F	1980	8	60	2.70

In the characteristics of the transport fleet, we can observe that there is a marked difference in the load capacity exploitation between Hyundai truck and the others; this is due to the improvements made by the truck manufacturers to the modern designs. The transport equipment has a load capacity offered by the manufacturer, but it is very difficult to achieve the maximum possible load in the delivery systems for multiple reasons. That is why we need to know how we can model the truck capacity.

4.3   Truck Capacity Modeling

From the operational behavior data, and with the aid of descriptive statistics, a cumulative frequency table is built for each truck, which includes values that are divided into non-overlapping classes. In this way, a set of n data can be summarized. For continuous data, the classes constitute value ranges called "class intervals." The classes are selected in a way that all data are totally classified; so, each data belongs in one and only one class. The definition and quantity of the classes varies from case to case. For continuous data, it is common to select the classes with equal amplitude h, as determined using the following equation:

$$h = \frac{X_{\max} - X_{\min}}{k} \tag{3}$$

where: $X_{\max}$ is the highest value of the data and $X_{\min}$ the smallest value of the data.

Each class is determined by a lower limit LI_i and an upper limit LS_i, as follows: the i class is the $[LI_i; LS_i)$ interval, where $LI_i = X_{\min} + (i - 1)\, h$ and $LS_i = X_{\min} + i\, h$. The last class is a closed interval at both ends. The relative cumulative frequency of the i class can be calculated as follows:

$$F_{ri} = \sum_{k=1}^{i} F_k \tag{4}$$

From the relative cumulative frequency, the probability associated with each class can be determined; therefore, in the case of an operational behavior of each truck, the associated probable occurrence of a certain level of capacity (CT) may be established. It is thus possible to simulate the behavior of the operational behavior of each truck by generating random numbers u_k that are evenly uniform distributed between [0; 1] as follows:

If $0 \leq u_k < P_1$ then the level of capacity is C_{T1}
If $P_1 \leq u_k < P_2$ then the level of capacity is C_{T2}
If $P_{i-1} \leq u_k < P_i$ then the level of capacity is C_{Ti}
$$\vdots \qquad\qquad\qquad\qquad\qquad\qquad\qquad \vdots$$
If $P_{i=n-1} \leq u_k \leq 1$ then the level of capacity is C_{Tn}

The truck operation is continuous, eventually fails and is repairable. Considering the operation effectiveness of the truck, we fix that the system and its components have two reliability states $z = 0, 1$. And consequently, at all operation states, we distinguish the following reliability states of the system and its components:

- a reliability state 1 – the truck operation is fully effective,
- a reliability state 0 – the truck is broken.

The stochastic capacity $C_{Tn,j}(t)$ at the time instant t of a truck j is determined by the TTF_j, TTR_j and $C_{Tn,j}$. The parameters TTF_j, TTR_j and $C_{Tn,j}$ allow to simulate with (3) the behavior of $C_{Tn,j}(t)$ generating kth independent random numbers, assuming $TTF_{j,k} \sim E(\lambda_j)$ and $TTR_{j,k} \sim E(\mu_j)$ in this paper, where λ_j and μ_j are parameters of the Exponential distribution function respectively, for each truck j.

In the modeling of the truck j, it is necessary that the sequence of random numerical chain $TTF_{j,k}$ and $TTR_{j,k}$, added, complete the 8 760 h of the year. Experimentally, it is determined in this work, that the integer numerical value MN_j defined in (4) depends on the numerical value of $MTTF_j$ of each truck j. The model proposed to simulate truck capacity is defined below:

$$C_{Tn,j}(t) = \begin{cases} C_{Tn,j} & \text{if } t < S_{1_{j,m}} + S_{2_{j,m-1}} \\ 0 & \text{if } S_{1_{j,m}} + S_{2_{j,m-1}} \leq t < S_{1_{j,m}} + S_{2_{j,m}} \end{cases} \qquad (5)$$

where:
   $j = 1, 2, ..., NT$ (Number of Truck).
   $S_{1_{j,m}} = \sum_{k=1}^{m} TTF_{j,k}$ for $m = 2, 3, ..., MN_j$.
   $S_{2_{j,m}} = \sum_{k=1}^{m} TTR_{j,k}$ for $m = 2, 3, ..., MN_j$.

The integer numerical value MN_j of the truck j necessary to guarantee the exposed conditions is defined below:

$$M_i = \frac{9015}{(\beta_i)^{0,955}}$$

$$N_j(MTTF_j, M_j) = \begin{cases} \dfrac{9015}{(MTTF_j)^{0,955}} & \text{if} \quad M_j > 50 \\ 50 & \text{if} \quad M_i < 50 \end{cases} \qquad (6)$$

$$MN_j = Z^+(N_j)$$

The system capacity $SC_j(t)$ defined in Eq. (5) is determined by adding the capacity of each truck $C_{Tn,j}(t)$

$$SC_j(t) = \sum_{j=1}^{N_T} C_{Tn,j}(t) \qquad (7)$$

On the other hand, one of the factors that affects the capacity of system, is not stochastic and is not considered a random phenomenon, it is preventive maintenance in the truck. Preventive maintenance is contemplated within the strategies of a system because it guarantees planned work time for the truck. Maintenance is the activity designed to prevent failures in the production process and in this way reduce the risks of unexpected stops due to system failures. In the case of preventive maintenance, it is the planned activity in the vulnerable points at the most opportune moment, destined to avoid failures in the system. It is carried out under normal conditions, that is, when the productive process works correctly. In this system, to perform some preventive maintenance tasks it is necessary that the truck does not work, and this causes loss of capacity in the system. Due to this reason, it is advisable that this preventive maintenance be carried out at the time of the year where the least demand exists, so that equilibrium and adequate flow are guaranteed in the system.

To consider this effect, in this work the parameters $TTM_{j,k}$ and $TDM_{j,k}$ are introduced and the Eq. (3) is redefined by Eq. (6), as shown below:

$$C_{Tn,j}(t) = \begin{cases} C_{Tn,j} & \text{if} \quad t < S_{1_{j,m}} + S_{2_{j,m-1}} \\ 0 & \text{if} \quad S_{1_{j,m}} + S_{2_{j,m-1}} \le t < S_{1_{j,m}} + S_{2_{j,m}} \\ 0 & \text{if} \quad A_{1_{j,n}} + A_{2_{j,n-1}} \le t < A_{1_{j,n}} + A_{2_{j,n}} \end{cases} \qquad (8)$$

where:

$j = 1, 2, \ldots, NT$ (Number of Truck).
$S_{1_{j,m}} = \sum_{k=1}^{m} TTF_{j,k}$ for $m = 2, 3, \ldots, MN_j$.
$S_{2_{j,m}} = \sum_{k=1}^{m} TTR_{j,k}$ for $m = 2, 3, \ldots, MN_j$.
$A_{1_{j,n}} = \sum_{k=1}^{n} TTM_{j,k}$ for $n = 2, 3, \ldots, NK_j$.
$A_{2_{j,n}} = \sum_{k=1}^{n} TDM_{j,k}$ for $n = 2, 3, \ldots, NK_j$.

4.4   Demand Behavior

The demand service of LPG is not the same all the time, so we can have different levels of demands service during the year. During the week there are peaks demand on Tuesdays and Thursdays, because the sales points on the outskirts of the city are open. Also, in holidays when students spend more time in home the demand increase. The more complex month are January, July, August and December as we can see in Fig. 3.

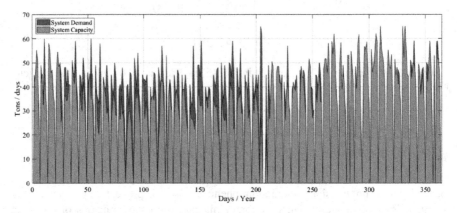

Fig. 3. Demand vs capacity of the system 2018 [own study]

4.5   Risk Indicator Modeling

We propose to evaluate the availability of the system expressed in terms of risk. The risk of shortfall occurs when the demand is above the capacity of the system by 8%. A margin of eight percent is used based on the experience of operating the system and the criteria of experts. The risk function denoted as $R(s)$ can be generated with the sum $X + Y$ of the random, independent and non-negative variables X and Y. The product of $R(s) = P(s)Q(s)$ is defined with the generating function $P(s) = \sum_{j=0}^{\infty} p_j s^j$ of X and the generating function $Q(s) = \sum_{j=0}^{\infty} q_j s^j$ of Y. Consequently, the generating function of $R(s)$ is defined by the convolution formula (7).

$$r_k = \sum_{j=1}^{k} p_j q_{k-j} \tag{9}$$

If $R(s)$ is a random, independent and not negative variable, the arithmetic mean $(R_1 + R_2 + \ldots + R_n)/n$ of a random sample $R_1, R_2, \ldots R_n$ of the variable $R(s)$ is approximately equal to the expected value $E[R(s)]$, for large values of n.

In this investigation, X is the truck capacity probability distribution function of the system defined in (8), and Y defined in (9) is the demand probability distribution function of the system.

$$X(t) = SC_j(t) \tag{10}$$

$$Y(t) = D(t) \tag{11}$$

where $D(t)$ is the demand of the system at instant t.

The risk function is denoted in this investigation as $R(t)$. This function is the convolution product of (8) and (9) defined in (10).

$$R(t) = \begin{cases} Y(t) - X(t) & \text{if } X(t) < Y(t) \text{ and } \frac{Y(t) - X(t)}{Y(t)} \geq 0,08 \\ 0 & \text{if } X(t) \geq Y(t) \end{cases} \tag{12}$$

The expected value of the risk function $E[R(t)]$ is defined in this paper as Shortfall, when $t = 1, 2, \ldots, T$ considers the 8760 h of the year.

In this work, to estimate $E[R(t)]$ the Monte Carlo simulation method is used. The convergence process is fluctuating in this method. However, the error level decreases when the number of samples increases, according to the law of large numbers. In this method it is not practical to run a simulation with many samples, because more calculation time is required. Therefore, it is necessary to balance the required precision and the calculation time. In this work, a stop criterion is used. This criterion guarantees that the simulation continues, until the risk indicator has the precision specified for the simulation. The parameter used as stopping criterion in the method is the coefficient of variation.

If $E[R(t)]$ is the estimated risk indicator, in the Monte Carlo simulation, the expected value and the variance of this indicator $R(t)$ are (11) and (12) respectively.

$$E[R(t)] = \frac{1}{N} \sum_{i=1}^{N} r_i(t) \tag{13}$$

$$V[R(t)] = \frac{1}{N-1} \sum_{i=1}^{N} (r_i(t) - E[R(t)])^2 \tag{14}$$

where $r_i(t)$ is the observed value of $R(t)$ in the simulation i, and N is the total number of simulations.

It is important to note that (11) only estimates the expected value of the risk indicator $R(t)$. However, the uncertainty around the indicator is measured by the variance (13) and standard deviation (14) of the expected value.

$$V(E[R(t)]) = \frac{V[R(t)]}{N} \tag{15}$$

$$\sigma(E[R(t)]) = \sqrt{V(E[R(t)])} = \sqrt{\frac{V[R(t)]}{N}} \tag{16}$$

The simulation precision level is expressed by the coefficient of variation β defined in (15). This coefficient is rewritten conveniently in (15), where $\sigma[R(t)] = \sqrt{V[R(t)]}$.

The simulation is controlled with the coefficient of variation β, selecting the error tolerance ε in the simulation (17). The error tolerance ε is the estimate maximum error. In the estimates it is typical to use 5% or 0.05.

$$\beta = \frac{\sigma(E[R(t)])}{E[R(t)]} \tag{17}$$

$$\beta = \frac{1}{E[R(t)]} \sqrt{\frac{V[R(t)]}{N}} = \frac{\sigma[R(t)]}{E[R(t)] \cdot \sqrt{N}} \tag{18}$$

$$\frac{\sigma[R(t)]}{E[R(t)] \cdot \sqrt{N}} \leq \varepsilon \tag{19}$$

The value of β decreases when the number of simulations N increases, as shown in (16). Therefore, the simulation process is stopped when β is less than ε.

The precision level of the Monte Carlo simulation method is related to the number of samples in the simulation and is independent of the system dimension. This condition is appropriate for handling systems with complex functions and large dimensions.

4.6   Truck Maintenance (Maintenance - Capacity Relation)

The incorrect planning of the maintenance causes that several equipment coincides in the same time in the workshop, the amount of mechanics to solve the problems of the trucks is limited, then unnecessary delays are caused in the maintenance process. When several transport equipment to carry out the maintenance match on the same day, the capacity of the delivery system decreases. Affecting customer satisfaction. The hypothesis is, *if we change the maintenance planning and taking in account the system demand, we can improve the delivery system, reducing the risk of shortfall* (Table 2).

Table 2. Maintenance data 2018 provide for the company [own study]

Index	TTF Time to Failure (days)	TTR Time to Repair (days)	TTM Time to Maintenance (days)	TDM Time Duration Maintenance (days)
Truck 7047	26, 3, 2	1, 1, 1	8, 21, 264, 19, 25, 19	3, 1, 2, 3, 2, 1
Truck 7048	55, 4, 1, 50, 36, 99	1, 1, 6, 12, 9	6, 21, 18, 17, 17, 34, 17, 25, 30, 24, 40, 21, 22, 19, 20, 18, 7	1, 2, 3, 4, 1, 2, 1, 1, 4, 4, 1, 2, 2, 2, 1, 3, 1
Truck 7061	106, 41, 87	1, 1, 1	8, 18, 17, 17, 9, 14, 23, 19, 23, 19, 16, 22, 30, 25, 18, 22, 18, 30	1, 1, 2, 1, 1, 3, 1, 1, 1, 2, 1, 4, 1, 1, 1, 1, 2, 1
Truck 7052	30, 30, 113, 43	1, 1, 1, 1	30, 29, 20, 35, 24, 19, 23, 18, 29, 19, 25, 28, 18, 17, 11	3, 1, 1, 1, 2, 1, 1, 1, 1, 1, 1, 1, 1, 1, 1
Truck 7156	90, 92, 54	1, 1, 1	18, 29, 24, 21, 26, 28, 23, 21, 32, 27, 25, 26, 29, 28	1, 2, 1, 2, 1, 2, 1, 2, 1, 3, 1, 2, 1, 1
Truck 7309	Not failure	Not repair	10, 283, 32, 37	4, 2, 4, 2
Truck 7358	13, 22, 2, 1, 88, 37, 50	1, 2, 1, 1, 1, 1, 1	29, 45, 142, 171, 204, 239	3, 1, 2, 1, 3, 1
Truck 7445	10, 28, 96, 77, 22	1, 1, 1, 1, 1	26, 19, 26, 19, 21, 33, 36, 32, 38, 66	2, 2, 1, 1, 2, 3, 2, 1, 4, 1
Truck 7720	19, 56, 6, 5, 47, 9, 9, 7, 23	1, 1, 1, 1, 1, 1, 1, 1, 1	10, 22, 27, 24, 18, 143, 27, 22, 10	1, 2, 3, 2, 1, 1, 1, 2, 1

4.7 Optimization Model

The detailed study of the process and its understanding allowed us to elaborate a model, where the variables of the capacity of the system, the demand and the times to failure and repair are related. As shown in Fig. 4.

The proposed model objective is to minimize the expected value of the convolution function, between the truck capacity probability distribution function of the system and the demand probability distribution function of the system. The model is defined below:

$$\min\{E[R(t)]\}$$

Where :
$$
\begin{aligned}
R(t) &\Rightarrow f[X(t), Y(t)] \\
X(t), Y(t) &\Rightarrow f[C_{Tn,j}(t)] \\
C_{Tn,j}(t) &\Rightarrow f(A_{1_{j,n}}, A_{2_{j,n}}) \\
A_{1_{j,n}}, A_{2_{j,n}} &\Rightarrow f(TTM_{j,k}, TDM_{j,k})
\end{aligned}
\tag{18}
$$

Subject to:
$$0 < TTM_{j,k} < 8760 - TDM_{j,k}$$

The stochastic non-linear optimization model proposed for the PMS problem solution of the trucks presents only continuous variables $x = TTM_{j,k}$ and is defined in the model constraint intervals. The independent variable of the objective function to be optimized $x = x_1, x_2, \ldots, x_{NKj}$ depends on the quantity of preventive maintenance NK_j to be coordinated for each truck j.

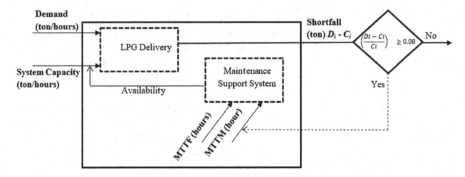

Fig. 4. Model proposal to optimize maintenance planning [own study]

4.8   Principal Result of the Research

The current system operation has a daily average deficit (Shortfall) between the demand and the capacity of the system of 4.65 ton. In addition, there is a risk that a deficit of 41% will occur, because 151 days met this condition.

Table 3. Principal result of the research. Note: *Simulation error ≤ 0.05 [own study]

	Shortfall	Days/year	% Risk Shortfall	Tons/year
Real operation	4.6514	151	41	1 697.7
Model simulation	4.7872*	145*	40	1 747.3*
Minimize Shortfall	4.1637	130	35	1 519.7

The model simulation result obtained a Shortfall expected value of 4.7872, so the error in the simulation is 2.84%, however, the deficit was reduced in 6 days (see Table 3).

In the second simulation, we use the proposed optimization model to improve the delivery system reducing the risk of shortfall. The expected shortfall is reduced by 15%, 15 days less without deficit and 228 tons save, are the results.

If we compare the maintenance planning of the system real operation, with the model proposed, the differences are significant in the maintenance schedule (see Table 4).

The use of the model to evaluate the system behaviors for different states, makes it a useful tool for the employer, because it does not run real risks to know future behaviors of the system. Which is useful for planning the process strategies.

The fact that the model conforms to the real behavior of the system allows the future application of telematics, by finding the different relationships between the variables of the system, which can be measured in real time.

Table 4. Preventive maintenances scheduling [own study]

Index	TTM Time to Maintenance (days) Optimization results	TTM Time to Maintenance (days) Real operation
Truck 7047	16	8
Truck 7048	3	6
Truck 7061	9	8
Truck 7052	0	30
Truck 7156	5	18
Truck 7309	0	10
Truck 7358	19	29
Truck 7445	27	26
Truck 7720	20	10

5 Conclusion

The art state review allowed us to know: Data mining is useful to find some patterns of behavior, mathematical modeling knowing how the system works, what are its critical components and find the system parameters identification to obtain a model proposal that represents the real problem, that we are trying to solve, PSO optimization method is chosen for the problem solution, because it is simple, practical, effective and easy to apply.

The proposed model presents a similar behavior to the real system operation (error 2.84%), so we can use the model proposed to evaluate the planning of the maintenance process. In fact, the model allows to the company know the shortfall possible result without running the risk of affecting the customer.

The selected control variable TTM have a significant influence on the average variation of the deficit between the system capacity and the demand (15% of variation).

Recommendation

It is recommended to analyze another system variable control and study the influence of the capital repairs and long-term repairs planning on the output variable of our system. Apply the model to data from the fleet of trucks of previous years, to corroborate the results obtained.

The use of telematics is something new in the Cuban business system and it is expected to achieve superior results in the availability of the transport fleets. This result may favor developing countries like Cuba. That is why the possibility of extending it to other underdeveloped countries, with similar conditions.

Acknowledgement. The work has been financially supported by the Polish Ministry of Science and Higher Education. The work has been also supported by the UNESCO AGH Chair for Science, Technology and Engineering Education, project ed. 2018A.

References

1. Chopard, B., Tomassini, T.: An Introduction to Metaheuristics for Optimization. Natural Computing Series. Springer, Cham (2018). https://doi.org/10.1007/978-3-319-93073-2. ISBN 978-3-319-93073-2. Series ISSN 1619-7127, Edition Number 1, Number of Pages XII, 226
2. Karaboga, D., Basturk, B.: Artificial Bee Colony (ABC) optimization algorithm for solving constrained optimization problems. In: Melin, P., Castillo, O., Aguilar, L.T., Kacprzyk, J., Pedrycz, W. (eds.) IFSA 2007. LNCS (LNAI), vol. 4529, pp. 789–798. Springer, Heidelberg (2007). https://doi.org/10.1007/978-3-540-72950-1_77
3. Becker, J., Rosemann, M., Scheutte, R.: Grundsätze ordnungsmäßiger Modellierung. Wirtschaftsinformatik **37**(5), 435–445 (1995)
4. Gorunescu, F.: Data Mining: Concepts, Models and Techniques. Intelligent Systems Reference Library, vol. 12. Springer, Heidelberg (2011). https://doi.org/10.1007/978-3-642-19721-5. ISBN 978-3-642-19721-5, Series ISSN 1868-4394. Edition Number 1. Number of Pages, XII, 360
5. Frederick, D.: Distribution Planning and Control: Managing in the Era of Supply Chain Management. Springer, New York (2015). https://doi.org/10.1007/978-1-4899-7578-2. ISBN 978-1-4899-7578-2 Edition Number 3. Number of Pages, XXV, 915
6. Kennedy, J., Eberhart, C.: Swarm Intelligence. Morgan Kaufmann Publishers Inc., San Francisco (2001). ISBN 1-55860-595-9
7. Karaboga, D.: An idea based on honey bee swarm for numerical optimization. Technical report-TR06, Erciyes University, Engineering Faculty, Computer Engineering Department, Turkey, pp. 1–10 (2005)
8. Maciocia, G.: The Foundations of Chinese Medicine. Elsevier, London (2005)
9. Manzini, R., et al.: Maintenance for Industrial Systems. Springer Series in Reliability Engineering. Springer, London (2010). https://doi.org/10.1007/978-1-84882-575-8
10. Peters, G., von Dresky, C., Gasser, I., Günzel, S.: Mathematische Modellierung: Eine Einführung in zwölf Fallstudien. Springer Spektrum, Wiesbaden (2013). https://doi.org/10.1007/978-3-658-00535-1. ISBN 978-3-658-00535-1, Edition Number 2. Number of pages, XI, 214
11. Georgieva, P., Mihaylova, L., Lakhmi, C.J. (eds.): Advances in Intelligent Signal Processing and Data Mining: Theory and Applications. Studies in Computational Intelligence, vol. 410. Springer, Heidelberg (2013). https://doi.org/10.1007/978-3-642-28696-4
12. Venkata, R., Savsani, V.J.: Mechanical Design Optimization Using Advanced Optimization Techniques. Springer, London (2012). https://doi.org/10.1007/978-1-4471-2748-2. ISBN 978-1-4471-2748-2. Series Print, ISSN 1860-5168
13. Ding, S.-H., Kamaruddin, S.: Maintenance policy optimization—literature review and directions. Int. J. Adv. Manuf. Technol. https://doi.org/10.1007/170.1433-3015. Print ISSN 0268-3768, Electronic ISSN 1433-3015, Issue 5-8/2015
14. Storn, R., Price, K.: Differential evolution, a simple and efficient heuristic for global optimization over continuous spaces. J. Glob. Optim. **11**, 341 (1997). https://doi.org/10.1023/A:1008202821328. Print ISSN 0925-5001. Online ISSN 1573-2916

15. Swanson, L.: Linking maintenance strategies to performance. Int. J. Prod. Econ. **70**(3), 237–244 (2001)
16. Simon, D.: Biogeography-based optimization. IEEE Trans. Evol. Comput. **12**(6), 702–713 (2008). https://doi.org/10.1109/TEVC.2008.919004
17. Feoktistov, V.: Differential Evolution. In Search of Solutions. Springer Optimization and Its Applications, vol. 5. Springer, Boston (2006). https://doi.org/10.1007/978-0-387-36896-2. eBook ISBN, 978-0-387-36896-2, Hardcover ISBN 978-0-387-36895-5. Softcover ISBN 978-1-4419-4234-0. Series ISSN 1931-6828, Edition Number 1, Number of Pages, XII, 196. ISBN 978-0-387-36896-2

The Intelligent Transport System Concept for Post - Disaster Infrastructure Under Reconstruction

Weam Nasan Agha[1,2]($\boxtimes$) and Janusz Szpytko[2]($\boxtimes$)

[1] Aleppo University, Aleppo, Syria
weam.agha@alepuniv.edu.sy
[2] AGH University of Science and Technology,
Ave A. Mickiewicza 30, Krakow, Poland
szpytko@agh.edu.pl

Abstract. Disasters that result from a complex combination of natural hazards and human actions, most often result in damage to infrastructure, in particular in built-up areas and in transport infrastructure. Transport infrastructure is critical for transporting the necessary humanitarian aid to affected communities and starting the reconstruction process. The paper is focused on an intelligent transport system concept for post - disaster infrastructure under reconstruction. On the basis of the information on needs in the field of humanitarian aid for the affected communities, the concept of a system of effective transport that fits into the existing infrastructure, terrain, climatic and environmental conditions was developed. In the construction of a flexible transport system in dynamically variable unpredictable conditions, it seems advisable to use tools of the intelligent type working on large databases (big data) acquired using information and communications technology (telematics, ICT).

Keywords: Post - disaster infrastructure · Transport telematics · Intelligent transport

1 Introduction

Disaster is defined as "a serious disruption of the functioning of a community or a society involving widespread human, material, economic or environmental losses and impacts, which exceeds the ability of the affected community or society to cope using its own resources" [1].

In the recent decades, the number of disasters as recorded by Centre for Research on the Epidemiology of Disasters (CRED), has been on the rise worldwide with destructive impacts [2]. Also, there has been a significant increase in the number of affected people due to the delay in relief operations [3], Fig. 1.

Disaster management is defined as "a multi-stage process that starts with pre-disaster mitigation and preparedness that focus on long-term measures for reducing or eliminating risk, and extends to post disaster response, recovery and reconstruction" [4].

© Springer Nature Switzerland AG 2019
J. Mikulski (Ed.): TST 2019, CCIS 1049, pp. 250–272, 2019.
https://doi.org/10.1007/978-3-030-27547-1_19

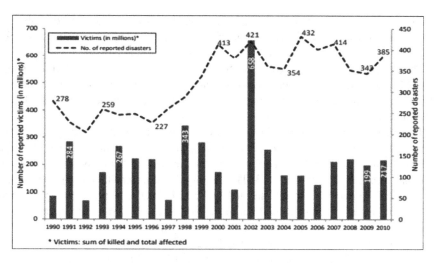

Fig. 1. Trends in disasters occurrence and victims [2]

In this paper, we will focus on Road Transport Infrastructure since road transport infrastructure plays a crucial role during all stages of disaster management cycle. On the other hand, road transport infrastructure has been considered as one of the development sectors with the most significant losses and damages [5].

In Pre-disaster stage, it is essential to prepare the optimal planning of resilient road transport infrastructure to avoid or reduce disaster impact and ensure sustainability concepts [5].

During disaster, road transport networks play a vital role in providing efficient response where most disaster deaths are the result of delay in relief operations to victims [2]. Where disaster render some of the links of the transportation network leading to the blockage of some routes and/or disconnectedness of some areas in need of aid [6]. This role is not limited to save lives, but also to all types of humanitarian aid [5]. In post-disaster stage, the effectiveness of road transport infrastructure plays an important role for accelerating the whole recovery processes [5].

A further review shows that post-disaster reconstruction of transport infrastructure is more complex than construction in normal situations due to its own characteristics and several challenges [7]. Where Post-disaster planning include several dynamic operations such as evacuation, emergency traffic management, emergency logistics deployment, performance assessment of surviving transport network, recovery-oriented resource allocation and restoration project programming [8].

Also, there are many essential issues regarding the post disaster reconstruction of traffic management system such as lack of information about damaged traffic facilities due to many obstacles hinder the process of data gathering, insufficiency of past studies on travel conditions in the aftermath of disasters, the need of traffic management systems with high capacity for responding to unexpected changes during disasters, weakness in the current structure of transport networks and insufficient plans for emergency facilities [9].

All above, there is an urgent need for more practical and advanced tools and technologies to overcome all critical challenges and provide victims with timely efficient aid.

The concept of Intelligent Transport Systems (ITS) has been adopted in this paper towards increasing the efficiency and availability of post disaster road transport infrastructure and systematic emergency response management in the future development.

This paper is organized as follows: In Sect. 2, we discuss firstly the concept and background of Intelligent Transport Systems (ITS) then we summarize related literature for developing intelligent transport systems in the aftermath of disasters. Research target has been introduced in Sect. 3. Then the used research methodology to meet the target of this research has been clarified in Sect. 4. Section 5 presents the research results represented by content analysis of previous related literature towards investigating the most common techniques for developing intelligent transport system after disasters. In addition, Sect. 5 presents detailed description of the design process of new integrated system for emergency transport management and its components. In Sect. 6, we summarize our contributions and the conclusions. Finally, we present some future works of this research in Sect. 7.

2 Intelligent Transport Systems (ITS)

In recent years, transportation sector witnesses the application of advanced sensor, computer, electronics and communications technologies. These applications are known as Intelligent Transportation Systems (ITS) and considered as one of the most important innovations to improve the management, maintenance, monitoring, control and safety of transport [10].

In this section, we will go through the concept of Intelligent Transportation Systems (ITS) and summarize briefly background Of ITS development process.

After that, we present an extensive review and highlight the most common techniques for developing intelligent transport systems in the aftermath of disasters.

2.1 ITS Concept & Background

Intelligent Transport Systems (ITS) Can be defined generally as "the application of advanced telecommunications, computing, and sensor technologies to improve the safety, efficiency and sustainability of the transportation system" [10].

Intelligent Transport Systems (ITS) has been around since the 30 s and it has been progressively developed in Europe, U.S. and Japan. The development process of Intelligent Transport Systems (ITS) has gone through three main phases as following, Fig. 2 [11]:

- Preparation (1930–1980);
- Feasibility Study (1980–1995);
- Product Development (1995–present).

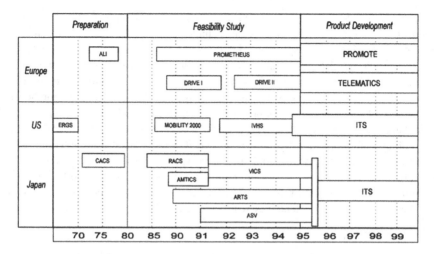

Fig. 2. ITS development chronology in Europe, US and Japan [11]

– Preparation (1930–1980):

In 1928, the Electric Traffic Signals implemented as the first original ITS system, then the concept of Automated Highway Systems (AHS) was presented at the General Motors' Futurama exhibit at the 1939 World's Fair in New York [10, 11].

Due to the absence of matured technologies in the first phase of ITS development process, the ITS movement did not take root until the 60 s, when appeared the first computer for controlling with traffic signals in US. After that, ERGS (Electronic Route Guidance Systems) was developed in US to the provide route guidance depending on two-way road vehicle communications [11].

During the 70s, CACS (Comprehensive Automobile Traffic Control System) and the ALI (Autofahrer Leit und Information System) were developed in Japan and Germany respectively. They are dynamic route guidance systems based on real traffic conditions. In addition, the microprocessor and the beginning of GPS development were introduced [11].

All above, this phase was so important for developing ITS where these basic technologies are now major components of many ITS systems.

– Feasibility Study (1980–1995):

This phase is characterised by rapid development of ITS programs in Europe, Japan and United States. Those programs were developed based on the basic technologies founded in previous phase.

In Europe, PROMETHEUS (Program for European Traffic with Efficiency and Unprecedented Safety) was established. Between 1987 and 1994, several ITS technologies and projects were developed in this program such as test vehicle VaMoRs, test vehicle VITA I1 and ARGO project. These technologies and projects were targeted to develop and test of innovative solutions for the vehicles of the future. After that, DRIVE (Dedicated Road Infrastructure for Vehicle Safety) program was established towards improving communication systems and traffic management [11].

In the United States, in the late OS, the Mobility 2000 study team laid the foundation of the IVHS America (Intelligent Vehicle Highway Systems) as an emerging concept for developing transportation facilities. After that, several ITS projects were developed such as AHS (Automated Highway System) towards fully automated test vehicles on highways. In 1994 s, the term "Intelligent Transportation Systems (ITS)" was coined by the U. S. Department of Transportation as a more comprehensive replacement of the "Intelligent Vehicle Highway Systems (IVHS)" [10, 11].

In Japan, in the 80 s, several ITS projects were developed such as RACS (Road Automobile Communication System) and AMTICS (Advanced Mobile Traffic Information and Communication System). In the 90 s, those two projects were combined into VICS (Vehicle Information and Communication System) towards improving communication systems and route planning. Other developed projects were developed as a result of information exchanges with Europe and United States [11].

– Product Development (1995–present):

This phase is characterised by high level development as well as large-scale integration and deployment of ITS programs in Europe, Japan and United States. Where ERTICO (European Road Transport Telematics Implementation Coordination Organization) was set up to provide the required support towards refining and implementing the Europe's Transport Telematics Project. In addition, unified policy was adopted to deal with ITS in a consistent and harmonious manner [11].

After that, Intelligent Transport Systems (ITS) have been known worldwide for their feasible applications towards improving the performance of the transportation systems. Where broad range of principal enabling technologies for Intelligent Transport Systems have been developed such as: Network data, Tree-building algorithms, Geographical Information Systems, Location referencing systems, Digital communications, Global Navigation Satellite Systems, Digital image processing, Roadway sensor technologies, Traffic detectors, Vehicle proximity sensors, Position sensors, Speed and braking sensors Occupant comfort (sleepy driver) sensors, Signs, in-vehicle units, voice recognition, Nomadic devices, handsets and Dynamic maps (local, regional, and national) [12].

Moreover, Intelligent Transport Systems (ITS) are being identified as a domain of high potential to solve many problems facing the transportation sector such as, traffic congestion, safety, transport efficiency and environmental conservation [11].

Intelligent Transport Systems (ITS) integrate four fundamental subsystems [13, 14]:

(1) Infrastructure subsystem;
(2) Vehicular subsystem;
(3) Users subsystem;
(4) Communications subsystem.

These subsystems must work together in cooperative manner in order to achieve the targets of utilizing ITS. Figure 3 shows the conceptual model of intelligent transportation systems.

Due to the rapid advances in the area of telematics, there has been more concentrated efforts and resources to the development, implementation and deployment of several applications and services of intelligent transport systems [12, 13]; among many others, the following can be mentioned:

– Advanced Traffic Management Systems (ATMS) [11–13];
– Advanced Traveller Information Systems (ATIS) [11–13];
– Advanced Vehicle Control Systems (AVCS) [11–13]
– Commercial Vehicle Operations (CVO) [11, 12];
– Advanced Public Transport Systems (APTS) [11–13];
– Fleet Management and Location systems (FMLS) [12, 13]
– Security and Safety Systems (SSS) [12, 13];
– Electronic Payment Systems (EP) [12, 13];
– Emergency Management (EM) [12, 13];
– Advanced Rural Transports Systems (ARTS) [11];
– Weather and Environmental Conditions Monitoring [12];
– Disaster Response Management and Coordination [12].

It is worth noting the diversity of ITS applications and services towards improving efficiency and reliability of offered services to users, increasing safety and reducing environmental impacts [13].

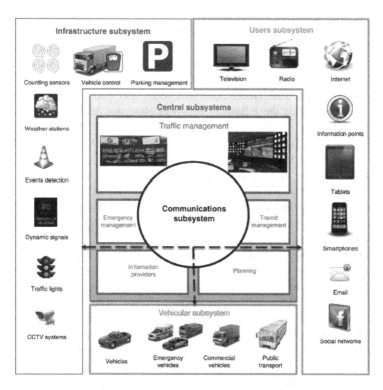

Fig. 3. Intelligent transport systems conceptual model [13]

2.2   Literature Review

In the recent years, the world has witnessed unprecedented advancements in information and communications technology (Telematics, ICT).

Several researchers highlighted the concept of intelligent transport systems (ITS), where they developed innovations and conducted many projects towards increasing the efficiency and availability of post disaster transport infrastructure and emergency response management.

An extensive review was conducted towards investigating the used techniques for developing intelligent transport systems in the aftermath of disasters. In the following, we will present this review and show the evolution of the concerns according to the year of publication of the works.

The authors in [6] developed an integrated multi-objective model using genetic algorithms incorporated with traffic assignment and K-shortest path methods. The model aimed to find the optimal rescue path and traffic controlled arcs for disaster relief processes under complex and unpredicted conditions. For dealing with uncertain information and measure the access reliability of rescue path, fuzzy system reliability theory was adopted. In addition, genetic algorithms and K-shortest path methods were used to determine optimal rescue path and controlled arcs. The proposed model included three sub-models: (1) rescue shortest path model, (2) post-disaster traffic assignment model & (3) traffic controlled arcs selection model. A case study approach was used to verify the applicability of this proposed model; the results showed the efficiency of this model in reduction the demand on police officers as well as the impacts to the ordinary trips, with only a small increment in travel time of rescue team.

The authors in [15] designed a wireless infrastructure for monitoring sensitive areas and enabling intercommunication between all rescue teams in the aftermath of the disaster. The authors developed an Integrated Emergency Communication System (IECS) to support local and remote communications and information collection. The proposed system included the following networks elements: Mobile Ad hoc Network (MANET), Mobile Terminals, Wireless Sensor Network (WSN), Local Gateways, Satellite Terminal and Terrestrial Gateways. Firstly, WSN and MANET were deployed on the disaster site for local communication and information collection. To communicate with the remote disaster-safe areas, satellite gateway was used for the local networks to interconnect with the satellite mobile network. In addition, cellular gateway was used as an alternative remote communication. The proposed system played a vital role in reducing the network deployment time, supporting more terminal types, and providing emergency management services.

The authors in [16] exploited the advancements in the ICT technologies through merging the following technologies: VANETs (Vehicular Ad hoc Networks) and Cloud computing technologies for developing an intelligent emergency response system. The proposed system architecture included three main layers: (1) the cloud infrastructure layer that represent the base platform for this system, (2) the intelligence layer which contains computational models and algorithm for choosing the optimal emergency procedures & (3) the system interface which acquires data from different ports. The system was characterized by its capacity of collection data from several sources and locations, making the best decisions and transference the information to vehicles and other nodes in real-time. This study used a case-study approach to measure the efficiency of this system by comparing two scenarios for emergency response system in the aftermath of disaster. The first was the traditional emergency response system while the second was the proposed Intelligent VANET Cloud Emergency Response System. The results showed the essential role of the proposed system in terms of improved dynamic traffic management and evacuation in the aftermath of disasters.

The author in [17] used Geographic Information Systems (GIS) data for modelling the optimal vehicle route in terrain in emergency situations. Where in the aftermath of disasters, it is so necessary to find the optimal paths (shortest or fastest) in terrain for transport as well as investigate point, line and area obstacles. This study considered only trees as the most common point obstacles in terrain, then the author analyses the typical structure of tree stands in the forest, their characteristics in GIS databases, as well as dimensional parameters of vehicles moving in the forest. Where the quality of the data is so necessary for finding routes between point obstacles. To search the optimal shortest route of movement among line obstructions and area obstructions, the following algorithms were used: Voronoi graph and Delaunay triangulation; Dijkstra algorithm of optimal route search and optimization of fractional line.

The authors in [18] used Geospatial technologies such as Remote Sensing, and Geographic Information Systems (GIS) integrated with valuable near/real time field information to provide a comprehensive platform for emergency management. Where authors focused on implementing Dijkstra algorithm to find the shortest distance between event location and resource location for Disaster management. This study explained standards for taking decision to transfer the resources form one place to another in emergency situation. In addition, authors developed software components for finding the shortest route between two locations. Where OpenLayers java Script framework was adopted by implementing Web Map Service (WMS) integrated in the system includes a spatial database PostGIS, pgRouting, a GIS server Geo Server and front-end technology PHP and Open Layers. This study used a case-study approach to measure the applicability of this software, the analysis results show the efficiency in finding the shortest route and displaying the route details in table as well as on the geospatial map.

The authors in [19] developed an Intelligent Disaster Decision Support System (IDDSS) to provide emergency managers and drivers with a platform for integrating spatial data (including road network, traffic, geographic, economic and meteorological data) as well as models (including disaster and traffic simulation) that can be used for managing road transport systems. The proposed system was characterized with its capability supporting homogenous data aggregation, manipulation and visualisation towards investigating a wide range of disaster management issues. Also, authors developed a conceptual framework for Traffic Management Points (TMP) optimization. Where genetic algorithm has been used to determine the best location of Traffic Management Points (TMP) taking into account available police resources, capacity of road network, estimated demand levels, risks to road users as well as traffic disruption. A case study approach was used to verify the applicability of this IDDSS system during bushfire and floods events, the results showed the efficiency of this proposed system in optimal location planning of Traffic Management Points based on the residual capacity of road network and estimated demand levels.

The authors in [20] emphaized the vital role of Intelligent Transport Systems (ITS) in providing flexible solutions towards improving traffic safety and emergency services in the aftermath of disasters. Authors proposed a new cloud computing model for Vehicular Ad-hoc networks (VANETs) called VANET-Cloud. This proposed model includes three layers: The client layer, the cloud layer, and communication layer to ensure communication between the client and the cloud layer. The proposed model can support several services (processing, storage, web services, bandwidth, and others) for traffic management and emergency systems.

The authors in [21] confirmed on the essential role of Vehicular Ad-hoc networks (VANETs) in traffic management and transport. Also, authors presented Cloud Computing as an advanced platform to provide vastly manageable and scalable virtual servers, virtual networks, computing resources, storage resources, and network resources. However, Vehicular cloud computing cannot meet all the requirements of quality of service in VANETs, so new technologies are needed. This study introduced Fog Computing as a frontier concept for VANETs that extends cloud computing and services to the edge of the network. Also, Fog Computing is characterized by its platform that provides the compute, storage, and networking services between end devices and data centres. In VANETs, fog nodes closest to the network edge ingest the data from different types of devices, and developers decide how to use them. The authors pointed out that merging fog computing with VANETs opens an area of possibilities for applications and services on the edge of the cloud computing. Also, they mentioned some opportunities for challenges and issues about research directions of potential future work for fog computing in VANETs towards more efficient traffic management.

The authors in [22] confirmed on the importance of conducting resilient communication transport infrastructure for relief operations in the aftermath of disasters. This study presented an extensive literature review for multi-hop device-to-device (D2D) communication in disaster scenarios. Then, the authors concluded a list of design guidelines, from the reviewed literature as well as their observations, for post-disaster resilient communication infrastructure. These design guidelines can be summarized as the following: The system must operate in a fully distributed manner, Instantly self-activated, Operable without electrical grid system, Applicable by smart phones or mobile devices, Interoperable and Geographically widespread. In addition, the authors debated the applicability of vehicular ad-hoc networks VANETs for communication scheme through experimental analysis on the impact of radio range in post-disaster communication infrastructure and drew conclusions for its applicability to real-world scenarios for rescue operations.

The authors in [23] proposed a new mobility model using Ad Hoc Wireless Networks for recovery operations and minimize the required time to reach the destroyed areas after disasters. The proposed model works in two stages, the first stage contain three steps: In the beginning, the disaster area will be split into hexagonal grids, then the tracked path during node's movement in the disaster area will be found, taking into consideration the spread of these nodes in hexa-cells, by using Three common algorithms: Breadth first search that explores in all directions equally, the second algorithm is the Dijkstra's Algorithm that seeks the lower cost paths by avoiding the blocked ways, the A* is a modified algorithm of the Dijkstra's where it was optimized for a single location. Finally, the weight for any cell that depends on the desired number of nodes in any cell will be defined. While during the second stage, re-weighting algorithm will be conducting in the case of new disaster shock or new emergency situation later after the first strike. Moreover, the authors stated that the Ad hoc nodes is characterized by its capacity to repair any distortion or interruption in the communication channels in the disaster areas and therefore help in the recovery and rescuing in such areas.

The authors in [24] addressed many problems in rescue processes and delays in the effective response to the victim areas. Authors confirmed on the crucial role of response actions in the aftermath of disaster, where large amount of properties and valuable lives are depending on it. Authors proposed an effective system to solve these problems. This system was developed using Global Position system (GPS) and Geographic Information Systems (GIS). Also Modified Dijkstra's was used to find the optimal route for emergency vehicles. The proposed system provided emergency rescue teams with the precise location of disaster area and the optimal evacuation routes to transport people from the hazard location to the safe places. In addition, this study presented a web-based application for the best evacuation route assessment during natural disaster. A case study approach was used to verify the applicability of this system during natural disaster, the results showed the system's capacity in Damage Location Identification and Defining the Close Emergency Services as well as Showing the Best Evacuation Routes.

The authors in [25] emphasized the vital role of emergency systems in the rescue operations in disaster situations. Authors designed a framework of a new emergency system based on Global Position Systems (GPS) and Geographic Information Systems (GIS). the system contains three structural layers: Access Layer, Business Logic Layer, and Data Layer. In addition, this system includes several basic functions towards achieving the optimal path planning and real-time location through the heuristic algorithm and improved genetic algorithm. The proposed system has been experimented through a case study, the results showed its capacity in collecting the information accurately and rapidly as well as providing effective services for emergency rescue command.

The authors in [26] emphasized the vital role of transportation and communication in Catastrophic natural disasters. The authors designed an emergency response system using Global Positioning System (GPS) and Vehicular Ad hoc Networks (VANETs). Firstly, Emergency control plan was developed, then Alert messages, their types and transferred message codes were set. In addition, a centralized server (control room) was established. The main function of this room is managing all alerts and information for relief operations as well as gathering all the information about the disaster area like collapsed bridges, road blocked etc. Also, this room connect with mobile nodes (hospitals, first aid teams, volunteers, expert-team-members for relief operations etc.) to deliver the desired services according to the request. The proposed system is characterized by its ability to fulfil the main communication requirements for land transport vessels and aid services in early hours after a disaster.

The authors in [27] proposed a new methodology for urban emergency planning using Geographic Information Systems (GIS) platform. this proposed methodology aims to overcome one of the biggest challenges after disasters represented by the impossibility of reaching the affected areas due to obstructions on road infrastructures. This proposed methodology can be used for the planning of optimal connections in the case of limit conditions. Also, it can be used for identification and planning of safety interventions, assigning appropriate priorities to various buildings on the basis of their relevance compared to road use and cost considerations. The proposed methodology has been experimented through a case study approach, the results showed the its capacity in finding the optimal routes.

The author in [28] emphasized the vital role of road transportation network in the management of disaster situations despite its' vulnerability to disasters. Ghavami developed a Multi-Criteria Spatial Decision Support System (MC-SDSS) to evaluate the transportation network performance in disaster situations. This system was developed using Geographic Information Systems (GIS) for storing the data, performing the analyses in order to produce the required criteria and displaying the results. Also, Analytical Hierarchy Process (AHP) is used to determine priorities and preferences of decision-makers about the criteria. This study adopted four criteria as indicators for evaluating the transportation network performance in disaster situations as the following: capacity, accessibility, vulnerability, and importance criteria. The proposed MC-SDSS is comprised of the four main modules: spatial analysis model, MCDM model, user interface, and a database. A case study approach was used to verify the applicability of this system, the results showed the system s' capacity in identifying strategic roads in disaster situations.

All above, this review emphasized the vital role of road transportation networks in supporting of emergency systems and rescue processes in disaster areas. In addition, this review revealed the crucial role of Information and Communications Technology (Telematics, ICT) for post disaster relief operations and emergency transport management systems.

It is worth noting that Information and Communications Technology (Telematics, ICT) is growing at immense rate [29]. Where diversity of techniques is being developed and adopted for developing intelligent transport systems in the aftermath of disasters.

Through our previous extensive review, we found several techniques has been adopted towards developing several intelligent systems for managing emergency systems and rescue operations, identifying the optimal shortest rescue routes, and optimal location planning of Traffic Management Points .... etc.; among many others, the following techniques can be mentioned:

Geographic Information System (GIS), Global Positioning System (GPS), Genetic Algorithms, Fuzzy Logic, Wireless Sensor Network (WSN), Mobile ad-hoc networks (MANETs), Vehicular ad-hoc networks (VANETs), Cloud Computing and Fog Computing.

Moreover, Here the following question arises: "What are the best techniques for dealing with big data under the dynamically variable unpredictable conditions???"

In this paper, we will investigate the most common techniques and develop a new integrated system for emergency transport management in the aftermath of disasters.

3   Research Target

This paper is focused on intelligent transport systems concept for post - disaster infrastructure under reconstruction. This paper aims to define the most common techniques for Emergency Response Management in the aftermath of disasters and develop a new integrated system for Emergency Transport Management on the basis of the information on needs in the field of humanitarian aid for the affected communities.

The Proposed Multi-Objective System fits into the existing infrastructure, terrain, climatic and environmental conditions. Moreover, this system is based on the latest telematics, web and phone applications to help users (emergency mangers, drivers, victims…etc.) for timely relief operations in the aftermath of disasters.

4   Research Methodology

An exploratory mixed approach has been used to meet the target of this research, this methodology is divided into three main stages: The first stage is qualitative in nature where data is collected via Literature Review of 26 related research materials ranging from 2008 to 2018 to detect the used techniques for Emergency Response Management in the aftermath of disasters.

While the second stage is Content Analysis where data obtained from the first stage will be analyzed to determine the trend of research materials during the selected period and the most common techniques for developing ITS after disasters.

The third stage is System Design where data and results from previous stages will be adopted to develop the proposed integrated system for Emergency Transport Management in dynamically variable unpredictable conditions, these stages are illustrated in Fig. 4.

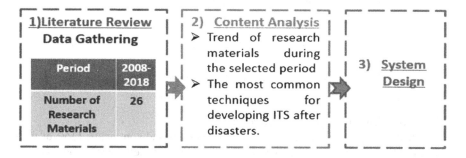

Fig. 4. Research methodology [own study]

5 Research Results

5.1 General Information About Research Materials

Altogether 26 research materials of using intelligent transport systems (ITS) for post disaster emergency transport management has been reviewed. In this section, we will present the results of descriptive analysis of these materials:

5.1.1 Year of Publication

Altogether 26 research materials of using intelligent transport systems (ITS) for post disaster emergency transport management, during the period from 2008 until 2018, has been reviewed.

Figure 5 shows the number of reviewed research materials per year, Although the vital role of ITS towards achieving efficient relief operations, the research in this field is relatively recent.

Also, the number of research materials per year is still not representative. However, it is worth noting the increasing number of research materials with the progress in years.

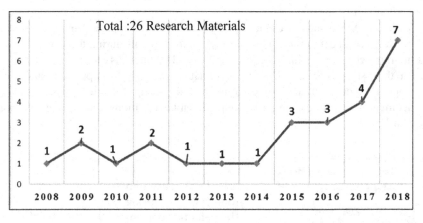

Fig. 5. Number of research materials between 2008 and 2018 [own study]

5.1.2 Geography of Research Materials

Related research materials were from different countries and continents. Most of them are based in the Asia (61%), followed by Europe (27%), America (8%) and Australia (4%), Fig. 6 shows the Geography of research materials.

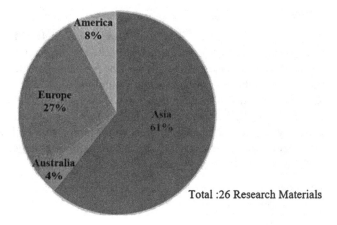

Fig. 6. Geography of research materials [own study]

5.1.3   Used Techniques for ITS in Research Materials

To meet research objectives, Different types of techniques for developing ITS after disasters have been investigated. Figure 7 shows the most common techniques for Emergency Response Management in the aftermath of disasters. where (GPS & GIS) and (VANETs) are the most common techniques in the reviewed research materials (15%), followed by (GPS& GIS& Algorithms); (VANETs& Cloud Computing) and which are (12%).

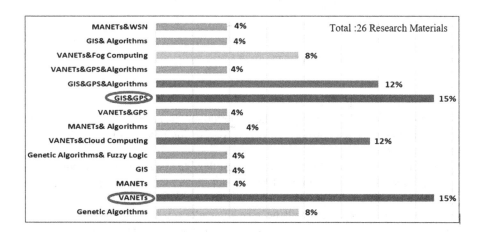

Fig. 7. The most common techniques for developing ITS after disasters [own study]

5.2   System Design

The Integrated System for Emergency Transport Management (IS4ETM) is designed depending on the most common telematics techniques, web and phone applications. Also, the proposed system is designed to fit into the humanitarian needs, existing infrastructure, terrain, climatic and environmental conditions.

The Proposed System aims to manage timely relief operations in the aftermath of disasters through the broadcast information to the users (emergency mangers, drivers, victims...etc.). This system would provide all users with a prototype mobile application & web platform to define the shortest rescue route and all required emergency services.

IS4ETM is composed of three sub-systems, Fig. 8:

I. Input sub-system
II. Processing & Control sub-system
III. Output sub-system

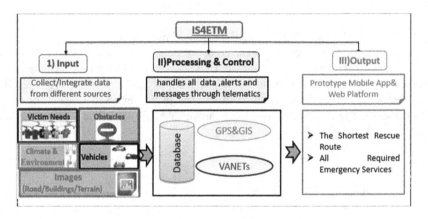

Fig. 8. IS4ETM- architecture [own study]

5.2.1   The Input Sub-system

The proposed Input sub-system will collect all required data from different sources and store in databases to develop the Integrated System for Emergency Transport Management *IS4ETM*.

The purpose of this sub- system is to design flexible system fit into the emergency situations after disasters through involving all stakeholder in gathering and exchanging data.

Moreover, affected people will be able to send/receive the updated information regarding the disaster situation. In addition, these data will be available to anyone who can provide a rescue services in the aftermath of disasters.

These data materials will include five main categories as following: Victim/Affected People Needs, Obstacles, Climate & Environment, Vehicles and Images. Figure 9 shows the input sub-system.

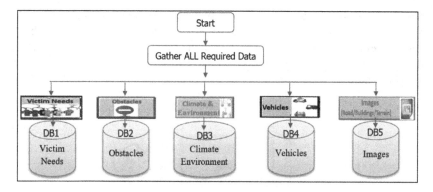

Fig. 9. The input sub-system [own study]

An abstract view will be explained for each category: Firstly, Victim/Affected People Needs category contains 9 nine keypad buttons for simple inputs. Since small size packets are quicker and easier to transfer in the network [26], short message label of the alert message has been mapped to each button. The alert message labels of Victim Needs Interface buttons are designed as the following: (1) First Aid, (2) Volunteers, (3) Food, (4) Water, (5) Clothes, (6) Camp, (*) Message, (#) Ok, and (0) Cancel. Figure 10 shows the interface of Victim Needs.

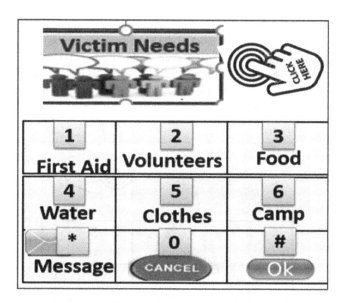

Fig. 10. The interface of victim needs [own study]

Secondly, Obstacles category contains 6 six keypad buttons for simple inputs. Also, short message label of the alert message has been mapped to each button. The alert message labels of Obstacles Interface buttons are designed as the following: (1) Blocked Road, (2) Broken Bridge, (3) Collapsed Building, (*) Message, (#) Ok, and (0) Cancel. Figure 11 shows the interface of Obstacles.

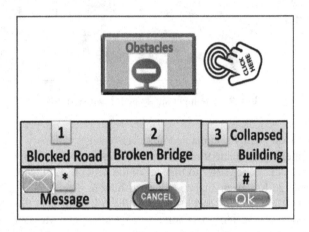

Fig. 11. The interface of obstacles [own study]

Thirdly, Climate & Environment category contains 9 nine keypad buttons for simple inputs. Also, short message label of the alert message has been mapped to each button. The alert message labels of Climate & Environment Interface buttons are designed as the following: (1) Temperature, (2) Drought, (3) Ice, (4) Tropical Cyclone, (5) Precipitation, (6) Gases Emissions, (*) Message, (#) Ok, and (0) Cancel. Figure 12 shows the interface of Climate & Environment.

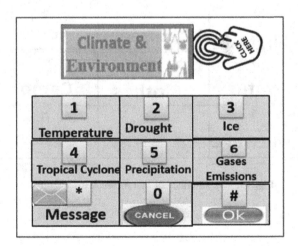

Fig. 12. The interface of climate & environment [own study]

Fourthly, Vehicles category contains 9 nine keypad buttons for simple inputs. Also, short message label of the alert message has been mapped to each button. The alert message labels of Vehicles Interface buttons are designed as the following: (1) Ambulance, (2) Truck, (3) BUS, (4) Van, (5) Car, (?) Number, (*) Message, (#) Ok, and (0) Cancel. Figure 13 shows the interface of Vehicles

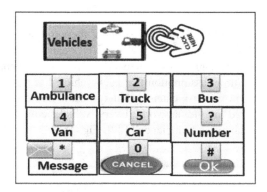

Fig. 13. The interface of vehicles [own study]

Finally, Images category contains 4 four keypad buttons for simple inputs and inserting GPS Images for displaying Disaster Area included (roads, buildings, etc.). Also, short message label of the alert message has been mapped to each button. The alert message labels of Images Interface buttons are designed as the following: (1) Area, (*) Message, (#) Ok, and (0) Cancel. Figure 14 shows the interface of Images.

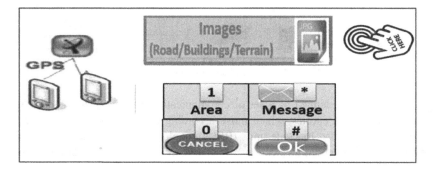

Fig. 14. The interface of images [own study]

5.2.2   The Processing & Control Sub-system

The proposed Processing & Control sub-system will handle all input data stored in various databases according to the previous categories to develop the Integrated System for Emergency Transport Management IS4ETM.

The purpose of this sub- system is to determine the shortest rescue route and all required emergency services through adopting the most common techniques of telematics. Figure 7 revealed that (GPS & GIS) and (VANETs) are ranked firstly as the most common of the reviewed research materials.

In this paper, this proposed sub-system is developed depending on the three most common techniques (GPS, GIS and VANETs).

– VANETs:

Vehicular ad-hoc networks (VANETs) is one of the wireless technologies and the most prominent enabling technology for ITS. VANETs can be defined as:

"An emerging field of mobile ad-hoc network. It is built for enhancing the traffic safety and efficiency with an assumption that each vehicle has the capability to communicate with others via wireless channel. Safety-related and traffic information are disseminated and shared in the network. Every vehicle collects information and cooperates to achieve safety and efficiency" [29], Fig. 15.

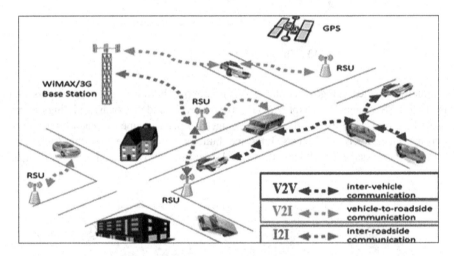

Fig. 15. Vehicular ad-hoc networks (VANETs) [30]

VANETs is also defined as a set of communication nodes consisting of vehicles considered as mobile entities, which move according to a restricted mobility pattern, and fixed entities called roadside units (RSUs), deployed at critical locations such as slippery roads, dangerous intersections, or places well known for hazardous weather conditions [20].

More importantly, VANETs requires no additional infrastructure, so it is comparably cheaper and provides good coverage [26].

VANETs often using Global Positioning System (GPS) devices for location determination and supports communication among vehicles known as vehicle-to-vehicle communication (V2V), and between vehicles and the RSU infrastructure, known also as vehicle-to-infrastructure communication (V2I), and among RSU infrastructure known as (I2I) [20].

The connected vehicles play a very significant role in the aftermath of disasters as they have on-board batteries and many sensors including cameras providing valuable images. The vehicular network is considered as emergency communication mechanism [21].

Under special conditions in the aftermath of disasters, the major Challenge in rescue operation is the partial or fully dis-connectivity of the already deployed network and with the critical need for many emergency vehicles, which will require more advanced communication technology to exchange the information between vehicles and avoid congestion. Moreover, (VANETs) has been adopted as an advanced technique enabled hand-devices or vehicle that are used in rescue emergency for effective telecommunications in the proposed system.

– GPS:

Global Positioning System (GPS) has been adopted as the most common location information technique worldwide. Also, GPS has high advantages over other location techniques in less infrastructure expenses [25]. GPS was used in the previous input sub-system as we stated above.

– GIS:

Geographic Information System (GIS) is the most powerful information system for analysing, modelling, and displaying the disaster situations [18].

GIS has capability to handle and process spatial data in a large volume. Also, GIS becomes a widespread technique that can create maps, integrate information, visualize and solve problems, and develop valuable solutions [31].

In addition, Applying GIS for disaster management is an effective technique to monitor all the activities that occur on the roads and store the records for future development.

In this paper, after determining disaster locations and taking the required images using Global Positioning System (GPS).

Geographic Information System (GIS) has been adopted to conduct spatial planning by organizing, analysing and mapping large sets of data. These data have been gathered in the previous input sub-system and through applying VANET s technique. Then, these data have be stored in database and will organized in several layers in GIS. After that spatial planning processes will be performed towards producing thematic maps for Emergency Systems and determining the Shortest Rescue Route, Fig. 16.

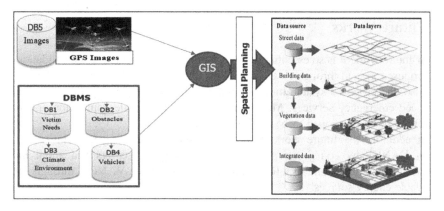

Fig. 16. The processing & control sub-system [own study]

5.2.3   The Output Sub-system

The expected results of Integrated System for Emergency Transport Management (IS4ETM) are represented by: determining the shortest rescue route and all required emergency services.

To make this proposed system IS4ETS available to all stakeholders, the information should be presented through End users: broadcast to the vehicles, prototype mobile application, and web platform.

National Database for Emergency Management (NDEM) will be adopted as web platform. Where NDEM is a Web based GIS application that provides client-side applications using http protocols running on the ISRO-VPN Network which can embed geographic information data as well as non-geographic data [18].

6   Conclusion

One of the most problems that occur in the case of a disaster events represents by the impossibility of reaching the affected places due to the inaccessibility of routes which have been obstructed by collapses. The integration of computers and other technologies (ICT) into transport infrastructure will create more advanced techniques towards more efficient timely relief operations.

In this research, we defined the most common techniques in intelligent transport systems (ITS) for effective emergency response management in the aftermath of disasters.

This research will contribute to practical knowledge by integrating the most prominent technologies: GPS, GIS and VANETs to propose a new Integrated System for Emergency Transport Management (IS4ETM) towards determining the shortest rescue route and emergency services.

The proposed system (IS4ETM) is characterized by its capacity to gather information from multiple sources and locations as well as provide the valuable images and alert messages for more effective emergency transport management.

In addition, this system will provide emergency managers, drivers and victims with integrating spatial data (including infrastructure and terrain) through prototype mobile application, and web platform.

7   Future Works

In our future work, it is so essential to focus more on further analysis and validation of the proposed system through case studies.

Also, the proposed system must be configured using suitable algorithms for more advanced emergency services. Moreover, the prototype mobile application and web platform will be developed to be used worldwide.

In addition, the future work may seek to broaden the scope of this work to Green VANET by combining permanent and temporary servers and adopt more advanced design procedure of a Road Side Unit (RSU) in the VANETs through using renewable energy sources.

Acknowledgement. The work has been financially supported by the Polish Ministry of Science and Higher Education. The work has been also supported by the UNESCO AGH Chair for Science, Technology and Engineering Education, project ed. 2018A.

References

1. United Nations, UNISDR Terminology on Disaster Risk Reduction, United Nations International Strategy for Disaster Reduction (UNISDR), Geneva, Switzerland, p. 35 (2009)
2. Guha-Sapir, D., et al.: Annual Disaster Statistical Review 2010: The Numbers and Trends, p. 50. CRED, Brussels (2010)
3. Baraka, J., Yadavalli, V., Singh, R.: A transportation model for an effective disaster relief operation in the SADC region. S. Afr. J. Ind. Eng. **28**(2), 46–58 (2017)
4. Peeta, S., et al.: Pre-disaster investment decisions for strengthening a highway network. Comput. Oper. Res. **37**(10), 1708–1719 (2010). https://doi.org/10.1016/j.cor.2009.12.006
5. Hayat, E., Amaratunga, D.: Road Reconstruction in Post Disaster Recovery; The Challenges and Obstacles, p. 15. University of Salford (2011)
6. Chiou, Y.-C., Lai, Y.-H.: An integrated multi-objective model to determine the optimal rescue path and traffic controlled arcs for disaster relief operations under uncertainty environments. J. Adv. Transp. **42**(4), 493–519 (2008)
7. Hayat, E., Amaratunga, D., Haigh, R.: The challenges and obstacles of post-disaster road infrastructure reconstruction in the pre-construction phase. In: The 6th International Conference on Structural Engineering and Construction Management 2015, Kandy, Sri Lanka, p. 11 (2015)
8. Konstantinidou, M., Kepaptsoglou, K., Karlaftis, M.: Transportation network post-disaster planning and management: a review part I: post-disaster transportation network performance. Int. J. Transp. **2**(3), 1–16 (2014)
9. Iida, Y., Kurauchi, F., Shimada, H.: Traffic management system against major earthquakes. IATSS Res. **24**(2), 6–17 (2000)
10. Williams, B.: Intelligent Transportation Systems, Sustainable Built Environment, vol. II, p. 409. Eolss Publishers Co. Ltd, UK (2009)
11. Figueiredo, L., et al.: Towards the development of intelligent transportation systems. In: IEEE Intelligent Transportation Systems Conference Proceedings - Oakland (CA) USA (2001). https://doi.org/10.1109/itsc.2001.948835
12. Miles, J.: Intelligent Transport Systems: Overview and Structure (History, Applications, and Architectures). Encyclopedia of Automotive Engineering, p. 16. Wiley, Chichester (2014)
13. Perallos, A., et al.: Intelligent Transport Systems Technologies and Applications, p. 468. Wiley, Chichester (2016)
14. Kelly, T., Choe, Y.: Intelligent transport systems and CALM. In: International Telecommunication Union, ITU-T Technology Watch Report 1, p. 13 (2007)
15. Bai, Y., et al.: Emergency communication system by heterogeneous wireless networking. In: 2010 IEEE International Conference on Wireless Communications, Networking and Information Security, pp. 488–492 (2010). https://doi.org/10.1109/wcins.2010.5541719
16. Alazawi, Z., et al.: Intelligent disaster management system based on cloud-enabled vehicular networks. In: 2011 11th International Conference on ITS Telecommunications, pp. 361–368 (2011)
17. Rybansky, M.: Modelling of the optimal vehicle route in terrain in emergency situations using GIS data. In: IOP Conference Series: Earth and Environmental Science, vol. 18, p. 6 (2014). https://doi.org/10.1088/1755-1315/18/1/012131

18. Bhanumurthy, V., et al.: Route analysis for decision support system in emergency management through GIS technologies. Int. J. Adv. Eng. Glob. Technol. **03**(02), 6 (2015)
19. Kaviani, A., et al.: A decision support system for improving the management of traffic networks during disasters. In: Australasian Transport Research Forum 2015 Proceedings, p. 14 (2015)
20. Bitam, S., Mellouk, A., Zeadally, S.: VANET-cloud: a generic cloud computing model for vehicular ad hoc networks. IEEE Wireless Commun. **22**(1), 96–102 (2015). https://doi.org/10.1109/mwc.2015.7054724
21. Kai, K., Cong, W., Tao, L.: Fog computing for vehicular Ad-hoc networks: paradigms, scenarios, and issues. J. China Univ. Posts Telecommun. **23**(2), 56–96 (2016). https://doi.org/10.1016/s1005-8885(16)60021-3
22. Dargahi, T., Momeni, S., Shafiei, H.: Post disaster resilient networks: design guidelines for rescue operations. In: INetSec 2017, Rome, Italy, p. 14 (2017)
23. Manaseer, S., Alawneh, A.: A new mobility model for ad hoc networks in disaster recovery areas. Int. J. Online Biomed. Eng. (iJOE) **13**(6), 8 (2017)
24. Phyo, K., Sein, M.: Effective evacuation route strategy during natural disaster. In: Proceedings of the APAN – Research Workshop 2017, p. 6 (2017). ISBN 978-4-9905448-7-4
25. Chen, Y., Zeng, X., Yuan, T.: Design and development of earthquake emergency rescue command system based on GIS and GPS. In: Zeng, X., Xie, X., Sun, J., Ma, L., Chen, Y. (eds.) ITASC 2017. SIST, vol. 62, pp. 126–138. Springer, Singapore (2017). https://doi.org/10.1007/978-981-10-3575-3_14
26. Khaliq, K.A., Chughtai, O., Qayyum, A., Pannek, J.: Design of emergency response system for disaster management using VANET. In: Freitag, M., Kotzab, H., Pannek, J. (eds.) LDIC 2018. LNL, pp. 310–317. Springer, Cham (2018). https://doi.org/10.1007/978-3-319-74225-0_42
27. Francini, M., et al.: To support urban emergency planning: a GIS instrument for the choice of optimal routes based on seismic hazards. Int. J. Disaster Risk Reduction **31**, 121–134 (2018)
28. Ghavami, S.M.: Multi-criteria spatial decision support system for identifying strategic roads in disaster situations. Int. J. Crit. Infrastruct. Prot. **24**, 23–36 (2018). https://doi.org/10.1016/j.ijcip.2018.10.004
29. Al-Azawi, Z.: Transportation evacuation strategies based on vehicular disaster management system in urban network environment, Ph.D. thesis, School of Computing, Science and Engineering Salford University Manchester, UK, p. 252 (2014)
30. Seliem, H., Shaaban, E.: Enhancing AOMDV routing protocol for V2V communication. In: Conference Paper, p. 9 (2012)
31. Lesage, S.S., Ayral, P.A.: Using GIS for emergency management: a case study during the 2002 and 2003 flooding in South-East France. Int. J. Emer. Manage. **4**(4), 682 (2007). https://doi.org/10.1504/ijem.2007.015738

Selected Problems of a Motor Vehicle Motion in a Turn After Steering Wheel Release

Jarosław Zalewski$^{(\boxtimes)}$

Warsaw University of Technology, Pl. Politechniki 1, Warsaw, Poland
j.zalewski@ans.pw.edu.pl

Abstract. In the paper selected phenomena related to lateral motion of a motor vehicle have been considered. The adopted maneuver, selected for the simulation in MSC Adams/Car environment, based on vehicle model realizing a turn with steering wheel release with the instant speed of 50 km/h. The most important issue is observing the phenomenon right after releasing the steering wheel. For the road with random inequalities, the same profiles were assumed for the left and right wheels of the vehicle, with two values of the coefficient determining the maximum height of irregularities assumed for the simulation purposes: 0,3 and 0,9. Thanks to this, the quality of the road surface could be considered as one of the potential factors disturbing the curvilinear movement of the motor vehicle.

Keywords: Lateral motion · Steering release · Vehicle dynamics ·
Uneven road

1 Introduction

The aim of this paper is to present the selected phenomena occurring while simulating the motor vehicle motion in a turn. Special attention has been paid to the first seconds after releasing the steering wheel, hence the duration time was about 5 s, during which the simulated vehicle traveled the distance of about 60 m. Different road conditions have been taken into account with the selected maneuver parameters and loading configuration adopted as an exemplary analysis of possible response of a motor vehicle in the specific traffic conditions.

As for the maneuver, vehicle cornering with steering wheel release has been selected, because it seems obvious that in such conditions the vehicle response would be difficult to predict. A double seater vehicle structure used also in previous papers (e.g. [2, 10–12]) has been laden as presented in the assumptions section and used for the adopted maneuver simulation in MSC Adams/Car software.

Certain aspects of lateral motion of a motor vehicle has been previously used e.g. in [5, 9] and for rail vehicles in [1].

As for the random road irregularities, several works have been devoted to the problem, e.g. [4]. Another scope of issues has been related to road – wheel cooperation, which has been the subject of multiple works, e.g. [6, 8]. In general there are numerous publications treating the problems of motor vehicle dynamics covering many problems in one publication, e.g. [3, 7].

© Springer Nature Switzerland AG 2019
J. Mikulski (Ed.): TST 2019, CCIS 1049, pp. 273–286, 2019.
https://doi.org/10.1007/978-3-030-27547-1_20

2 Assumptions and Vehicle Configuration

For the purpose of analysis of the selected phenomena during the vehicle cornering with the release of a steering wheel some essential assumptions concerning both the vehicle loading and the road surface have been made.

The mass of vehicle body has been increased from 995 kg to 1155 kg according to Figs. 1 and 2. The mass of the driver has been assumed at 80 kg, passenger at 60 kg and the baggage at 20 kg.

Initial coordinates of the body of the vehicle without any additional mass, in relation to the so-called "origo" point (marked in Figs. 1 and 2), are as follows [2]:

$x_C = 1.5$ m, $y_C = 0$, $z_C = 0.45$ m.

Initial values of the moments of inertia and deviation in relation to the axes passing through "origo" are as follows [2]:

$I_x = 401$ kgm^2, $I_y = 2940$ kgm^2, $I_z = 2838$ kgm^2, $I_{xy} = 0$, $I_{xz} = 671$ kgm^2, $I_{yz} = 0$.

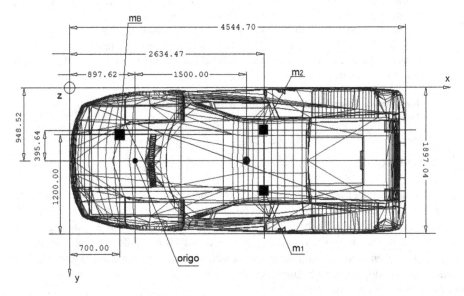

Fig. 1. Location of the masses loading the vehicle body: driver (m_1), passenger (m_2) and baggage (m_B), plan view [11]

By adding masses of the driver (m_1, Figs. 1 and 2), the passenger (m_2, Figs. 1 and 2) and the baggage (m_B, Figs. 1 and 2) mentioned above, new values of the mass – inertia parameters have been obtained, which enabled providing the additional factor disturbing vehicle motion, especially in lateral direction. These new parameters are as follows:

– center of mass coordinates:

$x_C = 1.499$ m, $y_C = 0.007$ m, $z_C = 0.452$ m.

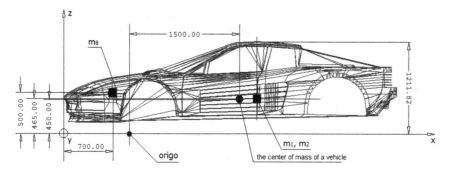

Fig. 2. Location of the loading masses, left side view [11]

– moments of inertia and deviation:

$I_x = 436$ kgm^2, $I_y = 3333$ kgm^2, $I_z = 3196$ kgm^2;
$I_{xy} = 118$ kgm^2, $I_{xz} = 783$ kgm^2, $I_{yz} = 36$ kgm^2.

The vehicle model which has been used for the simulations presented in this paper and the road irregularities generation have been described more exactly, among others, in [2]. Some necessary changes had to be made in this model in order to run simulations on a randomly uneven road surface. Hence the tires have been switched from standard PAC89 to FTire flexible tire models able to cooperate with the random road irregularities. Also certain assumptions concerning the road surface itself have been made, which is presented in the section concerning simulation of the adopted maneuver.

Other assumptions concern the partial nonlinearity of suspension, which has been presented in [11] i.e. the spring in a MacPherson column remained linear, whereas the damper was nonlinear. Quasi-rigidity of the vehicle body has also been assumed, because in order to understand the potential consequences of vehicle response to disturbances in turning maneuvers such simplification as lack of elasticity in a vehicle body seems understandable, especially when concerning the vehicle as a whole, e.g. [10].

3 Simulation of Vehicle Cornering with the Steering Wheel Release

Simulation of a cornering maneuver with steering wheel release has been performed along the randomly uneven road at an initial longitudinal velocity 50 km/h on 3rd gear. The initial radius of a turn has been set at 500 m. It is necessary to mention that the driver reaction to the occurring disturbances has not been taken into account due to the author's desire to provide simulation results corresponding with the vehicle reaction as a technical means of transport.

As for the road conditions four configurations has been adopted, which is presented in Table 1. The maneuver lasted 5 s which stresses the attention to the first few seconds after releasing the steering wheel and the phenomena occurring afterwards. The vehicle moved across randomly uneven road with different coefficient of adhesion reflecting dry (0,8) and icy (0,3) surface as well as the "intensity parameter" reflecting lower (0,3) and higher (0,9) amplitudes of the irregularities on the road surface. In Figs. 3 and 4 those irregularities along the road covered by the vehicle are presented.

Table 1. Configurations of both the vehicle and the road surface for the straight line, constant speed maneuver [own study]

Vehicle	Laden according to Figs. 1 and 2			
Simulation time	5 s			
Road surface condition	dry ($\mu = 0,8$)		icy ($\mu = 0,3$)	
Speed	50 km/h		50 km/h	
Intensity of road irregularities	0,3	0,9	0,3	0,9

Irregularities of the road profile for left and right wheels has been assumed to be similar, so the value of a coefficient determining this similarity (*corrl* in Adams/Car) has been set at close to 1.

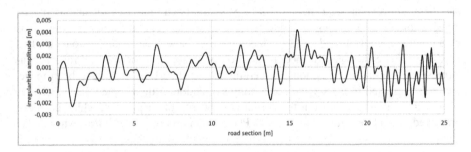

Fig. 3. Random profile for the selected road section, intensity 0,3 [own study]

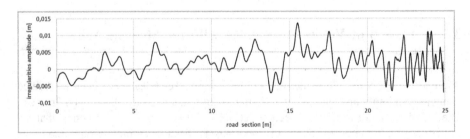

Fig. 4. Random profile for the selected road section, intensity 0,9 [own study]

In Figs. 3 and 4 exemplary road profiles of the selected road sections used in the simulation have been presented, depending on the value of the "intensity" parameter. One of the purposes of this paper is to present the possible consequences of the impact of lower (maximum height about 0,004 m) and higher (maximum height about 0,014 m) road irregularities on the response of the simulated vehicle.

The main goal of analyses presented in this paper was to discuss the selected phenomena occurring in curvilinear motion, especially when entering a turn and releasing the steering wheel at the same time. Of course, many examples of different road, velocity and load conditions are possible. However, here only the selected examples have been presented due to certain requirements concerning the paper length.

4   Discussion on the Selected Results Obtained for the Adopted Maneuver

Before discussing certain phenomena of a vehicle performing the selected maneuver it seems important to remind its duration of 5 s which indicates that the author has focused on the first crucial seconds of the beginning of curvilinear motion performed by the vehicle during the simulation. These first seconds can have essential impact on the further course of the vehicle, especially if only the vehicle response to disturbances originating from uneven loading and random road irregularities matters.

In Fig. 5 the lateral displacement in the first 5 s has been presented for four different configurations shown in Table 1. As in can be seen the vehicle travelled the distance of about 60 m at the initial speed of 50 km/h If the vehicle travelled at constant speed, it would cover about 80 – 90 m, so the braking nature of road irregularities is clearly visible as a factor preventing the vehicle from maintaining the speed.

It is worth noticing that the driver model which would increase the speed to defeat the resistance of the irregularities has not been included. The differences between the final position of the simulated vehicle are very small, but the tendency to move along a more straight line on an icy surface is clearly visible. However this figure is only for qualitative assessment of the vehicle trajectories, because further part of the paper is related to the selected characteristic features which can be observed mainly in lateral motion.

In Fig. 6 the lateral velocity versus the covered distance for dry road and in Fig. 7 – for icy road has been presented. It is worth noticing that for both road conditions the velocity was greater for the higher amplitudes of irregularities (intensity 0,9). However on dry surface the increase in lateral velocity for higher irregularities has been more rapid than on an icy road. On the other hand, the velocity value decreased more rapidly on dry road for lower irregularities and on an icy road this phenomena occurred on further distance, a about 55th meter of the covered road. This means that the transitional process of entering the curve and stabilizing the lateral motion takes more time and longer distance for worse traffic conditions (icy road).

Also the maximum value of lateral velocity for icy road was a little greater than for dry road surface in both cases – lower (intensity 0,3) and higher (intensity 0,9) amplitudes of road irregularities.

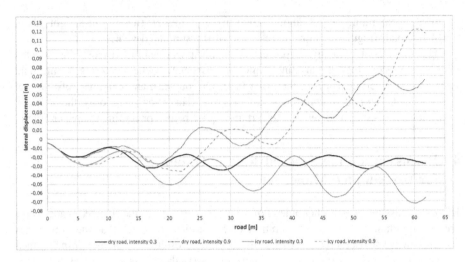

Fig. 5. Lateral displacement versus the covered distance [own study]

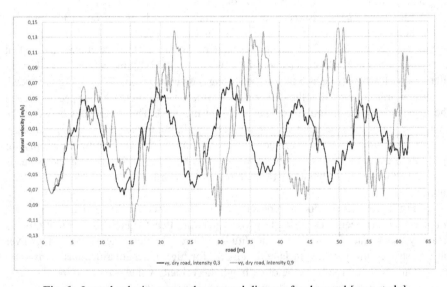

Fig. 6. Lateral velocity versus the covered distance for dry road [own study]

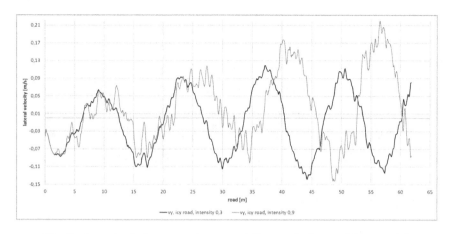

Fig. 7. Lateral velocity versus the covered distance for icy road [own study]

In Figs. 8 and 9 the lateral acceleration for the discussed vehicle – road configurations has been presented. As for this feature the changes occurred similarly for both higher and lower irregularities of the road, which allows a supposition that in the lateral motion only turns with relatively small radius and negotiated with high speeds can cause rapid increase in lateral acceleration, although for higher irregularities (intensity 0,9) its values are 2 or 3 times greater than in case of lower irregularities (intensity 0,3).

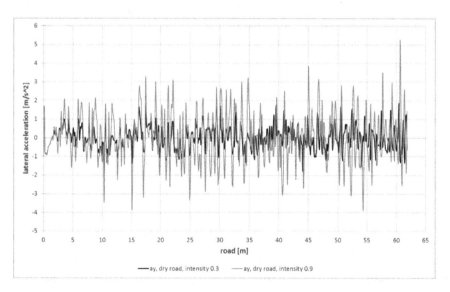

Fig. 8. Lateral acceleration versus the covered distance for dry road [own study]

Angular velocity of the simulated vehicle relative to its vertical axis passing through the center of mass versus the covered distance has been presented in Figs. 10

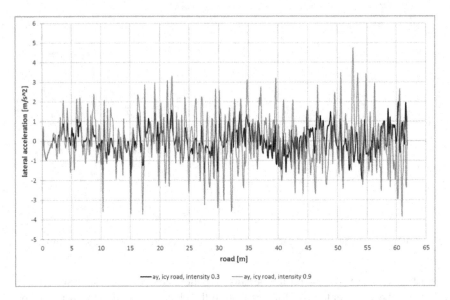

Fig. 9. Lateral acceleration versus the covered distance for icy road [own study]

and 11 for the dry and icy road surface respectively. For the dry surface a slight decrease can be observed, especially for the smaller irregularities of the road (intensity 0,3) which indicates the disappearance of the vehicle yaw motion in the turning maneuver after steering wheel release. The maximum angular velocity here is about 0,04 rad/s (which is about 2,2 degree/s) for lower and 0,06 rad/s (about 3,4 degree/s). This may seem not great, but what matters here is the nature of the changes.

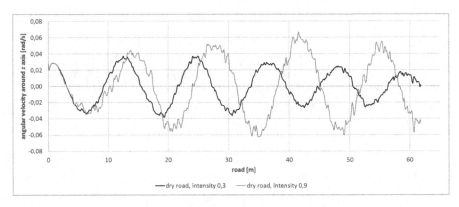

Fig. 10. Angular velocity around z axis versus the covered distance for dry road [own study]

However, it can be seen that the process of steadying the vehicle motion is slower for the more uneven road with worse surface condition (intensity 0,9). The maximum angular velocity on icy surface is about 0,07 rad/s (which is about 4 degrees/s) for lower and 0,1 rad/s (about 5,7 degree/s). Hence the worse road conditions, the more visible and non-steady can become a vehicle yaw motion.

As for the motion on the icy road it is clear that the tendency is similar to that for the dry surface, but the maximum values of the angular velocity (Fig. 11) are about 0,04 rad/s greater than those for the better traffic conditions (dry road). Moreover the steadying process of vehicle motion is visible only for lower amplitudes of road irregularities (intensity 0,3), because at the end of the covered distance the angular velocity for higher irregularities tend to increase, which means that the vehicle needs to travel further to stabilize its yawing motion.

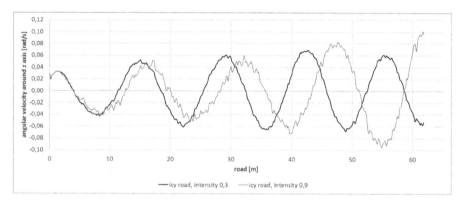

Fig. 11. Angular velocity around z axis versus the covered distance for icy road [own study]

The changes in roll angle of the simulated vehicle travelling on a randomly uneven road has been presented in Figs. 12 and 13 During the maneuver on dry surface the roll angle changed more rapidly for higher irregularities (intensity 0,9) which indicated the correctness of the vehicle behavior while moving on the road with poor surface condition. The maximum value of roll angle for smaller extorsions originating from the road (intensity 0,3) amounted to about 12–13°, while for the greater irregularities they rose even to 25° which can affect both safety and ride comfort.

As for the icy road, this tendency is similar, however maximum roll angle values for lower irregularities are close to 20° and for higher – even about 28°. The changes in the value of this parameter is characterized by similar tendency as on the dry road, but the decrease in magnitude observed previously cannot be noticed here, as the lack of adhesion between the wheels and the road can cause the increase in roll angle and at the same time the continuation of non – steady state motion for the simulated vehicle. As previously mentioned, only first few seconds of this maneuver have been considered.

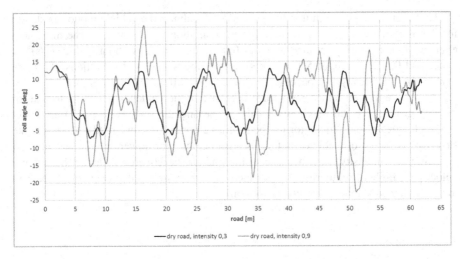

Fig. 12. Roll angle around x axis versus the covered distance for dry road [own study]

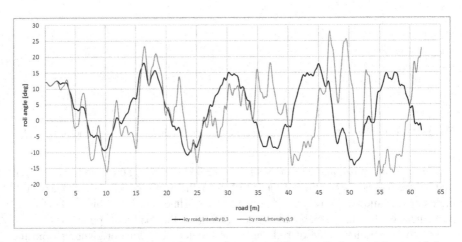

Fig. 13. Roll angle around x axis versus the covered distance for icy road [own study]

When discussing the roll phenomena, i.e. vehicle rotating around its x axis passing through the center of mass, it seems worth considering changes in the angular velocity around this axis. Let it be called the roll velocity. In Fig. 14 these changes for the motion on a dry road has been presented. This figure shows that the maximum values of the roll angle for the less uneven road (intensity 0,3) were about 0,05 rad/s (about 2,86 degree/s). However, for the less smooth road (intensity 0,9) it amounted even to 0,17 rad/s (about 9,74°) in the absolute value (neglecting minus in Figs. 14 or 15 as the information of the different direction of a velocity vector).

For the icy road conditions the tendency remained the same, although the maximum value for the higher road irregularities (intensity 0,9) was 0,15 rad/s (about 8,59 degree/s). It indicates that the lower adhesion between the icy road and wheels can slightly reduce the phenomena of vehicle rolling around x axis, but very insignificantly.

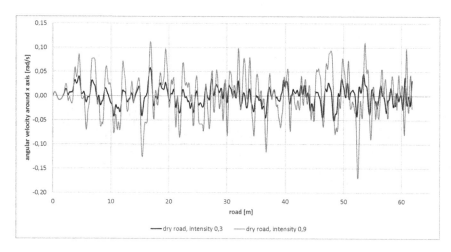

Fig. 14. Angular velocity around x axis versus the covered distance for dry road [own study]

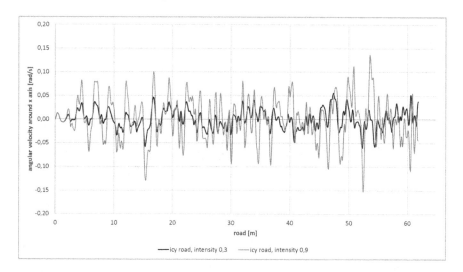

Fig. 15. Angular velocity around x axis versus the covered distance for icy road [own study]

As some kind of curiosity and the need to exhaust the discussed topic both angular accelerations around z and x axis passing through the center of mass has been presented in Figs. 16, 17, 18 and 19. In Figs. 16 and 17 the angular acceleration around the vertical z axis versus the covered distance has been presented, where the tendency of these changes is similar, however insignificantly smaller values occurred for the icy road, but the course of acceleration seems more condensed, maybe because of the lack of grip, slower steadying of the yaw motion and slower decrease in angular velocity during the motion on ice.

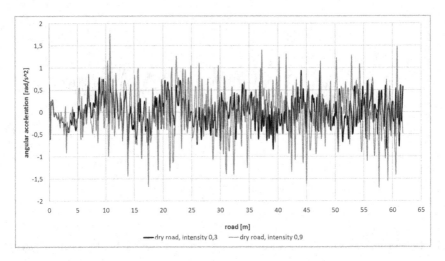

Fig. 16. Angular acceleration around z axis versus the covered distance for dry road [own study]

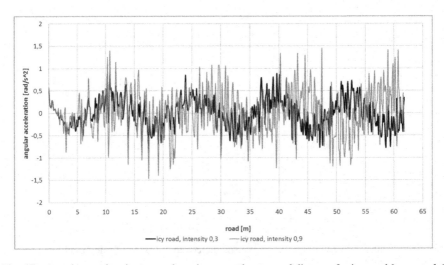

Fig. 17. Angular acceleration around z axis versus the covered distance for icy road [own study]

As for the angular acceleration of the vehicle around the x axis passing through the center of mass both figures (18 for dry and 19 for icy road) indicate the same changes which means that until different road irregularity profiles will be provided, no interesting phenomena can be observed.

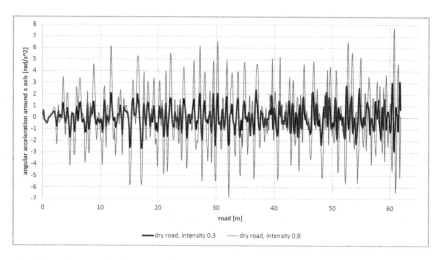

Fig. 18. Angular acceleration around x axis versus the covered distance for dry road [own study]

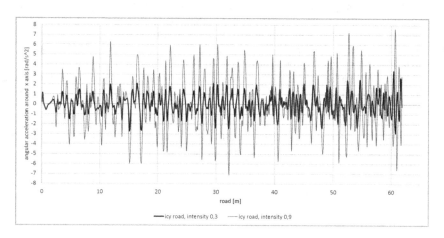

Fig. 19. Angular acceleration around x axis versus the covered distance for icy road [own study]

5 Conclusion

For simplification a similar profile of the randomly uneven road for left and right wheels of the given vehicle has been assumed, which in turn can be understood as lack of realism. However in further research different profiles for the left and right wheels will be taken into account. Especially in Figs. 18 and 19 it is clearly visible.

The aim of this paper was to present the selected considerations concerning the lateral motion of a motor vehicle based on computer simulations. In the future more factors disturbing the motion will be provided along with different road profiles for left and right wheels of a vehicle realizing maneuvers on a randomly uneven road.

References

1. Kisilowski, J., Kowalik, R.: The vision system for diagnostics of railway turnout elements. In: Mikulski, J. (ed.) TST 2018. CCIS, vol. 897, pp. 221–233. Springer, Cham (2018). https://doi.org/10.1007/978-3-319-97955-7_15
2. Kisilowski, J., Zalewski, J.: Analysis of the stochastic technical stability of engineering structures on example of moving car. J. Theor. Appl. Mech. **54**(4), 1157–1167 (2016)
3. Mastinu, G., Plochl, M.: Handbook of Road Vehicle Dynamics. CRC Press, Boca Raton (2013)
4. Múčka, P.: Current approaches to quantify the longitudinal road roughness. Int. J. Pavement Eng. **17**(8), 659–679 (2016)
5. Ni, L., et al.: Vehicle lateral motion control with performance and safety guarantees. IFAC–Papers On Line **49**(11), 285–290 (2016)
6. Riehm, P., et al.: 3D brush model to predict longitudinal tyre characteristics. Veh. Syst. Dyn. **57**(1), 17–43 (2019)
7. Rill, G.: Road Vehicle Dynamics: Fundamentals and Modeling. CRC Press, Boca Raton (2011)
8. Shi, Y., et al.: A practical identifier design of road variations for anti-lock brake system. Veh. Syst. Dyn. **57**(3), 336–368 (2019)
9. Zalewski, J.: Analysis of the motor vehicle dynamics on the example of a fish hook maneuver simulation. In: Mikulski, J. (ed.) TST 2017. CCIS, vol. 715, pp. 248–259. Springer, Cham (2017). https://doi.org/10.1007/978-3-319-66251-0_20
10. Zalewski, J.: Impact of the selected road parameters on a road vehicle motion. In: Proceedings of the Institute of Vehicles, no. 2(111) (2017)
11. Zalewski, J.: Influence of randomly uneven roads on selected problems of motor vehicle motion. In: Mikulski, J. (ed.) TST 2018. CCIS, vol. 897, pp. 185–196. Springer, Cham (2018). https://doi.org/10.1007/978-3-319-97955-7_13
12. Zalewski, J.: Impact of road conditions on the normal reaction forces on the wheels of a motor vehicle performing a straightforward braking maneuver. In: Mikulski, J. (ed.) TST 2015. CCIS, vol. 531, pp. 24–33. Springer, Cham (2015). https://doi.org/10.1007/978-3-319-24577-5_3

Application of Telematics Solutions for Improvement the Availability of Electric Vehicles Charging Stations

Mariusz Nürnberg and Stanisław Iwan[✉]

Maritime University of Szczecin, Pobożnego 11, Szczecin, Poland
{m.nurnberg, s.iwan}@am.szczecin.pl

Abstract. Electric vehicles (EV) are becoming more popular, therefore its number is increasing especially in large cities, the advantages of such vehicles are most noticeable there - lack of local emission and negligible noise. Following the popularity of EV, there is an increasingly dynamic development of charging infrastructure. The number, power and availability of the charging stations increases. The physical access to the charging station is becoming a real problem, the specificity of charging an EV means that in practice the place next to the station is a parking space and despite the markings it is occupied by other vehicles. The paper presents the concept of solving the problem of unauthorized use of charging stations by using a telematics system based on proximity detectors, whose main purpose is signaling the availability of stations and cases of unauthorized use of the charging station.

Keywords: Electric vehicles (EV) · Telematics systems · Charging stations

1 Introduction

Development of electric vehicles and electromobility is one of he most important challenge for road transport systems and transportation companies. It's not new idea. An interest in alternative fuels utilization in road transport is still increasing since the 1970s [1, 2]. It mostly effects due to problems with atmospheric emissions of anthropogenic origin [3]. The road transport, especially at urban areas, is the main source of emissions [4, 5]. Electromobility seems to be a good alternative for traditional fuels. The most important advantage in this case is the reduction of local pollutions, like carbon monoxide (CO), nitrogen oxides (NOx), sulphur dioxide (SO2), hydrocarbons (CHx, including polycyclic aromatic hydrocarbons – PAH), dioxins and benzene, as well as particulate matter (PM, mainly carbon, cadmium, zinc, nickel, platinum and chromium) [6].

One of the most important conditions of efficient utilization and development of electric vehicles is the charging stations infrastructure. This is critical important challenge for decision makers, on both governmental and business level. However, even if the charging stations infrastructure is appropriate for the needs of the EV users, it doesn't means that it will be utilized on the proper way. Many times the problem of the inappropriate usage of the parking slots equipped with the charging stations can be

© Springer Nature Switzerland AG 2019
J. Mikulski (Ed.): TST 2019, CCIS 1049, pp. 287–301, 2019.
https://doi.org/10.1007/978-3-030-27547-1_21

observed. In this case these places are occupied by non-electric vehicles just as a typical parking slots.

The solution, which could solve this problems is utilization of telematics systems. Based on the data sharing, the analysis of utilization of charging stations can be realized. Also, the advanced slots booking systems could be implemented. Moreover, telematics-based charging stations management system can help to provide the appropriate technical parameters for the needs of EV users.

2 Electric Vehicles Charging Station Network as a Telematic System

2.1 General Description of Transport Telematics Systems

The telematic system in general is spatially distributed physical systems with dedicated functionality, integrated by means of communication technologies into a whole, the purpose of which is to provide the recipient with designed services and information [7]. Transport telematics systems are those whose functional area is restricted to serve users of infra- and transport superstructure of a specific area.

The general principle of operation of telematics systems is the collection, processing, transmission and analysis of data within three functional subsystems [7]:

- data acquisition subsystem – designed to provide all information about the status of distributed system components. These can be static data such as spatial location of the system, parameters of services provided or level of availability as well as dynamic data such as: temporary system operation parameters, failure reports, etc.
- data processing and communication subsystem – in essence, is an algorithm designed by the operator of the telematics system that processes the input data collected by the acquisition system in the manner desired by the operator. In other words, the way data is processed is closely related to the system's functionality and the services it is intended to provide. Certainly the characteristic feature of this subsystem is the network sharing of information by means of appropriate transmission protocols between system elements. This is one of the most important features of the telematics system, allowing the planning and optimization of operations of both the user and the system operator in the area of operation of this system.
- dissemination subsystem for users – responsible for providing the output of the processing subsystem to users and operators. Due to the specificity of telematics systems, that is their spatial dispersion, it is desirable to provide information online in real time. This allows you to download this data both by mobile users (smartphones, OBU of vehicles), local (VMS) and central (ITS, websites).

2.2 Charging Stations as a Part of Telematics System

The network of EV charging stations certainly has features of the transport telematics system - it consists of spatially dispersed objects between which communication and management is necessary in order to achieve any system functionality, i.e. to enable charging the EV. Here should be quoted the definition of the charging station included in the Act on electromobility and alternative fuels which defines the charging station as "a construction device, including a normal-duty charging point or a high-capacity charging point, associated with a construction object, or detached building with at least one normal-sized charging point or a high-capacity charging point installed - equipped with software enabling the provision of charging services, including a parking stand and an installation leading from the charging point to the power connection" [18].

The authors propose that in the system approach the network of charging stations should be presented in the form of a telematics system consisting of the following elements:

- data acquisition subsystem as connections (plug-ins) and detectors of charging stations considered of the law;
- communication and data processing subsystem understood as an integrated data exchange and processing protocol allowing their transmission between system elements, in this article OCPP 2.0;
- dissemination/service providing subsystem considered as physical terminal devices allowing for the provision of vehicle charging services and data presenting the availability and technical parameters of the charging station for purpose of dissemination via mobile devices, on-board devices of electric cars and websites.

One of the major challenge for all kind of telematics systems is to deliver the proper data sets, according to the needs of the users and system administrators. The basis of the efficient and devices-independent data transmission is the utilization of the appropriate data transfer protocols. For this purpose the specialized protocol has been established for charging stations management – Open Charge Point Protocol, developed by Open Charge Alliance.

2.3 Open Charge Alliance – The Developer of Open Charge Point Protocol

Open Charge Alliance started in 2009 as an initiative from E-Laad foundation (now ElaadNL) in the Netherlands and was first formed as the Open Charge Point Protocol Forum. The aim was to create an open communication standard that would allow the Dutch Charging Stations (CS) and Charing Station Management Systems (CSMS) from different vendors to easily communicate with each other. The newly named Open Charge Alliance (OCA) which was founded by E-laad foundation, Greenlots (North America) and ESB (Ireland) maintains the original vision of the OCPP Forum: to further develop OCPP to guide open and flexible EV networks worldwide. It is a proven way to optimize the cost and risk of networked infrastructure investments.

The mission of OCA is to foster global development, adoption, and compliance of communication protocols in the EV charging infrastructure and related standards through collaboration, education, testing, and certification [11].

The Open Charge Point Protocol (OCPP) is the industry-supported de facto standard for communication between a Charging Station and a Charging Station

Management System (CSMS) and is designed to accommodate any type of charging technique. OCPP is an open standard with no cost or licensing barriers for adoption [14].

2.4 OCPP 2.0 as a Framework of Charging Stations Telematics Systems

Open Charge Point Protocol specification uses the term Charging Station as the physical system where an EV can be charged. A Charging Station can have one or more EVSEs (Electric Vehicle Supply Equipment). An EVSE is considered as a part of the Charging Station that can deliver energy to one EV at a time. The term Connector, as used in this specification, refers to an independently operated and managed electrical outlet on a Charging Station, in other words, this corresponds to a single physical Connector. In some cases an EVSE may have multiple physical socket types and/or tethered cable/connector arrangements to facilitate different vehicle types, this is a manufacturer's choice. For example, the EVSE might be integrated into a Charging Station and to look as just a part of that device, but it might just as well have its own casing and live outside of the physical entity Charging Station, for example a charging plaza with 20 EVSEs and Connectors which communicates via 1 modem as 1 Charging Station to the CSMS is seen by OCPP as 1 Charging Station [15]. The logical structure of OCPP is referred to as the 3-tier model and visualized in the Fig. 1.

In OCPP 2.0, a Charging Station is modelled as a set of "components", typically representing physical devices (including any external equipment to which it is connected for data gathering and/or control), logical functionality, or logical data entities. Components of different types are primarily identified by a ComponentName, that is either the name of a standardized component, or a custom/non-standardized component name, for new, pre-standardized equipment, vendor specific, extensions, etc.

ChargingStation (TopLevel), EVSE, and Connector represent the three major "tiers" of a Charging Station, and constitute an implicit "location-based" addressing scheme that is widely used in many OCPP data structures. By default, all components are located at the ChargingStation tier, but individual instances of any component can be associated with a specific EVSE, or a specific Connector (on a specific EVSE) by including EVSE or EVSE and Connector identification numbers as part of a component addressing reference. Every component has a number of variables, that can, as appropriate, be used to hold, set, read, and/or report on all (externally visible) data applicable to that component, including configuration parameters, measured values (e.g. a current or a temperature) [15].

This data structure allows efficient management of the CSMS (Charging Station Management System), as telematics system by the CSO (Charging System Operator) due to data integration, addressing (defining the location), defining the functionality and precise determination of variables and units of measure. What's more, CSMS has a large interoperability considered as the ability to easily integrate third party systems, such as the operator of the power distribution system. The Fig. 2 shows possible system components based on the OCPP 2.0 protocol.

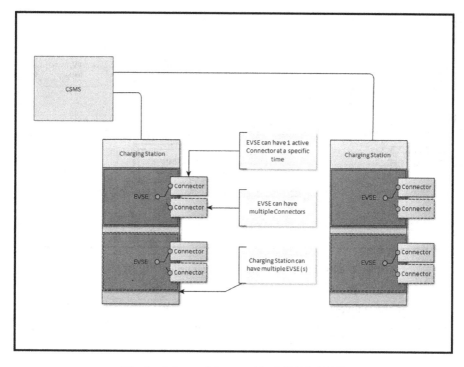

Fig. 1. 3-tier model as used in OCPP 2.0 [15]

Protocol OCPP 2.0 consist of following functional blocks:

- Security
- Provisioning
- Authorization
- Local authorization list management
- Transactions
- Remote control
- Availability
- Reservation
- Tariff and cost
- Metering
- Smart charging
- Firmware management
- ISO 15118 certificate management
- Diagnostics
- Display massage
- Data transfer

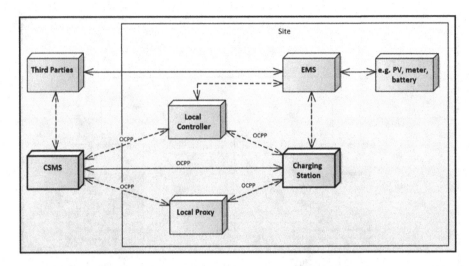

Fig. 2. Possible components in a setup using OCPP 2.0 [15]

Each of the above functional blocks requires separate devices installed on the charging station, separate units of measurement and an integrated data exchange protocol, in this case OCPP 2.0, for managing the EV charging process in real time.

3   EV Charging Methods

3.1   Charging Modes and Standards of the Most Popular Connectors

It should be emphasized that the process of charging EV batteries is not only about connecting the voltage to the vehicle's socket. The charging station establishes communication with the vehicle's charging module to determine the charging parameters and to protect the process itself in terms of user safety. An example may be charging with DC which, depending on the battery charge level, runs in the "constant current - constant voltage" mode. This means charging with constant current at increasing voltage up to 80% of the battery capacity, which allows you to quickly recharge it. After exceeding 80% of the battery capacity, the current is decreased, with constant voltage, so the charging time becomes significantly longer. This protects the cells against overheating and irreparable damage.

Charging plug-in can be divided into charging with DC and AC in the following modes:

- Mode 2 - slow charging - Charging with alternating current is easily available from the mains power supply with 230 V AC supplying power up to 3.7 kW;
- Mode 3 - accelerated charging - three-phase alternating current up to 22 kW. The limitation here is the vehicle charger, which is a "bottleneck" and parameters of charging process depends on its parameters;

– Mode 4 - rapid charging - in the case of DC charging, the vehicle battery is directly charged, without the use of a charger. The standard is 50 kW, but there are already available 150–350 kW chargers provisioning ultra rapid charging [19].

Table 1. EV charging modes and plugs comparison [own study]

Charging mode	Charging parameters	Charging time – from 0% to 80% of 40 kWh battery	Connectors type – plug and socket
Mode 2	Current: AC 230V, 16 A Power: 3,7 kW	11 hours	Standard electric plug and socket
Mode 3	Current: AC 3x230V/ 400V, 32 A Power: 22 kW	6 hours	Type 1 Type 2
Mode 4	Current : DC 400V, max. 250A Power: 50 kW	48 minutes	ChAdeMo CCS Combo

Connection of the vehicle to the charging station is carried out via a cable with the appropriate plug, the most popular connector standards, along with the power and charging time are presented in Table 1. Charging the plug-in is the most common, but not the only way to charging battery. The use of pantographs is reasonable when recharging vehicles equipped with a suitable connector, repeats at the same stations. Usually used for charging electric buses on bus loops. The disadvantage of this solution is necessity to equip the vehicle with a pantograph, which makes sense only in larger vehicles, while the advantage is the speed of service and available charging with a DC current of up to 150 kW [17].

Inductive charging involves the cooperation of two coils, one located in the vehicle and the other at the charging point, both coils being magnetically coupled and forming a transformer. The coil placed in the charging station produces a variable magnetic field, while the coil in the vehicle induces a current charging the vehicle batteries. Induction charging technology is not widely used, and currently manufactured vehicles are not equipped with coils and circuits allowing such charging.

3.2 Construction and Functional Elements of the Charging Station

The previously mentioned definition of the EV charging station allows to distinguish three basic structural elements:

- Electrical installations and power connections;
- Charging point - a device allowing for safe transmission of electric energy to vehicle batteries;
- Parking stand (parking bay) occupied by the vehicle while charging the batteries.

In terms of the telematics system, the charging point is treated as Charging Station (TopLevel) in the 3-tier OCPP structure and contains at least 1 EVSE (EV Supply Equipment), which sequently contains at least 1 connector. EVSE is in fact an electrical device that supplies the connector with the appropriate parameters set up during the vehicle - charging station communication process. At Fig. 3 you can see the AC charging point equipped with 2 connectors, and 1 ESVE on the left and DC charging point equipped with 2 ESVE (separate for DC and AC) and 3 connectors (2 for DC ESVE and 1 for AC ESVE) on the right side. Both devices manufactured by Garo [20]. In the charging point housing there is a significant number of additional devices enabling operation such as:

- communication module in 3G, LAN or WiFi technology;
- users interface allowing for authorization via RFID cards, tokens or logging in the application provided by the station operator and terminal of commercial transactions;
- control system managing the energy transfer to the vehicle (Smart Charging);
- measurement system controlling the amount of energy sold;
- physical components such as ventilation/heating system, lighting, external sensors

All data from these devices are integrated using the OCPP protocol and available in the CSMS (Charging Station Management System).

Fig. 3. Charging points manufactured by Garo [20]

Thus, the basic functionality of the charging station is provided by an appropriate system of controlling the transmission of current to the vehicle. However, improving the availability of charging stations considered as an increase in the quality of customer service using the Charging Station Operator (CSO) services are provided by additional systems installed at the charging station, integrated into the telematic system through the OCPP 2.0 protocol.

Particularly noticeable are the external sensors of the charging point which allows to collect data about the situation within the entire charging station and thus provide it available for system users. They will be discussed in detail in Sect. 5.

4 The Idea of Improvement the Availability of Electric Vehicles Charging Stations by Telematics System

4.1 Problem of Availability of Charging Stations

Electric cars are becoming the new mobility standard in the world. A growing group of drivers are convinced of their economic and functional advantages. Also, the governments especially of European countries decide to broadly support the implementation of EV by introducing subsidies and tax deductions for purchasing such means of transport. These are important activities that encourage drivers to switch traditional internal combustion cars to electric ones, however easy access to electric power is a prerequisite for the widespread use of EV. The development of electromobility is possible only when the charging station is properly available because each EV driver expects the full availability of his vehicle and must be sure that he will be able to quickly charge the battery at any time without losing mobility.

It should be noted that the duration of the EV charging process varies depending on the charging mode as shown in Table 1. At the same time, only one vehicle can use one EVSE. Therefore, not only the spatial arrangement of the charging station determines the access to the charging station, but also the power delivered by them and, as a result, the time needed to charge the batteries. Moreover, an integral part of the charging station is a parking bay that can be occupied by internal combustion car, thus preventing the proper use of the station.

Currently, there are about 400 different EV charging stations in Poland, unfortunately they do not constitute a consistent system that would support the development of electromobility. This number consists of:

– commercial charging stations of GreenWay network consist of 100 stations of various types [10], which form a system managed by the operator;
– commercial charging stations within traditional gas stations;
– charging stations provided by local authorities, as part of local support for electromobility, often linked to municipal companies which purchased EV;
– charging stations of service entities, e.g. hotels or supermarket stores providing the EV charging service as an incentive for customers of their core business;
– charging stations of entities supporting electromobility as a part of their commercial activities, electric car dealers, e.g. Polmotor [22] or manufacturers of charging points [20];
– electrical connections provided by private persons, which can not be treated as charging points, because they are not provide communication between the charging station and the car, and thus do not ensure safe charging, but proving high enthusiasm for electromobility.

The following figures shows examples of improper use of charging stations found during test drives performed at Nissan New Leaf in April 2018 in Szczecin. Figure 4 shows a public charging station at Golisza Street in Szczecin in the front of the office building of Water Supply and Sewerage Facility. This company simultaneously with purchase of EV established 2 charging points at the parking lot. It should be emphasized that despite the two sockets which can work simultaneously, only one parking bay is marked (in green) as a charging station. What's more, EV which is parked there, is not charging at the time!

Fig. 4. Improper use of charging station at Golisza Street [own study] (Color figure online)

Figure 5 illustrates the public free charger at the Leroy Merlin store parking lot. In this case, there is also only one parking bay around the charging station, treated by the drivers of the internal combustion cars as an ordinary parking space, thus completely preventing the use of the charging station.

Fig. 5. Charging station blocked by internal combustion cars [own study]

Figure 6 presents DC rapid charger next to the Nissan showroom of Polmotor at Struga Street in Szczecin. We can observe the correct determination of two places, but the charger has only 1 ChAdeMo connector. Therefore, it is possible to charge only one vehicle at a time, however this case should be considered as an example of lack of information rather than improper use.

Fig. 6. Two parking bays attached to one charging station [own study]

4.2 Information Systems to Facilitate the Availability of Charging Stations

Locations of the charging stations mentioned above, regardless of their technical parameters, ownership status and current availability are presented online by various websites of entities related to electromobility. The basic function of these sites is to indicate the location and provide information about the type of plugins and charging mode, but they cannot be considered part of the telematics system, because the information is not collected in real time from the station and doesn't report about its current state.

In general, three types of information systems should be distinguished:

- services of charging station operators providing data from their own stations, e.g. GreenWay [10];
- websites that aggregate all charging stations, for example Plug Share [12] supplied by Recargo Inc., Next Charge [9] provided by Go Electric Stations S.r.l.s. or Chargemap [8];

– embeddings of the aforementioned services by organizations involved in the development of electromobility such as the Polish Alternative Fuels Association, www.elektrowoz.pl or www.wysokienapiecie.pl;

The first two of these services allows to register as a user and logging in using the mobile application or website into the service. This allows to significantly expand the range of services offered. In the case of mobile devices, it enables navigation to the charging point and sending feedback about the use of the station, so-called "check in" to inform about the temporary unavailability of charging station.

Logged in users can add new charging points to the Plug Share type services. In case of charging station system operators (CSO) logging in allows users to subscribe contracts and use preferential tariffs for energy.

As mentioned above, despite the simplification of the services offered to drivers using charging stations, they cannot be considered as a substitute of the telematics system because they are based on voluntary reporting of station occupancy and are not verifiable.

4.3   Solutions Improving the Availability of Charging Stations

Charging station management systems (CSMS) based on the OCPP 2.0 protocol have the features of a telematic system as described above but their functionality is mainly limited to managing the process of safe provisioning of electric power with appropriate parameters to EV. The reason is not the lack of OCPP 2.0 potential [16], but the lack of a sufficient various set of detectors that charging station could be equipped with.

As described above, the real problem of EV drivers is the shortage of reliable real-time information about the availability of a parking bay within the charging station. Information of this type can be easily delivered to CSMS by means of detectors scanning the occupancy of parking bay by any vehicle.

There are number of types of motion detectors of vehicles that can be distinguish according to [13]:

– physical principle of operation - contact, acoustic, magnetic, inductive, electro-magnetic and vision;
– installation method - into road surface, onto road surface, under road surface and next to the road surface;
– the method of making measurements - in the cross-section of a road or on certain surface of the area.

In the case of a charging station, the decisive criterion is the way the measurement is performed, because the detection concerns a specific area and is not related to the movement of the vehicle. Therefore, magnetic, inductive or electromagnetic detectors are recommended choice. Due to the fact that the charging point may have several parking spaces, the best choice seems to be detectors placed under the road surface.

Data from parking bay availability detectors at the charging station in combination with technical parameters and station location will provide EV drivers access to real-time reliable information regarding the quality and availability of the EV charging service. Thus, it will significantly increase the functionality of information systems currently used by EV drivers and presented in Sect. 4.2.

However, much more important it's ability to aggregate this data with other transport telematics systems, such as ITS or FMS. This will allow achieving the synergy effect by coordinating information from the vehicle about current energy consumption, availability of charging stations and planned routes shared within the ITS telematics system.

5 Conclusion

Electromobility is still developing phenomenon but it develops faster year by year. The technical parameters of cars are improving, not only the capacity of batteries, energy density but also the speed of on-board chargers. An example is the Nissan New Leaf, introduced in spring of 2018, had batteries with a capacity of 240 kWh and a range of 270 km [22], while Hyundai Kona introduced a year later offers 64 kWh batteries and 449 km of range [21].

Thus, the charging time is shortened and therefore availability of the station increases. Recently installed public charging stations are more and more often rapid chargers requiring only a few-minute charge station occupancy. These facts combined with reliable information on the availability of stations increases the quality of service for drivers and provide driving of EV without worrying about short range or long-lasting battery charging. Unfortunately, infrastructure investments are not connected, therefore currently it's difficult to achieve synergy effect.

The authors postulate an increasingly implementation of detectors providing the real-time physical state of the charging station (bay occupancy, current charging sessions and their duration, connection failures, availability of the facility, etc.) that will provide station status data to the management system. Reliable and specific data will allow to share this data within transport telematics systems dedicated to EV support, thus supporting the development of electromobility and the convenience of using EV.

Acknowledgments. The paper has been prepared as the activity of the project Low Carbon Logistics, founded under Interreg South Baltic Programme.

European Regional Development Fund

References

1. Brinkman, N.D.: Vehicle evaluation of neat methanol—compromises among exhaust emissions, fuel economy and driveability. Int. J. Energy Res. **3**(3), 243–274 (1979)
2. Lucas, G.G., Richards, W.L.: Alternative fuels for transportation. Transp. Plan. Technol. **7** (3), 167–170 (1982)
3. Kijewska, K., Konicki, W., Iwan, S.: Freight transport pollution propagation at urban areas based on Szczecin example. Transp. Res. Procedia **14**, 1543–1552 (2016)

4. Huo, M.Q., et al.: Characteristics of carbonaceous components in precipitation and atmospheric particle at Japanese sites. Atmos. Environ. **146**, 164–173 (2016)
5. Piloto-Rodríguez, R., et al.: Assessment of diesel engine performance when fueled with biodiesel from algae and microalgae: an overview. Renew. Sustain. Energy Rev. **69**, 833–842 (2017)
6. Iwan, S., et al.: Analysis of the environmental impacts of unloading bays based on cellular automata simulation. Transp. Res. Part D: Transp. Environ. **61, Part A**, 104–117 (2018)
7. Iwan, S.: Wdrażanie dobrych praktyk w obszarze transportu dostawczego w miastach. Wydawnictwo Naukowe Akademii Morskiej w Szczecinie, Szczecin (2013)
8. https://fr.chargemap.com/map. Accessed 15 Feb 2019
9. https://goelectricstations.com/nextcharge.html. Accessed 15 Feb 2019
10. https://greenwaypolska.pl/nasze-stacje/. Accessed 14 Feb 2019
11. https://www.openchargealliance.org/about-us/. Accessed 13 Feb 2019
12. https://www.plugshare.com. Accessed 15 Feb 2019
13. Leśko, M., Guzik, J.: Sterowanie ruchem drogowym. Sygnalizacja świetlna i detektory ruchu pojazdów, Wydawnictwo Politechniki Śląskiej, Katowice (2000)
14. Open Charge Alliance, OCPP 2.0 Part 0 (2018)
15. Open Charge Alliance, OCPP 2.0 Part 1 (2018)
16. Open Charge Alliance, OCPP 2.0 Part 2 (2018)
17. Sidorski, F.: Charakterystyka pracy stacji ładowania autobusów Elektrycznych, Przegląd Elektrotechniczny, ISSN 0033-2097, R. 94 NR 10/2018
18. Ustawa z dnia 11 stycznia 2018 r. o elektromobilności i paliwach alternatywnych, Dz.U. 2018 poz. 317
19. www.abb.com/cawp/seitp202/c2ed43a8ef2e1de2c12581ae002d26b8.aspx. Accessed 13 Feb 2019
20. www.garo.com. Accessed 12 Feb 2019
21. https://www.hyundai.koreamotors.pl/uploads_hyundai/cenniki/Cennik_KONA_Electric_2019.pdf. Accessed 15 Feb 2019
22. https://nissan.polmotor.pl/wp-content/uploads/2017/10/NEW_LEAF_PL-3.pdf. Accessed 15 Feb 2019

How to Implement Telematics into the Urban Public Transportation System in Addis Ababa, Concept Study

Frehaileab Admasu Gidebo[1,2(✉)] and Janusz Szpytko[1(✉)]

[1] AGH University of Science and Technology,
Ave A. Mickiewicza 30, Krakow, Poland
admasu@student.agh.edu.pl, szpytko@agh.edu.pl
[2] Addis Ababa Science and Technology University, Addis Ababa, Ethiopia

Abstract. Transport is one of the basic elements in economic and social development of mankind. The today public transport system in Addis Ababa (Ethiopia) is characterized with many challenges: lacks of safety, availability and reliability, as well as unscheduled travel time, emissions. Another key barrier of the transport system development in the city is lack of proper transport policy, bus fleet exploitation management problem, strategy to adapt new technological solutions. The aim of this paper is the concept study how to improve the public transportation system in Addis Ababa with use of the new management solutions and technology based on telematics solutions.

Keywords: Public transport · Transport fleet availability ·
Transport telematics · Intelligent transport

1 Introduction

Transport is one of the basic elements in economic and social development of mankind. Transport system is one of the complex sub-systems as result of involving various technologies, working mechanisms and systems in order to transport passengers and goods from one point to another. The today public transport system in Addis Ababa (Ethiopia) is characterized with many challenges: lacks of safety, availability and reliability, as well as unscheduled travel time, emissions Ethiopian transportation system is dominated by informal and back warded system since its advancement with reference to passenger's interest and accessibility is very low. People most of time prefers used to walk long distance as result of shortage and inadequacy of transport infrastructure with different corridors of the city.

This minimizes the productivity of work as well as has an impact on keeping proper working time. There is government direction in order to solve the problem through expanding the existing road infrastructure to connect with different corridors. An expansion of road network capacity has been taken as major solution as a result of resolving traffic congestion and provides smooth traffic flow. Apart this, transport system should adapt and entertain modern technologies in order to make the transport system more efficient, attractive and effective. According to various studies, transport

J. Mikulski (Ed.): TST 2019, CCIS 1049, pp. 302–318, 2019.
https://doi.org/10.1007/978-3-030-27547-1_22

telematics is a part of modern transport technology which could support and facilitate the decision making process in real time phenomena through providing data analysis and information [15]. Transport telematics has been used in various transportation activities, air transport (air traffic control), shipping and logistics (haulage productivity and safety), road transport (route guidance, passenger information, protection against theft)... etc. are some of basic application areas of the technology (Fig. 1).

(a)

(b)

Fig. 1. a. Addis Ababa road network and current situation [27] **b.** Passenger vs. transport fleet exploitation management problem [25]

Moreover, loss of time, CO_2 emission has also another impacting issue on development and wellbeing of society. The inconsistent characteristics of transport system should be supported by modern transport technologies such as transport telematics, ITS, highway management system in order to heighten the quality of service. The study of paper [11] agreeing that in order to promote public transport; quality, availability and reliability of transport services should be taken into account as an increasingly important parameter due to needs of different level of societies. The main features of high-quality services are: attractive schedule, comfort, easy access, reliability of services and integration with other means of transport.

In different countries we can observe many practical importance of telematics in transport system, for instance, improvement in safety, reduction in environmental pollution, improving effectiveness of transportation activities; which manifests in reduction in the costs of managing the road vehicle stock, maintaining and modernization of the road surface, fuel consumption [6, 16]. According to Federal Ministry of Transport, Building and Housing of Germany (2004), transport telematics provides intelligent technological solutions for managing the high volume traffic and will help the transport infrastructure more efficient and enhance traffic safety.

In paper [4] Authors deal with that African transportation system is left behind in terms of using IT (information Type) technologies to ensure safe and accessible transport system to the users. Their study concluded that the benefit of using telematics in transport system is unsuspicious if properly implemented in transport sector. It is one of important tool to measure the availability and reliability of transport system in order to ensure safe travel and efficient mobility. The increase in population and urbanization is one of the biggest challenges in the cities of developing countries. This may be cause to open the gap between transport demand and available transport facilities. The transport system should be supported by ICT infrastructure in order to assure safe, efficient, and accessible transport system [21].

Nowadays it is possible to see intelligently connected things/societies such as people with cars and road infrastructures, vehicle with vehicle and environment by the help of information and technology (Fig. 2).

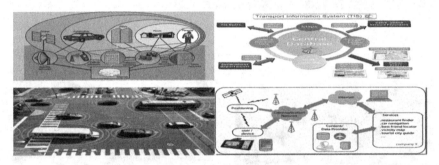

Fig. 2. Interconnected advanced transport system [22, 28]

1.1 Motivation/Problem Formulation

The movement of peoples and goods in day to day activities are influenced by the available transport facilities. Effective, efficient and safe transport system can bring potential benefits for the public good. The today public transport system in Addis Ababa (Ethiopia) is characterized with many challenges:

- lacks of safety,
- availability and reliability,
- unscheduled travel time and emissions.

Moreover, lack of proper transport policy, bus fleet exploitation management problem, strategy to adapt new technological solutions could be taken as key barrier of the transport system development in the city. The problem of using existing infrastructure and transport devices to increase efficiency and safety of transport users would be explored as undisputable issue. The culture of peoples in to proper using of transport system is insufficiently trained. This results accidents, traffic jams or congestions and reduction of transport productivity. Therefore, this research is focusing to answer these problems and introducing the concept of transport telematics solution as a key technology tool to change above mentioned bottle necks in transport system (Fig. 3).

Fig. 3. Transportation system in Addis Ababa [27]

1.2   Target of the Research

The main target of this research is to develop concept study of implementation of transport telematics solution in to public transport system in city of Addis Ababa, Ethiopia.

1.3   Objective of the Research

The primary objective of this paper is the concept study how to improve the public transportation system in Addis Ababa with use of the new management solutions and technology based on telematics solutions.

1.4   Research Study Area

Addis Ababa is one of the fastest growing metropolises in Africa, and it is Ethiopia's political and economic center. The city is the seat for African Union (AU) and United Nations Economic commission for Africa (UNECA). The city is experiencing with unexpected amount of transport demand that could be generated as result of rapid urbanization and increase of population. The number of population in Addis Ababa city will be expected more than 8 million in 2020 (Fig. 4).

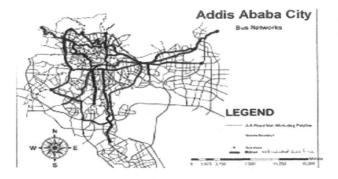

Fig. 4. Study area, Addis Ababa city [17]

1.5   Research Materials and Methodology

In developing countries, the transport system that concerns the whole society is public transport. Its service can be assessed by different criteria, such as:

– accessibility,
– good service,
– travel time,
– waiting time,
– quality of operational performance,
– reliability and availability.

In order to achieve the objective of this research study some basic methods and techniques has been developed. Reviewing various states of arts to develop concept study in existing knowledge and practice was conducted. The current policy document of Addis Ababa transport authority has been deeply reviewed. Availability and reliability assessment methods were also used in order to study the exploitation of fleet management of transport system. The concept study for integrated multimodal urban transport and intelligent public transport system was developed based on some existing data. Also, the use of intelligent transport system, transport telematics and the development of related transport technologies in different country perspectives has been studied.

2   Bus Fleet Exploitation Management Problem in Addis Ababa

The concept of bus fleet management is primarily used to get information about location of bus and to control activity of the bus in the given route. The problem of managing bus fleet is one of the crucial factors that impacting negatively the overall flow of traffic system. The possibility to see all types of vehicles is high at one time in Addis Ababa city and makes public transport system unattractive. It is as a result of bus fleet exploitation management problem. Uncontrolled behavior of driver, unnecessary fuel consumption, and unexpected delay of departure and arrival time is also contributing factor in transport fleet management. Moreover, controlling and monitoring the mobility of vehicles without task is, majorly taken as a challenge unless proper fleet management system implemented [9].

Hence implementing telematics is found as a proper solution to minimize this problem and in other hand it is used to realize the vehicle tracking, increase efficiency and productivity and reduce risks. The intelligent transport telematics system based on the real-time tele-information allows monitoring and controlling the drivers, vehicles and goods movement in variable environmental conditions [16]. Authors in paper [5] states that poor quality service of public transportation system impact socio-economic development, growth and wellbeing of people; hinder the day to day movement of people and goods. It is also critical to take an action as result of introducing new technology supported transport system as well as promoting modern public transport system to the urban dwellers. In the other hand bus fleet availability management is one of the physically challenging issues in urban transportation service. Control of traffic flow, emission, and travel times are of a part of fleet management tasks. Several technologies have been in use in order to increase operational availability of bus fleet.

During operation, cost is the major impacting parameter of transport system which is related with safety, accident and maintenances issues. Transport object should be free or minimum risk and aware of the preventive risks related with fleet operation:

- unplanned maintenance,
- safety-related risks,
- risk of decreasing fleet accessibility.

Operational availability of bus fleet is becoming in subject of when unplanned repair/maintenance schedule exist.

The reliability of the system will be reduced as result of unscheduled servicing and spare part changing activities. Many developing cities are dominated by old and fuel-intensive buses with high operating costs. Therefore, it is necessary to improve the efficiency and enhance the attractiveness of bus transportation. Fuel costs can be reduced by improving the driving style of bus drivers and through sound maintenance practices. A safe and economical driving style can reduce variable costs, decrease down time due to repair work and maintenance, mitigate negative environmental impacts and improve road safety.

A sustainable fleet management strategy is one that aims to reduce environmental impacts through a combination of cleaner vehicles and fuels, fuel-efficient operation and driving; and by reducing the amount of road traffic it generates.

3 Urban Public Transport Policy for Government, Passengers and Drivers

Inclusive transport policy should be prepared and implemented in a way to attract drivers and passengers to use alternative solutions. Government authorities could consider different opinions and utilization mechanisms in order to have shared responsibility of the transport users. Lack of inclusive and proper transport policy marks the transport system back warded and technologically unfit and uncompetitive. As a policy document, technology transfer shall refer to in the process of transferring to receivers a technology or method of manufacturing created by others and particularly tested through capital and intermediary good or skilled man power in technical and commercial information. The process of transfer includes direct use, coping or adaption of technologies [13]. In development of transport policy having principled strategy and implementation mechanism with respect to city development plan is crucial. Adopting city development strategy with city transport policy takes place a particular direction and enables method for the development of an existing transport system [11].

Transport policy of the city involves the following important tasks [12]:

- determination of the communication needs of the city in the time-space system,
- determination of the fundamental direction of the development of infrastructure,
- establishing rules for financial management (fees, tariffs, subsidies),
- organization and management of urban transport (selection of structures, systems and forms of ownership).

City transport policy should take into account various aspects, including in particular:

- psychological and social, guaranteeing citizens' access to sources of traffic,
- environmental, resulting from the need to protect the environment,
- spatial, taking into account the need for proper deployment of destinations and sources of traffic within the city and the existing infrastructure,
- economic, resulting from the need to accumulate financial resources to develop a transport system,
- temporal, associated with the need to achieve the desired result in a given time.

Transport authorities are responsible to rank attributes such as travel time, frequency, safety, availability, reliability and comfort of transport system. By doing this the probability of affecting service quality in public transport system will be reduced and increase the availability and reliability of transport system. The performance analysis of transport system has become an essential element in the public transport companies. However, the performance concept is extended. It covers at the same time; the costs, the transport quality, the user satisfaction and the financial results.

4 Existing Transport Infrastructure of the Addis Ababa City

The key problems of Addis Ababa transport system are:

- insufficient number of buses (high demand of transportation),
- passenger insecurity at transport and freight terminals,
- sub-standard traffic management system,
- absence of infrastructure for non-motorized transport modes,
- traffic congestion and road safety issues.

The existing road network cannot sustain the demand of transportation and it is increased with unprecedented scale. The problems related with this clearly indicate at paper [5] are:

- rapid urbanization and increase of population and physical expansion of the city,
- less service quality, effectiveness, efficiency and high cost,
- inappropriate number of public transport facility with respect to demand,
- absence of contemporary and privatized public transport system,
- poor quality of road network, traffic congestion and pollution,
- lack of technological support transport system such as vehicle tracking system, GPS.

The city also lacks the effective exploitation of public transport system based on existing population density. The urban land-use planning and transport infrastructure development are inseparable and should be balanced. So, the today transport infrastructure in Addis Ababa city is featured by growing demand and with limited supply of

85–95%, is based on road transport system. This means, increasing demand only with expansion of infrastructure, for instance, road and vehicles, does not seem to be a sustainable strategy. As a result of this, transport users are exposed to extra cost, safety problem, and delay and increased waiting time. The integrated infrastructure planning is vital for enhancement of city development.

Linking several parallel means of transportation such as air, rail, road, tram, bus, bicycle, and pedestrian provides multiple alternatives and quick access. However investment in physical infrastructure is become costly and not attractive in terms of funding and causes environmental degradation. Simultaneously, a new pattern of transport transformation is pushing global economy in to digitization for both goods and people [18]. The potential to improve the use of current transport capacity is the use of integrated modern information and communication technology, known as telematics systems for road transport, and it is an important component of intelligent transport systems (ITS) [10] (Fig. 5).

(a)

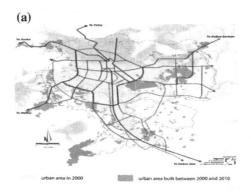

(b)

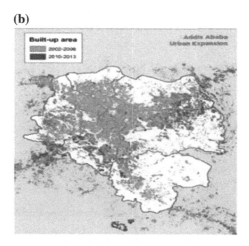

Fig. 5. a. Addis Ababa City Road Infrastructure expansion corridors [17] **b**. Addis Ababa City expansion; Addis Ababa, Ethiopia enhancing urban resilience [29]

5 Intelligent Transport System Development and Transport Telematics

General objectives of ITS in transport system is

- to increase transport efficiency,
- to improve traffic safety and
- to reduce traffic related pollution.

In fact our society nowadays is quickly advanced towards information technology. Information is one of the important quality criteria in modern world. Information systems in passenger transport companies and information systems for passengers can improve service quality and stimulate passenger demand [8]. Transport manufacturers are equipped vehicles with wireless technology in order to have efficient, effective and proper information of vehicle with vehicle and vehicle with infrastructure communication. Telematics, therefore is one of the widely used ITS component in transport system. Telematics techniques and intelligent transport services reduces imperfect decision making process as a result of availability of various information from various sources [20]. The benefit of telematics is multifunctional which not only support of decision making but also it has been used to increase road capacity as well as safety in traffic system.

The functions of transport telematics are to offer intelligent services to traffic users, which must be considered at several levels [7] and they are services for travellers and drivers, infrastructure administrators, transport operators (carriers), for public administration, for security and rescue system, for financial and control institutions. Passengers should have also proper information to plan travels accordingly. By using telematics solution of ITS, passenger can receive real time information about, road safety, traffic congestion, weather condition, and road infrastructure. The connected society as a result of information and technology could easily practice the concept of intelligent transport system (Fig. 6).

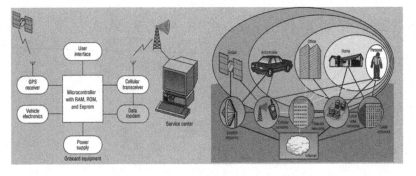

Fig. 6. A basic telematics system and connected information society [22]

The effects on individual driving behavior of other ITS functions, such as trip planning, travel information, road-pricing and fleet-management, are expected to be more indirect and therefore the impact of those support systems are also less clear.

The effective utilization of road network is an important function of ITS since it providing wide range of information to drivers and passengers in the vehicles. Information about direction, routes and driver services are sent directly into the vehicle. The connection of communication between the vehicle and the data center will produce information about traffic jams and information to dynamic navigation [7].

6 Implementation of Transport Telematics in to Public Transport

Public transport information system is very useful for transport users in order to align the passengers demand and available resources. In order to utilize road network the information must be updated in real-time, accurate and reliable that allows the system more effective. Information about traffic congestion, direction, routes and transport services for drivers and passengers could be transmitted in the form intelligent service known as telematics. Various efficiency indicators and performance parameters demonstrate that Addis Ababa city public bus transportation is influenced by lack of intelligent information. The conceptual integration of the light rail train, free bus lane and other transport infrastructures should be developed to increase the efficiency of public transport. Public transportation can be attracted when there is increase in availability of quality service of electronic pricing system, vehicle tracking system and ICT infrastructure [1]. Basically, the function of transport telematics described as follows to characterize multi-task application of ITS (Fig. 7).

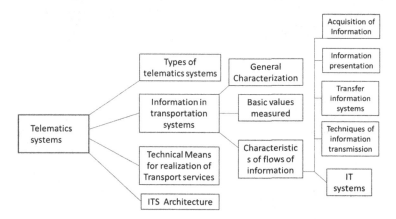

Fig. 7. System components of transport telematics [12]

The study of document [10] maintained that planning to meet the needs of different stakeholders is critical to successful introduction of telematics systems in road transport. However in other hand, the gap of skill to proper use of this system in both drivers and passenger could be a barrier. Electronic pricing machines might be placed safely in order to give accessible service to all users. But the problem is there is no properly installed security camera in streets in order to protect thefts. Public transport buses should be equipped with all the necessary facilities including telematics solutions. Having all this lacks, public transportation is still serving the city people as a major transport source.

Some of public buses currently giving transport service in Addis Ababa city is outdated, not environment friendly, not comfortable and problem of punctuality. Modern buses should provide quality service to satisfy and attract more passengers. Using public transport has a lot of benefits in terms of economy, safety and fast travel. Finding innovative ways of moving goods and people can create new business opportunities, generate value for travellers and help to build a flexible and adaptable economy [14, 19]. Implementing transport telematics in to public transport system can provide intelligent technological solutions to manage the capacity/volume of traffic jams. Sustainable, efficient and safe mobility is a part of transport telematics application (Fig. 8).

Fig. 8. Use of telematics in transport system [24]

Transport telematics can also enhance the efficiency of and optimize the transport system as whole where as managing transport demand to ensure sustainable mobility is one of challenging issues of transport sector. Thus, the importance implementing telematics solution is indisputable.

7   Use of Transport Devices in Decision Making Process

Transport devices are used to maintain availability of fleet. These devices are not only to maintain availability of fleet but also safety and security of the fleet. Many devices introduced in transport system is to facilitate the decision making process though receiving various information from various sources. Communication devices in vehicle monitoring application, wireless vehicle connections are the solutions of telematics used to transfer information. The roles of these devices are very significant in transport system. Fleet vehicles can be equipped with GPS and similar devices to log routes and time spent at various locations [22].

Vehicle mileage and other aging measurements can also be logged then transmitted wirelessly to the fleet manager's computerized system. Vehicles can automatically transmit the day's logged information when entering the fleet yard [9]. Alternatively, the same information can be gathered up-to-the-minute from out in the field when a city deploys a wireless municipal private network. Vehicle to vehicle connection, vehicle to road infrastructure connection and others internet of things can be used to improve the bus fleet management in transport industry.

8   Integrated Multi-modal Urban Transport System

In order to connect several transport systems in to the city the concept of multimodal transport system can play vital role. Transport telematics would be also useful to provide integrated parking management system with users, traffic controllers and transport planners. The demand can be distributed easily, the traffic flow will be smooth and the location access will be easy.

The capacity of existing Addis Ababa road network cannot manage all the integrated multimodal urban transport system for example bike, pedestrian, rail, public transport and shared transport. Majorly the city is dominated by "blue donkeys or small minibuses" which are not enough to give proper transport service. Its fleet is not managed and impossible to control its operation too. Therefore, it is regular to see accidents, traffic congestion, and emission in the city. The road network is not situated to consider all pedestrians walk ways, bike paths, free bus lanes. The light railway is situated from two congested lines from north south and east west direction. But integration of the available resources to optimize the service and to satisfy demand is obligatory in order to enhance multimodal urban transport (Fig. 9).

Fig. 9. (a) Blue donkeys (minibus); (b) Taxi; (c) Light rail train [23, 26] (Color figure online)

It is believed that multimodal transportation is an attractive alternative if the access and egress distance is not too large. Access and egress (together with waiting and transfer times) appear as factors that affect the effectiveness and performance of a multimodal transportation system to a larger extent as unacceptable distances are likely to reduce rider-ship patronage. In this regard accessibility is primary factor to make urban public transportation integrated and attractive for users. Accessibility could be explained as result of time accessibility, space and speed accessibility.

Basically, land use management to create possible connectivity is the primary task in order to achieve the multimodal urban transport system. In the city like Addis Ababa, lacks planned land use management which is key barrier for accessibility and promote multimodal transport system. This concept will help to introduce and implement integration of multimodal transport system.

9   Economic Benefit of Using Public Transportation

It is believed that transport is an essential component of life and a basis for providing access to goods and services. Transportation is the foundation of the economy and society, and the mobility is extremely important for the internal economy and for the quality of life of citizens. To enables economic growth and job creation transportation can play important role [11]. The future economy would be dependent on digital technology and will be impacting every part of government and the life of the entire societies. Government should work to improve the existing system in order to accommodate possible technologies for the benefit of people. The provision of adequate and appropriate transportation services helps for growing and expanding urban transport system and economy of the society [2]. Moreover, promoting efficient use of transport service (public transport, bike lane, pedestrian walk ways) in terms of:

– improving accessibility and travel time,
– minimizing environment degradation,
– reducing risks and accidents,
– reduction of adverse environmental impact (pollution, land use, traffic jams) of transport,
– increasing safety.

These can produce potential benefit on economy of the users (Fig. 10).

According to the practical experience of developed countries, using public transport as mass transit option has potential benefit economically as well socially. Though, safety and availability of the transport system and operational availability of the fleet of transport devices are the major measuring factors of public transport system in terms productivity and performance. Although, using public transport can save cost related with vehicles, such as vehicle operating cost (fuel, oil and servicing cost), long-term mileage-related costs (depreciation costs), special costs (parking, insurance, toll), vehicle ownership costs, and need for residential parking. This is can be achieved by implementing proper urban transportation service with technology deployment.

However, the record of safety/accident in Ethiopia is alarming issue and based on study more than 4000 people per year died in traffic accident [17]. This shows that the country is losing a lot of money due to accidents and as result of it contributes for economic loss and instability.

	Improved Transit Service	Increased Transit Travel	Reduced Automobile Travel	Transit-Oriented Development
	Service Quality (speed, reliability, comfort, safety, etc.)	Transit Ridership (passenger-miles or mode share)	Mode Shifts or Automobile Travel Reductions	Portion of Development With TOD Design Features
Potential Benefits	• Improved convenience and comfort for existing users. • Equity benefits (since existing users tend to be disadvantaged). • Option value (the value of having an option for possible future use). • Improved operating efficiency (if service speed increases). • Improved security (reduced crime risk)	• Mobility benefits to new users. • Increased fare revenue. • Increased public fitness and health (by stimulating more walking or cycling trips). • Increased security as more non-criminals ride transit and wait at stops and stations.	• Reduced traffic congestion. • Road and parking facility cost savings. • Consumer savings. • Reduced chauffeuring burdens. • Increased traffic safety. • Energy conservation. • Air and noise pollution reductions.	• Additional vehicle travel reductions ("leverage effects"). • Improved accessibility, particularly for non-drivers. • Reduced crime risk. • More efficient development (reduced infrastructure costs). • Farmland and habitat preservation.
Potential Costs	• Higher capital and operating costs, and therefore subsidies. • Land and road space. • Traffic congestion and accident risk imposed by transit vehicles.	• Transit vehicle crowding.	• Reduced automobile business activity.	• Various problems associated with more compact development.

Fig. 10. Summary of the benefit and cost of using public transport [30]

In the Fig. 11 it is used to show the block schematic diagram of Addis Ababa city transport system.

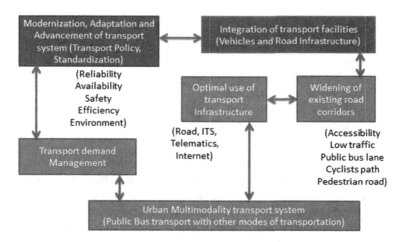

Fig. 11. Block scheme diagram of public transport system in Addis Ababa

According to study of document [10], the economic benefit of implementing transport telematics in terms of high societal attributes are described as following critical indicators in order to evaluate the costs of the transport services:

- fuel costs,
- distance based costs,
- time based costs,
- transport administration costs,
- infrastructure maintenance cost,
- accidents costs,
- noise and related costs,
- building new infrastructure costs,

Hence the reductions in cost in general have been seen based on the indicators set here as well as and particularly for e-commerce (toll payments, parking place payments, mobile payments) activities are major economic benefits of transport telematics services.

10 Promoting Sustainable Transportation

Public transport is vital for sustainable development [3]. Transport-related challenges in developing countries is pollution, congestion, accidents, public transport decline, environmental degradation, climate change, energy depletion, visual intrusion, and lack of accessibility for the urban poor. These are critical challenges and must be avoided or minimized from transport system. In order to maintain the principle of sustainable transport system in developing countries and others the following points should be kept in mind [15]:

- efficient management of traffic congestion,
- reliable and affordable public transport,
- safe transportation system,
- discouraging the use of private cars and encouraging the use of public transport,
- minimizing car-dominant society,
- providing access to passengers with special needs,
- developing transportation legislations,
- protecting the environment.

In addition to this sustainability of transport system can be ensured by supporting non-motorized zones, integration of public transport with bike lane and free walk ways, providing green technology or emission free cars, and implementing technological solutions such as transport telematics (ITS). However, urban areas across the world, in both developed and developing countries, have become increasingly automobile-dominated and less sustainable.

There is also need for sustainable fleet management. There is three key sustainable fleet management systems, namely: transport demand management, cleaner fuels and technologies (lowest emission vehicles), and efficient vehicle use (least amount of fuel).

Minimizing need for unnecessary travel or otherwise replacing with other means of travel such tele-video conferencing would be an option to promote sustainable fleet management.

11 Conclusion

This study was limited in less collecting of real data. It is the study to develop the concept in order to see the possibility of implementing the transport telematics technology in case of Addis Ababa. However, this paper has strongly examined that benefit of using transport technology in urban public transport sector. It is indisputable and believed that it can bring a potential impact into day to day activities of peoples and goods. Based on some practical analysis of conceptual study, implementation of transport telematics into public transport is found as crucial solution in order to increase the efficiency, effectiveness and to optimize the appropriate travel time and ease of accessibility.

The public transportation system would be more efficient, environment friendly and attractive to the users since it is based on real time information provided telematics. But developing countries like Ethiopia do not have full coverage of internet access as well as not fully connected cross roads. This could be challenge to proper implementation of this new transports system.

In the other hand the society perception/level of awareness and readiness to accept new technology, commitment of government to change existing policy and transport infrastructure might be affecting problem to implement the technology.

Acknowledgement. The work has been financially supported by the Polish Ministry of Science and Higher Education. The work has been also supported by the UNESCO AGH Chair for Science, Technology and Engineering Education, project ed. 2018A.

References

1. Abreha, D.: Analyzing public transport performance using efficiency measures and spatial analysis, the case of Addis Ababa Ethiopia. International Institute of Geo-information Science and Earth Observation, Enschede, The Netherlands, March 2007
2. Murray, A.T., et al.: Public transportation access. Transp. Res. -D **3**(5), 319–328 (1998)
3. Oranga, B.: Addis Ababa on the frontier of sustainable transport for African cities, Addis Ababa, Ethiopia (2015)
4. Boris, T., Szpytko, J.: Telematics is it useful and safety? African perspectives. Arch. Transp. Syst. Telemat. **8**(2), 5–7 (2015)
5. Fenta, T.: Demands for urban public transportation in Addis Ababa. J. Intell. Transp. Urban Plan. **2**(3), 81–88 (2014)
6. Janecki, R.: Formula of integrated territorial investments as an instrument to stimulate applications of intelligent transportation systems. Silesian University of Technology, Katowice, Poland (2014)

7. Kalasova, A., Krchova Z.: University of Zilina, The Faculty of Operation and Economics of Transport and Communications, Department of Road and Urban Transport, Zilina, Slovakia (2012)
8. Kostolná, M., Konecny, V.: Improving the service quality in public passenger transport by using information systems. University of Zilina, Zilina, Slovakia (2014)
9. Kosmanis, T.: Urban Transport Fleet Management, Department of Vehicles. Alexander Technological Educational Institute of Thessaloniki, Greece (2011)
10. Mbiydzenyuy, G.: Assessment of telematic systems for road freight transport. School of Computing Blekinge, Institute of Technology, Sweden, Blekinge Institute of Technology Licentiate Dissertation Series No. 10 (2010)
11. Mikulski, J.: The possibility of using telematics in urban transportation. In: Mikulski, J. (ed.) TST 2011. CCIS, vol. 239, pp. 54–69. Springer, Heidelberg (2011). https://doi.org/10.1007/978-3-642-24660-9_7
12. Mikulski, J., Introduction of Telematics for Transport. Faculty of Transport, Silesian University of Technology, Katowice, Poland (2012)
13. Ministry of Science and Technology (MoST), Policy document for innovation and technology transfer. Addis Ababa, Ethiopia (2013)
14. National Policy Framework for Land Transport Technology. Common Wealth Authority Australia (2016)
15. Pojani, D., Stead, D.: Sustainable urban transport in the developing world, beyond megacities (2015). www.mdpi.com/journal/sustainability. Accessed 14 Jan 2019
16. Rosinski, A.: Modeling of exploitation process of highway toll collection system. Warsaw University of Technology, Faculty of Transport, Warsaw, Poland (2016)
17. Samson, F.: Analysis of Traffic Accident In Addis Ababa: Traffic Simulation. Addis Ababa University Faculty of Technology, Mechanical Engineering Department, Addis Ababa (2006)
18. Smith, J., Clayton, E., Hanson, D.: Building sustainable, inclusive transportation systems and a framework for the future. Jakarta, Indonesia (2017). www.strategyand.pwc.com. Accessed 14 Jan 2019
19. Svitek, M., Zelinka, T., Jerabek, M.: Advanced Model of Intelligent Transport Systems. Faculty of Transportation Sciences, Czech Technical University, Prague (2016)
20. Szpytko, J.: Integrated decision making supporting the exploitation and control of transport devices, Krakow, Poland (2004)
21. Tavares, C.M., Szpytko, J.: The use of ICT technology for reliable transport control, Cape Verde case study. Arch. Transp. Syst. Telemat. **10**(3), 22–23 (2017)
22. Zhao, Y.: Telematics: safe and fun driving. intelligent transportation systems. IEEE Intell. Syst. (2002). https://www.computer.org/csdl/magazine/ex. Accessed 14 Jan 2019
23. https://www.ezega.com. Accessed 14 Jan 2019
24. https://civitas.eu/TG/transport-telematics. Accessed 14 Jan 2019
25. http://mereja.com/album/728. Accessed 14 Jan 2019
26. https://www.bbc.com/news/world-africa-38607986. Accessed 14 Jan 2019
27. https://use.metropolis.org/case-studies/sustainable-transport-in-addis-ababa. Accessed 14 Jan 2019
28. https://www.td.gov.hk/en/transport. Accessed 14 Jan 2019
29. World Bank (2015). Accessed 14 Jan 2019
30. www.vtpi.org. Accessed 14 Jan 2019

Telematics in Marine Transport

AIS Data Acquisition for Intelligent System for Obtaining Statistics

Mariusz Dramski[(✉)] and Marcin Mąka[(✉)]

Maritime University of Szczecin, Wały Chrobrego 1-2, Szczecin, Poland
{m.dramski,m.maka}@am.szczecin.pl

Abstract. In this paper the AIS data acquisition procedure for intelligent system for obtaining statistics is described. During this procedure several problems occurred and the way to solve them is presented. The aim of such data acquisition is to prepare them for an intelligent system which can be applied by different institutions responsible for creating the transport politics in Poland. This paper is also the introduction to the new project realized by the Maritime University of Szczecin with other cooperating institutions.

Keywords: AIS · Data mining · Intelligent systems · Intelligent statistics

1 Introduction

The share of maritime transport in the global economy is constantly growing. The official data presented by different institutions says that over 80% of the world trade volume was moved by sea. This fact leads to the natural conclusion that the total number of ships increases each year and it causes a lot of problems related to traffic management, safety etc.

In this paper authors touch upon the topic of obtaining statistics on maritime transport. Most ships are equipped with appropriate devices to register various types of informations. It should also be mentioned that this kind of equipment is mandatory on almost all marine units and it is regulated by law. Thus, there are no obstacles to acquire and process transport data and to draw conclusions. These conclusions may be useful in areas such:

- port state control,
- emergency/incident management,
- coastal monitoring,
- risk analysis and control,
- statistics,
- customs control,
- security monitoring,
- and more...

J. Mikulski (Ed.): TST 2019, CCIS 1049, pp. 321–332, 2019.
https://doi.org/10.1007/978-3-030-27547-1_23

The source of such data in this paper is AIS (Automatic Identification System) which devices are present on almost all the ships. It allows to acquire a data related to each vessel. Then the data may be used to further research and analysis.

2 Automatic Identification System (AIS)

AIS [1] is a system of automatic communication allowing for data exchange between ships and/or ships and onshore units. This system becomes popular also on private vessels such yachts, motorboats etc. Simple AIS receivers are cheap and can be easily installed on each unit.

Fig. 1. Simple AIS receiver [2]

Figure 1 illustrates a simple AIS receiver allowing for data acquisition. The only thing that is required by the vessel owner is to connect it with and antenna and laptop.
The features of professional commercial systems are:

- the system should automatically broadcast ships dynamic and some other informations in a self-organized manner,
- the system installation should be capable of receiving and processing specified interrogating calls,
- the system should be capable of transmitting additional safety information on request,
- the system installation should be able to operate continuously while under way or at anchor,
- the system should use TDMA (Time Division Multiple Access) techniques in a synchronized manner,
- the system should be capable of three modes of operation, autonomous, assigned and polled.

Automatic identification system equipment is listed in the table below. Besides, Fig. 2 illustrates a professional AIS device - ComNav Voyager X3. The full description of AIS can be found in [xxx] (Table 1).

Table 1. Automatic identification system equipment [1]

Automatic identification system VHF data link non-controlling stations	
1	Automatic identification system shipborne station
2	Aids to navigation-automatic identification system station
3	Limited base station (no VHF data link control functionality)
4	Search and rescue mobile aircraft equipment
5	Repeater station
6	Automatic identification system search and rescue transmitter
7	Man overboard-automatic identification system
8	Emergency position indicating radio beacon-automatic identification system
Automatic identification system VHF data link controlling stations	
1	Base station

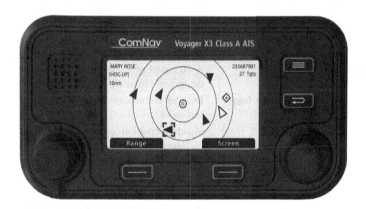

Fig. 2. ComNav Voyager X3 automatic identification system [3]

3 AIS Messages

To obtain some statistics it is necessary to analyze and process the data recorded thanks to automatic identification system. AIS provides 27 types of messages. These types are presented in Table 2 (M – mobile station, B – base station).

Table 2. The types of AIS messages [1]

Message ID	Name	Description	M/B
1	Position report	Scheduled position report	M
2	Position report	Assigned scheduled position report	M
3	Position report	Special position report, response to interrogation	M
4	Base station report	Position, UTC, date and current slot number of base station	B

(*continued*)

Table 2. (*continued*)

Message ID	Name	Description	M/B
5	Static and voyage related data	Scheduled static and voyage related vessel data report	M
6	Binary addressed message	Binary data for addressed communication	M/B
7	Binary acknowledgement	Acknowledgement of received addressed binary data	M/B
8	Binary broadcast message	Binary data for broadcast communication	M/B
9	Standard SAR aircraft position report	Position report for airborne stations involved in SAR operations, only	M
10	UTC/date inquiry	Request UTC and date	M/B
11	UTC/date response	Current UTC and date if available	M
12	Addressed safety related message	Safety related data for addressed communication	M/B
13	Safety related acknowledgement	Acknowledgement of received addressed safety related message	M/B
14	Safety related broadcast message	Safety related data for broadcast communication	M/B
15	Interrogation	Request for a specific message type	M/B
16	Assignment mode command	Assignment of a specific report behavior by competent authority using a base station	B
17	DGNSS broadcast binary message	DGNSS corrections provided by a base station	B
18	Standard Class B equipment position report	Standard position report for Class B shipborne mobile equipment to be used instead of Messages 1, 2, 3	M
19	Extended Class B equipment position report	No longer required; Extended position report for Class B shipborne mobile equipment; contains additional static information	M
20	Data link management message	Reserve slots for Base station(s)	B
21	Aids-to-navigation report	Position and status report for aids-to-navigation	M/B
22	Channel management	Management of channels and transceiver modes by a Base station	B
23	Group assignment command	Assignment of a specific report behaviour by competent authority using a Base station to a specific group of mobiles	B
24	Static data report	Additional data assigned to an MMSI Part A: Name Part B: Static Data	M/B
25	Single slot binary message	Short unscheduled binary data transmission (Broadcast or addressed)	M/B
26	Multiple slot binary message with Communications State	Scheduled binary data transmission (Broadcast or addressed)	M/B
27	Position report for long-range applications	Class A and Class B "SO" shipborne mobile equipment outside base station coverage	M

Extracting data from AIS message depends of course on it's type. First it is necessary to determine what type of message is received and then to decode it in appropriate way. The example AIS messages may look like (data recorded at Maritime University of Szczecin on 7th January 2019 – the data represents 10 min recording phase):

07.01.2019 11:03:26 !BSVDM,1,1,,B,H3pro50QTA8tM84J3;800000000,2*1E
07.01.2019 11:03:27 !BSVDM,1,1,,B,23q5DlhP00Q2pfRNSNq<<?v>RH4>,0*0B
07.01.2019 11:03:27 !BSVDM,1,1,,B,33prjPP01KQ2llVNUa>7Lmr<00lQ,0*0A
07.01.2019 11:03:27 !BSVDM,1,1,,A,13q5UfPP00Q2bKjNT`jbPgv>2@4L,0*6D
07.01.2019 11:03:27 !BSVDM,1,1,,B,13iit20001Q2hCTNU;oqr0P@0@4P,0*1D
07.01.2019 11:03:28 !BSVDM,1,1,,A,13h;VCgP0012j4`NTMNdRgvB0L0s,0*32
07.01.2019 11:03:29 !BSVDM,1,1,,A,13h;`9?P0012j2tNTMS:5OvB0<11,0*0B
07.01.2019 11:03:29 !BSVDM,1,1,,A,B3uHsQ000@@cPtWa=:SQ3wwTSP06,0*77
07.01.2019 11:03:29 !BSVDM,1,1,,A,D>j`;iQoD@fp00@01op@00A<hfp,2*2E
07.01.2019 11:03:30 !BSVDM,1,1,,B,13q5KQSP00Q3092NSMa00?vB0l0h,0*04
07.01.2019 11:03:30 !BSVDM,1,1,,A,33prjPP01KQ2ll8NUa1WKmr@0000,0*4E
07.01.2019 11:03:30 !BSVDM,1,1,,B,13pr<nP001Q2m`DNV5qWga@B0PSM,0*54
07.01.2019 11:03:30 !BSVDM,1,1,,A,G>j`;iP8aLvg@@b1tF600000;00,2*14
07.01.2019 11:03:31 !BSVDM,1,1,,A,29NWv7001UQ2`lFNdSjEO4J@0@6I,0*09
07.01.2019 11:03:31 !BSVDM,1,1,,B,33q5DShP01Q2ifbNUMWVk?vBP0VQ,0*08
07.01.2019 11:03:31 !BSVDM,1,1,,B,23q5DlhP00Q2pfPNSNph0?vFRH6R,0*46
07.01.2019 11:03:31 !BSVDM,1,1,,A,13q5Bm@P0bQ2eDFNR9w3OwvFR<0g,0*40
07.01.2019 11:03:31 !BSVDM,1,1,,B,23q5D<hP00Q2VejNT57P0?vF2@6b,0*52
07.01.2019 11:03:31 !BSVDM,1,1,,B,13pr=30000Q2sj8NW6eW7VLD086o,0*55
07.01.2019 11:03:31 !BSVDM,1,1,,B,G>j`;g08aHvg@@b1tF000000000,2*70
07.01.2019   11:03:32
!BSVDM,2,1,0,B,A>j`;g08KPvAp0@02bbN2OvP02d3w4D0>Q3uk01T7gnd058Mw
1L07@Gtrh0e,0*7B
07.01.2019 11:03:33 !BSVDM,1,1,,B,33prjPP01KQ2lkNNU`g7IErF012P,0*44
07.01.2019 11:03:33 !BSVDM,1,1,,A,23q5DlhP00Q2pfHNSNph0?vJRH7k,0*69
07.01.2019 11:03:33 !BSVDM,1,1,,A,23q5D<hP00Q2VenNT57h0?vJ2@7s,0*71
07.01.2019 11:03:33 !BSVDM,1,1,,A,139@`B0P00Q2VkPNT6Iv4?vJR87v,0*07
07.01.2019 11:03:33 !BSVDM,1,1,,B,D>j`;g02t@fp00A6F8D@028hhfp,2*13
07.01.2019 11:03:34 !BSVDM,1,1,,A,13q5DwHP00Q2h8`NU1;f4?vJR<0h,0*77
07.01.2019 11:03:34 !BSVDM,1,1,,B,13h;`R?P0012j9dNTMcFVgvL00RU,0*7A
07.01.2019 11:03:34 !BSVDM,1,1,,A,13q5SK@00012scdNW5p03V`6081d,0*64
07.01.2019 11:03:34 !BSVDM,1,1,,A,13aQe5000012m?8NSvorT`vN05@<,0*37
07.01.2019 11:03:34 !BSVDM,1,1,,A,402OfA1v<Cb3=Q2hf>NTsBG000S:,0*53
07.01.2019 11:03:35 !BSVDM,1,1,,B,4>j`;g1v<Cb3>Q1nf@NJ=jQ020S:,0*46
07.01.2019 11:03:35 !BSVDM,1,1,,B,13q5DShP01Q2if`NUMWFpgvJP000,0*54
07.01.2019 11:03:35 !BSVDM,1,1,,B,23q5DlhP00Q2pfDNSNph0?vNRH8q,0*77
07.01.2019 11:03:35 !BSVDM,1,1,,B,23q5D<hP00Q2VerNT57h0?vN2@8t,0*62
07.01.2019 11:03:35 !BSVDM,1,1,,A,13q5UfPP00Q2bKdNT`jbJ?vN2L0V,0*43
07.01.2019 11:03:36 $PSTXI,INFO,2,0,3,1,62*4C
07.01.2019 11:03:36 !BSVDM,1,1,,A,13q5Hm?P00Q2h`2NTV41HOvN0D0s,0*2B
07.01.2019 11:03:36 !BSVDM,1,1,,B,H3pro54m3?=5QQQC@Cjinn0h4310,0*0E
07.01.2019   11:03:37
!BSVDM,2,1,1,A,A>j`;iP8RpvWh0@02g:N4?nE06@7wdt0IQotV@0M0wkB03`5w
FP0;@;w5P1H,0*64

07.01.2019 11:03:37 !BSVDM,1,1,,A,23q5DlhP00Q2pf@NSNpP0?vRRH:7,0*10
07.01.2019 11:03:37 !BSVDM,1,1,,A,13iit20000Q2hCTNU;oar0PT0<0q,0*42
07.01.2019 11:03:37 !BSVDM,1,1,,A,29NWv7001UQ2`rpNdS<EO4JN00Rv,0*52
07.01.2019 11:03:37 !BSVDM,1,1,,B,H3pr;J4l653hhhiCA6EPPP0p33=0,0*31
07.01.2019 11:03:38 !BSVDM,1,1,,B,D02OfA24<Nfp00N000,4*0A
07.01.2019 11:03:38 !BSVDM,1,1,,A,13q5KQSP00Q3092NSMa00?vT0PS?,0*19
07.01.2019 11:03:39 !BSVDM,1,1,,A,13h;`9?P0012j2tNTMSrJgvV0H;8,0*77
07.01.2019 11:03:39 !BSVDM,1,1,,B,23q5DlhP00Q2pf<NSNp00?vVRH;>,0*03
07.01.2019 11:03:39 !BSVDM,1,1,,B,B3pr;J0008@e73Wa@MfqrJ9UWP06,0*6E
07.01.2019 11:03:39 !BSVDM,1,1,,A,13pr?I000012sUFNW57JdVNT05@<,0*2A
07.01.2019 11:03:40 !BSVDM,1,1,,B,33prjPP01KQ2lilNU`4oMUrT0000,0*0A

3.1   Reporting Intervals

Each type of information is valid for different period, so there is a need to update the data.

- Static information – every 6 min, when data has been amended, on request
- Dynamic information – dependent on speed and course but never more than 3 min (in Table 3 periods for Class A devices are shown, Table 4 contains values for non Class A devices)
- Voyage related information – every 6 min, when data has been amended, on request
- Safety related message – as required

The values presented in Table 3 are chosen to minimize unnecessary loading of the radio channels while maintaining compliance within the IMO AIS performance standards.

Table 3. Class A shipborne mobile equipment reporting intervals [1]

Ship's dynamic conditions	Nominal reporting interval
Ship at anchor or moored and not moving faster than 3 knots	2 s–3 min
Ship at anchor or moored and moving faster than 3 knots	2 s–10 s
Ship 0–14 knots	2 s–10 s
Ship 0–14 knots and changing course	2 s–3 1/3 s
Ship 14–23 knots	2 s–6 s
Ship 14–23 knots and changing course	2 s
Ship > 23 knots	2 s
Ship > 23 knots and changing course	2 s

Table 4. Reporting intervals for equipment other than Class A shipborne mobile equipment [1]

Platform's condition	Nominal reporting interval	Increased reporting interval
Class B "SO" shipborne mobile equipment not moving faster than 2 knots	3 min	3 min
Class B "SO" shipborne mobile equipment moving 2–14 knots	30 s	30 s
Class B "SO" shipborne mobile equipment moving 14–23 knots	15 s	30 s
Class B "SO" shipborne mobile equipment moving > 23 knots	5 s	15 s
Class B "CS" shipborne mobile equipment not moving faster than 2 knots	3 min	–
Class B "CS" shipborne mobile equipment moving faster than 2 knots	30 s	–
Search and rescue aircraft (airborne mobile equipment)	10 s	–
Aids to navigation	3 min	–
AIS base station	10 s	–

4 Research Results

As mentioned in the abstract this paper initiates a new project realized by Maritime University of Szczecin. To extract data, first thing is to record them. Several records were done in a period of one month from 10th December 2018 to 10th January 2019. It turned out that the pure acquisition of data is not an easy task. Some problems occurred and all of them are described in this paper. After recording the data was decoded to extract the informations.

4.1 Types of Messages

In Example 1 we took into consideration the example text file containing AIS data taken on 7th January 2019. Download started at 11:03AM and stopped at 17:40PM on this day. In total 76 471 messages of different types were received. It is illustrated in the Fig. 3. During the 6 h of recording following types of messages were received: 1, 2, 3, 4, 6, 7, 8, 18 and 24. The total number of each type is also visible in the figure.

Type 1, 2 and 3 messages contain basic information on the ship movement parameters of the vessel. They should be send periodically by mobile stations (vessels) equipped with Class A AIS devices. The equivalent of these messages for vessels equipped with Class B AIS is message 18. Message number 24 contains static data of ship such as name, call sign and others. Message 4 is sent by local base stations (VTS Szczecin in our case) and is used to synchronize the time of transmission. The number of messages 6 and 7 is the same because 7 is an acknowledge of 6. Message 8 doesn't have such confirmation.

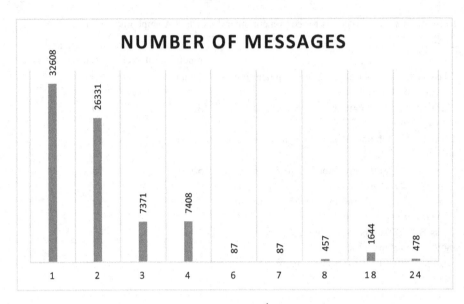

Fig. 3. Statistics of received messages 7th January 2019 [own study]

Let's consider now other data set taken on 3rd January 2019 from 8:37AM to midnight (Example 2). It can be observed that more message types were detected. This time the types 5, 17, 20 and 23 were also present. 5474 messages were decoded as wrong or unreadable. Message 5 represents the static data of ship's voyage. Messages 17, 20 and 23 were sent by base stations.

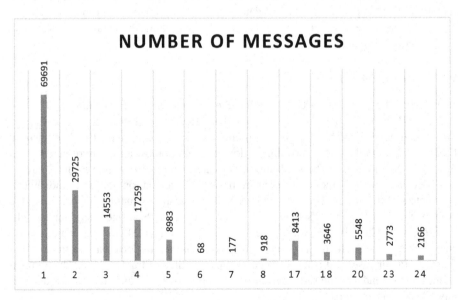

Fig. 4. Statistics of received messages 3rd January 2019 [own study]

Example 3–7th February 2019 from 0:00AM to 10:37AM (Figs. 4 and 5).

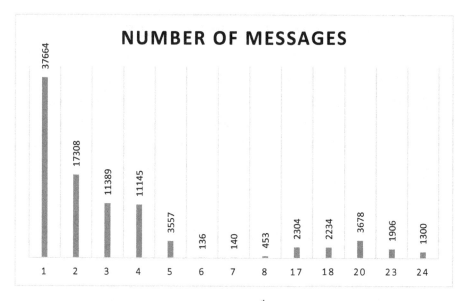

Fig. 5. Statistics of received messages 7th February 2019 [own study]

Example 4 from 22th February 2019 from 11:42AM to 12:18AM. This time it can be seen that additionally messages 21 and 27 were detected (Fig. 6).

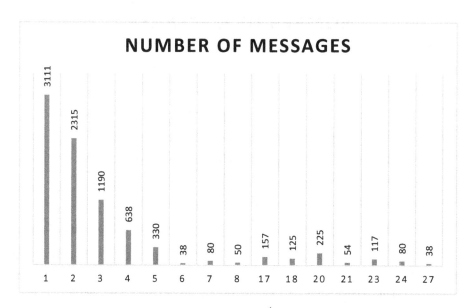

Fig. 6. Statistics of received messages 22th February 2019 [own study]

Example 5 from 25th February from 9:36AM to 12:38PM (Fig. 7).

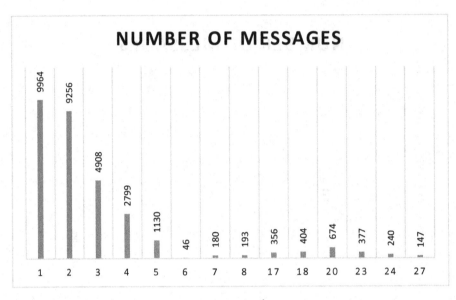

Fig. 7. Statistics of received messages 25th February 2019 [own study]

Example 6 28th February from 9:36AM to 2:44PM (Fig. 8).

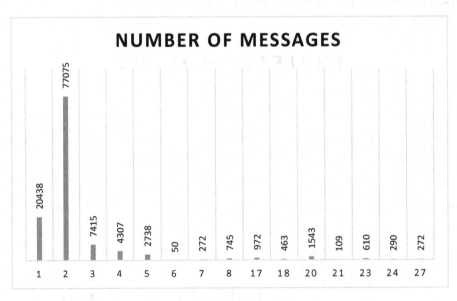

Fig. 8. Statistics of received messages 28th February 2019 [own study]

4.2   Problems, Errors etc.

The problems which occurred can be divided into two types: technical and human ones. First obstacles were observed during the recording process:

- power outage – although in modern countries such problems occur not very often, but it is necessary to add to the server an additional power supply (UPS),
- the stability of the computer system – this problem should be solved by using modern devices and software (including supported operation system, antivirus software etc.); sometimes computer restarted suddenly and the data recording was stopped,
- short VPN sessions – AIS device installed at Maritime University of Szczecin supports data sharing through the computer network. There is also the possibility to have the access to this network from outside using VPN (Virtual Private Network); VPN sessions took only 8 h and it was necessary to retrieve the session manually to start the download again,
- AIS malfunction – this problem didn't occur but has to be taken into the consideration,
- internal communication problems – all problems related to the LAN network installed at Maritime University of Szczecin,
- external communication problems – similar problems like above but only when VPN sessions were used.
- as shown in the figures above not always the same types of messages were detected – so the conclusion is that there is a need review more data that only from one limited short period.

Even if we ensure the total free of errors communication, there is no warranty that each message will be correct. Errors in the messages can be caused by human or can have direct technical source. Here are some examples of decoded messages containing some errors (error is italic and underlined, data recorded on 15th January 2019) (Table 5):

Table 5. Errors in AIS messages [own study]

No.	Ship	Description
1	Hydrograf22	AIS brand name transmitted incorrectly
0110000000111110001110101101110001010001001101010000100111100110100010110000110000110 0001010011010000010011110010110001110110110100000001100000010000001100000010000 15/01/2019 22:15:15 261011220 24 53 *COME!!!* SPS2166 6 4 3 1		
2	Kasia	Lacks of data (type of the message is correct)
0110000000111110001110101101110101101001001001010101000100100101010001010010000001000 0111100*00000000000000000000000000000000000000000000000000000000000000000000000000*00 15/01/2019 22:19:00 261011290 24 37 TRUEHDG *@@@@@@@ 0 0 0 0*		
3	Imoros1	Incorrect dimensions of the vessel. According to the AIS message the dimensions are: 10 × 26 [m] which is not reliable. Probably this data was written manually
0110000000111110001110100010110110100001001101000001100001010000111100011000011000011 000010100110100010001100101011000001000001000000000001110000000110000110011010000 15/01/2019 22:20:42 261000040 24 52 FEC0001 SQFU *7 3 3 13*		
4	Syriusz	Incorrect width of the vessel (the value is correct but it is measured by calculating the distance from the antenna – it's location is wrong in this message. It can be checked by looking at any Syriusz picture)
0110000000111110001110101101101111011001001110000000110011110011010000010100100000000 0000010011010000010011110010110001110110110011000001001000010010000000000100000000 15/01/2019 22:18:32 261011190 24 56 COMAR@@ SPS2163 *9 18 0 4*		

5 Conclusion

In this paper the data acquisition from AIS receiver is described. First section treats about AIS equipment and type of transmitted messages. Recording data is not an easy task. A lot of errors occurred and these cases need to be interpreted. The main problem is not technical because the equipment can be always fixed or replaced. The weakest point is always the human factor what is showed in the Sect. 4 of this paper.

The aim of recording AIS data is not only to illustrate the vessel's voyage. The data can be analyzed and processed to obtain a complete image of the maritime traffic in given area. The project which currently starts at Maritime University of Szczecin focuses on the Polish sea waters (most of all the region of Szczecin and Świnoujście ports).

References

1. Recommendation ITU-R M.1371-5 (02/2014). Technical characteristic for an automatic identification system using time division multiple access in the VHF maritime mobile frequency band (2014)
2. http://www.ft-tec.com. Accessed 15 Nov 2018
3. http://www.comnavmarine.com. Accessed 15 Nov 2018

The Determination of the Sea Navigator Safety Profile Using Data Mining

Zbigniew Pietrzykowski[✉], Mirosław Wielgosz,
and Marcin Breitsprecher

Maritime University of Szczecin, Wały Chrobrego 1-2, 70-500 Szczecin, Poland
{z.pietrzykowski, m.wielgosz,
m.breitsprecher}@am.szczecin.pl

Abstract. A person steering a transport vehicle needs to have qualifications confirmed by appropriate certificates. The holder of the certificates has to satisfy the criteria for a transport vehicle operator set under mandatory examination procedures. The operator safety profile, identified on the basis of psychological assessment, can essentially complement these criteria. The profile can be broadened from a comprehensive analysis of operator's actual behaviour, based on electronic data from recorders installed in the vehicle. In shipping, the data would come mainly from the automatic identification system and voyage data recorders. This article proposes to use data mining tools for an analysis and identification of selected characteristics of sea navigator's safety profile.

Keywords: Sea navigation · Navigator · Safety profile · Data mining

1 Introduction

Human factor is one of the most frequent causes of navigational accidents. Therefore, various actions are taken to reduce human errors. These are, inter alia improvement of navigators' training process and certification of qualifications for conducting various type ships, the improvement and construction of navigational equipment and systems that enhance the situational awareness of decision-makers. A lot of attention is paid to the problem of workload, and external factors such as hydro-meteorological conditions, the area, vessel traffic in the area, that vitally affect the quality of decision-making. Besides, the number of various types of recorders increases in ships and land-based centres. They enable registration of a growing number of ship and environment parameters used in the on-line mode (enhancing the situational awareness) and off-line, e.g. for voyage analysis based on adopted criteria (e.g. time, fuel consumption, operational decisions taken).

Like in other modes of transport, work continues on examining mental and physical characteristics of transport vehicle operators and their impact on accident risk. Other essential factors include manoeuvring characteristics of the ship in current shipping conditions. For these reasons it is purposeful to consider a ship as a socio-technical object: the ship and the crew. The above factors gain importance in the light of the

© Springer Nature Switzerland AG 2019
J. Mikulski (Ed.): TST 2019, CCIS 1049, pp. 333–345, 2019.
https://doi.org/10.1007/978-3-030-27547-1_24

advancing automation of control and management processes on a ship and the anticipated introduction of ships of various levels of autonomy with a skeleton crew on board. The analysis and assessment of ship's 'behaviour' is also important for vessel traffic service centres. The results make it possible to identify and counteract risks.

Ship's behaviour is understood as the manner in which the navigator performs specific manoeuvres, e.g. collision avoiding manoeuvres. A manoeuvre executed too late or passing another ship at a very close distance may indicate the ship conduct that does not conform with good sea practice at the very moment and in the near future. The proper identification of such ship would allow the centre and other ships concerned to observe it particularly closely, especially in approach channels, traffic separation schemes and routes with heavy traffic. Instead of the term ship 'behaviour', we propose to use the term navigator's safety profile.

Given the lack of data on the psychological profile and the current mental-physical condition of the navigator in charge, his safety profile may be determined on the basis of a comprehensive analysis of the real behaviour, based on electronic data obtained from recorders installed on the ship, e.g. data the automatic identification system (AIS). For this purpose, methods and tools of data mining are used, serving for automated discovery of relationships and patterns derived from very large data sets.

The Sect. 2 discusses, available in the literature, methods of analysis and assessment of safety taking into account the human factor in marine shipping compared to other modes of transport. The Sect. 3 presents the concept of determining the navigator's safety profile. Section 4 describes the applied method of data collection for the identification of the navigator's safety profile. Section 5 contains the results of the navigator's safety profile identification using data mining tools. The summary formulates the conclusions drawn from the research.

2   The Human Factor in the Analysis and Assessment of Navigation Safety

The analysis and assessment of safety in sea shipping is generally done separately for open sea and restricted areas. This division is based on the criterion of the geometry of the area available for the ship (length, width, sea depth) due to its manoeuvring capability. The basic criteria of the assessment of the navigational situation in the open sea include the closest point of approach (CPA) and time to CPA, ship domain, safety indicators, collision risk [1–10]. For restricted areas, additionally taken into account are the safe manoeuvring area, safe underkeel clearance, time of manoeuvre performance [11]. The human factor (professionalism, competence and mental and physical strength) is important in assessing safety, affects the above criteria and is difficult to account for. This concerns such issues as the identification of the situation as dangerous, defining the moment to commence an anti-collision manoeuvre, how apparent the manoeuvre is, passing distance to an object etc.

In sociotechnical systems three categories of the human factor are distinguished [12]:

- individual factors such as competence level, stress, motivation,
- group factors, inter alia management weaknesses, supervision and crew factors,
- organizational factors including standards, systems and procedures.

An approach often used is an analysis of individual factors, including psychophysical traits of a human being. Types of personality are considered in this context. The Big Five Traits model distinguishes five types of personality: neuroticism, openness, extraversion, conscientiousness and agreeableness [13] in relation to job performance. The objective is to identify the causes of human errors and the probability of error occurrence.

These issues are the subject of research in other modes of transport. For example, in air transport five hazardous attitudes leading to dangerous decisions are distinguished [14]:

- anti-authority (people who do not like anyone telling them what to do),
- impulsivity (the need to do something/anything immediately),
- invulnerability (believe that accidents only happen to others),
- macho (believe to be better than anyone else are thinking),
- resignation (leave the action to others, for better or worse).

An interesting approach to the identification of driver behaviour in road traffic is presented in [15]. A system of a comprehensive assessment of the operation of the vehicle and truck driver is proposed. The system has a layered nature. Types of drivers' behaviour and estimators identifying the driver's driving style are defined. The following types of driver are distinguished: calm, neutral, active. In the proposed method, driving style is identified based on recorded vehicle movement parameters: change in the acceleration (gas) pedal position. In the works [16, 17] the proposed model identifies driver types as mild, average, aggressive, based on changes in the position of acceleration and brake pedals.

In the work [18], this approach was used for the risk assessment of port manoeuvers. Three groups of navigator's (pilot's) attitudes towards risk were identified and distinguished:

- chancer, eager to take a risk,
- neutral, conservative,
- passive, reluctant to take a risk.

The identification was made using simulation tests and questionnaire surveys. The evaluation takes into account the following factors: the knowledge of the area and the navigator's experience, length of sea service as a captain and as a sea pilot. Based on the developed model of the human factor, the probability of making a wrong decision by the navigator is determined.

The quantities that characterize the navigator's manner of operation may be passing distance, maintained distance to navigational dangers and the type and parameters of manoeuvres performed for this purpose. Work [19] analyses factors affecting navigator's decisions. Individual personality traits, acquired skills, external conditions and other are distinguished. The percentage share of these factors has been determined based on the questionnaires conducted among professionally active navigators. The respective figures were estimated at 10%, 22%, 60% and 8%. Of the personal traits of character, the participants attributed 54% to personality, while among the acquired skills experience was recognized in the first place (59%). As for external conditions, the respondents considered the ship type and size as essential (28%), then the type of area (18%), traffic intensity (15%), hydro-meteorological conditions (13%) and ship manoeuvring capability (10%).

3 The Navigator's Safety Profile

One of the basic requirements of safety is the assurance of the composition of the crew with proper qualifications. The ship's minimum safe manning certificate specifies the number of crew members and certificates they should hold. The scope of the certificates and the crew composition depend mainly on the type and size of the ship, and its trading area. The qualification exams for ship's personnel include psychological tests, but their scope is limited. The actual number of crew members is determined by the shipowner, nevertheless it cannot be lower than that specified in the said manning certificate. To ensure a high level of safety in shipping, shipowners introduce tests of competence for the confirmation of the qualifications of the employees. While these tests allow the verification of the professional knowledge level, they do not identify the psychological profile in terms of safe behaviour and the use of good sea practice. The performance of a visible, substantial and early manoeuvre is an example of such good sea practice. In road traffic, good practices include overtaking other cars on a straight section of the road or adjusting the driving speed to conditions on the road.

Professional aptitude can be determined through psychological tests, which require qualified personnel to conduct them and interpret the results. However, such tests are conducted rarely. In this case, the navigator's safety profile will be useful, drawn on the basis of his actual behaviour by analysing electronic data from shipboard or land-based centre recorders. The identification of the navigator's safety profile may be an essential aid and hint to keep an eye on ships that may pose potential risk.

The work [20] attempts to determine navigators' behaviour profiles. Relevant research using questionnaires involved employed navigators. The respondents were requested to name the terms they use to describe navigators' behaviour at sea. The navigators distinguished 13 types of behaviour. The most frequent ones were: professional (15.3%), decisive (15.3%), risk-taker (1.4%), careful (13.9%), very careful (11.1%). The above terms are proposed for the navigator's profile description. The behaviour of navigators in ship encounter situations was analysed based on their own declared behaviour profiles and stated by them, considered as safe, passing distances (Fig. 1).

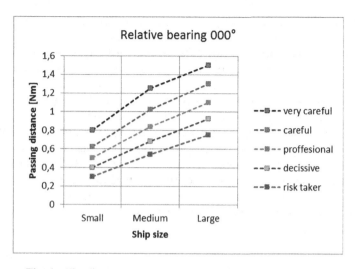

Fig. 1. The distances to other ships on 000° heading angle [20]

In an encounter of ships on opposite courses (Fig. 1) there was a visible relationship between navigator-declared profiles and passing distances they considered as safe. At sea many factors affect navigators' behaviour, i.e. the manner of performing a manoeuvre. The maintained passing distance is not the only criterion describing the navigator's safety profile. Other criteria may include: the manoeuvre extent – readily apparent or not, moment of its start, or the duration of the entire manoeuvre. The identification of the navigator's safety profile might be an essential aid and prompt to start more careful observation of ships that may potentially create risk.

This was the premise to undertake research on the possibility of identifying the navigator's safety profile based on recorded data.

4 The Research

The navigator's performance (as well as plane pilot's or driver's) can be assessed by current monitoring of actions taken by an individual on a simulator (very time-consuming) or the evaluation of recorded data (less stressful for the person assessed, guarantees more natural behaviour). The recorded data may come from data bases of land-based vessel traffic centres (e.g. AIS PL, VTS) or simulation. This analysis of navigators' performance makes use of the records of simulation tests using non-autonomous ship models.

The tests were conducted on a Transas-made simulator of Electronic Chart Display and Information System (ECDIS), widely used in marine navigation, with eight independent stations. The simulator allows recording standard data transmitted by ships in the AIS system at one second intervals. Installed at the Maritime University of Szczecin, the simulator has a capability to carry out virtually any scenario. The models of ships have full ability to manoeuvre by course or speed alteration, and there is a choice of sea areas and hydro-meteorological conditions.

The tests were conducted in two different restricted navigationally similar areas (Singapore Strait, Dover Strait). Six encounter situations and three models of vessels were selected for the tests. For these, scenarios were created and saved, allowing multiple reproduction of the initial situation from which each navigator could perform at his discretion. Each scenario was executed five times, resulting in 30 or 35 individual passages of ships manoeuvring in each scenario (depending on the number of ECDIS course participants). In total, 160 passages (performed scenarios) were recorded, which multiplied by six or seven (number of participants) gave 1036 individual passages. A single scenario, depending on the encounter and type of ship, took 10 to 20 min.

Three models of ships of different sizes were used, further referred to as large, medium and small (Table 1). Three speed variations were examined, designated as full-slow, the same, slow-full.

Table 1. The technical and operational parameters of ships used in the tests [21]

Ship model	Length [m]	Breadth [m]	Draft [m]	Displacement [t]	Speed [kn]
Small	95.0	13.0	3.7	3 510	11.1
Medium	173.5	23.0	8.1	19 512	18.9
Large	261.3	48.0	9.0	63 430	16.3

The first step to the analysis and further calculations for all scenarios was to determine the true trajectories of the ships. The true trajectories in the scenario 045° is shown in Fig. 2, presenting a single track of a ship maintaining a steady course and speed (190°, 18.9 knots) and a set of 35 trajectories of manoeuvring ships, all starting their passages with the same movement parameters (280°, v0 = 18.9 knots). The trajectories show a diversity of the manoeuvres performed in respect to the direction and extent of course alteration, time of starting the alteration and speed alterations. Three groups of ships are visible:

- ships altering course only (turn to starboard, detail 1);
- ships altering course and speed (speed reduction, turn to starboard, detail 2);
- ships altering course only (turn to port, detail 3).

After the assessment and acceptance of the recorded data, relative trajectories were determined, the first step to identify the ship domain. The relative trajectories were determined separately for the non-manoeuvring and manoeuvring ships. They are presented, respectively, in Figs. 2 and 3.

Figure 3 presents a ship located in the centre of a coordinate system with visible contours of the manoeuvring ships. The described scenario 045° simulates the situation where ships preparing for a collision avoiding manoeuvre see another ship on the relative bearing 045° (in 360° notation, calculated from ship's centre line). This is the relative head-up display, often used by navigators in radar and electronic chart systems, offering prompt assessment of the true passing distance.

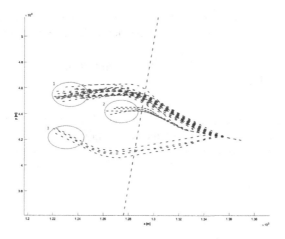

Fig. 2. True trajectories of medium ships, scenario 045° [own study]

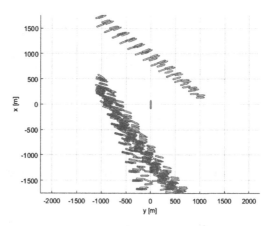

Fig. 3. Relative trajectories of the ships in the scenario 045° [own study]

Figure 3 presents a situation where a ship is placed in the middle of the coordinate system with visible contours of the manoeuvring ships.

5   The Navigator's Safety Profile – Research

The recorded data presented in the form of graphs (Fig. 4) are presented to expert-navigators for the assessment of the performance of manoeuvres.

It should be noted that the same effect, in this case the passing distance, can be obtained by manoeuvring in a number of ways. For instance:

– only one course alteration and a decisive or gradual return to the course;
– two or more subsequent course alterations and a decisive or gradual return to the course;
– speed alteration – reduction or increase of ship's speed (the latter is rare as ships generally sail at full ahead);
– speed and course alterations.

Depending on the manoeuvres performed, the other ship can be passed on port or starboard side, i.e. ahead or astern of the other ship, which in some cases will be interpreted as complying or not complying with the Collision Regulations. For course and speed manoeuvres, assessment refers to the extent of alteration (visible or not) and the time of commencement.

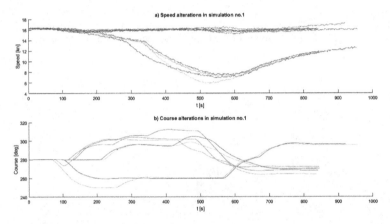

Fig. 4. Selected anti-collision manoeuvres in the scenario 045°: (a) speed alterations; (b) course alterations [own study]

Five navigator's safety profiles were adopted (see Sect. 4): professional, decisive, risk-taker, careful, very careful. The experts assessed the passages and the performance of manoeuvres. On this basis, they assigned one of the said profiles to each of them. The experts considered the risk-taker profile as a hazardous attitude.

The obtained data were used for the identification of navigators' safety profiles using data mining tools for the discovery of patterns in large data sets. The basic aim of data mining is to extract the searched-for piece of information and display the results, the discovered relations, in a clear and readable form, e.g. as an algorithm or model. Data mining is possible using computers. A number of tools and techniques are used for this purpose: algorithms for machine learning, genetic and neural algorithms, fuzzy logic and approximate sets, statistical methods. Data mining basically aims at classification, prediction, association and detection. Classification means the identification of classes or clusters that are then used for the categorization of data. Prediction is intended to identify key characteristics or attributes to create a formula for examining unknown cases (future values). Association makes it possible to determine the relationships between objects, the basis for the creation of rules describing a phenomenon. Finally, detection is to indicate specific anomalies or irregularities in data. Data mining has a number of applications in such fields as medicine and technology (diagnostics), trade and economy (analysis and forecasting), business and banking (customer segmentation, detection of fraud), astronomy and genetic science (research) [22–24].

6 The Navigator's Safety Profile Identification

One of the tools of data mining is the RapidMiner platform created by a company with the same name. RapidMiner software integrates a number of tools, including a module of preliminary data processing, algorithms of machine learning, and statistical and analytical tools [25, 26]. RapidMiner use consists in constructing, by means of the graphical interface, a suitable process for an analysis and visualization of the explored data. It is also possible to verify and optimize a model that is generated by the software after an input data analysis.

The collected AIS data recorded in simulation tests, together with expert assessments, were used for the construction of the navigator's safety profile model. To this end, the data were preprocessed, i.e. checked for completeness and additional parameters describing the behaviour of navigators were calculated, e.g. the time of manoeuvre performance, manner of ship manoeuvring (course and/or speed alterations), chosen direction of manoeuvre (to port or starboard). The process of identifying navigator's safety profile was defined (Fig. 5).

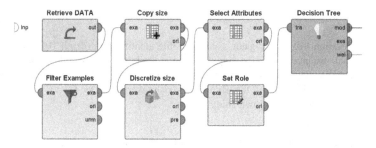

Fig. 5. The process of identifying navigator's safety profile [own study]

Based on this, the decision trees of navigator's safety profile identification were generated for various tree depths. The decision trees were generated with and without using the pruning technique. All adopted navigator's safety profiles were taken into account. Two basic groups of profiles were distinguished: hazardous (risk-taker) and safe - professional, decisive, careful, very careful).

Figure 6 presents a generated decision tree with depth 10 using the pruning technique.

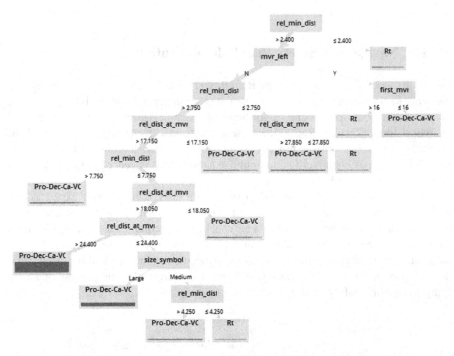

Fig. 6. The decision tree of navigator's safety profile identification (depth 10); rel_min_dist – relative minimal distance during passing the ship; mvr_left – manoeuvre to the left [Y/N]; first_mvr – first manoeuvre in degrees; rel_dist_at_mvr – relative distance at first manoeuvre; size_symbol – symbolic size of the ship; Rt – risk-taker, Pro-Dec-Ca-VC – Professional, Decisive, Careful, Very careful [own study]

The division was based on the most significant attributes: relative distance of ship passing, type of manoeuvre, relative distance at the moment of starting the manoeuvre, the manoeuvre visibility in [°] and ship size. The weights of each attribute are presented in Table 2.

Figure 7 presents a decision tree with depth 5, generated using pruning. The division made was based on the same attributes as above, except for the ship size parameter. This considerably simplified the decision tree.

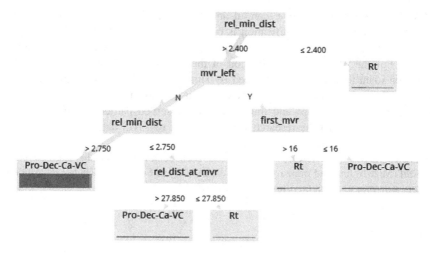

Fig. 7. The decision tree of navigator's safety profile identification (depth 5); rel_min_dist – relative minimal distance during passing the ship; mvr_left – manoeuvre to the left [Y/N]; first_mvr – first manoeuvre in degrees; rel_dist_at_mvr – relative distance at first manoeuvre; Rt – risk-taker, Pro-Dec-Ca-VC – Professional, Decisive, Careful, Very careful [own study]

The weights of each attribute are presented in Table 2.

Table 2. Weights of the attributes in the process of navigator's safety profile identification [own study]

Attribute (short name in brackets)	Tree 10 (depth) weight	Tree 5 (depth) weight
Relative minimal distance during passing the ship (rel_min_dist)	0.389	0.168
Relative distance at first manoeuvre (rel_dist_at_mvr)	0.334	0.473
First manoeuvre in degrees (first_mvr)	0.160	0.272
Symbolic size of the ship (size_symbol)	0.067	n/a
Manoeuvre to the left [Y/N] (mvr_left)	0.051	0.086

The most significant attributes in the presented decision trees were the relative distance of ship passing, relative distance at the moment of starting the manoeuvre and the manoeuvre visibility.

7 Conclusion

The possibilities of navigators' behaviour identification have been analysed based on recorded data from the AIS system. The concept of navigator's safety profile has been defined and classified. Two general profiles are distinguished: hazardous (risk-taker) and safe (professional, decisive, careful and very careful). The presented method of navigator's safety profile identification is based on the above-mentioned data supplemented by data obtained by preprocessing. Data mining tools have been used for the purpose. For the preliminary verification of the proposed method the safety profiles have been identified from data obtained by simulation tests on an ECDIS simulator. The identified navigator's safety profile allows us to indicate a ship that may pose a potential risk to other ships and thus should be observed particularly carefully. The authors plan to conduct the research with the use of real AIS data.

Acknowledgments. This research outcome has been achieved under the research project No. 1/S/ITM/2016 financed from a subsidy of the Ministry of Science and Higher Education for statutory activities of Maritime University of Szczecin.

References

1. Bukhari, A.C., et al.: An intelligent realtime multi-vessel collision risk assessment system from VTS view point based on fuzzy inference system. Expert Syst. Appl. **40**, 1220 (2013)
2. Fujii, Y., Tanaka, K.: Traffic capacity. J. Navig. **24**, 543 (1971)
3. Goerlandt, F., et al.: A risk-informed ship collision alert system: framework and application. Saf. Sci. **77**, 182 (2015)
4. Goodwin, E.M.: A statistical study of ship domain. J. Navig. **28**, 328 (1975)
5. Kearon, J.: Computer program for collision avoidance and track keeping. In: Hollingdale, S. H. (ed.) Conference on Mathematics Aspects of Marine Traffic. Academic Press (1979)
6. Kijima, K., Furukawa, Y.: Design of automatic collision avoidance system using fuzzy inference. In: IFAC Conference Computer Applications in Marine Systems, CAMS 2001. Elsevier (2002)
7. MCA, Report No.: PP092663/1-1/2 Rev. 2 EMSA/OP/10/2013 Risk Level and Acceptance Criteria for Passenger Ships. First interim report, part 2: Risk Acceptance Criteria European Maritime Safety Agency, 20
8. Pietrzykowski, Z., Uriasz, J.: The ship domain – a criterion of navigational safety assessment in an open sea area. J. Navig. **62**, 93 (2009)
9. Wang, N.: An intelligent spatial collision risk based on the quaternion ship domain. J. Navig. **63**, 733 (2010)
10. Zhao, J., et al.: A statistical study of mariners behaviour in collision avoidance at sea. In: Marine Simulation and Ship Manoeuvrability. Balkema, Rotterdam (1996)
11. Gucma, L., et al.: Integrated dynamic UKC assessment system for Polish ports. Sci. J. Maritime Univ. Szczecin **32**(104), **2**, 41–47 (2012)
12. Reason, J.: Achieving a safe culture: theory and practice. Work Stress **12**(3), 293 (1998)
13. McCare, R., Costa, P.: Personality trait structure as a human universal. Am. Psychol. **52**(5), 509 (1997)
14. U.S. Department of Transportation, Federal Aviation Administration, Flight Standards Service: Aviation instructor's handbook, United States Government Printing Office, Washington (2008). http://www.faa.gov/regulations_policies/handbooks_manuals/aviation/aviation_instructors_handbook/media/faa-h-8083-9a.pdf. Accessed 21 Jan 2019
15. Augustynowicz, A.: Modelowanie typu kierowcy samochodu. Oficyna Wydawnicza Politechniki Opolskiej, Opole (2008). (in Polish)

16. Aliefendioglu, O., Küçükay, F.: Real-time statistical-based test environment for transmission control unit of passenger cars. SAE Technical paper Series, 1999-01-1047 (1999)
17. Kücükay, F., Bergholz, J.: Driver assistant systems. In: ICAT 2004 International Conference on Automotive Technology "Future Automotive Technologies on Powertrain and Vehicle", Istanbul, Turkey (2004)
18. Abramowicz-Gerigk, T., Hejmlich, A.: Human factor modelling in the risk assessment of Port Manoeuvers. Transnav Int. J. Mar. Navig. Saf. Sea Transp. 9(3) (2015)
19. Wielgosz, M.: Profil bezpieczeństwa nawigatora morskiego i jego znaczenie dla bezpieczeństwa ruchu jednostek pływających, Prace Naukowe Politechniki Warszawskiej, Transport, Zeszyt 114. (prezentacja Konf. Transport XXI wieku, 2016, Arłamów) (2016)
20. Wielgosz, M.: Profil bezpieczeństwa nawigatora jako kryterium selekcji i doboru osób odpowiedzialnych za bezpieczne prowadzenie żeglugi, Gospodarka Materiałowa i Logistyka, nr 12/2016, str. 849–858 (2016). (in Polish)
21. Wielgosz, M.: Analiza symulowanych manewrów antykolizyjnych dla określenia spodziewanego działania nawigatora morskiego, Autobusy, nr 12/2016 (prezentacja na Konferencji Transcomp) (2016). (in Polish)
22. Han, K., et al.: Data Mining: Concepts and Techniques, 3rd edn. Morgan Kaufmann, San Francisco (2011)
23. Olson, D.L.: Data mining in business services. Serv. Bus. (2007). https://doi.org/10.1007/s11628-006-0014-7
24. Witten, I.H., Frank, E., Hall, M.A.: Data Mining: Practical Machine Learning Tools and Techniques, 3rd edn. Elsevier, San Francisco (2011)
25. Hofmann, M., Klinkenberg, R.: RapidMiner: Data Mining Use Cases and Business Analytics Applications (Chapman & Hall/CRC Data Mining and Knowledge Discovery Series). CRC Press, Boca Raton (2013)
26. https://rapidminer.com. Accessed 21 Jan 2019

Comparative Analysis of the Usefulness of AIS and ARPA for Anti-collision Purposes and Detection of Ship Manoeuvres

Ryszard Wawruch[✉]

Gdynia Maritime University, Avenue of John Paul II 3, 81-345 Gdynia, Poland
r.wawruch@wn.umg.edu.pl

Abstract. At the previous TST Conference in 2018, the paper "Use of automatic identification system as a source of information to avoid ships' collisions at sea" was presented. It discussed the results of research conducted on sea-going vessels to verify the accuracy of data transmitted by AIS ship's equipment and compare it with the accuracy of radar tracking devices. This paper expands and summarizes the information it contains and compares the results of measurements with the accuracy requirements defined in the recommendation of the International Maritime Organization and the standards of the International Electrotechnical Commission. In addition, it contains remarks on the possibility of detecting manoeuvres of ships using AIS and radar tracking devices.

Keywords: Automatic identification system · Radar tracking · Data accuracy

1 Introduction

At the previous TST Conference in 2018, the paper "Use of automatic identification system as a source of information to avoid ships' collisions at sea" was presented [1]. It discussed the results of research conducted on sea-going vessels to verify the accuracy of data transmitted by automatic identification system (AIS) ship's equipment and compare it with the accuracy of indications of on board radar tracking devices. Measurements were carried out on very large, large and medium-sized cargo ships listed in columns two, three and four in Table 1 and fitted with AIS and radar with automatic plotting aid (ARPA) described in this table too. Their results were presented comprehensively at the 19th International Radar Symposium (IRS) in 2018 and in two articles published in The International Journal on Marine Navigation and Safety of Sea Transportation "TransNav" [2–4]. This paper extends the information contained in the aforementioned publications, adding the results of measurements carried out on a small cargo vessel "Listerland" employed in international shipping on the Baltic Sea, also described in the last (fifth) column of Table 1 and shown in Fig. 1 [9].

The division of vessels into size categories was made conventionally by the author of the paper.

© Springer Nature Switzerland AG 2019
J. Mikulski (Ed.): TST 2019, CCIS 1049, pp. 346–360, 2019.
https://doi.org/10.1007/978-3-030-27547-1_25

Table 1. Ships on which tests were carried out with the indication of the size category [5–8]

Ship's name	Magdalena Odendorff	Pampero	ESL Africa	Listerland
Size category	Very large (V)	Large (L)	Medium (M)	Small (S)
Ship's type	Bulk carrier	LPG tanker	Multipurpose vessel	Bulk carrier
Gross tonnage	106884	46789	11864	2735
Length [m]	299.9 m	226.0 m	143.0 m	89.4 m
Service speed [kn/m/s]	15.6/8.0	16.7/8.6	13.2/6.8	11.0/5.7
Utilised radar and ARPA equipment/ manufacturer	JMA-9132-SA, JMA-9122-9XA/JRC	JMA-9172-SA, JMA-9122-9XA/JRC	GR3017 (X-Band), GR3018 (S-Band), ARPA Multipilot 1100/SAM Electronics GmbH	FAR-28 × 7 model FAR-21 × 7 (-BB)/Furuno
Utilised AIS/manufacturer	JHS-183/JRC	JHS-183/JRC	DEBEG 3400/SAM Electronics GmbH	R4/SAAB

Fig. 1. Cargo ship "Listerland" [9]

The results of measurements carried out on this ships have been compared with the results of earlier studies done on larger ships and accuracy requirements set out in the recommendation of the International Maritime Organization (IMO) and the standards of the International Electrotechnical Commission (IEC) presented at the previous TST Conference and recalled in brief in the Table 2. In addition, paper contains remarks on the possibility of detecting manoeuvres of ships using AIS and radar tracking devices.

In this paper, as in the previous one, distances and speeds are presented both in kilometres and m/s as well as in used in maritime navigation nautical miles and knots (1 M = 1.852 km; 1 knot = 1 M/h ≈ 0.514 m/s).

The analyses described in this paper were carried out as part of the statutory research No. 440 conducted at the Navigation Department of the Maritime University in Gdynia.

Table 2. Required tracking accuracy after three minutes of steady state tracking (95% probability figures) [10–12]

Time of steady state tracking	True course	True speed	CPA
3 min: motion	5°	0.5 knot (0.3 m/s) or 1% (whichever is greater)	0.3 M (0.56 km)

2 Description of the Measurements

All measurements were carried out on marine merchant ships by students of the Faculty of Navigation of the Gdynia Maritime University as part of their engineering thesis listed in [5–8]. During each test were recorded, simultaneously every 30 s, following parameters of the observed vessel indicated by AIS and ARPA: bearing, distance, true course, true speed, closest point of approach (CPA) and time to reach CPA (TCPA). In order to meet the conditions of steady state tracking set out in the IMO resolution and the IEC standard, observed ships were tracked by ARPAs for at least 5 min before the beginning of registration and both vessels (own and opposite) did not take any manoeuvres at this time and later during the registration.

Table 3 presents information on all ships tracked during measurements, type of recorded meeting situations and sea conditions during research. In the case of very large, large and medium-sized vessels, it is a repetition of the table placed in earlier publications, e.g. in [3].

Table 3. Ships observed during tests divided according to the meeting situation and size category of the vessel from which the tests were conducted [5–8]

No./size category	Ship's name	T	L [m]	Speed [kn/m/s]	Distance [M/km]	Sea state
Parallel courses – overtaking						
1/V	Belgian Express	C	180	13.0/6,7	1.0-0.7/1.9-1.3	4
2/V	China Peace	B	289	0/0	16.8-14.5/31.1-26.9	3
3/V	Lena River	T	290	0/0	6.7-3.4/12.4-6.3	2
4/V	Ocean Trader	CS	180	11.1/5.7	19.8-19.6/36.7-36.3	4
5/V	Regio Mar	FV	21	8.0/4.1	6.5-3.0/12.0-5.6	2
6/V	Tian Zhu Feng	B	225	10.8/5.6	16.8-16.4/31.1-30.4	7
7/L	F.D. Gennaro Aurilia	B	225	12.0/6.2	14.1-13.2/26.1-24.4	3
8/L	Hyundai Unity	C	294	13.3/6.8	9.3/17.2	3
9/L	Suez Vasilis	T	274	14.0/7.2	2.0-1.8/3.7-3.3	4
10/M	Alexandra	CS	270	17.5/9.0	2.5-2.2/4.6-4.1	2
11/M	Celtic Ambasador	CS	88	9.1/4.7	13.4-12.4/24.8-23.0	5
12/M	Christopher	CS	171	15.1/7.8	1.8-1.6/3.3-3.0	5
13/M	Coral Meandra	T	91	11.1/5.7	1.5-1.4/2.8-2.6	4

(*continued*)

Table 3. (*continued*)

No./size category	Ship's name	T	L [m]	Speed [kn/m/s]	Distance [M/km]	Sea state
14/M	Corcovado	CS	207	0.5/0.3	18.9-15.8/35.0-29.3	1
15/M	CSCL Jupiter	CS	366	18.2/9.4	3.6-2.6/6.7-4.8	3
16/M	Flinter Aland	CS	132	10.7/5.5	7.9-7.1/14.6-13.1	4
17/M	Heinrich	T	114	11.9/6.1	18.6-18.1/34.4-33.5	2
18/M	Histria Ivory	T	179	10.8/5.6	17.1-17.0/31.7-31.5	6
19/M	Navin Kestrel	CS	116	10.2/5.3	5.2-4.4/9.6-8.1	3
20/M	Pacific Heron	SP	88	4.8/2.5	9.0-7.8/16.7-14.4	1
21/M	Panther	CS	207	16.1/8.3	11.4-10.9/21.1-20.2	3
22/M	Union Ranger	CS	185	11.7/6.0	18.7-18.4/34.6-34.1	1
23/M	Varvara	CS	225	11.2/5.8	5.7-5.1/10.6-9.4	3
24/S	Britannia	P	329	17.0/8.7	2.2-4.1/4.1-7.6	1
25/S	Finnstar	P	219	22.7/11.7	6.4-0.5/11.9-0.9	4
26/S	Gilingham	CS	190	13.0/6.7	5.7-4.7/10.6-8.7	4
27/S	Hafnia Sea	CS	187	18.5/9.5	2.6-6.0/4.8-11.1	2
28/S	Kompozitor Rakhmaninov	CS	126	9.6/4.9	2.2-2.1/4.0-3.9	1
29/S	Navi Star	CS	110	11.5/5.9	1.8-1.7/3.3-3.1	1
30/S	Sea Explorer	CS	110	11.5/5.9	0.8-0.9/1.5-1.7	2
Reciprocal courses						
31/V	APL Vancuver	C	328	19.2/9.9	18.4-13.1/34.1-24.3	4
32/V	Jacamar Arrow	B	199	14.0/7.2	5.5-1.3/10.2-2.4	5
33/L	Cosco Jinggangshan	B	177	10.0/5.1	13.1-6.6/24.3-12.2	5
34/L	HSC	B	289	11.6/6.0	7.6-5.7/14.1-10.6	3
35/L	Maersk Cape Coast	C	249	15.0/7.7	6.5-2.6/12.0-4.8	1
36/L	NYK Altair	C	333	14.1/7.3	12.5/23.2	4
37/L	Port Shanghai	B	190	10.0/5.1	7.7-2.5/14.3-4.6	5
38/L	Varamo	C	166	25.3/13.0	6.9-1.2/12.8-2.2	4
39/M	Ara Antwerpen	CS	145	11.2/5.8	9.2-3.0/17.0-5.6	4
40/M	Beatriz B	CS	159	12.9/6.6	19.0-12.9/35.2-24.0	6
41/M	Bomar Resolute	CS	232	15.4/7.9	7.0-1.8/13.0-3.3	1
42/M	Eken	T	135	12/6,2	4.7-2.0/8.7-3.7	2
43/M	Gas Pasha	CS	96	9.3/4.8	14.1-8.4/26.1-15.6	3
44/M	Hoegh Shanghai	CS	229	9.2/4.7	17.1-11.3/31.7-20.9	2
45/M	Rome Trader	CS	179	14.4/7.4	19.5-12.6/36.1-23.3	2
46/M	Rome Trader	CS	179	14.4/7.4	10.1-3.4/18.7-6.3	2
47/M	Thorco Legion	CS	132	12.35/6.4	13.5-6.8/25.0-12.6	3
48/S	Baltic Advance	T	182	11.1/5.7	10.9-1.4/20.2-2.6	3
49/S	Genco Thunder	CS	225	10.2/5.2	10.3-3.5/19.1-6.5	4
50/S	Seabourn Ovation	P	211	16.9/8.7	11.0-4.9/20.4-9.1	2
51/S	Tidan	CS	88	10.5/5.4	9.8-1.8/18.1-3.3	2

(*continued*)

Table 3. (*continued*)

No./size category	Ship's name	T	L [m]	Speed [kn/m/s]	Distance [M/km]	Sea state
Crossing courses						
52/V	Bulk Switzerland	B	289	9.5/4.9	20.0-18.0/37.0-33.3	5
53/V	Free Neptune	CS	185	11.5/5.9	14.2-11.5/26.2-21.3	2
54/V	MSC Rachele	C	334	19.5/10.0	23.4-17.5/43.3-32.4	5
55/V	NCC Danah	T	183	13.5/6.9	5.6-3.3/10.4-6.1	7
56/V	OOCL Korea	C	366	15.8/8.1	5.7-1.6/10.6-3.0	7 sw
57/V	Spirit of Britain	F	213	23.5/12.1	9.1-8.3/16.9-22.4	3
58/L	Cap San Marco	C	333	20.0/10.3	4.3-2.7/8.0-5.0	4
59/L	Carnival Valor	P	292	18.2/9.4	3.4-2.9/6.3-5.4	4
60/L	Horncap	C	153	14.5/7.5	5.6-2.9/10.4-5.4	3
61/L	JS Columbia	B	199	14.4/7.4	16.7-12.8/30.9-23.7	2
62/M	Abis Calais	CS	115	9.4/4.8	16-13.7/29.6-25.4	4
63/M	Arklow Cadet	CS	87	10.6/5.4	6.7-4.3/12.4-8.0	3
64/M	Coral Lophelia	T	109	13.4/6.9	17.1-16.3/31.7-30.2	5
65/M	Ilyas Efendiyev	CS	140	8.4/4.3	9.6-4.9/17.8-9.1	2
66/M	Rio de Janeiro Express	CS	260	13.4/7.4	19.5-15.4/36.1-28.5	2
67/S	Ekfjord	T	144	11.7/6.0	8.6-2.4/15.9-4.4	3
68/S	Freya	CS	118	17.5/9.0	8.8-5.8/16.3-10.7	1
69/S	John August Essberger	T	120	12.2/6.3	10.3-5.5/19.1-10.2	1
70/S	King Gregory	T	183	11.7/6.0	8.6-3.1/15.9-5.7	3

The terms and abbreviations used in Table 3 mean:

- No./size category – measurement series number/ship size category;
- Ship size category: V – very large, L – large, M – medium-sized, S – small;
- T – type of the ship indicated by AIS: B – bulk carrier, C – container vessel, CS – cargo ship, F – ferry boat, FV – fishing vessel, P – passenger ship, SP – special purpose ship, T – tanker;
- L – the length of the vessel presented on the web-site;
- Distance – distance between the ships (own and observed) during the measurement; and
- Sea state – state of the sea expressed in degrees of the Douglas scale, sw means swell.

3   Results of the Measurements

Tables 4 and 5 present results of tests conducted on small ship only. They contain information about mean values (M) and standard deviations (σ) of true motion vectors (true courses and true speeds) and CPA of observed vessels presented by ARPA and

AIS in particular measurement series. Values of standard deviations exceeding their limits specified in Table 2 are printed in these tables in bold and underlined. The results of measurements carried out on larger vessels were presented at the TST Conference in 2018 [1].

Table 4. Results of tests conducted on small ship. True course and true speed (95% probability figures) [own study]

No./size category	ARPA				AIS			
	True course		True speed		True course		True speed	
	M	2σ	M	2σ	M	2σ	M	2σ
	[°]	[°]	[kn/m/s]	[kn/m/s]	[°]	[°]	[kn/m/s]	[kn/m/s]
Parallel courses – overtaking								
24/S	037.1	3.1	17.00/8.74	0.18/0.09	037.5	2.0	17.00/8.74	0.16/0.08
25/S	249.8	0.6	22.80/11.7	0.36/0.19	249.6	1.1	22.70/11.67	0.16/0.08
26/S	034.3	1.8	13.0/6.68	0.16/0.08	033.9	1.8	13.00/6.68	0.12/0.06
27/S	051.1	0.8	18.5/9.51	0.34/0.17	051.1	1.0	18.40/9.46	0.34/0.17
28/S	231.5	0.3	9.71/4.99	**1.2/0.62**	231.6	0.9	9.60/4.93	0.14/0.07
29/S	034.8	1.8	11.50/5.91	**1.5/0.78**	034.8	2.0	11.50/5.91	0.18/0.09
30/S	061.0	2.4	11.60/5.96	0.40/0.21	060.9	1.8	12.00/6.17	0.18/0.09
Reciprocal courses								
48/S	058.7	1.6	11.30/5.81	**1.14/0.59**	058.3	0.9	11.11/5.71	**0.80/0.41**
49/S	070.9	0.7	10.30/5.29	0.28/0.14	070.2	0.4	10.20/5.24	0.1/0.05
50/S	037.5	1.2	17.05/8.76	**0.56/0.29**	037.3	0.7	16.90/8.69	0.24/0.12
51/S	268.1	0.8	10.58/5.44	0.28/0.14	268.8	0.6	10.45/5.37	0.10/0.05
Crossing courses								
67/S	237.7	1.0	11.86/6.10	0.22/0.11	238.5	1.1	11.62/5.97	0.08/0.04
68/S	017.3	2.4	17.60/9.05	**0.60/0.31**	017.7	0.1	17.50/9.00	0.16/0.08
69/S	015.8	3.2	12.20/6.27	0.44/0.23	016.6	0.9	12.17/6.27	0.18/0.09
71/S	254.2	2.4	11.90/6.12	**1.58/0.81**	255.2	0.8	11.70/6.01	0.28/0.14

Table 5. Results of tests conducted on small ship. CPA (95% probability figures) [own study]

No./size category	CPA (ARPA)		CPA (AIS)	
	Mean value	2σ	Mean value	2σ
	[M/km]	[M/km]	[M/km]	[M/km]
Parallel courses - overtaking				
24/S	1.94/3.59	**0.36/0.67**	1.90/3.52	0.22/0.41
25/S	0.46/0.85	0.11/0.20	0.45/0.83	0.14/0.30
26/S	1.11/2.06	**0.64/1.19**	0.63/1.17	**0.92/1.70**
27/S	0.53/0.98	0.02/0.04	0.80/1.48	0,16/0.30

(continued)

Table 5. (*continued*)

No./size category	CPA (ARPA)		CPA (AIS)	
	Mean value	2σ	Mean value	2σ
	[M/km]	[M/km]	[M/km]	[M/km]
28/S	1.08/2.00	**1.89/3.50**	1.36/2.52	**0.96/1.78**
29/S	0.85/1.57	**1.43/2.65**	0.92/1.70	**1.24/2.30**
30/S	0.77/1.43	0.02/0.04	0.80/1.48	0.14/0.26
Reciprocal courses				
48/S	1.37/2.54	0.19/0.36	1.2/2.22	0.06/0.11
49/S	3.50/6.48	0.04/0.07	3.50/6.48	0.08/0.15
50/S	5.02/9.30	0.08/0.15	5.01/9.28	0.24/0.44
51/S	1.81/3.35	**0.94/1.74**	1.69/3.13	0.01/0.02
Crossing courses				
67/S	2.39/4.43	0.04/0.07	2.37/4.39	0.10/0.19
68/S	5.38/9.96	**0.32/0.59**	5.67/10.50	0.18/0.33
69/S	5.50/10.19	0.12/0.22	5.41/10.02	0.10/0.18
70/S	3.20/5.93	0.04/0.07	3.13/5.80	0.16/0.30

4   Discussion of Tests Results

Table 6 combines data from Tables 4 and 5 and from tables with errors of indications presented during the previous conference. It shows if the values of the courses, speeds and CPA presented by ARPA and AIS meet the accuracy requirements. The information is presented separately for each meeting situation and each size category of the vessel on which the measurements were conducted. The results of measurements carried out on ships larger than small were taken into account and are presented in the table to indicate a possible dependence of the accuracy of data of the opposite ship received with ARPA and AIS on the size of the vessel keeping the observation.

Table 6. Compliance with accuracy requirements for a probability equal to 95% [own study]

No./size category	Compliance with accuracy requirements						Sea state
	True course		True speed		CPA		
	ARPA	AIS	ARPA	AIS	ARPA	AIS	
Parallel courses – overtaking							
1/V	Yes	Yes	Yes	Yes	Yes	Yes	4
2/V	No	No	No	Yes	No	No	3
3/V	No	Yes	Yes	Yes	Yes	Yes	2
4/V	No	No	No	Yes	No	No	4
5/V	Yes	Yes	Yes	Yes	Yes	Yes	2
6/V	No	No	No	Yes	No	No	7

(*continued*)

Table 6. (*continued*)

No./size category	Compliance with accuracy requirements						Sea state
	True course		True speed		CPA		
	ARPA	AIS	ARPA	AIS	ARPA	AIS	
7/L	**No**	Yes	**No**	Yes	**No**	No	3
8/L	Yes	Yes	**No**	Yes	Yes	Yes	3
9/L	Yes	Yes	Yes	Yes	Yes	Yes	4
10/M	Yes	Yes	Yes	Yes	Yes	Yes	2
11/M	**No**	Yes	Yes	Yes	**No**	No	5
12/M	Yes	Yes	Yes	Yes	Yes	No	5
13/M	Yes	Yes	Yes	Yes	Yes	Yes	4
14/M	**No**	No	Yes	Yes	**No**	No	1
15/M	Yes	Yes	**No**	Yes	**No**	No	3
16/M	Yes	Yes	Yes	Yes	**No**	No	4
17/M	Yes	Yes	**No**	Yes	**No**	No	2
18/M	Yes	Yes	**No**	Yes	**No**	No	6
19/M	Yes	Yes	Yes	Yes	**No**	Yes	3
20/M	Yes	Yes	Yes	Yes	Yes	Yes	1
21/M	Yes	Yes	Yes	Yes	**No**	No	3
22/M	Yes	Yes	**No**	Yes	**No**	No	1
23/M	Yes	Yes	**No**	Yes	**No**	No	3
24/S	Yes	Yes	Yes	Yes	**No**	Yes	1
25/S	Yes	Yes	Yes	Yes	Yes	Yes	4
26/S	Yes	Yes	Yes	Yes	**No**	No	4
27/S	Yes	Yes	Yes	Yes	Yes	Yes	2
28/S	Yes	Yes	**No**	Yes	**No**	No	1
29/S	Yes	Yes	**No**	Yes	**No**	No	1
30/S	Yes	Yes	Yes	Yes	Yes	Yes	2
Reciprocal courses							
31/V	**No**	Yes	**No**	Yes	**No**	Yes	4
32/V	Yes	Yes	Yes	Yes	Yes	Yes	5
33/L	**No**	Yes	Yes	Yes	**No**	Yes	5
34/L	Yes	Yes	Yes	Yes	Yes	Yes	3
35/L	Yes	Yes	Yes	Yes	Yes	Yes	1
36/L	Yes	Yes	**No**	Yes	**No**	No	4
37/L	Yes	Yes	Yes	Yes	Yes	Yes	5
38/L	Yes	Yes	Yes	Yes	Yes	Yes	4
39/M	Yes	Yes	**No**	Yes	Yes	Yes	4
40/M	Yes	Yes	**No**	Yes	**No**	Yes	6
41/M	**No**	Yes	**No**	Yes	**No**	Yes	1
42/M	Yes	Yes	**No**	Yes	Yes	Yes	2
43/M	Yes	Yes	**No**	Yes	Yes	Yes	3

(*continued*)

Table 6. (*continued*)

No./size category	Compliance with accuracy requirements						Sea state
	True course		True speed		CPA		
	ARPA	AIS	ARPA	AIS	ARPA	AIS	
44/M	No	Yes	Yes	Yes	No	Yes	2
45/M	Yes	Yes	Yes	Yes	No	No	2
46/M	Yes	Yes	Yes	Yes	No	Yes	2
47/M	No	Yes	Yes	Yes	No	Yes	3
48/S	Yes	Yes	No	No	Yes	Yes	3
49/S	Yes	Yes	Yes	Yes	Yes	Yes	4
50/S	Yes	Yes	No	Yes	Yes	Yes	2
51/S	Yes	Yes	Yes	Yes	No	Yes	2
Crossing courses							
52/V	No	No	No	Yes	No	No	5
53/V	No	Yes	No	Yes	No	Yes	2
54/V	No	Yes	No	Yes	No	Yes	5
55/V	Yes	No	Yes	Yes	Yes	Yes	7
56/V	Yes	Yes	No	Yes	Yes	Yes	7 sw
57/V	No	No	No	Yes	Yes	Yes	3
58/L	Yes	Yes	Yes	Yes	Yes	Yes	4
59/L	Yes	Yes	No	Yes	Yes	Yes	4
60/L	Yes	Yes	Yes	Yes	Yes	Yes	3
61/L	Yes	Yes	No	Yes	No	No	2
62/M	Yes	Yes	No	Yes	No	No	4
63/M	Yes	Yes	Yes	Yes	Yes	Yes	3
64/M	No	Yes	No	Yes	No	No	5
65/M	No	Yes	No	Yes	No	Yes	2
66/M	Yes	Yes	No	Yes	No	No	2
67/S	Yes	Yes	Yes	Yes	Yes	Yes	3
68/S	Yes	Yes	No	Yes	No	Yes	1
69/S	Yes	Yes	Yes	Yes	Yes	Yes	1
70/S	Yes	Yes	No	Yes	Yes	Yes	3

Table 7 summarizes the information given in Table 6 and shows the number of particular types of investigated meeting situations of two ships where standard deviation (for 95% probability) of the presented data was greater than its allowable value specified in the international standards.

It should be emphasized that in all tests, except one, on board AIS presented instantaneous value of the opposite ship's true speed with the dispersion smaller than maximum allowable value for error of the true speed indication by radar tracking devices. In 7 tests AIS presented instantaneous value of the opposite ship's true course with the dispersion greater than its maximum allowable value. The reason could be too much yawing angle of the observed ship. For all these 7 tests ARPA had problems with the true course calculation too. In two situations, too large variation of the actual value of true course indication did not affect the accuracy of the CPA presentation by AIS. In 19 meeting situations, AIS had a problem with presenting with the required accuracy the CPA value only. It means that in these cases the reason for too high error of the CPA indication by AIS was not too much instability of the movement of the opposite vessel.

Table 7. The number of meeting situations where standard deviation of data presented by AIS and ARPA (CPA, true course and/or true speed) were greater than their allowable values (for 95% probability figures) [own study]

Data	Number of meeting situations with data errors greater than allowed							
	ARPA				AIS			
	1	2	3	All	1	2	3	All
TC	1	0	0	1	0	0	2	2
TSp	1	5	3	9	0	1	0	1
TC and TSp	0	0	1	1	0	0	0	0
CPA	5	3	0	8	13	2	4	19
CPA and TC	2	3	0	5	4	0	1	5
CPA and TSp	7	2	3	12	0	0	0	0
All data	4	2	6	12	0	o	0	0
Σ/Σ_T	20/30	15/21	13/19	48/70	17/30	3/21	7/19	27/70

Abbreviations used in Table 5 mean:

- 1 - parallel courses – overtaking;
- 2 - reciprocal courses;
- 3 - crossing courses;
- All - all meeting situations;
- TC - true course;
- TSp - true speed; and
- Σ/Σ_T - number of meeting situations of a given type with data errors greater than allowed/total number of all meeting situations of this type.

Collective information on the state of the sea during particular measurement series is presented in Table 8. Too few measurements in storm conditions make it impossible to draw conclusions about the relationship between the accuracy of ARPA and AIS indications and the state of the sea.

Table 8. State of the sea expressed in degrees of the Douglas scale during the particular measurement series [own study]

State of the sea (Douglas scale)	1	2	3	4	5	6	7
Number of measurement series	10	16	16	15	8	2	3

Table 9 shows correlation between the errors of ARPA calculations and standard deviation of the true course, true speed and/or CPA indications by AIS.

Table 9. Correlation between the errors of ARPA calculations and standard deviations of the true course and/or true speed and/or CPA indications by AIS (abbreviations as in Table 7) [own study]

Data presented by ARPA with standard deviation bigger than acceptable	The number of tests during which AIS showed true course, true speed and/or CPA with too large standard deviation and, at the same time, ARPA calculated individual data with too large errors					The total number of tests with ARPA indication errors greater than the allowable
	TC	TSp	CPA	TC + CPA	Total	
TC	0	0	0	0	0	1
TSp	0	1	0	0	1	9
TC and TSp	1	0	0	0	1	1
CPA	0	0	4	0	4	8
CP and TC	0	0	1	1	2	5
CPA and TSp	0	0	10	1	11	12
All data	0	0	3	4	7	12
ARPA data without unacceptable errors	1	0	1	0	2	Not applicable
Total	2	1	19	6	28	48

5   Detection of Ship's Manoeuvres

During the measurements carried out at sea, 32 meeting situations were recorded, in which the observed vessel performed a manoeuvre altering its course and/or speed. Data presented by ARPA and AIS were recorded at 30-s intervals. Such a low discretization of recorded indications makes it impossible to accurately determine the time delay of visual detection by radar observer of the opposite vessel's manoeuvre by comparison of the instantaneous values of its true course and true speed shown by radar equipment and AIS. It can only be said that the maximum time delay was between one – one and a half and three minutes.

Examples of the time delay of ARPA's indication of the tracked ship's manoeuvres for observers on ships of various sizes are shown in Figs. 2, 3, 4 and 5.

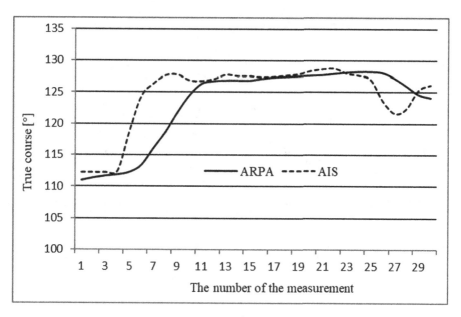

Fig. 2. An example of the time delay of ARPA's indication on a very large bulk carrier "Magdalena Oldendorff" of the course alterations made by 347 m long container vessel "Caroline Maersk" sailing at the distances of 3.95–2.98 M (7.32–5.52 km) at a mean speed of 18.9 knts (9.7 m/s), state of the sea 5 [8]

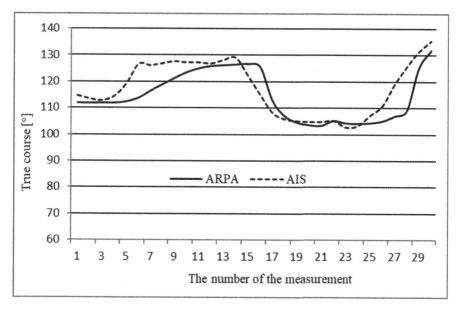

Fig. 3. An example of the time delay of ARPA's indication on a large LPG tanker "Pampero" of the course alterations made by 333 m long tanker "New Harmony" sailing at the distances of 4.04–3.13 M (7.48–5.80 km) at a mean speed of 14.7 knts (7.6 m/s), state of the sea 6 [7]

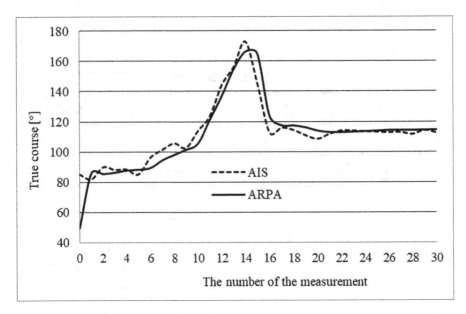

Fig. 4. An example of the time delay of ARPA's indication on a medium-sized multipurpose vessel "ESL Africa" of the course and speed alterations made by 43 m long war ship "HDMS Diana" sailing at the distances of 6.59–3.23 M (12.21–5.98 km) at a speed of 24.1–12.6 knts (12.4–6.5 m/s), state of the sea 3 [5]

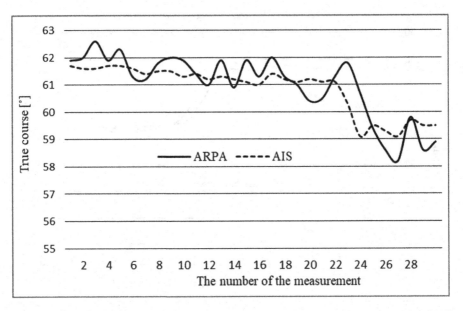

Fig. 5. An example of the time delay of ARPA's indication on a small bulk carrier "Listerland" of the course alteration made by 110 m long cargo ship "Sea Explorer" sailing at the distances of 0.90–0.78 M (1.67–1.44 km) at a mean speed of 11.6 knts (6.0 m/s), state of the sea 2 [6]

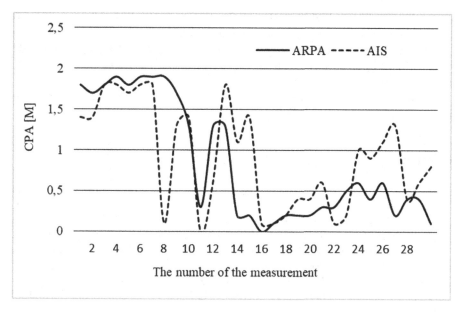

Fig. 6. Changes in the ship's CPA value as a function of measurement time in the meeting situation No. 29 [6]

6 Conclusion

Measurements described in this paper were carried out on four different merchant ships using popular, often used on the vessels AIS and radar on board equipment but produced by three manufacturers only. Due to that and due to the limited number of conducted tests (70 series of measurements), it is still impossible to formulate on their basis general conclusions about the stability and accuracy of the AIS and ARPA indications and their dependence on hydro meteorological conditions.

Nevertheless, it should be emphasized that the measurements carried out on a relatively small ship (bulk carrier "Listerland") confirmed the conclusions presented on the previous TST Conference and formulated on the basis of tests carried out on very large, large and medium-sized cargo ships passing other vessels at greater distances. Particular attention should be paid to the accuracy of CPA indications by ARPA and AIS in the case when ships are sailing in a short distance between them.

For example, such a case took place in the meeting situation No. 29. Own ship - bulk carrier "Listerland" sailing the course of 035° at the speed of 11.8 knots (6.1 m/s) was overtaking slowly a cargo ship "Navi Star" proceeding the course 033° at a speed of 11.3 knots (5.8 m/s). The distance between ships during the measurements decreased from 1.92 M to 1.79 M (from 3.56 km to 3.32 km) according to ARPA data and from 1.83 M to 1.71 M (from 3.39 km to 3.17 km) according to AIS data. Although both vessels kept all the time steady courses and speeds, the CPA value indicated by ARPA and AIS fluctuated between 0.0 M and 1.9 M (0.0 km–3.52 km) (ARPA) and between 0.1 M and 1.8 M (0.16 km–3.33 km) (AIS). This example proves the correctness of the conclusion formulated on the basis of previous measurements saying that systematic observation of the relative or true motion vector of the other vessel and the digital value of its CPA indicated by both ARPA and AIS should be carried out. In practice, you cannot rely on a one-off reading of the current CPA value shown by both ARPA and AIS.

Changes in the ship's CPA value as a function of measurement time in the meeting situation No. 29 are presented in Fig. 6.

References

1. Wawruch, R.: Use of Automatic Identification System as a Source of Information to Avoid Ships' Collisions at Sea. In: Mikulski, J. (ed.) TST 2018. CCIS, vol. 897, pp. 411–425. Springer, Cham (2018). https://doi.org/10.1007/978-3-319-97955-7_28
2. Wawruch, R.: Tests of the accuracy of indications by ARPA and AIS of the opposite vessel true course, true speed and CPA. In: The 19th International Radar Symposium "IRS 2018", Bonn, 22 June 2018, Proceedings, DGON, Bonn (CD) (2018)
3. Wawruch, R.: Comparative study of the accuracy of AIS and ARPA indications. Part 1: accuracy of the CPA indications. Int. J. Mar. Navig. Saf. Sea Transp. TransNav 12(3), 439–443 (2018)
4. Wawruch, R.: Comparative study of the accuracy of AIS and ARPA indications. Part 2: accuracy of the opposite vessel true course and true speed indication. Int. J. Mar. Navig. Saf. Sea Transp. TransNav 12(4), 1–4 (2018)
5. Kalamon, M.: AIS jako dodatkowy środek obserwacji i oceny ryzyka zderzenia, engineering thesis. Gdynia Maritime University, Gdynia (2017)
6. Piekarska, M.K.: Badania eksperymentalne dokładności i stabilności wskazań wektorów ruchu statku przeciwnego przez AIS i urządzenie radarowe, engineering thesis. Gdynia Maritime University, Gdynia (2019)
7. Wesołowski, J.: Analiza porównawcza dokładności danych o parametrach ruchu względnego i rzeczywistego statku obcego prezentowanych przez ARPA i AIS, engineering thesis. Gdynia Maritime University, Gdynia (2016)
8. Wilczyński, M.: Analiza porównawcza dokładności śledzenia systemów AIS i ARPA. Engineering Thesis. Gdynia Maritime University, Gdynia (2015)
9. http://www.shipspotting.com/gallery/photo. Accessed 20 Jan 2019
10. Resolution MSC.192(79) Adoption of the revised performance standards for radar equipment, IMO, London (2004)
11. IEC Standard 61993-2 ED 3 Maritime navigation and radiocommunication equipment and systems – Automatic identification systems (AIS) – Part 2: Class A ship borne equipment of the automatic identification system (AIS) – Operational and performance requirements, methods of test and required test results, IEC, Geneva (2017)
12. IEC 62388 Maritime navigation and radio communication equipment and systems – Shipborne radar – Performance requirements, methods of testing and required test results. IEC, Geneva (2012)

Telematics in Air Transport

A Method of Evaluating Air Traffic Controller Time Workload

Piotr Andrzej Dmochowski[1,2] and Jacek Skorupski[2(✉)]

[1] Polish Air Navigation Services Agency, Wieżowa 8, Warsaw, Poland
piotr.dmochowski@pw.edu.pl
[2] Warsaw University of Technology, Koszykowa 75, Warsaw, Poland
jacek.skorupski@pw.edu.pl

Abstract. Aircraft enroute flights are supervised by area air traffic controllers supported by telematics systems, ensuring communication and visualization. Based on them, controllers make decisions regarding the aircraft movement. The air traffic controller workload is the basic factor determining the safety of flight operations. The aim of this research was to develop a simulation method for assessing the controller time workload. The method presented in the paper uses a mathematical model that simultaneously considers the air traffic and the work of the controller. The model created as a colored timed Petri net, allows for estimating the controller time workload for various parameters of the traffic flow, infrastructure and support systems. As part of simulation experiments, the quantitative dependence of time workload on the traffic volume was demonstrated. It has been shown that, for the modeled sector, maintaining the traffic in accordance with a predetermined flight plans reduces the controller's workload, and granting clearances for direct flights, although beneficial for flight economics, increases workload and, therefore, may affect traffic safety.

Keywords: Air traffic management · Air traffic controller workload · Colored Petri nets · Air traffic safety

1 Introduction

The Air Traffic Control (ATC) sector, in which aircraft enroute flight operations are primarily carried out, is the area of interest in this paper. It is a complicated sociotechnical system in which humans are aided by telematics systems. The main area of support is the acquisition, processing, visualization and distribution of information to be able to use them in decision making processes.

The capacity of the control sector depends on its size, air routes layout and the technical equipment. These factors, together with the characteristics of the traffic stream, determine the air traffic controller (ATCo) workload. It has a direct impact on the safety of traffic. Therefore, it is extremely important to assess the workload of the controller for any traffic conditions.

The ATCo workload can be examined directly by observing his/her work and measuring time necessary to complete all actions. On this basis, we can specify the percentage of time spent on handling aircraft during the hour. This analysis was used in

© Springer Nature Switzerland AG 2019
J. Mikulski (Ed.): TST 2019, CCIS 1049, pp. 363–376, 2019.
https://doi.org/10.1007/978-3-030-27547-1_26

[4, 5]. However, this method can be used to investigate the ATCo workload only for the existing traffic organization, air routes layout etc. It cannot be used for planned organization, other traffic conditions or equipment. Additionally, it is not possible to conduct experiments on the current traffic for safety reasons.

The above-mentioned circumstances make it necessary to develop a method for analyzing the ATCo workload based on the use of models. In the current research, a discreet mesoscale model based on colored, timed, hierarchical Petri nets was developed.

1.1 Literature Review

The problem of controller work analysis is present in the literature. The most common are papers related to the controller workload and its relation to the sector capacity, safety and impact of the supporting devices and systems on the capacity. A lot of attention is also devoted to the methodology of air traffic modeling.

The psychological aspects of the ATCo work were discussed by Nealley and Gawron [13], Langan-Fox et al. [10], Inoue et al. [8] or Bekier et al. [1]. In turn Zhang et al. [21] and Tobaruela [19] studied the sector capacity. Relationships between the controller's workload and the sector capacity and safety were analyzed in [17], and between the ATC and FMP services, relevant to this article, were investigated by Lehouillier et al. [11]. The problem of the impact of supporting systems on work of the ATCo was undertaken by Szamel and Szabo [18], Westin et al. [20] and Ferduła and Skorupski [7]. An extensive overview of the challenges for air traffic safety related to air traffic management issues can be found in [2]. Direct measurements of the controller workload were used in the work of Rohacs et al. [15] and Dmochowski and Skorupski [5], while modeling of air traffic in the sector in terms of assessing the ATCo workload was studied by Saez Nieto et al. [16], Zohrevandi et al. [22] and Corver et al. [3].

1.2 The Concept of Work

ATCo adjusts the aircraft flow in the sector to prevailing conditions by providing pilots with instructions describing necessary changes of the direction, level or cruise speed. The decision is made after verifying flight parameters and the planned route. On this basis, the ATCo foresees future traffic situation, examines its safety and then coordinates the decision with other controllers.

It is possible to identify repetitive elementary activities in the basic types of actions mentioned above. Some of them can be performed in parallel, but there are situations when they block each other. The controller then works in a shortage of time to carry out certain activities. Hence, time as a limited resource is of interest in this article.

The developed method is based on discrete simulation, using a model describing both the dynamics of aircraft and the work of the controller. In relation to previous work, we have extended research by using a discrete mesoscale model tracing all situations when the critical resource – controller's time is blocked. As a result, it is possible to indicate not only the traffic flow parameters and the ATC sector parameters affecting the ATCo workload, but also the critical sequences of events causing a potential threat to the safety of air traffic.

The model is continuous in time and discrete in state and has been implemented in CPN Tools 4.0 environment as the hierarchical, colored, timed Petri net. It allows conducting simulation experiments towards looking for a dependency between the ATCo workload and the complexity of traffic and sector parameters.

2   Analysis of Air Traffic Controller Work

2.1   Controller Work Technology

The control team responsible for the ATC sector consists of two persons: the executive (or radar) controller (EC) and planning (or assistant) controller (PC). The former conducts direct radio correspondence with aircraft. Providing separations EC follows the general plan prepared by the latter. As part of our research, we first proposed a method for assessing the time workload of a radar controller. In his/her work we can distinguish several basic types of tasks.

1. Entrance of an aircraft into the sector. In this task the aircraft is identified, and the crew establishes communication with the ATCo.
2. Flight monitoring. During the flight through the sector, the ATCo periodically checks the flight parameters of the aircraft paying attention to the location, speed, direction and flight level. ATCo assesses the situation in the sector and takes appropriate actions.
3. Change of flight parameters. Following the decision-making process described above or at the request of the pilot, the ATCo may grant permission to change flight parameters. These activities must be coordinated with neighboring sectors.
4. Leaving the ATC sector. Upon reaching the sector border, radio correspondence takes place, as a result of which the pilot switches to communication with the controller of the next sector, which is equivalent to the transfer of control over it.
5. Change of flight speed. Such a task is carried out when, due to the need to maintain safe separation, the aircraft must have arrived at the navigation point within a strictly defined time.
6. Changing of the transponder code, used to identify the aircraft. It can occur when two aircraft in the sector have the same code.

2.2   ATCo Support Systems

The main tool supporting controllers work is the air traffic management system (ATMS). A typical ATMS usually consists of the following modules [12].

1. Surveillance data processing module. It is also called the tracker. Its task is to obtain aircraft position data.
2. Flight plan processing module. Its tasks consist of reception of messages from Aeronautical Fixed Telecommunication Network (AFTN) and On-Line Data Interchange (OLDI) system, calculating trajectory, determining the sectors sequence and looking for possible collisions with forbidden airspace.

3. Data visualization module. It presents data about of the position of aircraft and the state of the airspace.
4. Surveillance data and flight plans correlation module. Its task is to provide the information from the flight plan relating to the aircraft identified by the tracker.
5. Alarm modules. Their task is to assist the controller in monitoring the traffic situation by generating safety alarms and warnings.
6. Auxiliary modules. They consist of applications that do not require direct access to radar data visualization.
7. Air traffic simulator module used for training.

2.3 Communications Systems Used in Air Traffic Control

A lot of information is exchanged between the aircraft crew and the ATCo to provide safe flight. Especially important is the traditional radio communication, during which messages are forwarded concerning the subsequent clearances (permitted pilot actions).

An important element of telematic support for ATCos are systems of bidirectional digital communication with aircraft, aircraft position self-reporting systems, systems of controller-pilot digital communication. They are an important complement to the ongoing mostly analog communication methods.

3 Model of the Air Traffic Control Process

3.1 Area Control Sector Traffic Model

The object of the analysis is the area control sector where enroute flight are carried out. Typically, elementary sectors are determined based on an important air route or intersection of air routes. In our model we have taken the second approach into consideration, as this is how the sectors are defined in Polish airspace.

The following assumptions were defined during the model development. Relevant rules governing traffic in the sector and the ATCo work were included. Among the most important are:

1. The sector is of convex shape, the projection of which is shown in Fig. 1. In the vertical plane, the sector includes flight levels from FL 100 to FL 400.
2. There are three entry points called the input and output gates of the sector. They are marked with the letters A, B and C.
3. Within the sector, there is a point (marked by D), which is the intersection of three air routes AD, BD and CD. These are two-way routes with disjoint flight levels intended for eastbound and westbound flights.
4. A typical flight is planned on one of the following routes: ADC, ADB, BDA, BDC, CDA or CDB. Alternatively, at the request of the aircraft crew, the ATCo may clear the aircraft to use the direct route (so called shortcut) – AB, AC, BC, BA, CA or CB. The ATCo may also issue such a clearance on his own to improve flight economics.
5. The crew may request permission to use different cruising altitude. Again, the ATCo may also issue such a clearance on his own.

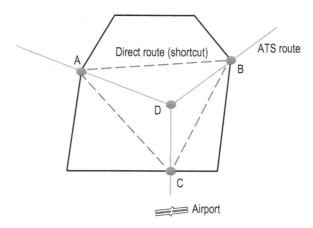

Fig. 1. Top projection of the modeled area control sector [own study]

6. There is an airport near the point C, but already outside the sector. Aircraft whose initial or final point of the route is C are treated as landing or taking off at that airport. Therefore, all aircraft flying on the routes ending at point C are descending from the cruising level (FL 370 or FL 380) to the agreed FL 100. Similarly, aircraft flying on the routes beginning in point C are climbing from the FL 110 to the cruising level (FL 390 or FL 400). Other flights take place at a fixed altitude (FL 350 or FL 360).

7. Based on the flight plan, for each aircraft the position in three-dimensional space and the direction of flight and horizontal and vertical speeds are determined. The position is updated independently of other traffic events with a constant step $dt = 1$ s.

3.2   Model of Air Traffic Controller Work

In Sect. 2.1 the typical everyday ATCo tasks were described. In our model we considered the most common tasks, which include about 98% of activities carried out [5]. Traffic events included in the model that correspond to the typical ATCo tasks are shown in Table 1.

Table 1. Traffic events in the model [own study]

The type of event in the model	Description of the event
AC Entry	The aircraft enters the sector according to the flight plan
AC Hdg rqst	The pilot requests a change of the course
AC FL rqst	The pilot requests a change of the flight level
ATC Exit	The aircraft leaves the sector
ATC Hdg rqst	The ATCo initiates a course change
ATC FL rqst	The ATCo initiates the change of the flight level
ATC Observes	The controller analyzes the situation in the sector

Events *AC Entry* and *AC Exit* apply to any aircraft flying through the sector under consideration and the associated ATCo activities shall be carried out once, respectively, in the input and output gates of the sector. Event *ATC Observes* takes place when there are no other events requiring attention and the ATCo performs routine analysis of the traffic situation in the sector. This occurs regardless of the traffic volume, averaging approximately every 25 s. The remaining events occur randomly, and their frequency was determined based on measurements made in FIR Warszawa in 2015.

3.3   Elementary Activities in Tasks

The aim of our research was to determine an hourly ATCo workload. For this, it is necessary to specify the frequency of traffic events and the time required to perform adequate actions. Unlike other methods, we used a mesoscale model to consider the duration of elementary activities that make up traffic management tasks. The identified elementary activities are for instance: controller-pilot and pilot-controller radio correspondence, coordination of decisions with other sectors, measurement of distances using a radar indicator. The duration of each elementary activity is a random variable, and the total time necessary for handling the traffic is the sum of these random variables.

In the remaining part of this section we present traffic events with simplified description of the elementary activities and the corresponding times needed to execute them (Table 2). These times were adopted based on two sources: (i) of our own observations of ATCo work at the operational position in FIR Warsaw and (ii) according to the CAPAN method used to estimate the capacity of the area air traffic control sectors [6]. These times are random variables, but only mean values are presented for the shortness of the description.

Table 2. Average duration of activities in traffic events [own study]

Event	t_1 [s]	t_2 [s]	t_3 [s]	t_4 [s]	t_5 [s]
AC Entry	4	10	3	4	2
AC Hdg rqst	4	10	3	4	2
AC FL rqst	3	10	3	3	2
AC Exit	5	4	-	-	-
ATC Hdg rqst	10	3	5	5	-
ATC FL rqst	10	3	4	4	-
ATC Observes	3	-	-	-	-

Event *AC Entry*
The *AC Entry* event takes place when sector border is crossed. The incoming aircraft crew must contact the ATCo. This is possible if the communication channel is available. Handling of this event consists of the following elementary activities.

1. The pilot reports at the input gate (A, B or C) and the pilot-controller transmission takes place; it lasts t_1 seconds.
2. The ATCo analyses the situation in the sector. During this time, the communication channel is available, and another transmission may occur.

(a) In some cases, it is necessary to coordinate decision with other controllers; the activity lasts t_2 seconds.
(b) In other cases, only the analysis of the traffic situation takes place; the activity takes t_3 seconds.
3. The controller-pilot transmission occurs, within which the clearance to continue the flight is issued; the duration of the action is t_4 seconds.
4. The pilot repeats the message (readback), which is required for safety reasons, to verify whether it has been properly understood; it takes t_5 seconds.

Event *AC Hdg rqst*

The *AC Hdg rqst* event refers to the pilot's request to fly to the output gate of the sector directly, without having to fly over point D. This event usually takes place at a short distance from the input gate. The procedure of handling this event consists of the same elementary activities as in the *AC Entry* event. The average time for the execution of these elementary activities are shown in Table 2.

Event *AC FL rqst*

When the aircraft operates at the flight level, which is economically unfavorable, or when there are turbulences which are uncomfortable for passengers, the aircraft crew may ask to change their flight level. The *AC FL rqst* event handling consists of the same elementary activities as in the *AC Entry* event. However, the average times of executing elementary activities are different and are shown in Table 2.

Event *AC Exit*

The *AC Exit* event consists in short voice transmission, and it occurs during sector border crossing at the output gate. The event handling consists of the following elementary activities.

1. The ATCo passes a short message to the pilot; that lasts t_1 seconds.
2. The pilot repeats the message (readback); this takes t_2 seconds.

Event *ATC Hdg rqst*

Due to the need of flight economics improvement, the ATCo sometimes on its own suggests that the aircraft crew may use the shortcut and take a direct route to the output gate from the sector. In this case, an *ATC Hdg rqst* event occurs, which consists of the following elementary activities.

1. The ATCo analyses the situation in the sector. During this, the communication channel is available, and another transmission may occur.
(a) In some cases, it is necessary to coordinate decision with other controllers; the activity lasts t_1 seconds.
(b) In other cases, only the analysis of the traffic situation takes place; the activity takes t_2 seconds.
2. The controller-pilot transmission occurs, within which the clearance to go directly to the output gate is issued; the duration of the action is t_3 seconds.
3. The pilot repeats the message (readback); it takes t_4 seconds.

Event *ATC FL rqst*

Similarly, as in the *ATC Hdg rqst* event, the ATCo can on its own initiate the change of the cruising level of the aircraft. Handling of this events consist of the same elementary activities as in the event *ATC Hdg rqst*. However, the average times of elementary activities are different and are shown in Table 2.

Event *ATC Observes*

The *ATC Observes* event consists in analyzing the traffic situation in the sector. It also takes place in all other traffic events, but sometimes the ATCo wants to additionally ensure that all aircraft are separated sufficiently from other aircraft and prohibited airspaces. This event consists of one operation, which takes an average of t_1 seconds.

3.4   Validation of Input Data

In July 2015, various activities completed by the controller were measured. Measurements were carried out directly at the operational position and their more detailed analysis was presented in [5]. These measurements were used to verify durations of elementary activities adopted in the model. The results are presented in Table 3.

Table 3. Elementary activities of the EC controller [own study]

Elementary activities	Numbers of occurrences	Total time [s]	Average [s]
Aircraft identification	31	290	9.4
Transfer of control	31	301	9.7
Heading change (direct)	14	110	7.9
Coordination heading change	5	53	10.6
Flight level change	10	78	7.8
Coordination with PC	22	209	9.5
Different measurements	149	470	3,2

The input data to the model show good compliance with the measurement data for FIR Warsaw. For example, we compared the measurement data for the event *AC Entry* with the corresponding row of Table 2. The results are presented in Table 4.

Table 4. Data validation results for *AC Entry* event [own study]

Elementary activities	Measurement data [s]	Data in the model					
		t_1 [s]	t_2 [s]	t_3 [s]	t_4 [s]	t_5 [s]	Total [s]
Aircraft identification	9.4	4	-	-	4	2	10
Coordination with PC	9.5	-	10	-	-	-	10
Different measurements	3.2	-	-	3	-	-	3

3.5   Petri Nets

The model of air traffic in the area sector correlating with the model of ATCo work was implemented as hierarchical, colored, timed Petri net with priorities.

The general form of this net is as follows:

$$S_{ATC} = \{P, T, A, M_0, \tau, X, \Gamma, C, G, E, R, r_0, B\} \tag{1}$$

where:

P – set of places,
T – set of transitions $T \cap P = \varnothing$,
$A \subseteq (T \times P) \cup (P \times T)$ – set of arcs,
$M_0 : P \to \mathbb{Z}_+ \times R$ – marking which defines the initial state of the system,
$\tau : T \times P \to \mathbb{R}_+$ – function determining the static delay that of activity (event) t,
$X : T \times P \to \mathbb{R}_+$ – random time of carrying out an activity (event) t,
Γ – finite set of colors which correspond to the possible properties of tokens,
C – function determining what kinds of can be stored in a place: $C : P \to \Gamma$,
G – function which determines the conditions for a given event to occur,
E – function describing properties of tokens that are processed,
R – set of timestamps (also called time points) $R \subseteq \mathbb{R}$,
r_0 – initial time, $r_0 \in R$.
$B : T \to \mathbb{R}_+$ – function determining the priority of an event.

3.6   Model Implementation

The developed model has been computer implemented in the CPN Tools 4.0 programming environment [9, 14] as a hierarchical Petri net. The hierarchy consists of ten modules, with the "fused places" synchronization mechanism applied. The modules, called "pages", represent traffic events (*AC Entry, AC Hdg rqst, AC FL rqst, ATC Observes, ATC FL rqst, ATC Hdg rqst, AC Exit*), aircraft dynamics (*Position*), and perform initialization of simulation parameters (*Main*) and final calculations (*Results*).

To illustrate how the model is implemented one page will be presented – *AC Hdg rqst* modeling the actions after pilot's request to fly directly to the output gate from the sector (Fig. 2).

Figure 2 shows the situation after 1101 s from the beginning of the simulation. The flight heading change request was made by the aircraft with system number 9. The token with this information is visible in the *Hdg rqst* place. At the same time, the place *Ready* contains a token that indicates that the communication channel is available. Thus, pilot-controller voice transmission can be carried out within the transition *Heading change request AC-ATC*. In the following steps, coordination of the decision with neighboring controllers takes place (transition *Coordination*), then the controller-pilot radio correspondence with the appropriate clearance (transition *ATC-AC transmission*) and finally readback confirming understanding of the clearance (transition *RDBCK*). Each of these elementary activities takes some random time defined in the function *rnd()* and stored in variables *tm, tm1* and *tm2*. After finishing the event

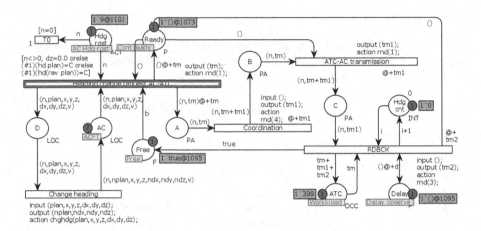

Fig. 2. Petri net modeling *AC Hdg rqst* traffic event [own study]

handling the ATCo workload time is updated and stored in place *ATC*. The actual change in the flight parameters is carried out within the transition *Change heading* by the function *chghdg()*.

4   Simulation Experiments

Several simulation experiments using the model were carried out as part of the research. Dependencies were sought between the parameters of the air traffic entering the sector and the parameters of the sector itself, and the time workload of the ATCo. In this section we will present only three experiments covering the following scenarios.

1. Basic scenario for typical traffic in FIR Warsaw for a sector like the one used in the model.
2. Scenario with similar air traffic characteristics but with decreased intensity.
3. Scenario in which a prohibited area was created in the central part of the sector (near the navigation point D).

4.1   Scenario 1 – Basic Version

In Scenario 1, we have analyzed the ATCo workload when the traffic is typical for the sector with the modeled size and structure. It is assumed that on average every 2 min an aircraft enters the sector through one of the input gates. The second hour of simulation was taken as the measuring period, the first being omitted, because at the beginning of the analysis we assume that the sector is empty. Thus, the first hour is used to saturate the traffic in the sector and stabilize it.

For this traffic volume, the values characterizing the time workload of the ATCo for five simulation runs are shown in Table 5.

4.2   Scenario 2 – Changing the Traffic Volume

In Scenario 2, we made an analysis of the ATCo workload depending on the traffic intensity. To this end, we modified the average time interval between successive aircraft arriving to the sector. Input data regarding the frequency of flight parameters changes was adopted at the same level as in the basic variant. The average hourly ATCo workload depending on the mean time between successive arrivals to the sector is shown in the Table 6.

Table 5. Results of experiments in Scenario 1 [own study]

Simulation run	The number of aircraft	Total ATCo work time [s]	Average ATCo work time per aircraft [s]	Hourly ATCo workload [%]
1	25	1366	54.6	38
2	26	1221	47.0	34
3	27	1434	53.1	40
4	26	1310	50.4	36
5	27	1429	52.9	40
Average	26.2	1352	51.6	37.6

Table 6. Results of experiments in Scenario 2 - hourly controller workload [own study]

Simulation run	The average time between arrivals to the sector [s]								
	60	75	90	105	120	135	150	165	180
1	69	52	48	44	38	35	30	30	27
2	75	51	46	40	34	34	33	31	26
3	66	57	47	43	40	35	32	32	29
4	68	53	47	43	36	34	33	32	31
5	75	51	48	42	40	34	31	31	30
Average	70.6	52.8	47.2	42.4	37.6	34.4	31.8	31.2	28.6

4.3   Scenario 3 – Prohibited Area

In Scenario 3, we analyzed the situation when a prohibited area was activated in the sector, which prevents standard flight through the waypoint D. In this case, all aircraft are routed in such a way that they go directly from the input to the output gate. On the one hand, it is beneficial for the economy of the flight, as the time of flight through the sector decreases, but on the other hand, it increases the ATCo workload. The other parameters were adopted as in the basic variant.

The values characterizing the time workload of the ATCo for five simulation runs are shown in Table 7.

Table 7. Results of experiments in Scenario 3 [own study]

Simulation run	The number of aircraft	Total ATCo work time [s]	Average ATCo work time per aircraft [s]	Hourly ATCo workload [%]
1	26	1527	58.7	42
2	26	1550	59.6	43
3	27	1608	59.6	45
4	25	1546	61.8	43
5	26	1552	59.7	43
Average	26	1557	59.9	43.2

5   Analysis of the Results

In Scenario 1 we analyzed the ATCo workload for typical traffic conditions. The results show that it equals to 38%. According to EUROCONTROL standards this corresponds to the average workload [6]. In our previous work [5] we analyzed real ATCo time workload, measured at the EPWWC and EPWWD control sectors. The results obtained were 38% and 43%, respectively. In our model, the sector has the size and structure like EPWWC sector. The experiment for the nominal variant allows positive validation of the results obtained from the model.

In Scenario 2, we analyzed the quantitative dependence of the ATCo time workload on the intensity of air traffic. Results presented in Fig. 3 clearly indicate that such a dependence exists, however, for an average interval between arrivals to the sector greater than 90 s the ATCo hourly workload remains at the *medium* level. At the interval of 75 s, it increases to the *heavy* level to reach the *overload* level at intervals of 60 s.

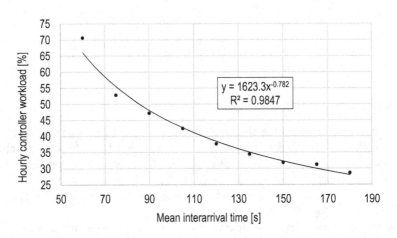

Fig. 3. Dependence of workload and interarrival time [own study]

The results of the experiment in Scenario 3 show the impact of flight plan changes on the ATCo workload. Because of direct flight clearance granted to each aircraft, the length of the route flown in the sector is shorter. The stay of each aircraft in the sector is thus shorter. This situation is therefore advantageous for the economy of the flight. Nevertheless, the average time spent on handling the aircraft changing the heading is approximately 16% longer and therefore the workload is higher to a similar extent.

6   Conclusion

The mesoscale model in the form of a colored Petri net, presented in this paper, was developed in the framework of the research aiming at determination of the quantitative relationship between air traffic smoothness and the sector capacity. The model represents both the air traffic in the sector and the work of the ATCo while handling this traffic. The capacity of the area control sector is usually determined by reference to the hourly workload of the air traffic controller.

The results of experiments confirm the dependence between the aircraft arrival stream intensity and the ATCo time workload. It is possible to determine this dependence in a quantitative way. The mesoscale model allows analyzing situations when the ATCo is busy handling an aircraft, and a new request is coming from other aircraft under control. This may happen when the communication channel is available but the ATCo is busy analyzing the traffic situation as part of routine monitoring or before taking the decision about changing the aircraft traffic parameters. Both cases, but especially the latter, constitute a safety risk and should be subject to further careful consideration.

Another important conclusion from this research is the importance of executing previously established flight plan. The pursuit of improving flight economics by granting clearances for direct flights is very common. It has a positive impact on the amount of fuel used, and thus on the costs of air operations, as well as the level of environmental pollution. However, it should be considered that with this traffic control strategy, the workload of the controller increases, and thus the capacity decreases, as demonstrated in one of the experiments. These issues will be developed in the next stage of our research on traffic smoothness.

References

1. Bekier, M., Molesworth, B., Williamson, A.: Tipping point: the narrow path between automation acceptance and rejection in air traffic management. Saf. Sci. **50**(2), 259–265 (2012)
2. Brooker, P.: Air traffic management safety challenges. In: 2nd Institution of Engineering and Technology System Safety Conference, pp. 1–45 (2007)
3. Corver, S., Unger, D., Grote, G.: Predicting air traffic controller workload: trajectory uncertainty as the moderator of the indirect effect of traffic density on controller workload through traffic conflict. Hum. Factors **58**(4), 560–573 (2016)
4. Dmochowski, P.A., Skorupski, J.: Air traffic smoothness as a universal measure for air traffic quality assessment. Procedia Eng. **134**, 237–244 (2016)
5. Dmochowski, P.A., Skorupski, J.: Air traffic smoothness. A new look at the air traffic flow management. Transp. Res. Procedia **28**, 127–132 (2017)

6. EUROCONTROL. Description of the CAPAN method, Bruxells. https://www.eurocontrol. int/sites/default/files/field_tabs/content/documents/nm/airspace/airspace-capan.pdf. Accessed 10 Dec 2018

7. Ferduła, P., Skorupski, J.: The influence of errors in visualization systems on the level of safety threat in air traffic. J. Adv. Transp. **2018**, 1–16 (2018). Article ID 1034301

8. Inoue, S., et al.: Cognitive process modelling of controllers in en route air traffic control. Ergonomics **55**(4), 450–464 (2012)

9. Jensen, K., Kristensen, L., Wells, L.: Coloured Petri nets and CPN tools for modelling and validation of concurrent systems. Int. J. Softw. Tools Technol. Transf. **9**(3–4), 213–254 (2007)

10. Langan-Fox, J., et al.: Human factors measurement for future air traffic control systems. Hum. Factors **51**(5), 595–637 (2010)

11. Lehouillier, T., et al.: Measuring the interactions between air traffic control and flow management using a simulation-based framework. Comput. Ind. Eng. **99**, 269–279 (2016)

12. Malarski, M., Walczak, K.: A contemporary approach to air traffic management systems on the example of the PEGASUS_21 system being implemented, vol. 89, pp. 109–134. Scientific Works of Warsaw University of Technology, Transport (2013). (in Polish)

13. Nealley, M., Gawron, V.: The effect of fatigue on air traffic controllers. Int. J. Aviat. Psychol. **25**(1), 14–47 (2015)

14. Ratzer, A.V., et al.: CPN tools for editing, simulating, and analysing coloured Petri nets. In: van der Aalst, W.M.P., Best, E. (eds.) ICATPN 2003. LNCS, vol. 2679, pp. 450–462. Springer, Heidelberg (2003). https://doi.org/10.1007/3-540-44919-1_28

15. Rohacs, J., Rohacs, D., Jankovics, I.: Conceptual development of an advanced air traffic controller workstation based on objective workload monitoring and augmented reality. J. Aerosp. Eng. **230**(9), 1747–1761 (2016)

16. Sáez Nieto, F., et al.: Development of a three-dimensional collision risk model tool to assess safety in high density en-route airspaces. J. Aerosp. Eng. **224**, 1119–1129 (2010)

17. Skorupski, J.: ATC sector capacity as a measure of air traffic safety. In: Safety, Reliability and Risk Analysis: Beyond the Horizon - Proceedings of the European Safety and Reliability Conference, ESREL 2013, pp. 1827–1835. Taylor & Francis, London (2014)

18. Számel, B., Szabó, G.: Supporting safety management systems of air traffic controllers by analyzing human-technical interactions. In: 25th European Safety and Reliability Conference, ESREL 2015, pp. 3119–3128 (2015)

19. Tobaruela, G.: Capacity estimation for the single european sky. In: 5th International Conference on Research and Air Transportation, Berkeley, USA, pp. 1–8 (2012)

20. Westin, C., Borst, C., Hilburn, B.: Automation transparency and personalized decision support: air traffic controller interaction with a resolution advisory system. IFAC-PapersOnLine **49**(19), 201–206 (2016)

21. Zhang, M., et al.: Terminal airspace sector capacity estimation method based on the ATC dynamical model. Kybernetes **45**(6), 884–899 (2016)

22. Zohrevandi, E., et al.: Modeling and analysis of controller's taskload in different predictability conditions. In: 6th SESAR Innovation Days, Delft, the Netherlands, pp. 1–8 (2016)

The Concept of Quality Assurance and Data Incompatibilities Management in Intelligent Air Transport Systems

Ewa Dudek[✉]

Warsaw University of Technology, Koszykowa 75, Warsaw, Poland
edudek@wt.pw.edu.pl

Abstract. This article is a continuation of the Author's work on the ways to ensure quality and safety of aeronautical data and information. This time, however, attention was paid to the steady increase in the amount of collected and processed data in intelligent air transport systems, its causes and the resulting consequences. Aeronautical data and information were described in details - documents in which they appear, proposed classification categories, types and their end users. It was noticed that the currently occurring excess of data in air telematic systems generates a problem with their adoption and processing. Consequently, the more important becomes the issue of their quality (timeliness, accuracy, completeness, origin, ...) assurance. That is why, in the following part of the paper, requirements were characterized as well as procedures, methods, principles and tools for quality assessment were described. Afterwards the case when requirements are not meet was considered, for which, taking into account the background obligation to implement Safety Management System and Quality Management System – Compliance Monitoring System by all air operators, the concept of data incompatibility management procedure was presented. Analysed issues will be the subject of Author's further study.

Keywords: Aeronautical data and information · Quality ·
Incompatibilities management

1 Introduction

This article is a continuation of the Author's work on the ways to ensure quality and safety of aeronautical data and information. It also refers to achievements of other authors in this area ([16, 19, 20] for example), although it must be honestly admitted that the issue of aeronautical data and information quality management is not broadly discussed neither in polish nor in foreign literature.

In this paper, however, attention was paid to the following relationship: development of air transport → increase in number of implemented intelligent air transport systems → more aeronautical data and information to be processed and verified → data quality assurance even more important → methods, procedures of quality assurance/incompatibilities management. The main focus is placed on quality assurance and in case when all methods and procedures fail, on the incompatibilities management.

© Springer Nature Switzerland AG 2019
J. Mikulski (Ed.): TST 2019, CCIS 1049, pp. 377–390, 2019.
https://doi.org/10.1007/978-3-030-27547-1_27

Air transport is a rapidly growing domain. This can be noticed in, for example: the growing number of air operations (263028 in 2013 versus 341199 in 2017), the growing number of attended passengers (24 982 623 in 2013 versus 39 972 247 in 2017) (see Fig. 1) or the growing number of foreign carriers operating to/from Poland (33 in 2015 versus 54 in 2017) [18].

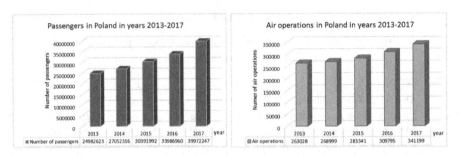

Fig. 1. Number of passengers attended and air operations in Poland in years 2013–2017 [18]

From the technical point of view, the dynamic development may be observed in the continuous implementation of new intelligent transport solutions, with the overriding objective to ensure continuous improvement of telematic systems and to increase the level of safety and quality of air traffic and transport. It is difficult nowadays to imagine modern manned aircrafts and BSP systems without smart computers on board, supported by various types of digital technology. Moreover, in the entire Air Traffic Management (ATM) the growing importance of immaterial assets, such as information, may be noticed, which results in the continuous implementation of new intelligent air transport systems solutions, allowing the exchange of data and information. What seems characteristic is that before air transport suffered from shortage of information while nowadays there are so many information that it is difficult to comprehend them, and even more difficult to verify, which are proper, valid or up to date. Furthermore, taking into account the specifics of flight operation (e.g. the approach or take-off phase) it must be considered that in numerous situations there is no time reserve to analyse the received data. That is why, taking into account the mentioned growth in operations', passengers' and telematic systems' numbers, which have direct impact on information to be processed, the issue of aeronautical data and information quality assurance in the aspects of operational risk and safety is still actual and important.

In this article the Author focused on three aspects:

1. aeronautical data and information description,
2. quality assurance – requirements, methods and procedures,
3. incompatibilities management.

The first one is to give a general background, the second one is essential and should be done as best as possible (according to rules and expectations) while the third point is a must in case when the preceding process fails.

2 Aeronautical Data and Information

The term "aeronautical data", according to [1, 10], stands for a representation of aeronautical facts, concepts or instructions in a formalized manner, suitable for communication, interpretation or processing. "Aeronautical information" can be defined as information resulting from the assembly, analysis and formatting of aeronautical data [1, 10]. The relation between data and information may be presented based on the aeronautical data chain (Fig. 2), which is a formalized manner of showing the following stages of data/information lifecycle.

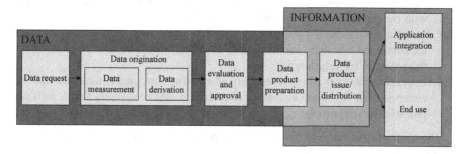

Fig. 2. Aeronautical data and information chain [own study based on 7]

Aeronautical data and information chain (as shown on Fig. 2) consists of six consecutive stages [7] from aeronautical data request and origination through to its operational use. The subsequent stages have already been analysed and described in other Author's works, for example [21]. However, it is worth mentioning that it is on the fourth chain's stage when accepted data are placed in the registry and they become Information.

Aeronautical information are divided into many different types as they serve different purposes and have different recipients (end users). Therefore, taking into account legal requirements and practical operational aspects, analysed data and information may be classified according to:

1. the document, in which they are published,
2. the level of data integrity, which must be assured,
3. the type of data, which is presented,
4. the entity/group of recipients that may use them.

Aeronautical documents, understood as aeronautical information and their carriers, can be divided into the following types:

(1a) legal acts, standards and international regulations,
(1b) Integrated Aeronautical Information Package (IAIP) – therein Aeronautical Information Publication – AIP, temporary operational documentation - NOTAM messages, supplements to AIP, Pre-Flight Information Bulletin and Aeronautical Information Circular,

(1c)   flight documentation for aircraft crews to be used in the cabin - prepared on the basis of IAIP often by different companies,

(1d)   manuals, handbooks, training materials, data sets, etc.

Integrity classification [10] (where data integrity is understood as a degree of assurance that an aeronautical data and its value has not been lost or altered since the data origination or authorized amendment) is based upon the potential risk resulting from the use of corrupted data. In this rating aeronautical data are classified into three groups:

(2a)   routine data: there is a very low probability when using corrupted routine data that the continued safe flight and landing of an aircraft would be severely at risk with the potential for catastrophe,

(2b)   essential data: there is a low probability when using corrupted essential data that the continued safe flight and landing of an aircraft would be severely at risk with the potential for catastrophe,

(2c)   critical data: there is a high probability when using corrupted critical data that the continued safe flight and landing of an aircraft would be severely at risk with the potential for catastrophe.

The third classification is based on the type of data, which is presented. It was created as a result of the documents' and requirements' analysis and based on the interviews with personnel responsible for air traffic as well as aerodrome traffic and it concerns the following data categories:

(3a)   geospatial, geographic and topographic data,

(3b)   meteorological data,

(3c)   aeronautical charts,

(3d)   data concerning birds and other animals that jeopardize the safety of air operations,

(3e)   data about radiation sources or objects that may interfere with air communication,

(3f)   traffic data for aircrafts on movement area and during the flight, including information for search and rescue services,

(3g)   organizational information, available at the aerodrome's passengers terminal.

The first three mentioned categories (3a) to (3c) constitute the biggest aeronautical data group. Usually when considering issues related to aeronautical data and information, geospatial data are dealt with, which means measured data, originated data or data calculated/obtained from other data. Moreover, in many cases, geographic, geospatial and topographic data, presented in a descriptive form, coincide with information contained in aeronautical charts. The following four groups, even if less numerous, and in case of (3f) and (3g) categories, containing rather operational data, not published in the AIRAC cycles but exchanged up to date (e.g.: through radiotelephone communication, ATIS, digital data connections), still constitute important data group affecting the safety of flight operations.

The analysed aeronautical data and information can also be considered from the point of view of the recipient groups for which they are intended. Bearing in mind the tasks performed by the air system's participants, the following four groups of recipients were distinguished:

(4a) 1st group: air traffic services units' personnel, aircraft crews, aerodrome's management services personnel, vehicle drivers on the movement area,

(4b) 2nd group: aircraft's passengers (and their accompanying persons), tour operators, etc.,

(4c) 3rd group: staff and service of ground handling agents,

(4d) 4th group: government administration bodies competent in aviation matters: appropriate ministry, Civil Aviation Authority and adequate in terms of competencies international organizations and agencies, e.g. ICAO, EURO-CONTROL, EASA, etc.

Figure 3 illustrates the relationship between the four data recipient groups (point 4) and the data categories identified in point 3.

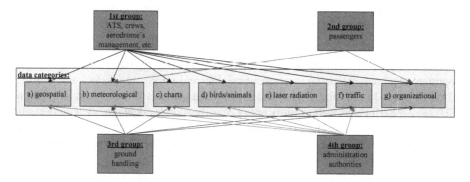

Fig. 3. Relationship between data categories and their recipients [own study]

The largest and most important recipient of aeronautical data and information is the 1st group. The use of adequate data as well as data of appropriate quality by its members has direct impact on the safety of air operations, both in the air and on the aerodrome's movement area. As natural consequence of this fact the members of this group use all seven described data categories. Similarly extensive use of data and information can be observed in case of the 3rd group - ground handling. Its personnel mainly uses data from categories (3a) to (c), (f) and (g).

The least amount of data and information are required by aircrafts' passengers and their companions. The information for this group is merely a facilitation and is intended to rationalize their movement in the aerodrome's passenger terminal. Therefore, it was identified that this group uses the data described in categories (3b) and (g).

The main purpose of aeronautical data and information creation and publication is to ensure safe and regular air navigation, in accordance with the detailed requirements of ICAO Annex 15 [10], which specifies the type of information to be disclosed and their quality requirements. Most of the aeronautical data and information is critical to safety, hence the special efforts to ensure their quality and safety in the whole process of their creation, collection, processing and publication, described in Author' previous works [e.g.: 3, 5, 21], for selected systems [e.g. 6] or cases [e.g. 14]. This time, however, in the following section of this article special attention is be paid to requirements, methods and procedures of quality assurance.

3 Quality Assurance

Data quality (according most of all to aeronautical data) is understood as a degree or level of confidence that the data provided meets the requirements of the data user in terms of accuracy, resolution and integrity [10]. Bearing this definition in mind it can be stated that quality assurance should have the following components:

1. precisely defined requirements (legal, technical, operational, contractual, etc.),
2. selected instruments for impact on quality (rules, methods, tools),
3. data quality evaluation.

Air transport is a discipline containing many legal regulations. As the most important legal acts, referring to aeronautical data and information safety and quality, ICAO Annexes 15 [10] and 19 [11] and their related manuals, Commission Regulation (EU) No 73/2010 [1] as well as Eurocontrol Specification for data quality requirements [8] should be considered. The list may of course be much longer when including other EU regulations, EASA or Eurocontrol specifications, etc. The idea is not to present all of them, but to show their great number and importance.

Data quality definition reveals one statement more, which finds confirmation in other quality definitions presented in literature, for example in ISO 9001 standard [12]. The unequivocal understanding of quality in a certain field (aeronautical data for example) is possible only by defining a set of attributes/features that describe it. The definition [10] lists three of them: integrity (described before), accuracy (the degree of conformance between the estimated or measured value and the true value) and resolution (number of units or digits to which a measured or calculated value is expressed and used). Whether this list is complete or not may be subject of discussion as regulation [1] reveals also other features such as:

(a) the accuracy and resolution of the data,
(b) the integrity level of the data,
(c) the ability to determine the origin of the data,
(d) the level of assurance that data is made available to the next intended user prior to its effective start date/time and not deleted before its effective end date/time.

To make it even less consistent the ISO19157 standard [17] names more attributes:

(a) completeness,
(b) logical consistency,
(c) positional accuracy,
(d) temporal quality,
(e) thematic accuracy.

To make a long story short after a detailed analysis of numerous aeronautical documents, as a general rule it is proposed to analyse data quality above all with reference to the three basic attributes: integrity, accuracy and resolution (as written in ICAO standards) supplemented with punctuality and ability to determine the data origin (as written in [1]) as well as with its completeness (accepted from [17]). Nevertheless, for particular analysis other features may be taken into account.

There are many instruments for impact on quality. Moreover, quality assessment is a part of a complicated quality management process, often based on Total Quality Management concept. On the other hand, an import rule being in force in aviation must be taken into account - namely, the principle of proceeding only in accordance with specified Standards and Recommended Practices – SARPs and Acceptable Means of Compliance – AMC. Which in practice means that when choosing methods (or rules or procedures), for data quality assessment for example, only methods which have been published in the form of international standards may be selected. Bearing this in mind instruments for quality management may be named and described. In literature rules/principles, methods and tools are distinguished, however, the distinction is often poorly defined and lack of precision is observed. Such situation may be explained by different author's approach as well as by the interrelations, linkages and dependencies between the above-mentioned groups. Nonetheless, the main distinguishing factor is the range of their influence:

– quality management rules define a long-term strategy and the approach to the overarching quality problems of the entire company, the results of their application are difficult to assess on an ongoing basis,
– quality management methods constitute a "medium-term" tool, they are based on generally accepted algorithms,
– quality management tools are operational instruments which results are visible in the short-term.

Rules and tools are used throughout the process cycle, and the use of methods is usually limited to one specific process stage. Examples of tools, methods and principles used in quality management are presented in Table 1.

Table 1. Classification of quality management instruments [own study based on 9, 15]

Quality instrument	Examples/Names
Rules/principles	Deming's 14 points philosophy Kaizen's continuous improvement "Zero defects" concept Teamwork Poka-Yoke (mistake-proofing) system
Methods	**Design methods**
	FMEA - Failure Modes and Effects Analysis DOE - design of experiments QFD - Quality Function Deployment
	Assessment and control methods
	Statistical process control Statistical acceptance control Statistical quality control
Tools	**Traditional tools**
	Histogram Ishikawa diagrams Pareto diagram, Pareto-Lorenz chart Shewhart control charts Flow diagram
	New tools
	Six-Sigma Entity relationship diagram Tree diagram Correlation diagram

The instruments from the above mentioned list may be selected freely. In some of the previous works, the Author proposed implementation of the FMEA analysis [2, 21], Shewhart control charts [14] or Six-Sigma method [3]. However, the appointment of tools should be based on the analysed data type, expected results and the analysis purpose.

Knowing the exact quality requirements (point 1) as well as the instrument for quality assessment (point 2) it is possible to continue with the procedure of data quality evaluation. Such procedure, according to [17] is understood as a sequence of steps, leading to the final data quality evaluation and may be presented in the schematic form shown on Fig. 4.

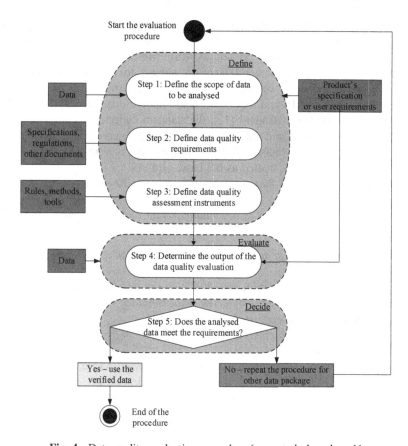

Fig. 4. Data quality evaluation procedure [own study based on 1]

The efforts to ensure adequate level of data quality should be continuous, cyclic and most of all effective. As mentioned before, most of aeronautical data and information have direct impact on operations safety, so their quality matters. However, a question can be posed: what should be done, if despite the effort to ensure adequate data quality, the requirements are not meet? The answer to this problem will be subject of the following paragraph.

4 Data Incompatibilities Management

Taking into account the existing legal rules in civil aviation, the obligation to implement and maintain a quality management system (QMS) can be identified. This requirement applies to all areas, administrative bodies and companies/institutions operating in civil aviation (civil aviation authorities, air carriers and aircrafts' operators, management of the certified public aerodromes, air traffic services providers, etc.) and is combined with the obligation to implement a safety management system (SMS) as well as Compliance Monitoring System (CMS). Moreover, the fulfilment of all applicable and legally defined requirements is subject to formal confirmation and compliance, which is done by certification. As far as the normative standard, defining the general principles, model and requirements in relation to the Quality Management System (QMS) is ISO 9001 standard [12], the standard concerning compliance management is ISO 19600 [13], and within the scope limited to compliance management, CMS is a component of the National Civil Aviation Safety Program [18], alongside and equally with SMS and QMS, treated as the basis of CMS.

As written in Annex VII Part A of the Commission Regulation [1]: *"A quality management system supporting the origination, production, storage, handling, processing, transfer and distribution of aeronautical data and aeronautical information shall:*

- *define the quality policy in such a way as to meet the needs of different users as close as possible,*
- *set up a quality assurance programme that contains procedures designed to verify that all operations are being conducted in accordance with applicable requirements, standards and procedures [...],*
- *provide evidence of the functioning of the quality system by means of manuals and monitoring documents,*
- *appoint management representatives to monitor compliance with, and adequacy of, procedures to ensure safe and efficient operational practices,*
- *perform reviews of the quality system in place and take remedial actions, as appropriate."*

Implementation of the above cited fragment in practice means that the overriding objective to be achieved by implementing a quality management system in the area of ensuring the safety and quality of aeronautical data and information is:

1. the incompatibilities management,
2. prevention of their occurrence and (last but not least),
3. identification and application of adequate corrective and preventive actions.

Those three suggestions are the exact answer to the question asked before - what should be done, if despite the effort to ensure adequate data quality, the requirements are not meet? The proposed proceeding diagram concerning data incompatibilities management procedure is shown on Fig. 5.

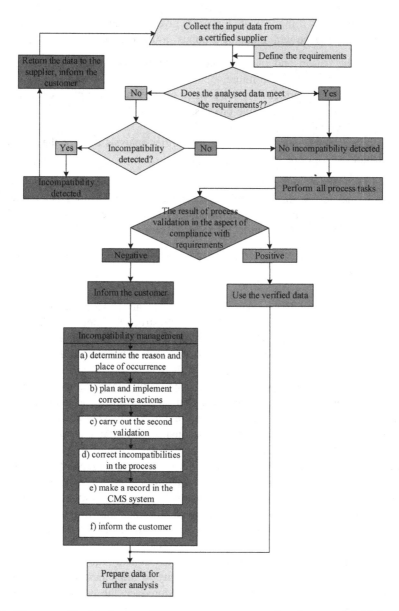

Fig. 5. Diagram with data incompatibility management procedure [own study] (Color figure online)

The expected route is shown in green – the requirements are meet, no incompatibilities are detected, all process tasks may be performed and in the end the result of process validation is positive. In this case, no incompatibilities management procedure is necessary. However, if the validation process gives a negative answer it is necessary to proceed in accordance with elaborated points (a) to (f) and:

- determine the reason and place of incompatibility's occurrence, in order not to repeat the same errors in the future,
- plan and implement corrective actions, based on the reason and place of occurrence, in order to improve the defective process,
- correct the faulty data,
- write down the necessary information for further analysis and for the customer's information.

Failure to detect incompatibilities, which results in lack of corrective and preventive actions, may cause that data with undetected non-conformities get through all stages of the aeronautical data and information chain and be used operationally. In some cases, this may cause threat to air operation safety.

5 Conclusion

The introduction of intelligent transport systems, in air transport also, is aimed at facilitating the use and functioning of transport infrastructure, improving the quality of services, the safety of traffic users as well as air operations themselves. At the same time, however, it evokes the necessity to process, understand and verify an increasing amount of data and information. The quality of these data and information is significant for the safety of operations performed, especially taking into account the enormous dynamics of operational activities occurring in air transport. The complete way of thinking presented in the article is summarized in Fig. 6. The main purpose is to ensure the proper aeronautical data and information quality, in accordance with the requirements set out in the corresponding literature and with the use of ICAO Standards and Recommended Practices. For unwanted but still occurring situations of non-compliances detection, the concept of incompatibilities management procedure was developed, which stands in line with the obligation to have and implement SMS, QMS and CMS systems in air transport. The developed procedure may in future be expanded to consider the occurrence of potential incompatibilities, bearing in mind that the participants of the aeronautical data and information chain are companies of different nature and goals, as well as the different competences and requirements set. Further potential research areas also include the possibility to implement other quality management instruments from the listed solutions. Moreover, the presented approach of compliance management is based and stays in accordance with risk management concerning compliance and may be broaden of such analysis in the future. These aspects will be subject of Author's further work.

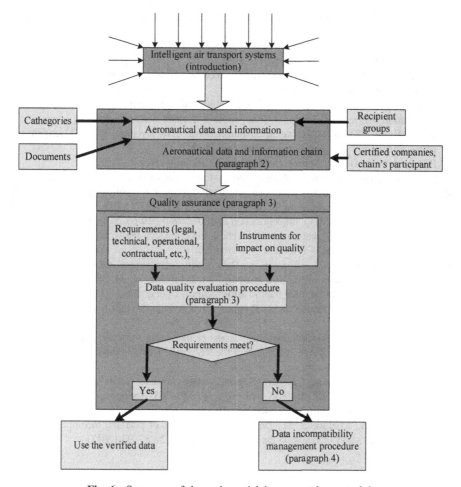

Fig. 6. Summary of the entire article's concept [own study]

References

1. Commission Regulation (EU) No 73/2010 of 26 January 2010 laying down requirements on the quality of aeronautical data and aeronautical information for the single European sky
2. Dudek, E.: The concept of DMAIC methodology application for diagnostics of potential incompatibilities in aeronautical data request process. Diagnostyka **19**(4), 33–38 (2018)
3. Dudek, E., Kozłowski, M.: The concept of a method ensuring aeronautical data quality. J. KONBiN **1**(37), 319–340 (2016)
4. Dudek, E., Kozłowski, M.: The concept of a method improving the process of aeronautical geospatial data creation. J. KONBiN **46**, 35–50 (2018)
5. Dudek, E., Kozłowski, M.: The concept of risk tolerability matrix determination for aeronautical data and information chain. J. KONBiN **43**, 69–94 (2017)
6. Dudek, E., Kozłowski, M.: The concept of the instrument landing system – ILS continuity risk analysis method. In: Mikulski, J. (ed.) TST 2018. CCIS, vol. 897, pp. 305–319. Springer, Cham (2018). https://doi.org/10.1007/978-3-319-97955-7_21

7. Eurocontrol Specification for Data Assurance Level, Reference no: EUROCONTROL-SPEC-148 (2012)
8. Eurocontrol Specification for data quality requirements, Reference no: EUROCONTROL-SPEC-152 (2014)
9. Hamrol, A., Mantura, W.: Zarządzanie jakością: Teoria i praktyka. Wydawnictwo Naukowe PWN, Warszawa (2013)
10. ICAO Annex 15 to the Convention on International Civil Aviation, Aeronautical Information Services, International Civil Aviation Organization, July 2013
11. ICAO Annex 19 to the Convention on International Civil Aviation, Safety Management, International Civil Aviation Organization, July 2013
12. ISO 9001:2015, Quality Management Systems – Requirements
13. ISO 19600:2014, Compliance Management Systems – Guidelines
14. Kozłowski, M., Dudek, E.: Risk analysis in air transport telematics systems based on Aircraft's Airbus A320 accident. In: Mikulski, J. (ed.) TST 2017. CCIS, vol. 715, pp. 385–395. Springer, Cham (2017). https://doi.org/10.1007/978-3-319-66251-0_31
15. Mazur, A., Gołaś, H.: Zasady, metody i techniki wykorzystywane w zarządzaniu jakością. Wydawnictwo Politechniki Poznańskiej, Poznań (2010)
16. Ohbyung, K., Namyeon, L., Bongsik, S.: Data quality management, data usage experience and acquisition intention of big data analytics. Int. J. Inf. Manag. **34**, 387–394 (2014)
17. PN-EN ISO19157:2014:04, Geographic information – Data quality
18. Polish National Civil Aviation Safety Program, Civil Aviation Authority of the Republic of Poland (2016)
19. Schroth, W.R.: Aeronautical data quality - a new challenge for surveyors. In: FIG Congress 2014 Engaging the Challenges - Enhancing the Relevance Kuala Lumpur, Malaysia, 16–21 June 2014
20. Siergiejczyk, M.: Assessing transport telematic systems in terms of data services quality. In: Mikulski, J. (ed.) TST 2012. CCIS, vol. 329, pp. 356–363. Springer, Heidelberg (2012). https://doi.org/10.1007/978-3-642-34050-5_40
21. Siergiejczyk, M., Kozłowski, M., Dudek, E.: Diagnostics of potential incompatibilities in aeronautical data and information chain. Diagnostyka **18**(2), 87–93 (2017)

Model Tests on an Integration Method of Collision Avoidance and Radio Communication Systems with Helmet-Mounted Imaging Systems in Order to Increase Safety of Air Transport Systems

Andrzej Szelmanowski, Andrzej Pazur, and Krzysztof Sajda[✉]

Air Force Institute of Technology, Księcia Bolesława 6, Warsaw, Poland
Krzysztof.sajda@itwl.pl

Abstract. Modern integrated avionic systems include, among others, helmet-mounted data presentation systems, the main objective of which is to improve situational and tactical awareness of a pilot on the modern battlefield. A completely new issue related to the helmet-mounted data imaging is the use of imaging the information obtained from collision avoidance and radio communication systems. The electronic (computer) integration of individual devices forming an integrated avionic system uses digital data buses, in which information (including alarm signals, radio operating parameters, voice commands) can be provided directly "in front of the pilot's eyes" in the helmet-mounted imaging systems. The paper presents the results of the model tests, within the framework of the reliability of information obtained from the selected collision avoidance and radio communication systems, carried out in the Air Force Institute of Technology. It also discusses the selected methods and systems applied in order to support the pilot in terms of warning of a collision risk situation (monitor imaging) and the selected analysis results of the probability of the aircraft collision in the controlled airspace. The SWPL-1 Cyklop helmet-mounted flight parameter display system (constructed in the Avionics Division of Air Force Institute of Technology) and proposals of imaging the selected parameters from the collision avoidance and radio communication systems on military helicopters of the Polish Armed Forces were presented.

Keywords: Communication systems · Air transport systems ·
Helmet-mounted imaging systems

1 Introduction

One of the modern elements to increase the safety of air transport systems is the use of the so-called collision avoidance systems supporting communication of an anthro-potechnical "human – aircraft" system. The modern integrated avionic systems (using the collision avoidance systems) including, among others, systems warning of a potential collision between aircraft (SP) in flight of the TCAS (Traffic Collision Avoidance System) type in terms of "air-air" and of a collision of the aircraft with the

© Springer Nature Switzerland AG 2019
J. Mikulski (Ed.): TST 2019, CCIS 1049, pp. 391–406, 2019.
https://doi.org/10.1007/978-3-030-27547-1_28

ground of the GPWS (Ground Proximity Warning System) type, in terms of "air-ground". They allow not only to directly inform the aircraft crew on the occurrence of the collision risk situation (which is very important during manoeuvring flights and the descent approach), but they also give directive commands (ordering the activities necessary to perform the obstacle "by-passing" manoeuvre). The aircraft is one of the most versatile tools of the modern battlefield. It performs fire missions, fights the enemy, recognises, patrols and protects its own activities. One of the most important conditions for the timely and accurate implementation of tasks is to ensure the proper radio communication system. The development of information and radio communication technology, and hence, functional parameters of the modern on-board radios in terms of their frequency, range, transmission of additional signals (among others, navigation and weapons) and the communication methods (e.g. with the use of helmet-mounted targeting systems) resulted in the formation of new concepts and the possibility of their organization on the aircraft board. The maintenance of the aircraft as valuable combat means on the modern battlefield requires a permanent increase in its operational capabilities and ability to survive. It involves the need to introduce the modern helmet-mounted imaging system to its board, among others, the possibility of presenting the radio communication data in the helmet-mounted targeting systems [1]. The currently carried out development works in the field of the collision avoidance systems indicate the possibilities of using the information on the collision risk situation in the so-called helmet-mounted data presentation. The technical solution of such an approach may be aviation helmets adjusted to operate in the so-called cyberspace. An example is the pilot's helmet with a built-in HMDS (Helmet Mounted Display Systems) system of the F-35 multi-task aircraft, which allows the pilot to observe the entire aircraft during the performance of an air task. A helmet-mounted display images all the information that is needed to complete the task without the necessity of taking eyes off the airspace; it is the only modern multi-task aircraft without a HUD (Head-Up Display) indicator. The F-35 aircraft is equipped in a multi-directional system of detecting and tracking infrared targets, consisting of six cameras, mounted on each side of the aircraft airframe. The cameras send the image to the pilot's helmet showing him a space sector observed by them. Therefore, the pilot has the opportunity to observe even this zone that is covered by the aircraft structural elements, warning and allowing him to make decisions adequate to the risk of action. This function is essential not only in combat but also during landings on the aircraft carrier board and during night vertical landings. The F-35 aircraft cockpit has one main screen, which the pilot integrates with by touch and a voice recognition system. By using this technique, the pilot can change the size, position and contents of the appearing windows with piloting-navigational data and the armament system on the screen, including the main TSD (Tactical Situation Display) panel with the imaged tactical situation [2–4]. The HMDS system allows not only to directly display the selected parameters in front of the pilot's eyes, but it also gives the directive commands ordering the performance of necessary activities in case of alarms and warnings of emergency situations or defects received from the control systems and its technical condition (Fig. 1).

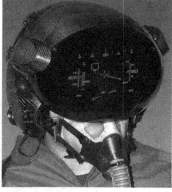

Fig. 1. F-35 aircraft cabin (on the left) and the pilot's helmet with HMDS (on the right) [2]

One of the elements to increase the safety of aircraft is the use of the so-called TCAS and GPWS collision avoidance systems. The TCAS system task is to reduce the possibility of a collision in the air by warning the pilot of the approach of other aircraft [8, 9]. In turn, the GPWS system is a system warning the pilots of a distance of their aircraft in relation to the ground [6, 7, 11]. The above-mentioned systems allow not only to directly inform the aircraft crew (pilot) on the occurrence of the collision risk situation (which is very important during manoeuvring flights and the descent approach), but they also give directive commands (ordering the activities necessary to perform the obstacle "by-passing" manoeuvre). The maintenance of the aircraft as valuable combat means on the modern battlefield requires a permanent increase in its operational capabilities and ability to survive. The currently carried out development works in the field of the collision avoidance systems and the radio communication systems indicate the possibilities of using this information in the helmet-mounted data presentation systems, among others, in the SWPL-1 Cyklop helmet-mounted flight parameter display system.

2 Analysis of the Data Imaging Method for Radio Communication and Collision Avoidance Systems

The data presentation systems have evolved from piloting-navigational instruments placed in the cockpit, requiring the pilot to look away, and the application of the latest technology through the helmet-mounted data imaging systems. Depending on the aircraft destination and complexity degree of the integrated avionic system, the pilot owing to the helmet-mounted imaging system receives data on the spatial position of the aircraft, radio navigation data, information on targets and owned weaponry. The helmet-mounted system provides the pilot with imagining the basic flight parameters, tracking the target and choosing the weaponry in different weather conditions.

One of the latest design solutions is a helmet with the HMDS system for the F-35 Lightning II Strike Fighter multi-task aircraft (Fig. 2).

Fig. 2. Data imaging on the helmet-mounted display of the F-35 aircraft (day-night) [4]

The possibilities of imaging data on radio communication in the helmet-mounted targeting systems were presented in the helmet with the HMDS of the F-35 multi-task aircraft (Fig. 3). In addition to an oxygen mask (1), the helmet has a built-in headset (2, 4) connected to the on-board computer of the aircraft with the use of a digital data cable (3). On the helmet viewfinder, owing to the image projectors (5), the information on radio data (radio frequency at which communication with command posts is maintained, flight speed, altitude and targeting data for all weaponry variants) is displayed. The display also shows the alarms and warnings occurring in an emergency situation, when the pilot is informed about potential dangers occurring during the mission performance, and this time, his sight is turned to the other side of the aircraft. Lighting green eyes, a round shape and a carbon structure of the helmet of the F-35 fighter pilot make it look important both in terms of safety and data imaged on the helmet-mounted display.

The image projectors display data on the helmet viewfinders in front of the pilot's eyes thus forming two green points [4]. The imaging of basic information, i.e. the radio operating parameters (radio channel, frequency) on the helmet-mounted display increases the so-called pilot's situational awareness, and the supply of more perfect navigation aids and more effective use of the weaponry system.

Fig. 3. Helmet with an in-built radio communication system for the F-35 multi-task aircraft [6] (Color figure online)

In order to meet these requirements, it is estimated that there is the possibility of presenting the data obtained from the collision avoidance system and radio communication system (Fig. 4) in the helmet-mounted targeting systems. However, the development of guidelines as to the way of imaging on the helmet-mounted displays requires a detailed analysis of the current method of presenting the data received from these systems and displayed on MFD multifunction displays (Multifunction Displays) [6].

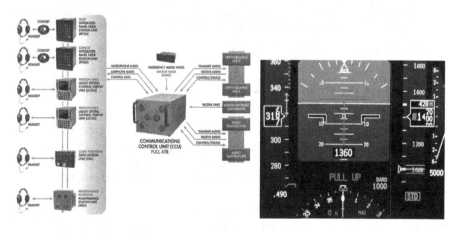

Fig. 4. View of the communication and collision avoidance systems [4]

2.1   Imaging of Data from the Radio Communication System on the MFD Multifunction Displays

The modern Western solutions in terms of the integrated communication system are based on IT solutions, and the typical radio communication system constitutes an analogy of the computer system. Aviation communication is one of the main tools on the aircraft board, and the essential requirements for it have been the same for many years (i.e. certainty and secrecy). It means securing the radio transmission from interception and deciphering of correspondence by the enemy. This system as the so-called intercom must provide communication on the aircraft board, and the pilot (crew) must maintain communication from the aircraft or helicopter board with other units (e.g. command post, convoy, and other aircraft, etc.) [3]. The imaging on the MFD multifunction displays of basic operating parameters of individual on-board radios (radio channel, frequency), provides the pilot with comfort during the performance of a flight operation, in which the radio communication is necessary (Fig. 5).

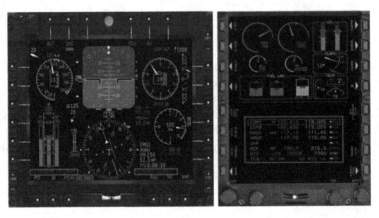

Fig. 5. Examples of imaging the basic radio communication parameters on MFD [4]

2.2   Imaging of Data from the Collision Avoidance System on the MFD Multifunction Displays

The signals received from the collision avoidance system, owing to ensuring the flight safety of the own aircraft and objects in its surrounding, should have a priority in the data presentation to the other information given to the pilot and should be presented in a special way with the maintenance of the so-called notification redundancy.

2.2.1   TCAS Collision Avoidance Warning System

Depending on the aircraft destination and complexity degree of the integrated avionic system, the pilot owing to the helmet-mounted imaging system receives data on the spatial position of the aircraft, piloting and radio navigation data, information on targets and owned weaponry. The modern Western solutions in terms of the collision avoidance systems are based on IT solutions, and typical TCAS constitutes an analogy of the computer system. The TCAS system monitors the airspace surrounding the aircraft by listening to signals from the radar transponders of other aircraft, which may pose a threat and communicate with other aircraft equipped with the TCAS system coordinating the manoeuvres appropriate to the situation. The system displays the information on the situation in the air on the multifunction displays, warns with voice messages of the possibility of a collision in the air, and if necessary, advises (orders) a horizontal manoeuvre necessary to avoid the collision [10].

The TCAS system sends and receives the following information on the aircraft posing a threat, i.e. a range between the own aircraft and the aircraft that can pose a threat, relative bearing to the aircraft posing a threat, altitude and vertical speed of the aircraft that may pose a threat and the approach speed of aircraft on collision courses. With the use of the data, the system predicts time and a distance from the potential collision point with the aircraft, the movement of which poses a threat. The system in the TCAS II version predicts, whether the safety border can be exceeded, and in this case, it generates TA (Traffic Advisory) in order to warn the pilot that the collision point is nearby. If the aircraft posing a threat continues the flight on the collision course, the system will give RA (Resolution Advisory) for ensuring safe vertical separation between aircraft on the collision courses. The TCAS system generates the alert and protected zones that provide safe separation assuming that the reaction time is 5 s [9, 10, 12]. The zones increasing the vertical separation or change in their direction require the reaction within 2.5 s (Fig. 6).

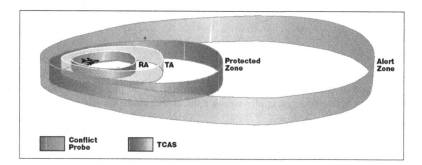

Fig. 6. TCAS system alert zones [9]

Two aircraft equipped with the TCAS system will coordinate their orders (RA) using the transponders operating in the S mode. This coordination ensures the generation of opposing warnings in the aircraft flying on the collision courses. The pilots should smoothly but strongly perform the recommended manoeuvres. The aircraft pilot is never allowed to perform manoeuvres in the opposite direction to the ones ordered by the TCAS system. The system can track up to 60 aircraft at the same time and display up to 30 aircraft on the indicators. Advisory indications include slight deviation from the calculated flight path at the time of the vertical separation generation.

On the MFD multifunction displays, the system can display four types of warnings depending on the position of the aircraft that may pose a threat and its approach speed to the own aircraft. These symbols change the color and shape so as to properly present a threat level and pay attention to the pilot. The symbols of movement can be also combined with the information on the altitude difference (relative altitude) between aircraft expressed in hundreds of feet.

In addition, the information, whether the "intruder" aircraft climbs, descends or keeps a constant flight level, can be additionally displayed. The "+" sign at the relative altitude digits means that the "intruder" aircraft is above, and the minus sign means that the "intruder" aircraft is below. An upwards arrow means that the "intruder" aircraft on the collision course climbs at the speed of 500 ft/min or more, however, a downwards arrow means that the "intruder" aircraft descends at the speed of 500 ft/min or more. The digits that mean the relative altitude and horizontal flight tendency (climb, descent) will not be displayed, if the intruder aircraft does not have a response function which contains an altitude report NAR (Non-Altitude Reporting).

If an error occurs in the determination of the "intruder" aircraft bearing, "NO BEARING" will be displayed on the multifunction display screen (Fig. 7).

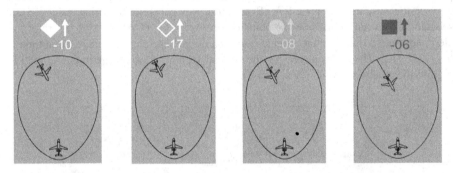

Fig. 7. Examples of the air situation imaging (movement not posing a threat, movement that may pose a threat, movement potentially posing a threat and resolution advisories) [7]

Each pilot has the ability to control the data overlapping from TCAS through the own MFD. The information displayed from the TCAS system is to ensure better imaging of air traffic and differentiation of threat levels (Fig. 8) [9, 10].

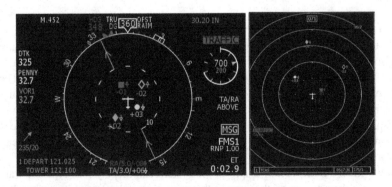

Fig. 8. Examples of imaging the air traffic and differentiation of the threat levels [9]

2.2.2   GPWS Warning System (EGPWS)

The GPWS system is designed to warn the pilot of the excessive speed of approaching the ground, a sudden decrease in the flight altitude without changing the aircraft vertical speed, a sudden decrease in speed without the aircraft altitude change, the need to release flaps, excessive low deviation of a glide path, too excessive tilting, the possibility of a collision with a terrain obstacle or a building obstacle, and it provides messages on the flight altitude during landing. The GPWS uses data from the field database, as well as piloting and radio navigation systems. Based on this information, the warnings of approaching the ground are developed. The pilots receive voice messages and light signals in advance, so as to make it possible to take the aircraft out of a dangerous situation [7, 8, 11].

Depending on the situation and the flight phase, six modes of the EGPWS operation were distinguished [11]:

1. Exceeding the descent speed – it provides "SINK RATE" warning with an excessively rapid decrease in the flight altitude. In the final approach phase, the warning is activated when exceeding the vertical speed of 1 000 ft/s (305 m/s).
2. Terrain elevation increase – At a distance of 90 s of flight from the expected intersection of the flight trajectory with the ground surface, the system provides the "CAUTION, TERRAIN" information and activates the "TERR" light. At a distance of 30 s from the forecast collision place, the "TERRAIN TERRAIN - PULL UP, PULL UP" warning and the "PULL UP" warning light are activated.
3. The loss of the altitude after take-off – The system provides the "DON'T SINK" warning ("TERR" light), if up to the altitude of 50 ft (15.2 m), the aircraft starts to descend. This mode is active until reaching the altitude of 700 ft (213 m) above the obstacles.
4. Exceeding the altitude of 500 ft (152.4 m) above the ground level – Decrease in the altitude up to 500 ft is signalled by voice: "FIVE HUNDRED". This mode is activated when the aircraft flies close to the ground and the modes 1 and 2 are inactive.
5. The approach below the glide path – indicates the descent below the 3-degree glide path. It is activated during the approach according to ILS, after the release of the landing gear.
6. The warning of excessive tilting – It is activated after exceeding the bank angle depending on the altitude: 40° in case of 150 ft (46 m) above the ground, and to 10° at the altitude of 30 ft (9 m).

The operation mode presented in Fig. 9 corresponds to the flight phase during the landing approach over a diverse terrain. During landing, the entry of the aircraft into the danger zone will be indicated by voice signalling with the repeating message "TERRAIN - TERRAIN" and activation of a red warning light.

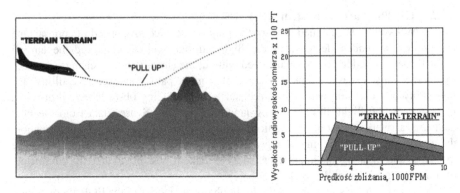

Fig. 9. Example of excessive speed of approaching the ground over a diverse terrain (Wysokość radiowysokościomierza – Radio altimeter height, Prędkość zbliżania – Approach speed) [11] (Color figure online)

After the signal lamp activation, the "PULL-UP" voice message is heard. After hearing any of the messages, it is important to immediately increase the altitude until switching off the light and voice signals. The signalling and messages of the EGPWS system are displayed on the display indicator below the horizon. The "PULL UP" message and the "GPWS" status are displayed in red, when the EGPWS system generates basic (like, e.g. the "SINK RATE" message) and terrain warnings. The messages blink for five seconds, and then, they are displayed in a continuous manner. The "GPWS" status is displayed in yellow, when the warning or terrain modes are active (Fig. 10).

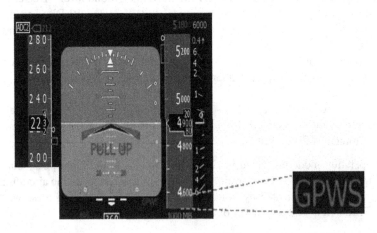

Fig. 10. View of the "PULL UP" message and the GPWS status of the EGPWS system on the display indicator below the horizon [7] (Color figure online)

The warning messages are generated individually and in case of the simultaneous occurrence of the several following messages, they are generated in the appropriate order starting from the message with the highest priority. The warning messages presented in Table 1 and generated in the appropriate operation mode of the system [11].

Table 1. Voice warning messages [11]

Item	Voice Messages	
1	**BANK ANGLE**	Boundary bank angle
2	**DON'T SINK**	Do not descend
3	**FIVE HUNDRED**	Exceeding the altitude of 500 ft AGL
4	**GLIDESLOPE**	Glide path (descent below the glide path)
5	**MINIMUS-MINIMUS**	Decision altitude achievement
6	**PULL UP**	Increase the altitude
7	**SINK RATE**	Excessive descent
8	**TERRAIN - TERRAIN**	Excessive speed of approaching the ground
9	**TOO LOW, FLAPS**	Low altitude, release the flaps
10	**TOO LOW, TERRAIN**	Insufficient separation over the terrain
11	**OBSTACLE, OBSTACLE**	Obstacle (structure, antenna, etc.)
12	**CAUTION TERRAIN**	Caution terrain
13	**CAUTION OBSTACLE**	Caution obstacle

3 Proposal of a Method for Data Presentation on the HMDS Displays

In order to meet these requirements and improve the so-called pilot's (crews') situational and tactical awareness in terms of the collision avoidance and radio communication systems, it is possible to image basic information, among others, on the situation in the air, collision possibility, and also warning the pilot (crew) of excessive speed of approaching the ground, on the helmet-mounted display. The provision of the pilot with more perfect radio navigation aids will allow for more efficient use of the data presentation system in the helmet-mounted systems and they will improve the safety of the performance of flights.

3.1 Imaging of the Radio Communication System Operating Parameters on the MFD Displays

In order to meet these requirements and improve the so-called crews' situational awareness in the field of radio communication of the Polish military helicopters in the Avionics Division of Air Force Institute of technology, an integrated avionic system (ZSA), which one of the elements is an integrated radio communication system (ZSŁ), was developed. It constitutes an IT set of the communication server, air and tactical radios necessary to implement each air task.

In order to control the integrated radio communication system, the MW-1 multi-function displays (Fig. 11), on which there are buttons to select the radio and subscribers in the internal and external communication, are used. The screen images the connection states, communication types and operating parameters of the selected on-board radio. The helicopter crew controls (by multifunction displays and devices dedicated for individual on-board radios) the integrated radio communication system elements having consistent contact with the environment by the internal and external communication. Depending on the tasks performed by the helicopter crew and the threat level, the parameters from individual radios and radio navigation data from other subsystems of the integrated avionic system (including the so-called warning signals) are transferred to the communication server [3].

Fig. 11. View of the multifunction display with elements of the integrate radio communication system built in the W-3PL Głuszec helicopter [3] (Color figure online)

The radio communication data presentation on the multifunction displays of the integrated avionic system (ZSA) confirmed that such a system can be integrated with the SWPL-1 Cyklop helmet-mounted flight parameter display system (Fig. 12). The standalone version of the helmet-mounted display will significantly affect the improvement of safety during the flight in a difficult terrain (e.g. in the mountains) or at night with the use of NVG (Night Vision Goggles) [5].

The main objective of the management integration of the helmet-mounted targeting system on the W-3PL helicopter board in terms of radio communication will be the improvement of a safety level of flights, as well as relief and improvement of the crew's situational awareness in the day-night conditions by improvement of imaging the radio navigation systems and systems of controlling the targeting system during the implementation of operational tasks.

Fig. 12. Example of the pilot's helmet of the SWPL-1 system with imaging the piloting-navigational parameters and elements of the radio communication system data presentation [5]

A characteristic feature of the helmet-mounted imaging system will be multi-functionality, which will result in the situation that also the crew will be able to use the radio system at the same time and choose the operating mode of other devices in the field of the so-called piloting-navigational signals, target data and weaponry selection. The open architecture of the SWPL-1 helmet-mounted flight parameter display and full control over its software allows to prepare the integration and management of the helicopter helmet-mounted system, creating a completely new system.

3.2 Imaging of the Collision Avoidance System Operating Parameters on the MFD Displays

The presentation of data from the warning collision avoidance systems in each aircraft with the built-in TCAS and GPWS (EGPWS) systems confirmed that such systems can be integrated with the SWPL-1 Cyklop helmet-mounted flight parameter display (Fig. 13). The standalone version of the helmet-mounted display will significantly affect the improvement of safety during the performance of flights in a difficult terrain (e.g. in the mountain area) or at night with the use of NVG (Night Vision Goggles) [5, 7].

The main objective of integration and management of the helmet-mounted flight parameter system on the military helicopter board in the field of the warning collision avoidance systems will be the autonomy and improvement of the crew's situational and tactical awareness in all flight conditions by imaging the warning signals from the above-mentioned collision avoidance systems.

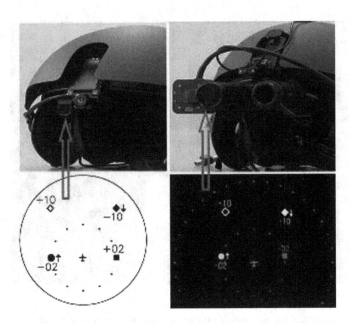

Fig. 13. SWPL-1 helmet-mounted flight parameter display and the example of imaging the emergency situation day and night [7] (Color figure online)

The day and night display of the helmet-mounted flight parameter display, the following intruder aircraft symbols are indicated.

- Depending on the configuration, there will be:
- harmless movement displayed as an open diamond (unfilled),
- close movement which may pose a threat displayed as a filled white diamond,
- close movement posing a threat TA (Traffic Advisory) displayed as a yellow filled circle,
- imminent threat RA (Resolution Advisory) displayed as a filled red square.

On the "OPER" operational board of the SWPL-1 helmet-mounted flight parameter display, the proposals of imaging the TCAS and GPWS warning collision avoidance systems. The pilot during the task performance can choose one of the available boards which is essential for him in a given flight phase (Fig. 14).

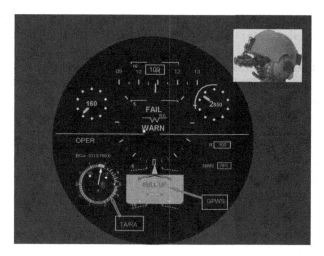

Fig. 14. SWPL-1 helmet-mounted flight parameter display and the example of imaging the emergency situation on the "OPER" board [7]

The above presented examples of the SWPL-1 helmet-mounted flight parameter display with the collision avoidance and radio communication systems constitute a basis for the development of the helmet-mounted targeting system dedicated for the military helicopters operated in the Polish Armed Forces.

4 Conclusion

Each older generation aircraft, after building the modern helmet-mounted data imaging system in, extends its operational capabilities with the application that has been unattainable so far, such as multi-functionality and ability to survive in the current battlefield. The display system (HMDS) built in the helmet of the F-35 multi-task aircraft pilot provides the pilots with a very high level of the situational and tactical awareness improvement. The possibility of detecting and locating the targets, deter-mination of the targets by direct looking at them and the built-in night-vision system with the use of the integrated cameras allow the pilot to perform each flight operation. The performed analyses and results of the model tests in terms of the reliability of information received from the selected collision avoidance and radio communication systems allowed for integration with the SWPL-1 Cyklop helmet-mounted flight parameter system. The SWPL-1 helmet-mounted system allows to directly image information from the warning collision avoidance systems and gives the directive commands related to the warning of dangerous situations during the flight. Each military helicopter equipped with the TCAS and EGPWS systems will expand its operational capabilities and gain multifunctionality in the field of performing the operational and tactical tasks. The imaging of important information which is, among others, warning the crew of a collision with another aircraft and warning of fast approaching the ground (obstacle) on the helmet-mounted display would not only increase the pilot's situational awareness within the framework of the performed task but it would also shorten the time to react in case of a danger, resulting in better use of this system.

The digital signal processing and the need for the presentation of data from on-board radios in the SWPL-1 helmet-mounted system will increase the safety and network-centric activities.

The open architecture of the SWPL-1 helmet-mounted flight parameter display and control of its integration software allows for preparation of integration with the collision avoidance systems and the integrated radio communication system and management, creating a modern helmet-mounted imaging system.

References

1. Russo, B.M., et al.: Helmet-Mounted Displays Sensation, Perception and Cognition Issues, USA (2009)
2. Vision Systems International (VSI, Elbit Systems/Rockwell Collins) F-35 Lightning II Strike Fighter, USA (2010)
3. Kowalczyk, H.: Technical description and Instructions for use of the integrated helicopter system W3PL, Communication System, Warsaw, AFIT (2008)
4. Lockheed Martin: Terminator Helmet for F-35 Pilots, USA (2009)
5. Borowski, J.: SWPL-1 flight parameters display system for Mi17 helicopters. Technical description and Instructions for use, Warsaw, AFIT (2010)
6. Pazur, A.: Possibilities and needs for the presentation of radio communication data in helmeted mounted systems used in air transport, LOGITRANS 2012, Szczyrk, Poland (2012)
7. Pazur, A.: Model studies of anti-collision systems in the field of improving the safety of air transport systems, LogiTrans Szczyrk, Buses, Techniques, Exploitation, Transport Systems No. 3/2013, Poland (2013)
8. Allied Signal Collision Avoidance System CAS 67 ACAS II Pilot's Guide. USA (1999)
9. Anti-collision system TCAS II CAS 67A. Technical Description of the Aircraft M28B/PT, Mielec Poland (2010)
10. Anti-collision system TCAS-4000. Technical Description of the Aircraft M28B/PT GLASS COCKPIT, Mielec Poland (2010)
11. Warning system EGPWS. Technical Description of the Aircraft M28B/PT, Mielec Poland (2010)
12. TCASII/ACASII, Collision Avoidance System User's Manual. USA (2000)

General About Telematics

Modern Telematics and Its Impact on Safety Development

Andrzej Bujak[✉]

WSB University in Wrocław, Fabryczna 29-31, Wrocław, Poland
andrzej.bujak@interia.pl

Abstract. Safety is not only one of the fundamental human needs but also a condition for economic and social development. The technological and industrial revolution of recent years has significantly affected the shaping of the level of safety, generating new threats on the one hand, and new opportunities on the other. Telematics has an essential place among these new possibilities, and, owing to the development of technology, miniaturisation and digital transformation of our world, has become a tool which has an essential impact on the shaping of the level of safety. However, an essential condition in this case, is the perception and recognition of these new possibilities, their proper implementation and use. The pace and scale of changes in the area of telematics solutions produces a need to carry out many analyses and studies, the aim of which is to identify the best technologies and solutions as well as the ways of their implementation. Many of today's organisations do not know how to implement specific solutions and in what order, how to build systems and relationships in the digital world using telematics. The article attempts to identify and comprehensively approach the factors determining the use of such solutions and their implementation into practice.

Keywords: Safety · Digital transformation · Development of telematics · Visibility · Logistic 4.0

1 Introduction

The beginning of the 21st century brought an unprecedented development of digital technology, which is proceeding at a revolutionary pace. In the market of telecommunications, digital services and computer hardware, completely new products are constantly appearing. As a result, we have completely new possibilities for entities producing and using telematics tools and systems. Currently, telematics is a field of knowledge that integrates telecommunications, IT, social, and economic systems with the flows of raw materials, which are bonded by first obtaining, then processing and finally using the information properly [1].

Based on the analysis of the literature on the subject, it can be concluded that the current development of telematics solutions is focused on continuous improvement of existing information and telecommunications solutions, as well as on the emergence of new telematics solutions. Currently, such technologies as IT, information, teleinformation and telecommunications are not only used to automate the control of various

© Springer Nature Switzerland AG 2019
J. Mikulski (Ed.): TST 2019, CCIS 1049, pp. 409–421, 2019.
https://doi.org/10.1007/978-3-030-27547-1_29

processes or to read information, because they have a much wider application in the economy. This is due to the fact that current telematic systems are adapted both to support human work and to mutual cooperation on the plane of the machine-man, human-machine or machine-machine. This means that the 21st century is based on integrated artificial intelligence systems with physical systems represented by the human species. Importantly, this cooperation takes place taking into account all possible technological developments known today, which, combined with an appropriate approach to the organization of tasks, process management, allows creating tasks that maximize the positive aspects of telematics. This state of affairs in combination with dynamically developing economies means that the competition on the telematic services market is growing, which is why companies are still looking for modern system solutions that aim to optimize processes and costs.

Bearing in mind that in the modern world of permanent exchange of goods in connection with the flow of information, participants of this exchange are required to pay particular attention to ensuring an adequate level of security for the ongoing processes of this exchange. It should be emphasized here that the development of technology in this area occurs at a previously unprecedented rate. It affects the creation of completely new technological solutions. And this translates into the generation of new threats unknown so far.

Just like telematics, security is a broad concept, and consequently the slogan is variously defined in the literature of the subject. Most authors believe that security serves to prevent undesirable states, i.e. threats that may create difficulties for a specific group of people or for some undertaking. Therefore, it is determined that ensuring appropriate conditions for survival and the pursuit of interests by a specific group of entities, or one entity, is possible through proper and effective use of the potential. The use of resources should take place in such a way that the level of risk during the implementation of a specific project/project was minimal. In connection with the above, while implementing specific strategies of business entities, one of the primary goals should be the objective of risk minimization and counteracting threats to tasks that they perform. It should be remembered here that the once achieved level of security is not given for eternity. Because the phenomenon of security is a dynamic creation, changing both in time and space. It can be determined that this phenomenon is multidimensional. Knowledge in the area of security requires combining theory with practice, while practical activity includes a very wide range of ways to organize conditions for ensuring security, respect for human rights and creating conditions for the effective use of resources [2].

Analyzing the dynamic development of telematics solutions in combination with the trend of miniaturizing everything and maximizing the use of resources, the question arises whether the direction in which telematics science is "going" is desirable and what impact it has on the security level of processes by various types of entities that they participate in business life.

In connection with the above, the purpose of the article is to present an analysis of the impact of telematic solutions used in everyday life of an ordinary person as well as an employee and state apparatus authorities on the level of security. The work is based on: literature analysis of the subject and statistical data obtained from enterprises offering their services in the TSL industry.

The study uses a method of system analysis of information focused on the analysis of secondary sources. The monographic method, statistical methods and methods of comparative analysis were also used. The results of the research were presented using descriptive techniques, tabular techniques and graphic techniques.

2 Telematics and Safety

The last decade of 20th century and the beginning of 21st century resulted in numerous revolutionary changes following a dynamic development of scientific and technical progress. As a consequence, a lot of phenomena, actions and processes as well as the entire global economy and the world have been perceived in a new way. New technological solutions very often generated new possibilities and solutions in many areas of our social and economic life. A wide application of new ICT technologies (in particular the internet) as a communication platform not only led to a different perception of globalization processes but also to further changes to organizational processes and management in business. They powered a lot of changes and constituted the basis for building new concepts and strategies of various scale and scope. Figure 2 is an example illustrating this process and showing trends related to management of the supply chain also indicating two basic factors of these changes such as new technologies and networks.

Obtaining the appropriate level of security that is acceptable to all entities, regardless of whether we are talking about a single person or a group of people is associated with the need to shape a kind of safety culture in enterprises. Building it both in a private and state organization and in the everyday life of people is a long and difficult process that requires strictly defined goals and tailored tools for a given situation and a group of people or individuals. In the study, the starting point for further considerations is the statement that safety is one of the basic needs of every human being. As of today, it is difficult to indicate the area of human activity in which security issues would not play a key role. This does not mean, however, that man always behaves in a way in which he ensures an adequate level of security. There are social units that are not able to act without proper supervision, in such a way that they do not cause harm to themselves or to someone, even by destroying their own property or someone else's property.

The perception of security will be different for each person and for each organization. Such a situation results, above all, from the difference of interest and from the fact that each unit has its own individual comfort zone. Therefore, it seems that tools in the form of telematic systems in the future will allow to achieve a certain security level that will be acceptable for the majority of the society. Before this happens, however, it should be noted that current telematic systems have different applications in various sectors of human, business and state activity. Today, these systems are usually autonomous/centrally controlled and not always related to each other in a rational and safe manner. This means that telematic systems are not fully used and constitute a source of potential threats and attacks/cyber-attacks for their users.

As a result, the question arises how telematics systems work, where and how they can be used and for what purpose?

In general, it is possible to assume thesis/hypothesis that telematics relies on the connection of telecommunications, IT, teleinformation and information solutions with the use of automatic reading solutions, which are then used to effectively control various types of physical systems. In addition, the main telematics tasks include the analysis of the infrastructure status to the possibility of organizing processes performed on this infrastructure. Thanks to these systems, maintenance, management and control become processes/systems more effective.

Consequently, the level of security increases and the operating costs of individual systems in enterprises decrease. Process optimization is possible by integrating the flow of information between particular subsystems. It should be noted that telematics systems have special properties. First of all, they are most often used for systems that are spatially dispersed and have a large number of elements. At the same time it is pointed out that the use of telematic solutions makes sense in cases in which there is a superior role of communication between the user and the environment. This is done through the continuous development of IT equipment capabilities and integrating the functions of electronic techniques with the capabilities of interoperability of various hardware with specific software [3]. Whereas today's unlimited possibilities of data processing practically allow for immediate reaction of changes, modernization and making corrections in the operation of systems and people participating in them. Indication of changes in operating conditions that take place around this processing would not be possible without the following components [3]:

- electronic communication, connecting individual elements of the telematics system (WAN sub-networks, LAN local networks, mobile telecommunications networks, satellite systems, GSM systems, etc.),
- obtaining information (measuring sensors, video cameras, radars, satellites, drones, RFID tags, etc.),
- information presentation for telematics system administrators (GIS systems, access control systems, etc.),
- presentation of information for system users (VMS variable signs, traffic lights, radio broadcasting, Internet technologies - WAP, WWW, SMS, MMS, VMI, etc.).

On the basis of the above, it can be concluded that the basic functions of telematics systems are the functions of effective information management, both at the stage of its acquisition, then processing, distribution along with transmission and its secondary use in decision-making processes. At the same time, these processes can be carried out automatically without human intervention, i.e. they are described in advance with appropriate algorithms. An example is automatic traffic control in the form of traffic lights at an early stage of development, currently used ITS, i.e. intelligent transport systems that control traffic based on traffic volume analysis, autonomously adjusting the time of great traffic to the current traffic. In the second variant, the use of telematics is based on controlling processes resulting from ad hoc situations, which are collected from readers registering then processed into data on the basis of which decisions are made by the dispatcher who manages the given infrastructure.

The speed with which technology is evolving today has a significant impact on telematic technologies and systems as well as their development. It is a response to an increase in the requirements of the participants in the supply chain, in terms of time of service provision, their flexibility, availability and reliability. On the other hand, there is a need to reduce costs and reduce the amount of frozen capital in companies as well as tailored products and services to their individual consumer needs. Modern telematics can meet this requirement and provides the ability to efficiently respond to potential threats occurring in the supply chain. The configuration of a smart network requires the use of a wide range of technologies and telematics solutions.'

Telematics, similarly to previously presented concepts, is constantly developing, especially in the area of transport. The evolution of these systems is shown in Fig. 1. According to the evaluations, the international telematics market will grow very rapidly. It is assumed that by 2025, 104 million new cars will be on the network. Penetration of global integrated telematics to touch 88% for new cars by 2025, while that of tethered telematics to flatten around 28% [4].

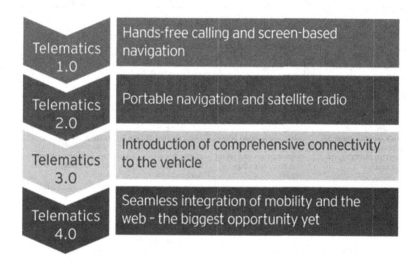

Fig. 1. Evolution of automotive telematics [4]

The use of telematics solutions and technologies in the digital transformation requires taking many actions related to, among others:

- defining the telematics system and its components consistent with the assumptions of this transformation;
- defining the needs, the scope of services and the necessary infrastructure for their implementation;
- identifying differences in telematics strategy operating in various sectors of the economy (vehicles, management, health, information, etc.)
- adoption of cost-effective development strategies, ensuring compatibility and implementation.

Along with digital transformation, new challenges and opportunities arise towards telematics. In particular, they concern the need and possibilities of building new customer interactions, expanding telematics services in various areas, practical implantation of concepts and considerations into business practice, and constitute the essence of this transformation.

The development of modern tools and telematics systems has accelerated dynamically at the start of the so-called Revolution 4.0, which in connection with the digitization of processes and cost reduction resulted in more and more access to modern telematics systems, which is illustrated in the figure below (Fig. 2).

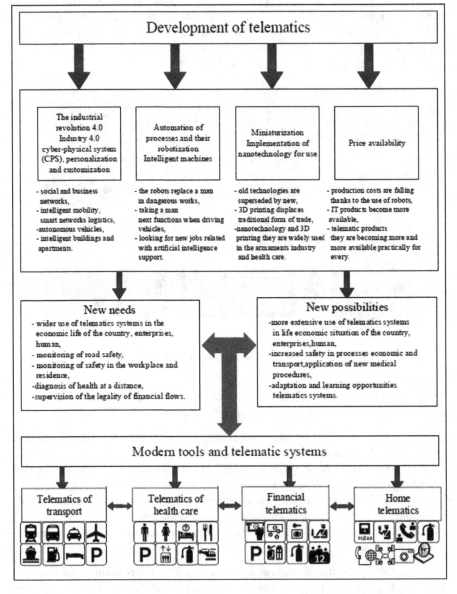

Fig. 2. Development of telematics tools and systems in terms of new opportunities as well as needs [own study]

Tools and telematics systems have both positive and negative sides, Table 1 shows the typical applications of thematic systems and the basic benefits of their implementation for use. It should be noted that the current world is no longer able to function without these solutions. This is due to the fact that telematics can support many functional areas of both the city, as well as transport and health services, and even a single citizen. Due to the above, its application should be considered in a multifaceted manner. The various applications of computer and telecommunications techniques coordinate the flow of information in principle for most spheres in which human beings are present. This means that these solutions can support both services that protect safety and support transport systems or parking cars in a given city. These solutions support the activities of state administration at least by introducing elements of electronic democracy [5].

Currently, telematic systems are necessary for the functioning of production, transport and social subsystems, which support the aspects of effective management of these subsystems in many areas of modern life.

Such actions result directly in the improvement of the quality of functioning of these subsystems, and thus of man. This happens, among others by increasing the ability to control the flows of human and material streams and financial flows throughout the entire economic system, while limiting the phenomenon of congestion, commonly occurring in the 21st century. The phenomenon of congestion is currently one of the most important problems occurring in supply chains. This phenomenon generates further difficulties such as environmental pollution, increased noise levels, increased accident rate, increased operating costs of logistic and social systems, and others. The increase in congestion is influenced on the one hand by the growing number of motor vehicles and the dynamic way of life and developed societies, which generates the need for frequent and rapid movement of people and loads. Thanks to the use of telematics solutions, it is possible to limit it even by replacing dispersed individual transport with collective transport (e.g. urban transport in relation to the transport of people, or solutions based on consolidation of cargo in relation to freight transport) [5].

The phenomenon of congestion has a significant impact on the level of security of users of a given system. For example, heavy traffic causes nervousness among drivers who become aggressive, the aggression translates into undesirable behavior, which in turn leads to accidents. In the case of health care, too long queues cause difficult access to a specialist, which results in a feeling of helplessness that makes him feel anxious. Excessive waiting times for a specialist appointment can even lead to life-threatening conditions in the patient. In the case of financial institutions, congestion can also have a negative impact on both the institutions themselves and their clients. In the case of an institution, this may be a loss of a client who waits too long for service or an outbreak of uncontrolled aggression among the serviced, which may expose a financial institution to material and reputational losses. In the case of customers, they are exposed to theft, which for some people become a tragedy in life. It should be remembered that every gathering of people is a perfect place to conduct business by people involved in theft.

Table 1. Positive and negative aspects of the use of telematics tools in various sectors of social life [own study]

Area of application	Transport sector (Telematics of transport)	Healthcare sector (Medical telematics)	Financial sector (Financial telematics)	Private sector (Home telematics)
The main application of telematics in the described sector	• Automatic Fee Collection. • Freight and Fleet Management Systems. • Public Transport. • Traffic and Traveller Information • Traffic Control. • Road Traffic Data. • Automatic Vehicle Identification. • After Theft Systems for Recovery of Stolen Vehicle. • Use in insurance for billing that depends on your driving style.	• IT systems supporting documentation. Decision support systems in medicine, regional • IT systems in health care management. Medical teleconference and teleconsultation systems; • Internet systems and applications supporting diagnostics, treatment and monitoring of patients. • Internet services for patients, the public and healthcare professionals. • Access to scientific articles on the medical cases discussed • No possibility to wait in two queues for the same type.	• Performing financial operations without the need to visit financial institutions. • Remote payment processing systems, • Virtual stores. • e-money, e-bank • Electronic form of banknotes or coins. • The ability to make payments between different countries in a short time. • The ability to monitor transactions by each participant	• Control and support systems for the use of various technical building systems and separate rooms. • Control systems for lighting, heating, ventilation and air conditioning. • Control systems for communication means (telephone, television, computer), • Home access security control systems (person identification, robbery or burglary signalling) • Safety control systems (gas, water, fire). • Home supply sustenance systems (cooking, washing, vacuuming, mowing etc.).
The main benefits of using telematics in the sector described	• Traffic control and optimal control • Reduced costs of infrastructure and vehicle use. • Decrease in the number of adverse behaviours. • Access to vehicle information and traffic situation in real time. • Optimal use of technical means of transport. • Management of driver fatigue.	• Reduction in the queue lengths for specialists in the system. • A summary of the entire patient's medical history from each specialist in one place. • Possibility to analyse the patient's condition without the participation of a doctor and at a distance. • Reduction of system operation costs. • Access to medical knowledge from various medical centres.	• Reduction of transaction costs. • Extended access to financial services • Monitored transactions from the application level without leaving your home. • Transaction automation. • Facilitated access to financial resources.	• Increased living safety of residents. • Possibility of remote monitoring of the house status. • Automatic notification of emergency services. • Informing users about threats (fire, burglary, flood, etc.). • Saves time.
Typical threats resulting from the use of telematics in the sector described	• Depriving the driver of the ability to assess the traffic situation. • Erroneous indications of telematic devices. • Drop in driver vigilance on the road while driving. • Negative feelings and reactions to permanent monitoring of activity.	• Addiction of users from e-diagnosis. • Declining confidence in diagnoses given by people. • A decrease in the level of medical knowledge of a traditional doctor	• Loss of control over finances as a result of giving up access to traditional money. • Lack of payment means in the absence of energy supply. • Permanent state surveillance regarding consumer financial activity.	• Loss of vigilance resulting from a sense of too high level of security. • The possibility of outside attacks on telematics systems at home. • The disappearance of social relations as a result of the virtualization of the life of social units. • The closure of social units within their telematic fortresses.
Typical hazards resulting from the use of telematics in the described sector (common for all sectors)	• High costs of creating new telematic solutions. • Over-dependence of people on telematics solutions. • Depriving the user of the systems of the right to self-determination and decision-making. • Depriving people of decision-making and executive skills. • Possibility of taking control over a human by artificial intelligence systems and telematic systems. • No possibility of action in the event of a system failure or lack of access to energy sources. • Lack of integration of information flow between individual telematic systems.	• Over-dependence of people on telematic solutions. • Depriving the user of the right to self-determination and decision-making.	• High costs of creating new telematic solutions. • Over-dependence of people on telematics solutions. • Depriving the user of the systems of the right to self-determination and decision-making. • Depriving people of decision-making and executive skills. • Possibility of taking control over a human by artificial intelligence systems and telematic systems. • No possibility of action in the event of a system failure or lack of access to energy sources. • Be vulnerable to external attacks (e.g. hacking attack, cutting off power sources).	

It should be emphasized here that the use of telematics systems in the above-mentioned systems reduces the risk of undesirable behavior, thus increasing the level of security. It should be noted, however, that other factors also influence the level of safety in various types of economic subsystems. We are talking here about economic security created by political spheres. The political circumstances of economic security are closely related to economic conditions, because they depend on each other and cannot occur independently. Therefore, there can be no question of increasing security without taking into account the role of the state in this phenomenon [6].

It should be noted that the state, apart from the security and economic aspects, creates an important role in regulating the rules of using existing telematics solutions as well as implementing new ones. At the same time, the state should remember that these regulations do not hinder the creative and constructive shaping of economic and technical-organizational security policy. This does not change the fact that the rules for the use of telematic systems should take the form of institutionalized determinants of shaping security. This is due to the fact that the width and depth of connections between telematics systems and security determinants make them mutually verifiable.

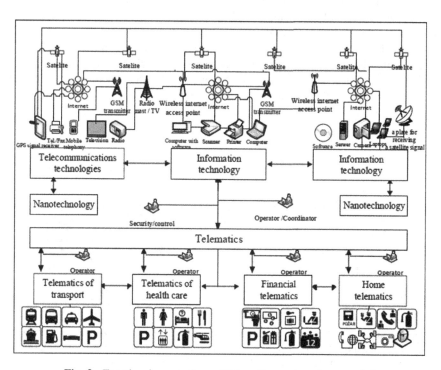

Fig. 3. Functional connections of telematics systems [own study]

In connection with the above, the question arises how should the process of implementing new telematics solutions look like and verify those already in force? It should be remembered that implementing new solutions is not always safe for their users. Whereas functioning telematic systems, from safe ones, may no longer meet safety requirements. Each such action requires a well-prepared procedure that will check the efficiency of telematics systems, their communication methods and tools to ensure an adequate level of security. The concept of applying telematics solutions and monitoring of already functioning telematics systems for selected areas of society functioning will be presented below (Fig. 3).

When designing implementation procedures and checking telematics systems, it should be remembered that these systems and applications are constructed for specific processes and an important feature of telematics applications is the ability to effectively associate various subsystems and introduce them into a coordinated operating mode. This means that currently implemented solutions are intelligent and have the ability to learn, and thus they are able to adapt to changes of the environment. In connection with the above, each algorithm/procedure should take into account measures to prevent loss of control over telematics systems and the possibility of their hard shutdown. And hence, it should also be remembered to create procedures in the event of the inability to use telematic devices and systems.

For the purposes of this article, research has been carried out in Lower Silesian enterprises that have their own transport fleets. These were companies that use their vehicles for a variety of tasks, including both manufacturing and service companies as well as those that provide transport services. The survey was conducted at the turn of January and February 2019. A total of 85 respondents were questioned using an interview questionnaire. The aim of the study was to check the level of awareness in enterprises in Lower Silesia about the possibility of using telematics devices and systems, and whether they are aware of the hazards resulting from it.

(a)   **(b)**

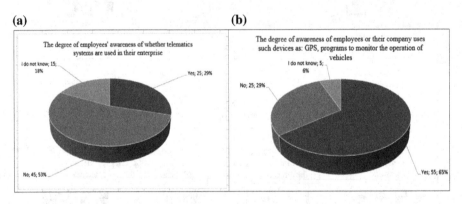

Fig. 4. a. The degree of employees' awareness of whether telematics systems are used in their enterprise [own study]. **b.** The degree of employees' awareness of whether their company uses such devices as: GPS, programs to monitor the operation of vehicles [own study].

In the first question, the respondents were asked if their systems and telematic devices are used in their enterprise. Most of the respondents, 53% said that they do not use such devices in their organization (Fig. 4a.). The results obtained in the second question are very interestingly combined with these answers, in which they asked whether the devices used to monitor vehicle activity are used in the company and whether specific computer programs that support this monitoring are used for this purpose. For the question asked, as many as 65% of the answers were positive (Fig. 4b).

In the third question, respondents were asked to determine the benefits for their company in the implementation of telematics systems and devices. On the basis of collected answers, it can be concluded that in almost every enterprise there was a group of similar benefits in the form of: drop of kilometers driven by drivers, decrease of fuel consumption, reduction of number of accidents, reduction of accidents and road collisions, increase of tire life, reduction of untimely deliveries/meetings. The differences achieved after the implementation of telematics solutions range from 9% on the decrease in the number of accidents to 20% with a decrease in the number of untimely deliveries (Fig. 5).

In the next question, the awareness regarding threats resulting from the use of telematic devices and systems was checked. It turns out that it is on a fairly good level. Practically in each company, the respondents pointed to specific groups of threats. The most frequently mentioned include: lack of autonomy for the driver, unlimited trust in telematics systems, suspension of the telematics system, failure of devices for data transmission, cyber-attacks, which unfortunately are negligible in many enterprises (Fig. 6).

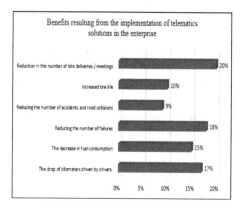

Fig. 5. Benefits resulting from the implementation of telematics solutions in the enterprise [own study].

Fig. 6. The degree of awareness about the risks that telematics solutions bring [own study].

3 Conclusion

It can be said that the place of security in the entire telematics system is extremely important and requires many more analyzes that will support this sector of the economy. From literature research it can be seen that this undertaking is not easy. This is due to the fact that there are many factors that create a typical telematic system.

And this combined with the economic aspect significantly affects the structure of these systems and the level of security during the use of these facilities. This is noticed by many authors. For example, J. Świniarski claims that: 'In the tradition of thinking about security, abundance, prosperity and wealth are often placed among its conditions. For a long time, happiness, prosperity and certainty of people's efforts to implement their lives (its prolongation and improvement) were made conditional upon economic circumstances. They were and are an element, a pillar and a factor and a premise of security. They are expressed by the component known today as economic security. On the other hand, it is based on some wealth, prosperity and abundance as well as income (national) or product (global) both produced and divided. Quite common is the belief that wealth and prosperity significantly complement happiness and security. Hence the situation of this component among the cardinal pillars on which security is supported, understood as a form of existence and life that ensures survival and increases the chances for its development, as a certainty of survival and freedom of development [7].

The aim of the article was an attempt to evaluate the impact of selected telematics subsystems, including particular emphasis on transport. It should be noted that the benefits of using telematics systems in transport as well as in other sectors are huge. Unfortunately, despite the many benefits, there is still a lot of resistance to their use. What is extremely important, the application of basic telematics solutions does not require large capital at all, and the benefits obtained from their implementation can significantly exceed the costs incurred for their implementation. Based on the literature, it can be concluded that both Japanese, European and Polish companies indicated a similar range of benefits from the use of telematics systems.

Summing up, on the basis of the conducted research, it can be assumed that both the use of telematics systems and devices increases the efficiency and effectiveness of using the company's resources, allowing for the optimization of expenses.

The presented research results allowed to formulate general conclusions in a very narrow scope of telematics application in the economic life of a human being. In the next stage, more in-depth research will be carried out and the scope of this research will be extended to the possibility of using other telematics tools towards a greater degree of their integration.

References

1. Badzińska, E., Ichorek, S.z.: Telematics systems in support of fleet management in road transport - case study. In: Scientific Papers of the University of Szczecin, No. 875 Problems of Management, Finance and Marketing No. 41, vol. 2 (2015)
2. Szymonik, A.: Management of economic security in the national security system, Logistics aspects, Monographs of the Lodz University of Technology, Łódź, p. 5 (2016)
3. Wydro, K.B.: Telematics - meanings and definitions of the term. In: Telecommunications and Information Technology, vol. 1–2, pp. 116–118 (2005)
4. http://www.ey.com/gl/en/industries/automotive/the-quest-for-telematics-4-0—overview. Accessed 4 Jan 2019

5. Małecki, K., Iwan, S.: Application of telematics solutions as a factor conditioning effective management of urban freight transport. In: Logistics - Science, Logistics, vol. 3, p. 4129 (2014)
6. Grosset, R.: Factors shaping the level of state security. In: Safety & Fire Technique, Józefów, p. 15 (2010)
7. Świniarski, J.: Military economics and the peace economy in the system of general security theory. In: Military Economics and Military Logistics - Similarities and Differences, Materials from the Symposium. AON, Warsaw, pp. 29–30 (1998)

Inclination for Customer Citizenship Behaviour on Transportation Market

Anna Dewalska-Opitek[(✉)]

University of Economics, 1 Maja 50, Katowice, Poland
a.dewalska-opitek@ue.katowice.pl

Abstract. Passenger transportation has been undergoing serious changes towards more ICT based and customer-oriented services. Customers are not only purchasers, but participate in added value co-creation in transportation market, which bring benefits to others. This extra-role behaviour is defined as customer citizenship behaviour (CCB) and may be described as voluntary performance. It consist of several dimensions, nevertheless some seem to be of high importance, i.e.: providing information, encouraging and helping other customers. In the transportation market CCB would refer to providing real-time information to other road users via mobile apps, car sharing and ride sharing. To identify the inclination for customer citizenship behaviour a quantitative research (a survey) was conducted on a group of 241 customers. Research data gathered from a sample of Silesian customers and analyzed on the basis of exploratory factor analysis allowed extracting a 4-item construct of key drivers for helping behaviour, i.e.: social influence (i.e. the extent to which customers are influenced by others), economic and environmental awareness (saving the natural environment, time and money) CCB inclination (as a tendency to engage in citizenship behaviour in future) and intrinsic motivation (i.e. pursuing an activity for the enjoyment of performing it or a sense of obligation). Average variance extracted (AVE) and composite reliability (CR) allowed to verify that measures of latent variables were valid and reliable in case of all four constructs.

Keywords: Customer Citizenship Behaviour (CCB) · Transportation

1 Introduction

Transportation is one of the most important services of a developed society. The growing need for mobility of people (and goods) may be observed due to increasing accumulation and concentration of business activities at some places, increasing value of international trade and generally the passenger mobility. According to the European Environment Agency (EEA), the passenger transport demand in the EU-28 increased by 3% yearly between 2014 and 2017. Car passenger travel remains the dominant transport mode accounting for well over 70% of total transport [21].

Efficient transportation system, as well as convenient communication becomes important challenges for contemporary global economy. They determine the quality of living perceived by inhabitants and become an important element of cost accounting including time and money spent on transport.

© Springer Nature Switzerland AG 2019
J. Mikulski (Ed.): TST 2019, CCIS 1049, pp. 422–433, 2019.
https://doi.org/10.1007/978-3-030-27547-1_30

The transportation market has been undergoing serious changes towards customer-oriented services, on-demand solutions, collaborative consumption and customer-to-customer services. Customers play an active role on the market, not only as transportation service purchasers, but also as service providers or co-providers. Customers provide extra-role, voluntary behaviour, performed in favour of other customers. This behaviour is referred to in literature studies as customer citizenship behaviour [7].

New trends in customers' behaviour bring a significant change in the contemporary transport services consumption model. Although there are various factors discussed in the literature as drivers of CCB, our knowledge about mechanism leading consumers to engage in CCB is still weak, especially on empirical level.

This paper addresses the identified gap. This article aims to present the concept of CCB on the basis of literature studies as well as to identify the customers' inclination for citizenship behaviour based on empirical research in the form of direct quantitative research. A survey was conducted on a sample of 241 Silesian customers in 2016. The study allowed to propose a construct of latent variables explaining the intention to engage in customer citizenship behaviour on transportation market. Conclusions were drawn, possible limitations and future research areas were indicated.

2 Contemporary Trends on Passenger Transportation Market

Passenger transport refers to the total movement of passengers using inland transport on a given network [19]. The passenger transportation system is interrelated with other transportation systems and its expansion promotes urban economic development by increasing the spatial and time accessibility of economic activities. Transportation expansion also contributes to the transformation of centralized, high-density urban areas into decentralized, lower density (but larger) urban areas. As a consequence, workers and firms are more likely to take jobs further from home and to move to new locations, respectively. However, the expansion may also result in such negative urban environmental impacts as air and noise pollution [22].

There is a common consensus, that passenger transportation (as well as other forms of transportation) should be sustainable [9, 13, 17]. According to the Council of the European Union 2001 [5] and OECD 2001 [20], a sustainable transport system should be analysed from three different dimensions, i.e. [1]:

- Environmental: limiting emissions and waste, minimizing the negative impact on land and the generation of noise,
- Social: allowing the basic access and development needs of individuals, companies and societies to be met safely and in a manner consistent with human and ecosystem health,
- Economic: affordable, operating fairly and efficiently, offering choice of transport modes, and supporting a competitive economy, as well as balanced regional development.

According to Deloitte [6] the passenger transportation market has been undergoing serious changes. Nevertheless, the mobility field will look very different going forward. It will be:

- Massively networked, with ubiquitous connectivity throughout the system
- Dynamically priced, so as to balance supply and demand
- User cantered, taking into account users' needs, priorities, data flows, and dynamic responses to conditions
- Integrated, so that users can move easily from point A to point B, regardless of mode, service provider, or time of day.
- Reliant on new models of private-public collaboration, which take advantage of the increasingly diverse ecosystem of public, private, and nonprofit entities that are working to meet the mobility challenges of the 21st century.

Next generation urban transport systems will connect transportation modes, services, and technologies together in innovative new ways that pragmatically address a seemingly intractable problem. The vision of an passenger integrated transportation system is presented in Fig. 1.

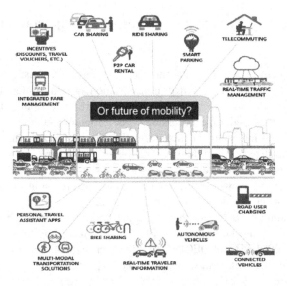

Fig. 1. The future of passenger transportation [6]

Some aspects of the system require addressing in the paper. Attention shall be drawn to car sharing, ride sharing and real-time travelling information. These activities are initiated and performed by customers and bring benefits to other customers, therefore may be described as customer citizenship behaviour (CCB).

3 Customer Citizenship Behaviour on Transportation Market

Citizenship behaviours are extra-role initiatives beyond the requirements of the customer roles usually performed. CCB may be defined as "discretionary and pro-social actions displayed by customers, that bring benefits both to other customers and companies" [4]. Hsieh, Yen and Chin [14] deem such helpful behaviours which are performed by customers as customer voluntary performance (CVP).

According to Fowler [8] customer citizenship behaviour derives from civic citizenship behaviour, as a subject of interest of various concepts, from ancient times, up till now. In the modern-day concept, civic citizenship behaviour is revealed in information exchange and opinion sharing among individuals, which fosters the development of social autonomy and self-governance. Customer citizenship behaviour (CCB) may also be based on the theory of social exchange where customer reciprocates positive behaviour from a sense of personal obligation or gratitude [7].

Literature studies [7] prove that customer citizenship behaviour is a multidimensional construct consisting of several forms, but three of them seem to be of high importance in the transportation market context. They are the following dimensions:

- providing information and (positive or negative) opinions on companies, their goods and services (often referred to as providing f feedback, voice, consultancy),
- encouraging other customers (friends, family members internet users etc.) to use a company's goods or services, positive Word-Of-Mouth and recommendations (referred to as advocacy),
- helping other customers when product or service usage or company's proceedings may be troublesome and uneasy for other customers; it is also described as benevolent acts of service facilitation towards other customers (referred to as helping others).

Among various dimensions of CCB, one seems to play an important role in the context of customer behaviour in passenger transport, i.e. helping other customers while using a mobile app for road navigation (GPS app). Due to data optimization in real time, users are informed, and inform other road users about possible traffic difficulties and burdens, congestions, traffic jams and road works, as well as speed controls, speed detectors and police patrols. All the information about current situation observed on the roads is provided by the application users who build a social network of traffic participants. Especially information about congestion may allow other car users to avoid traffic jams and save time and money, which sums up to economic effects of time loss in urban passenger transport. There are several apps available in Poland dedicated to road users. Yanosik, Coyote, RadarStop or AntyRadar are the most popular.

Another antecedent of customer citizenship behaviour that may be observed in transportation is collaborative consumption. It is an emerging social and economic phenomenon that is fuelled by development in information and communications technology (ICT), growing consumer awareness, proliferation of collaborative web communities as well as social commerce/sharing [3, 23, 24]. It may be defined as the peer-to-peer-based activity of obtaining, giving, or sharing the access to goods and services, coordinated through community-based online services [10]. In collaborative lifestyles, people with similar needs or interests band together to share and exchange less-tangible assets such as time, space, skills, and money. These exchanges happen mostly on a local or neighbourhood level, as people share working spaces, gardens, or parking spots. Collaborative lifestyle sharing happens on a global scale, too [3]. Consumers turn to their social networks in which the participants can be consumers, providers, or both. Such consumer behaviours may be driven by enjoyment, economic incentive or reputation, and yet additionally paired with collaboration. Participating in sharing can be emotional and rational, utility maximizing behaviour wherein the consumer replaces exclusive ownership of goods with lower-cost options from within a collaborative consumption. The service may be a source of enjoyment and may also enable gaining reputation among likeminded people.

BlaBlaCar as the world's largest long-distance ridesharing community, valued at 1.6 billion USD can be indicated as an example of collaborative consumption referring to passenger transportation. The main idea of the initiative is to connect drivers and passengers willing to travel together between cities, and share the cost of the journey. Members must register and create a personal online profile, which includes ratings and reviews by other members, social network verification, and rate of response. Profiles of members show how much experience they have of the service, which means that those more experienced, known as "ambassadors", attract more ride shares. It is also important that each user's profile includes comments and recommendations for both drivers and passengers.

BlaBlaCar was launched in 2008 in France and within 10 years it has spread into 20 countries, i.e. Brazil, Croatia, Czech Republic, Germany, Hungary, India, Italy, Mexico, the Netherlands, Poland, Portugal, Romania, Russia, Serbia, Slovakia, Spain, Turkey, UK and Ukraine. The service accessible via the web, mobile devices and also via apps for iOS and Android has exceeded 20 million members in January 2016 [24].

BlaBlaCar is the best known, but not the only service offering collaborative journeys. In Poland drivers and passengers may use other services, like Uber, Otodojazd or Yanosik Autostop [27], but the idea is very similar – drivers and passengers offer and search for journeys. After finding a match they contact each other to arrange all details like costs, meeting points, space for luggage etc. Then they meet and start their shared car journey as planned.

Another form of collaborative consumption referring to passenger transportation is carsharing (US) or car clubs (UK), a model of car rental where people rent cars for short periods of time, often for an hour. It is attractive to customers who make only occasional use of a vehicle, as well as others who would like occasional access to a vehicle of a different type than they use day-to-day.

Carsharing services are available in over a thousand cities in many countries and offered not only by traditional car rental companies, but car manufacturers (e.g. Daimler's Car2Go, BMW's DriveNow, Volkswagen's Quicar), as well as private car owners.

A typical carsharing organization places a network of shared-use vehicles at strategic parking locations throughout a dense city. Members usually reserve shared-use vehicles in advance. At the time of the rental, the users gain access to the vehicles, carry out their trip, and return the vehicles back to the same place they originally accessed them from (this is also known as a "two-way" rental because the user is required to rent and return a vehicle to the same lot during one continuous rental period).

There is also a "one-way" rental model, called multi-nodal shared-use vehicle system in which the vehicles are driven among multiple stations or nodes to travel from one activity centre to another. Such systems may be located at resorts, recreational areas, national parks, and corporate and university campuses. A specific presented shared-use vehicle system model is known as "station cars". A fleet of vehicles are deployed at passenger terminals and stations in metropolitan areas that are used by commuters primarily on the home – and – work end of a trip. A majority of these systems have been initiated by rail transit operators seeking to relieve parking short-ages, increase transit ridership and create a multimodal transport system.

Participants pay a usage fee (typically based on time and mileage) each time a vehicle is used. The carsharing organization as a whole maintains the vehicle fleet (including light trucks) throughout a network of locations, so users in neighbourhoods and business areas have relatively convenient access to vehicles. Usually there is also a small monthly subscription fee, a one-time deposit, or both. Internationally, carsharing organizations are the most prevalent type of shared-use vehicle system. The vehicles are most often placed in residential neighbourhoods; less frequently, they are located in downtown business areas and rural locations [2, 16].

Although the carshare service model has been well established over the past 20 years, significant growth has been observed in the market recently. According to Navigant Research, global carsharing services revenue is expected to grow from $1.1 billion in 2015 to $6.5 billion in 2024 [26].

Customer engagement in citizenship behaviour in transportation market, i.e. helping others by providing useful and necessary information, carsharing and ridesharing as forms of collaborative consumption, was the subject matter of the empirical part study.

4 Customers' Inclination for Citizenship Behaviour – Direct Research Findings

The purpose of this study was to identify correlates with the inclination of polish customers to help others, participate in ridesharing and carsharing. The research was in a form of a survey conducted in 2016. It was exploratory in nature, conducted in order to determine the nature of the problem, and was not intended to provide conclusive evidence, but to have a better understanding of the problem [12].

Data collection was accomplished through a survey among Silesian customers. Sampling procedures were based on a non-random technique. In total, 241 valid questionnaires were used in the analysis. 116 of the respondents were male (48%) and 125 female (52%), aged 25–34 (36%). They are professionally active (working) - 63%, with higher (45%) or secondary (35%) education (Table 1).

Table 1. Sample characteristics (N = 241) [own study]

Categories	Total sample (%)
1. Gender	
a. Male	48
b. Female	52
2. Age	
a. 18–24 years	26
b. 25–34 years	36
c. 35–44 years	19
d. 45–54 years	11
e. 55–64 years	7
f. 65 years and more	1
3. Professional activity	
a. working	63
b. not working	37
4. Education	
a. elementary	3
b. vocational	17
c. secondary	35
d. higher	45

Majority of survey participants (62%) declare owning a car. The respondents were asked to indicate the purposes of using their car. The answers of the respondents indicate that they use their cars daily to get to work and back home (89%), they use them daily for other purposes not connected with the professional work, like shopping, personal services etc. (63%), and for long distance journey (53%).

The respondents were asked whether they used mobile apps enabling using and sharing on-line information about traffic. The vast majority of them (95%) declared they did, mostly apps like *Yanosik* (62%), *Coyote* (22%) and *Rysiek* (11%). 5% of the respondents used traditional navigation devices.

When asked whether they would be willing to accept fellow passengers (apart from family members and friends) who have the same destination, the survey participants declared they would take them occasionally, for long-distance journeys or for everyday journeys to work and back home (71%). Only a third of respondents (29%) would not decide to accept or invite a fellow passenger. Respondents' opinions are presented in Fig. 2.

64% of respondents declared they would participate in collaborative journeys as passengers. The individuals who were open to this form of passenger transport, either as drivers or as passengers, were mainly young employed people (aged 18–34) with higher education. Only a quarter of respondents declared they had experience in that area, while using mostly two on-line services, i.e.: BlaBlaCar or Yanosik Autostop.

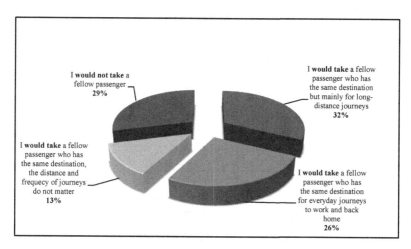

Fig. 2. Graphic presentation of respondents' opinion on their willingness to accept fellow passengers for ridesharing [own study]

The respondents were asked whether they knew the carsharing concept. From the answers of the subjects it can be indicated that this concept is rather popular among the respondents. 84% of respondents declared knowledge of carsharing, but only a third used this form of transport (Fig. 3).

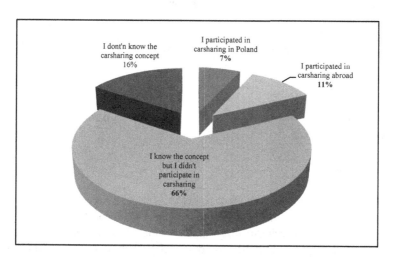

Fig. 3. Graphic presentation of respondents' knowledge and implementation of carsharing [own study]

In order to identify what the key drivers for customer citizenship behavior would be, exploratory factor analysis (EFA) was conducted on the basis of SPSS program. The Scree Plot (Fig. 4) indicated a four-factor solution. The Varimax results of EFA for previously identified 13 items used for the latent constructs. In general, all items loaded on the expected constructs and they had factor loadings higher than 0,6 with no cross loadings. The Varimax results are presented in Table 2.

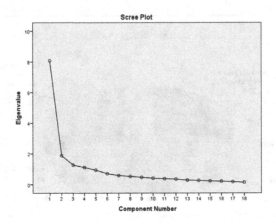

Fig. 4. Scree Plot indicating the number of components for CCB [own study]

Table 2. Rotated component matrix [own study results processed in SPSS package]

	Component			
	1	2	3	4
Will share information with other customers			0,636	
Will share a ride with other customers as a driver			0,711	
Will share a ride with other customers a passenger			0,705	
Other people recommend it	0,825			
Other people do it	0,792			
Other people appreciate it	0,842			
To reduce traffic jams and congestion		0,691		
To reduce pollution		0,623		
To reduce journey expenses		0,831		
To safe time		0,76		
Being a good person				0,779
Selflessness				0,832
Helping others				0,651

The rotated component matrix allows to indicate 4 main constructs determining the customers' inclination to perform citizenship behaviour. The first one refers to extrinsic motivation, i.e. doing something because other people behave this way, and it may be appreciated or even rewarded by other customers (SOCIAL_INFLUENCE) and covers other people's recommendation, appreciation and replication. The second construct (ECONOMIC_ENVIRONMENTAL_AWARENESS) refers to customers' environmental protection tendencies, i.e. reducing traffic jams and congestion, pollution, as well as economic attitude – saving time and money by performing customer citizenship behaviour. The third construct is the willingness to perform citizenship behaviour in future (CCB_INCLINATION), consisting of information sharing and car sharing with other customers. The fourth construct (INTRINSIC_MOTIVATION) refers to behavior that is driven by internal rewards, the motivation to engage in citizenship behavior arises from within the individual because it is naturally satisfying to customers.

Following Hair et al. [11], as well as Mitręga and Pfajfar [18], convergent validity was tested to determine whether the "indicators of a specific construct should coverage or share a high proportion of variance in common". Average variance extracted (AVE) and composite reliability (CR) asses convergent validity, according to the following criteria: AVE > 0,5 and CR > 0,6. The results of convergent validity are presented in Table 3.

Table 3. Convergent validity for 3-item construct [own study]

	Composite Reliability (CR)	Average Variance Extracted (AVE)
SOCIAL_INFLUENCE	0,8197	0,6723
ECONOMIC_ENVIRONMENTAL_AWARENESS	0,7263	0,53345
CCB_INCLINATION	0,784	0,6175
INTRINSIC_MOTIVATION	0,754	0,574267

The above mentioned criteria were met in case of all measured constructs. Taking this into consideration, as well as the results of conducted analysis, it may be assumed that measures of latent variables were valid and reliable in case of all four constructs: SOCIAL_INFLUENCE, ECONOMIC_ENVIRONMENTAL_AWARENESS, CCB_INCLINATION and INTRINSIC_MOTIVATION, which allows testing relationships between these constructs in future studies, using other analytical methods.

5 Conclusion

Summarizing the theoretical deliberation presented in the paper, CCB may be perceived as an important trend in customer behaviour in transportation market. It is a multidimensional construct consisting of several dimensions. As it was stated in the paper, three trends seem to be particularly significant.

One of them is helping other consumers as a form of consumer citizenship behaviour. Road users use and share traffic information on-line, making social networks of prosumers, which means being information or service consumer and supplier at the same time.

Another identified and described trend is collaborative journey as a part of collaborative consumption (ridesharing). People tend to share free space in their cars, invite fellow passengers or offer their companionship (and money in a form of co-covering the travel cost). Due to this trend, travellers have lower costs and fewer cars on roads. This means lower congestion as well as lower environmental damage.

The third trend that was a subject matter of the paper is carsharing, i.e. people rent cars for short periods of time, often for hours. It is attractive to customers who make only occasional use of a vehicle, as well as others who would like occasional access to a vehicle of a different type than they use day-to-day.

It needs to be stated that all described trends are supported or even delivered to the market due to information and communication technologies and could not appear without them.

There are various theories explaining what the key determinants of discretionary and voluntary behaviour may be. So far, customer citizenship behaviour in transportation market was not the subject of interest of many researchers, so the paper fills in the gap to some extent.

Research data gathered from a sample of Silesian customers and analyzed on the basis of exploratory factor analysis allowed extracting a 4-item construct of key drivers for helping behaviour, i.e.: social influence (i.e. the extent to which customers are influenced by others), economic and environmental awareness (saving the natural environment, time and money) CCB inclination (as a tendency to engage in citizenship behaviour in future) and intrinsic motivation (i.e. pursuing an activity for the enjoyment of performing it or a sense of obligation).

Although the paper presents findings which may be interesting for both researchers and transportation practitioners, some limitations are worth addressing. Firstly, research could be conducted on a bigger and more differentiated and representative sample. Secondly, the data analysis method may be extended. This leaves place for a future studies.

References

1. Alonso, A., Mozon, A., Cascajo, R.: Comparative analysis of passenger transport sustainability in European cities. Ecol. Ind. **48**, 578–592 (2015)
2. Barth, M., Shaheen, S.: Shared-use vehicle systems: a framework for classifying carsharing, station cars, and combined approaches. Trans. Res. Rec. (2014). http://trrjournalonline.trb.org. Accessed 12 Jan 2019
3. Botsman, R., Rogers, R.: Beyond Zipcar: collaborative consumption. Harvard Bus. Rev. **88** (10), 30 (2010)
4. Bove, L.L., et al.: Service worker role in encouraging customer organizational citizenship behaviours. J. Bus. Res. **63**, 698–705 (2009)
5. Council of the European Union: Council Resolution on the Integration of Environment and Sustainable Development into the Transport Policy, Report from the Committee of Permanent Representatives to the Council 7329/01. Council of the European Union, Goteborg (2001)
6. Deloitte Report 2013: Digital-Age Transportation. The Future of Urban Mobility, www2. deloitte.com
7. Dewalska–Opitek, A., Wiechoczek, J.: Customer citizenship behaviour towards customers and enterprises operating in medium high-tech sector. In: Tome, E., Neumann, G., Knezević, B. (eds.) Theory and Application in the Knowledge Economy, pp. 248–262. University of Zagreb, Zagreb (2017)

8. Fowler, J.G.: Customer citizenship behaviour: an expanded theoretical understanding. Int. J. Bus. Soc. Sci. **4**(5) (2013)
9. Haghshenas, H., Vaziri, M.: Urban sustainable transportation indicators for global comparison. Ecol. Ind. **15**, 115–121 (2012)
10. Hamari, J., Sjöklint, M., Ukkonen, A.: The sharing economy: why people participate in collaborative consumption? J. Assoc. Inform. Sci. Technol. **67**(9), 2047–2059 (2015)
11. Hair, J.F., et al.: Multivariate Data Analysis. Pearson Prentice Hall, Upper Saddle River (2006)
12. Henson, R.K., Roberts, J.K.: Use of exploratory factor analysis in published research common errors and some comment on improved practice. Educ. Psychol. Meas. **66**(3), 393–416 (2006)
13. Holden, E., Linnerud, K., Banister, D.: Sustainable passenger transport: back to Brundtland. Transp. Res. Part A: Policy Pract. **54**, 67–77 (2013)
14. Hsieh, A., Yen, C., Chin, K.: Participative customers as partial employees and service provider workload. Int. J. Serv. Ind. Manag. **15**(2), 187–199 (2004)
15. Kaplan, A.M., Haenlein, M.: Users of the world, unite! The challenges and opportunities of social media. Bus. Horiz. **53**(1), 59–68 (2010)
16. Martin, E., Shaneen, S., Lidickej, J.: Carsharing's Impact on Household Vehicle Holdings: Results From a North American Shared-Use Vehicle Survey, e-Scholarship University of California (2010). http://eprints.cdlib.org/
17. Miranda, H.D.F., Rodrigues da Silva, A.N.: Benchmarking sustainable urban mobility: the case of Curitiba, Brazil. Transp. Policy **21**, 141–151 (2012)
18. Mitręga, M., Pfajfar, G.: Business relationship process management as company dynamic capability improving relationship portfolio. Ind. Mark. Manag. **46**, 193–203 (2015)
19. OECD, Passenger transportation (2019). www.oecd.org. Accessed 29 Jan 2019
20. OECD, Policy instruments for Achieving Project Environmentally Sustainable Transport. Paris (2001)
21. Passenger transport demand. www.eea.europa.eu. Accessed 17 Jan 2019
22. Telly, W.K.: Classifying urban passenger transportation services. In: Millan, P.B., Inglade, V. (eds.) Esseys on Transportation Economics, pp. 65–77. Springer, Heidelberg (2007). https://doi.org/10.1007/978-3-7908-1765-2_5
23. Wang, C., Zhang, P.: The evolution of social commerce: the people, management, technology, and information dimensions. Commun. Assoc. Inf. Syst. **31**(1), 105–127 (2012)
24. Kalasova, A., Kuchova, L.: Telematics applications and their influence on the human factor. Transport Prob. **2**(2), 89–94 (2013)
25. www.blablacar.uk. Accessed 17 Jan 2019
26. www.navigantresearch.com. Accessed 17 Jan 2019
27. www.softonet.pl. Accessed 17 Jan 2019

Control of Compliance with the Ban on Illegal Work and Illegal Employment in the Sector of Road Freight Transport

Zuzana Otáhalová, Miloš Poliak, and Štefánia Semanová$^{(\boxtimes)}$

University of Žilina, Univerzitná 8215/1, 010 26 Žilina, Slovak Republic
zuzana.otahalova@gmail.com, {milos.poliak,
stefania.semanova}@fpedas.uniza.sk

Abstract. The form of doing work for a haulier as a self-employed person/company depends mainly on the type of work performed. In most cases, a haulier has two options: to employ an employee (employment relationship) or to hire a self-employed person which performs for him an order. According to the Labour Code, employee work (dependent work) can be carried out only under the employment relationship. The Labour Code explicitly prohibits the dependent work to be substituted with any contractual commercial or civil law relationship. However in practice, there are cases where the dependent work, mainly employment relationship, is confused with hiring self-employed persons. The legislation prohibits such cooperation (cooperation involving features of dependent work). Dependent work cannot be performed within a contractual civil law relationship or commercial law relationship under special regulations. In this case, this may represent a violation of Act No. 82/2005 Coll. on Illegal Work and Illegal Employment which defines illegal employment.

Keywords: Freight transport · Illegal work · Labour Code

1 Introduction

The issue of employing a driver of road freight transport is very complex. The paper describes the legal aspects of possibilities for such employment as well as their legal impact on the road freight driver performance. It is necessary to distinguish whether the driver is a self-employed person who is also a road transport entrepreneur who employees drivers or the driver carries out his activities on the basis of a trade licence which entitles him to drive a foreign motor vehicle [1].

In accordance with the Labour Code, employee work (dependent work) can be carried out only under the employment relationship. The Labour Code explicitly prohibits the dependent work to be substituted with any contractual commercial or civil law relationship. However in practice, there are cases where drivers carry out their activities as drivers of passenger and freight road transport on the basis of an unregulated trade (denoted as Service provision of personal nature with the scope of authorization involving Service provision of driving a foreign motor vehicle). The mentioned trade type can be used for the activities related to the provision of personal

© Springer Nature Switzerland AG 2019
J. Mikulski (Ed.): TST 2019, CCIS 1049, pp. 434–447, 2019.
https://doi.org/10.1007/978-3-030-27547-1_31

service having the character of operation (driving) a foreign motor vehicle and not for the activities related to transporting persons, animals, things or shipments by a haulier on the basis of the contract of carriage according to the established transport regulation and the tariffs or the agreed route. Based on the above fact, a self-employed person holding the trade licence for "Service provision of driving a foreign motor vehicle" is not entitled to perform the activity of a driver of the freight vehicle over 3.5 t of total weight for a transport company that owns freight vehicles. Also, the driver's activity can meet the characteristics of dependent work according to Act No. 311/2001 Coll. Labour Code. In this way, the drivers change their labour-law relationship to business relationship, even though these natural persons (drivers) carry out the same work as the drivers – employees [2].

The conditions for the operation of national and international transport are regulated by Act No. 56/2012 Coll. on Road Transport, the provisions of which refer in particular to:

- Regulation (EC) No. 1071/2009 of the European Parliament and of the Council of 21 October 2009 establishing common rules concerning the conditions to be complied with pursue the occupation of road transport operator and repealing Council Directive 96/26/EC
- Regulation (EC) No. 1072/2009 of the European Parliament and of the Council of 21 October 2009 on common rules for access to the international road haulage market.

These regulations regulate in particular the requirements for the occupation of road transport operator and the conditions of licensing [3–5].

Undertakings engaged in the occupation of road transport operator shall:

- have an effective and stable establishment in a Member State,
- be of good repute,
- have appropriate financial standing,
- have the requisite professional competence.

1.1 Characteristics of Illegal Work and Illegal Employment

Illegal work represents the dependent work which is performed by a natural person for a legal person or natural person, who is an entrepreneur, and:

- does not have a labour-law relationship with a legal person or a natural person that is an entrepreneur, or a civil service relationship under a special regulation,
- is a national of the country which is not a Member State of the EU, or another state that is a party to the Agreement on the European Economic Area or the Swiss Confederation, or a stateless person without a temporary residence permit for the purposes of employment and a work permit

Illegal employment is the employment by a legal person or a natural person who is an entrepreneur, provided they utilise dependent work:

- of a natural person and they do not have a labour-law relationship or a civil service relationship under a special regulation

- of a natural person and they have a labour-law relationship or a civil service relationship under a special regulation and they do not meet the obligation according to the special regulation
- of a third country national without a temporary residence permit for the purposes of employment and a work permit if a special regulation so requires and unless otherwise provided in the international treaty by which the Slovak Republic is bounded.

The repeated violation of the ban on illegal employment is considered to be particularly serious violation of Act No. 82/2005 Coll. on Illegal Work and Illegal Employment and on amendment of certain acts. Thus, this results in cancellation of the trade licence [3].

Sanctions imposed for illegal employment are regulated by Act No. 5/2007 Coll. on Employment Services and on amendment of certain acts [4].

2 The Form of Doing Work

The form of doing work for a haulier (a self-employed person/company) depends mainly on the type of work carried out. In most cases, a haulier has two options:

- to employ an employee (under employment relationship) or
- to hire a self-employed person which performs for him an order.

Doing work within employment relationship is often substituted with hiring a self-employed person due to employers' savings on compulsory levies because work done by an employee represents more costly way for employers in comparison with work carried out by a self-employed person. Under certain circumstances, such situation is even favorable for both parties, i.e. "employer" as well as "self-employed person", but the legislation prohibits such cooperation (cooperation involving the characteristics of dependent work) [5, 6].

If a haulier orders service provision, i.e. work performance, from a self-employed person, this person will issue an invoice for the services provided. The haulier does not have to pay neither compulsory levies to social and health insurance nor the withholding taxes for the self-employed person. He does not have to send notices, reports or other documents to insurance companies. He pays the agreed invoiced amount to the self-employed person. However, the haulier should pay high attention to the contractual terms of the cooperation because the conditions agreed in the contract are very important in the case of submission of a compensation claim for services provided by the self-employed person.

The self-employed persons are also significantly less protected compared to employees. If any injury occurs to a self-employed person, the company for which she/he works for will not be responsible because she/he is not its employee. The self-employed persons are also not entitled to meal vouchers, days off to visit a doctor and they are not entitled to paid leave unless it is agreed with the company (employer). The employer must provide the employee with the workplace and work tools. He must ensure initial training and regular education for employees at his own expense. Various administrative obligations towards Tax Office, the Social Insurance Agency or the health insurance company arise in relation to employing employees.

When operating a transport company, the rule that the entrepreneur must be registered in the Business Register of the Slovak Republic applies. Under the current legislation, any legal form of business, such as establishing a limited liability company, joint-stock company or doing business as a self-employed person (hereinafter referred to as "SEP") may be used.

In the case of a limited liability company, the advantage is the limited liability as well as the fact that the authorization and Community Licence are not statically linked to SEP.

Also, it is necessary to take into account the fact that an entrepreneur can only invoice what is the subject of his business. For this reason, obtaining the authorization and Community Licence is a prerequisite for starting business in transport. If an entrepreneur starts to provide transport services without relevant authorization, he/she will commit the infraction or in some cases even a crime.

In practice, it is necessary to distinguish between two options:

1. a driver as a self-employed person who is also a road transport entrepreneur, i.e. the authorisation to pursue the occupation of road transport operator (or Community Licence) is issued to his name and he is also a haulier,
2. a driver acting based on a trade licence which entitles him to drive a foreign motor vehicle; however, he carries out work for other haulier, i.e. the holder of the authorisation to pursue the occupation of road transport operator (or Community Licence) is another person or company – the driver is not a road transport carrier in this case.

According to § 2 (2) of Act No. 513/1991 Coll. Commercial Code as amended by later regulations, the following persons shall be regarded as an entrepreneur:

(a) a party registered in the Business Register,
(b) a party doing business pursuant to a trade licence,
(c) a party doing business pursuant to the special legislation and based on other authorization than a trade licence – this includes, for example, road transport area according to Act No. 56/2012 Coll. on Road Transport as amended by later regulations (hereinafter referred to as "Act No. 56/2012 Coll.)",
(d) a natural person engaged in agricultural production and she/he is registered according to the special legislation.

The only correct legal possibility for the operation of national or international road transport is to meet the requirements stipulated in Act No. 56/2012 Coll. The main prerequisites to obtain the authorization and Community Licence in road freight transport are [7, 8]:

– Authorization for business.
– Financial standing declared at the level of 9 000 € for the first vehicle + 5 000 € for each additional vehicle.
– Professional competence demonstrated by the responsible person (a professional competence guarantor, transport manager) who effectively and continuously

manages the transport activities in the undertaking and he/she is a holder of a valid certificate o professional competence. The transport manager may be a shareholder (at least 15% of the business share) or an employee of the undertaking.

- Technical base equipped for parking of vehicles, carrying out the necessary inspections, maintenance and minor repairs. The minimum area for a tractor unit is 60 m^2. This is declared either by ownership relationship or a tenancy agreement to the real estate.
- The company transport regulations compiled pursuant to § 4 of Act No. 56/2012 Coll. that reflect the way in which a transport company carries out its activities in the context of road freight transport.
- Vehicles intended for road freight transport. An entrepreneur demonstrates ownership, leasing or rental relationship to the vehicles. In the case of a leasing contract the subject of which is the vehicle owned by the leasing company, it is also necessary to submit the consent of the leasing company concerned.

Based on the above, a self-employed person holding the trade licence for "Service provision of driving a foreign motor vehicle" is not entitled to perform the activity of a driver of the freight vehicle over 3.5 t of total weight for a transport company that owns freight vehicles. Also, the driver's activity can meet the characteristics of dependent work according to Act No. 311/2001 Coll. Labour Code. In this way, the drivers change their labour-law relationship to business relationship, even though these natural persons (drivers) carry out the same work as the drivers – employees.

According to § 1 (2) of Act No. 311/2001 Coll. (Labour Code), dependent work is carried out in a relation where the employer is superior and the employee is subordinate, and in which the employee carries out work personally for the employer according to the employer's instructions, in the employer's name, during working time set by the employer. Also, it is necessary to note that dependent work can be carried out only:

- within employment relationship,
- in a similar labour relationship, or
- exceptionally in another form of labour-law relationship under the conditions laid down in the Labour Code.

Dependent work cannot be carried out in contractual civil-law relationship or in contractual commercial-law relationship according to the special regulations. In this case, it may also be a violation of Act No. 82/2005 Coll. on Illegal Work and Illegal Employment as amended by later regulations (hereinafter referred to as "Act No. 82/2005 Coll.") which defines illegal employment. According to § 2 (2) (a) of Act No. 82/2005 Coll., illegal employment is the employment by a legal person or a natural person who is an entrepreneur, provided they utilise dependent work of a natural person and do not have the labour-law relationship concluded according to the special regulation (Labour Code). Based on the above, a driver in road transport may act follows:

- a mobile worker – must be in employment relationship in relation to the employer according to § 7 (1) of Act No. 462/2007 Coll. on Organization of Working Time in Transport, or
- a self-employed person; however, the authorization and Community Licence must be issued to his name, i.e. the driver is also a road transport operator (haulier).

In accordance with the Labour Code, employee's work can be carried out only within employment relationship. The Labour Code explicitly prohibits the dependent work to be substituted with any contractual commercial or civil law relationship. However in practice, there are cases where the dependent work, mainly employment relationship, is confused with hiring self-employed persons. Dependent work cannot be carried out in contractual civil-law or commercial-law relationship according to the special regulations. This may result in a violation of Act No. 82/2005 Coll. which defines illegal employment.

However in practice, there are cases where drivers carry out their activities as drivers of passenger and freight road transport on the basis of the unregulated trade for Service provision of personal nature with the scope of authorization involving Service provision of driving a foreign motor vehicle. The mentioned trade type can be used for the activities related to the provision of personal service having the character of operation (driving) a foreign motor vehicle and not for the activities related to transporting persons, animals, things or shipments by a haulier on the basis of the contract of carriage according to the established transport regulation and the tariffs or the agreed route. No special education or training is required to obtain an unregulated trade licence as it is required for granting the authorization (licence) for hauliers. An applicant must meet only general conditions which must be met by anyone who wants to obtain a trade licence. These general conditions are the age of minimum 18 years, full legal capacity and no criminal record.

Based on the above, a self-employed person holding the trade licence for "Service provision of driving a foreign motor vehicle" is not entitled to perform the activity of a driver of the freight vehicle over 3.5 t of total weight for a transport company that owns freight vehicles. Also, the driver's activity can meet the characteristics of dependent work according to Act No. 311/2001 Coll. Labour Code. In this way, the drivers change their labour-law relationship to business relationship, even though these natural persons (drivers) carry out the same work as the drivers – employees.

3 Control of Illegal Work and Illegal Employment and Punishment for Illegal Employment

The control of illegal work and employment is generally carried out by the following control authorities:

- labour inspectorates,
- the Central Office of Labour, Social Affairs and Family,
- the competent Labour Office, Social Affairs and Family.

The control of illegal work and employment within the transport sector is carried out by the following control authorities:

- labour inspectorates,
- the competent District Office, Department of Road Transport and Infrastructure.

The inspected entity and the competent control authority are obligated to cooperate with each other and to provide all necessary information in the scope of their competence when controlling illegal work and employment.

The employer is obligated to provide the control authority with all documents related to the labour-law relationship of the employed person such as employment contract, etc. The consent of the inspected entity concerned is not required for the control carried out by the competent control authority.

3.1   Analysis of the Controls of Labour Inspectorates in the Sector of Road Transport

The National Labour Inspectorate is the state administrative body. The general director manages this organization and he is responsible for its activities. The minister of Labour, Social affairs and Family of the Slovak Republic appoints and dismisses the director of the National Labour Inspectorate.

The National Labour Inspectorate establishes an accreditation commission that performs the activities of a specialized advisory body. The details about composition of the accreditation commission and its activities are governed by the statute issued by the National Labour Inspectorate after approval by the Ministry.

The national Labour Inspectorate:

- manages and controls labour inspectorates,
- is the appellate body in matters over which the labour inspectorate decided at the first instance,
- ensures the operation of the information system of labour protection and its technical equipment,
- issues and withdraws authorizations of natural persons and legal persons.

Labour inspection is focused on searching and mending illegal work and employment. The purpose of the controls on compliance with the ban on illegal work and employment and the provisions of the Labour Code is to actively act on inspected entities in order to improve the unfavourable state of compliance with the legislation related to illegal work and employment as well as the Labour Code. Another important aspect emphasised by control authorities is the preventive effect on employers. There are 8 labour inspectorates in the Slovak Republic. In 2018, they were together with the National Labor Inspectorate in Košice contacted with a request to comment on the following questions in Table 1.

Table 1. Survey evaluation [own study]

Questions	Yes	No
Did the labour inspectorate carry out any inspection in this field in 2017/2018?	2	6
Was the mentioned problem (when a haulier substituted dependent work with a commercial-law relationship concluded with a self-employed person) identified during inspections?	1	7
If yes, how many cases were occurred?	2	6
Was any sanction/fine imposed?	0	8
Does the labour inspectorate have any plan prepared for monitoring or controls in this field in 2019 or for the future?	2	6

The National Labour Inspectorate, which is the supreme authority of all labour inspectorates, manages and regulates labour inspection in Slovakia. Labour inspection supervises compliance with labor-law regulations, occupational health and safety legislation, regulations related to social legislation in transport and compliance with the ban on illegal work and employment. Labour inspection is supervision over observance of the labour-law legislation that regulates labour-law relationships, in particular their establishment, change and termination, wage and working conditions of employees. In the field of road transport, the labour inspection focuses mainly on controlling compliance with social legislation, occupational health and safety legislation, labour-law and wage regulations as well as observance of the ban on illegal work and employment.

The labour inspectorates referred to the fact that they can quantify work performance as dependent work in the case that all characteristics of dependent work are cumulatively fulfilled. During the inspection carrying out by the labour inspectorate, attention is also paid to the will of contracting parties, i.e. if they enter into the commercial-law relationship by concluding the contract, whether their will (the will of the employee) actually lies in concluding such a contract or in fact they are interested in concluding an employment contract. The individual cases are considered individually and the labour inspection does not have to consider a particular relationship to be contrary to the provisions of the Labor Code.

The Labour Inspectorate Prešov stated that it is generally not possible to claim that dependent work is any work where someone follows the instructions of the other. For instance, the subcontractor fulfils the instructions of the contracting authority in a purely commercial relationship (e.g. the scope of work, the way of work performance, mutual coordination of work, etc.). Assessing particular work as dependent work is not easy especially if the situation suits both parties of the commercial-law relationship. It is also important where and how is work carried out when deciding on dependent work. The drivers of passenger and freight transport are not considered as persons who regularly and for long-term period go to one place to the same employer and where they fulfil employer's detailed instructions, use employer's working tools and adhere the working time set by the employer. The drivers are constantly on roads (on business trips); and therefore, it is practically impossible to demonstrate that they realize usually irregular transportations in a manner and on routes according to the detailed instruction of licence holders.

The National Labour Inspectorate in Košice stated that statistical data on this issue is not available. The inspection specifically aimed at self-employed drivers in freight transport was not carried out. Inspections of such drivers were carried out randomly during roadside inspections and inspections in transport companies. As legislation is largely unclear on this issue, the change in legislation is required in this regard. The government law draft amending Act No. 56/2012 Coll. has brought a change in the subject area. The law draft was approved on 6 December 2018 in National Council of the SR.

The general director of the National Labour Inspectorate Karol Habin mentioned that two types of employers exist. The first group includes the employers who employ their employers illegally, but they even do not know about this because their knowledge on the legislation is not at a sufficient level. The second group includes those employers who employe their employees in violation of the law despite the fact that they have knowledge of the legislation but they try to unfairly gain a competitive advantage in the market. However, this distorts the market not only on the side of employers but subsequently there is also a lack of pressure to increase wages for employees.

Labour inspection should continue to intensively control compliance with the ban on illegal employment. The possibility of publishing information on inspections and their focus is utilized to prevent purely punitive action. Preventive actions on employers not only from the side of labour inspections are important to understand the need for constantly improving the status of employees and their working conditions.

Labour inspection is focused on the control of illegal employment and it is made unannounced. Employers can expect the inspection at any time. Labour inspectors control the legality of employment also outside normal working hours. The objective of labour inspection is to achieve the state in which employees will be legally employed and they will receive an adequate reward for their work. This concerns both Slovak employees as well as foreigners. Therefore, the National Labour Inspectorate has been recently involved in the events accompanied by edification.

In the sector of road freight transport, the labour inspectorate has not included the control aimed at the drivers (employers), who substituted a labour-law relationship with a commercial-law relationship, into their main task plan by the end of 2018. No legislation obliges the labour inspection to do so.

Act No. 177/2018 Coll. was adopted as an amendment to Act No. 462/2007 Coll. on Organization of Working Time in Transport with effective date 1.1.2019. This amendment introduced a new duty for the labour inspectorate. The new section denoted by letter h) was added in §37 (3) and it stipulates that the labour inspectorate shall impose a fine from 20 000 to 100 000 Sk on a transport company which has not concluded an employment relationship with a driver who carries out transport services for this company, unless the driver is a self-employed person. By this provision, the labour inspectorate is obliged to control the employment contract conclusion from the side of the transport company with the driver who carries out road transport activities for it. This obligation was then immediately reflected in the main task plan of the National Labour Inspectorate. The National Labour Inspectorate has prepared the main task plan for 2019 in which one of the tasks is focused on the control in the road transport sector. This main task relates to: Control of social legislation in road transport in companies (employers) and on the roads (pursuant to Act No. 462/2007 Coll., as amended).

The objective of this task is to control compliance with working conditions laid down for drivers and employers in road transport sector at the workplaces of employers and on the roads as well as to provide advice and command the necessary measures to remedy shortcomings identified. The inspections will be particularly focused on adherence of minimum rest periods, maximum driving times, mandatory breaks as well as the use of recording equipment [9, 10].

3.2 Employment Contract Provisions

An employment contract is important when employing drivers. It represents an agreement between the employer and the employee, on the basis of which employment relationship is established. In the employment contract, the employer is obligated to agree with the employee essential contract provisions such as type of work, work of performance, day of work take up, and wage conditions. The contract is not valid without these provisions.

Under Act No. 311/2001 Coll. Labour Code, the labour-law relationships are regulated in relation to the performance of dependent work by natural persons for natural persons or legal persons. Dependent work is performed only within an employment relationship or a similar employment relationship. Dependent work cannot be performed within a contractual civil-law relationship or commercial-law relationship under special regulations [11].

The employment relationship is established by the mutual consent between the employer and the employee. This relationship is demonstrated by the conclusion of an employment contract in accordance with § 42 – § 44 of the Labour Code. The employment contract must be in a written form and must include the following essential provisions:

– type of work for which the employee was accepted, and its brief description,
– place of work performance (municipality or its part, or place otherwise determined)
– day of work take up,
– wage conditions, unless agreed in collective agreement.

Before signing the employment contract, the employer is obliged to inform the employee about his rights and obligations arising from the contract as well as the working and wage conditions under which work is to be carried out. The employment contract must be concluded at the latest on the date when employee takes up employment relationship.

Other employment contract provisions which are not necessary but it is appropriate to include them into the contract are further conditions concerning payment terms, working time, duration of paid leave and length of notice period. It is also recommended to include into the contract various benefits promised by the employer when negotiating for working conditions and whose later failure to fulfill them cannot be otherwise enforceable.

Employment contracts commonly include the various benefits and bonuses that can be obtained by the employee during the employment period. On the contrary, various sanctions and deductions from wages due to non-adherence to fuel consumption, scheduled loading and unloading, wear of brakes etc. are observed in practice when employing drivers. In fact, the wage conditions included in the contract often specify a basic (fixed) wage rate (frequently minimum wage) and then a part of wage as a bonus obtained after fulfilling the conditions set by the employer. The level of this benefit changes in terms of the results achieved. This means that if the driver adheres the fuel consumption (or consumes less fuel) and scheduled loading/unloading, the bonus will be paid in full to the driver. The contract compiled in such way is in accordance with the law.

The working time is the time from the start till the end of work. The time including "other work" (loading, unloading, handling) as well as any time spent travelling to a location to take charge of a vehicle from the company's headquarters is the working time and it is paid.

At present, the working time and rest periods are stipulated by several regulations:

- Regulation (EC) No. 561/2006 on the harmonisation of certain social legislation relating to road transport,
- Act No. 462/2007 Coll. on Organization of Working Time in Transport,
- Decree No. 208/1991 Coll. on Work Safety and Technical Equipment in Operation, Maintenance and Repair of Vehicles,
- European Agreement concerning the Work of Crews of Vehicles engaged in International Road Transport (AETR).

Wage conditions are agreed between the employer and employee in the employment contract. First of all, it is necessary to agree on the amount of a basic wage and variable wage components. The basic wage is provided to the employee based on the time worked or performance achieved. It is a fixed amount the level of which cannot be changed without a written agreement between the employer and the employee. The variable wage components (bonuses) are incentives the purpose of which is to motivate employees to higher performance, better work, better task fulfilment, etc. These bonuses as well as formulas to calculate their amount must be stated in the employment contract.

The following items are not considered as wage: wage compensation (e.g. for public holidays), severance allowances, travel compensations (per diems), contributions from a social fund, etc. According to the Labour Code, overtime work is work performed by an employee by the order of the employer or with his/her consent, beyond the determined weekly working time arising from the predetermined distribution of working time, and performed outside the scope of the timetable of work shifts. An employee may be charged overtime work up to the maximum extent of 150 h in a calendar year. For serious reasons, an employer may agree with an employee on another 250 h of overtime work [12].

3.3   Other Duties of Drivers During Transport

Besides the actual driving the vehicle, the additional requirements are imposed on drivers. In addition to supervision of the vehicle and goods being transported, the drivers are also responsible for the documents that must be present in the vehicle during transport. During roadside inspections, the drivers are the first persons who have to submit the documents to inspectors or to clarify the facts in relation to the submitted documents.

The documents that must be submitted by the driver at the roadside inspection can be divided into the following groups:

- driver documents,
- vehicle documents,
- documents related to the business activity,
- documents related to a particular shipment and carriage.

This paper focuses on the documents related to the business activity – a group of documents necessary to prove the authorization for doing business in road freight transport. During the inspection, the driver must be able to submit the following documents:

- Authorisation to operate national road freight transport – demonstrated by the authorization issued by District Office for Road Transport and Infrastructure. A certified copy of this authorization must be present in the vehicle.
- Authorisation to operate international road freight transport – demonstrated by the authorization issued by District Office for Road Transport and Infrastructure. A certified copy of this authorization must be present in each vehicle (it can be controlled during transport to non-EU countries).
- For transport within the EU countries, the drivers must also have Community Licence issued by the Ministry of Transport and Construction of the SR in addition to other mandatory documents in the vehicle. Without this Licence, it is not possible to carry out transport to other EU Member States despite the fact that there are no controls at borders after the entry of the SR into the Schengen Area. If it is found that the haulier carried out international transport within the EU without Community Licence, high fines are imposed on that haulier. The amount of the fine differs in terms of a particular EU Member State. The original of the License or a certified copy must be in the vehicle.
- Entry permit to non-EU countries – it is necessary so that an entry permit to each non-EU country the territory of which the route of transport leads through must be in the vehicle. These transport permits may be substituted with a permanent CEMT permit. CEMT permit entitles to transport within CEMT Member States in the system loco, including transit as well as third-country transport, where the place of loading and unloading is located in the CEMT Member States.
- In connection to Act 177/2018, the new amendment to Act 462/2007 Coll. on Organization of Working Time in Transport was adopted with effective date 1.1.2019. In this regard, it is a question of whether the employment contract is a document that the driver must have in the vehicle during transport.

4 Conclusion

Illegal work and illegal employment are a serious social problem. Seriousness primarily lies in an adverse impact on the revenue and expenditure side of the state budget and other public resources. Also, it is necessary to note that it contributes to the distortion of data on the number of unemployed persons and other statistical data.

The most frequent forms of illegal work and illegal employment represent a non-fulfillment of the obligatory to notify the Social Insurance Agency for purposes of social insurance and the use of dependent work of a natural person without concluding a labour-law relationship under Act No. 311/2001 Coll. Labour Code as amended.

The basic labour-law claims – claim for a wage, leave, per diems, personal protective work tools, sickness benefits at the time of illness or occupational accident are withholded to the persons who preform illegal work from the side of the entity that assigns them to work in an illegal way. However, they also encounter the problems related to entitlement to old age pension, early old age pension as well as invalidity pension because an applicant for a pension cannot count the period of illegal employment into the total insurance period needed for entitlement to pension.

Therefore, the illegally employed person does not utilize the standard level of legal protection that is provided within a conclude employment contract as well as by fulfilling the employer's notification obligation towards the Social Insurance Agency for social insurance purposes. The employer violating the ban on illegal employment is exposed to the possibility of imposing sanctions from the side of state authorities.

Another negative side of illegal work lies in the adverse impact on the national economy as entities violating the ban on illegal employment also avoid tax and levy obligation. Also, it can be stated that the action of employers towards to violation or circumvention of the ban on illegal employment causes a direct reduction of the level of labour-law relationships in the market.

In conclusion, it must be added that the occupation of a driver as self-employed person is illegal in our conditions; however, such cases occur in practice. A self-employed person itself has a lower burden in the first years of business compared to an employee. However, this person encounters worse conditions during the years when he/she pays full levies. The negative phenomenon of this form of business is that the drivers (employees) formally change in this way to entrepreneurs (self-employed drivers) in many cases, despite the fact that the basic characteristics of the business are not fulfilled [13, 14].

Acknowledgment. This paper was developed under the support of project: MSVVS SR VEGA No. 1/0143/17 POLIAK, M.: Increasing the competitiveness of Slovak carriers providing transport services in road transport in the common market of the European Union.

References

1. Gnap, J., Konečný, V., Poliak, M.: Demand elasticity of public transport. J. Econ. **54**(7), 668–684 (2006). ISSN 0013-3035
2. Gnap, J., Konečný, V.: Transport policy related to road transport and sustainable development. Commun. Sci. Lett. Univ. Žilina 52–61 (2003). ISSN 1335-4205
3. https://www.ip.gov.sk/podmienky-prevadzkovania-vnutrostatnej-a-medzinarodnej-dopravy/. Accessed 12 Jan 2019
4. Act No. 82/2005 Coll. on Illegal Work and Illegal Employment
5. Act No. 5/2007 Coll. on Employment Services According to § 2 (2)
6. Act No. 513/1991 Coll. Commercial Code § 1 (2) of Act No. 311/2001 Coll. (Labour Code)
7. Kalašová, A., Kubíková, S.: The interaction of safety and intelligent transport systems in road transport. In: Young Researches Seminar 2015 [electronic source], 17–19 June 2015, Sapienza - Universita di Roma. - [S.l.: S.n.], CD-ROM, s. 3–13 (2015)
8. https://www.upsvr.gov.sk/buxus/docs/urady/DS/aktualne_informacie/14_002_nelegalna_praca.pdf. Accessed 12 Jan 2019
9. Petro, F., Konečný, V.: Calculation of emissions from transport services and their use for the internalisation of external costs in road. Procedia Eng. [elektronický zdroj] **192**, 677–682 (2017). ISSN 1877-7058
10. Kubíková, S., Kalašová, A., Černický, Ľ.: Microscopic simulation of optimal use of communication network. In: Mikulski, J. (ed.) TST 2014. CCIS, vol. 471, pp. 414–423. Springer, Heidelberg (2014). https://doi.org/10.1007/978-3-662-45317-9_44

11. Cernicky, L., Kalasova, A., Kapusta, J.: Signal controlled junctions calculations in traffic-capacity assessment - Aimsun, Omnitrans, Webster and TP 10/2010 results comparison. Transp. Probl. **11**(1), 121–130 (2016)
12. Culik, K., Kalasova, A., Kubikova, S.: Simulation as an instrument for research of driver-vehicle interaction. In: Stopka, O. (ed.) 18th International Scientific Conference-Logi 2017, MATEC Web of Conferences. E D P Sciences, Cedex A (2017)
13. Berežný, R., Konečný, V.: The impact of the quality of transport services on passenger demand in the suburban bus transport. Procedia Eng. **192**, 40–45 (2017). ISSN 1877-7058
14. Gnap, J., Konečný, V.: The impact of a demographic trend on the demand for scheduled bus transport in the Slovak Republic. Commun. Sci. Lett. Univ. Žilina **10**(2), 55–59 (2008). ISSN 1335-4205
15. https://www.upsvr.gov.sk/buxus/docs/urady/DS/aktualne. Accessed 12 Jan 2019

Author Index